The

EYEWITNESS
HISTORY
of the CHURCH

Volume One
THE RESTORATION
1800–1833

W. JEFFREY MARSH
with
JENNIFER JOHNSON
CELESTE PITTMAN

CFI
Springville, Utah

ISBN: 1-55517-845-6

Published by CFI,
an imprint of Cedar Fort, Inc.
925 N. Main Springville, Utah, 84663
www.cedarfort.com

Distributed by:

Cover design by Nicole Williams
Cover design © 2005 by Lyle Mortimer

Printed in the United States of America
10 9 8 7 6 5 4 3 2

Printed on acid-free paper

Contents

⟡ Acknowledgments ⟡

The artistic Renaissance was launched when the great Italian paint-
ers and sculptors of that age determined that the objective of their work
was to "make it breathe!"

The Eyewitness History of the Church allows us to turn a similar
corner in the study of LDS Church history by using the words of those
who beheld firsthand the unfolding of the Restoration. Their eyewitness
accounts breathe new life into the events of the Restoration, enabling us
to watch Church history unfold just as they saw it. It is exhilarating and
inspiring to read their reminiscences. We stand on tall shoulders and
owe them an eternal debt of gratitude for their faith and sacrifices.

Collecting these wonderful first-person narratives has taken my
research assistants and me to archives at Brigham Young University,
the University of Utah, the Daughters of the Utah Pioneers Museum,
the LDS Church Archives in Salt Lake City, the RLDS Archives in
Independence, Missouri, and Church History sites in New York, Ohio,
Illinois, Nebraska, Iowa, and Utah. Thank you to all the archivists and
historians who helped make these treasured records available to us.

I have been gathering the eyewitness accounts found in this volume
over the course of many years. Preparing them for publication took
the combined efforts of many people, to whom I would like to express
appreciation.

First, I would like to thank my wife, Kathie, and my children for
their continued support and encouragement these many years while
I journeyed on research trips and conducted Church history tours to
many of the sites mentioned in this book. There is no greater joy than
sharing the LDS legacy with your own family.

I also express great thanks to Rachel Cope and Esther Barney, who
assisted in the typing and editing of the early drafts of the manuscript.

Cami Moore, Kristen Kelley, and Natalie Ross proved themselves invaluable as they tirelessly searched through archives and the

microscopic print of aged manuscripts to reproduce the original texts that made this book possible. I owe a debt of gratitude to Claire Koltko for her meticulous and professional work editing the hundreds of journals and articles we brought to her to ensure the historical accuracy of the text.

I gratefully acknowledge the contributions of those at Cedar Fort, especially Lyle Mortimer and Lee Nelson for their willingness to publish *The Eyewitness History of the Church*. Thanks also to Michael Morris for his insightful editing and tireless efforts, and to Nikki Williams for her beautiful work on the cover and aesthetics of the book.

I would also like to offer special thanks to Bobbie Reynolds and those at the LDS Church Archives for their generosity in allowing us use of the photographs seen throughout the book.

Finally, I would like to give a special thanks to two of my students who worked as research assistants through the entire project. Because of their huge investment of time, I invited Jennifer Johnson and Celeste Pittman to join me as coauthors. I thank them both for their willingness to join me on this journey through eyewitness Church history.

✠ INTRODUCTION ✠

The year 2005 is an important year of commemoration for Latter-day Saints. It is the 185th anniversary of the First Vision, the 175th anniversary of the publication of the Book of the Mormon, the 175th anniversary of the organization of the Church, and the 200th anniversary of the Prophet Joseph Smith's birth. This is the perfect time to reflect on and celebrate the legacy left by the Prophet Joseph Smith and the early Saints.

Many who knew Joseph Smith personally—who were there when the curtain on this final dispensation was lifted—left written records of their experiences. The Prophet encouraged them to write about their involvement in the momentous events that transpired:

> The blessing of the Most High will rest upon our tabernacles, and our name will be handed down to future ages; our children will rise up and call us blessed, and *generations yet unborn will dwell with peculiar delight, upon the scenes that we have passed through, the privations that we have endured, the untiring zeal that we have manifested, the all but insurmountable difficulties that we have overcome,* in laying the foundation of a work that will bring about the glory and blessing which they [future generations] will realize; a work which God and Angels have contemplated with delight for generations past; a work that fired the souls of the ancient patriarchs and prophets; *a work that is destined to bring about the destruction of the powers of darkness, the renovation of the earth, the glory of God, and the salvation of the human family.* (*History of The Church of Jesus Christ of Latter-day Saints,* ed. B. H. Roberts, 2d ed. rev., 7 vols. [Salt Lake City: The Church of Jesus Christ of Latter-day Saints, 1932–51], 4:609)

Those who witnessed the dawning of this final dispensation were compelled to write about it. This is a story that needs to be told, and as eyewitnesses and personal friends of the prophet, they are the ones who must tell it (paraphrased from Ted Gibbons, ed., *I Witnessed the Carthage Massacre—The Testimony of Willard Richards* [Orem, Utah: Keepsake Paperbacks, 1988], 1, 42–43).

This kind of "eye-witness history is much more vivid than the sifted, sorted words of recorded history. . . . The pure joy of eye-witness history lies in the vicarious thrill of experiencing the event. Sometimes it can even allow intimate eavesdropping over time. . . . Many of the eye-witnesses themselves are the movers and shakers of history. . . . Others are people caught up by chance in the great affairs of their time" (Jon E. Lewis, ed., *The Mammoth Book of Eyewitness History 2000* [New York: Carroll & Graf Publishers, Inc., 2000], xiii–xiv).

Beginning with Adam and Eve, the Lord's people have always been a record-keeping people. Indeed, they have been commanded to be. God taught Adam and Eve how to write and instructed them and their posterity to keep a book of remembrance: "For a book of remembrance we have written among us, according to the pattern given by the finger of God; and it is given in our own language" (Moses 6:46). Many of Adam and Eve's children kept records of sacred events, "for it was given unto as many as called upon God to write by the spirit of inspiration" (Moses 6:5). Records were kept by the righteous in every dispensation (Helaman 3:13, 15).

As quickly as the gospel of Jesus Christ was restored in our day, the Saints were again commanded to keep records. Some were called to be scribes for the Prophet Joseph Smith (D&C 9:4; 35:23; 124:12), and they were told that their writings were to be inspired: "You cannot write that which is sacred save it be given you from me" (D&C 9:9); "And it shall be given thee in the very moment what thou shalt speak and write" (D&C 24:6); "Wherefore, it shall be given him, inasmuch as he is faithful, by the Comforter, to write these things" (D&C 47:4).

The Lord said it was "expedient" that a record keeper be called to "write and keep a regular history, and assist . . . [His] servant Joseph, in transcribing all things which shall be given" (D&C 47:1). The Lord also commanded the Saints to write a description of the land of Zion under the influence of the Spirit (D&C 58:50). Visions were to be written by the power of the Spirit (D&C 76:28, 49, 80, 113, 115; Official Declaration 1). The commandments received from the Lord were to be similarly recorded (D&C 90:32; 104:81; 127:10).

Original records help preserve memory of important events. Sacred experiences and significant events can be forgotten if they are not recorded, and the gospel insights received from them lost.

These eyewitness accounts not only bear testimony of what occurred, but they also plant seeds of belief. When these eyewitness accounts are read and pondered, they blossom and grow in the hearts of the readers. For the past two hundred years, these eyewitness accounts helped shape the spiritual heritage of the Church around the world. They form the basis for all that we are about. They bear witness that we are indeed about our Father's business, that we are helping to build the kingdom of God, and that God is directing this work. It is thrilling to read the experiences and feelings of those who were caught up in such significant events. Their experiences can reconfirm a spiritual commitment in our own lives and help us with the important events in our own day.

The first two volumes of *The Eyewitness History of the Church* contain thirty-eight chapters in honor of Joseph Smith's thirty-eight years of life. Each chapter consists of eyewitness, first-person narratives of central events of Joseph's life and character, and of the history of the early Church. Reading these accounts will enable you to see and feel history as it occurred, providing you with an armchair-view of the unfolding drama that ushered in the dispensation of the fulness of all times. You will experience Church history through snapshots of specific moments captured by those who were there. The diaries, letters, and reminiscences of those eyewitnesses will enable you to view history through the lives of those who saw, heard, and participated in the events themselves. Mosiah Lyman Hancock, for example, was twelve years old when the Prophet Joseph Smith was martyred in Carthage Jail. He wrote a detailed and moving account of his experience:

> I saw the Prophet and the rest when they departed from Nauvoo for the last time; and I went out to meet their martyred bodies when they were brought from Carthage with Apostle John Taylor, who was himself so badly wounded that he could not stir. There were many of the Saints who went out to meet them, and their hearts were full of sorrow. I went to see those noble martyrs after they were laid out in the mansion. Their heads were placed to the north. As we came in at the door, we came to the feet of the Prophet

> Joseph, then passed up by his left side, around his head, then down by his right side. Next we turned to the right and came to the feet of Hyrum, then up by his left side and around his head and down by his right side; then we filed out of the other door. So the great stream of people continued until the Saints all had the privilege of taking their last look at the martyred bodies.
>
> After the people had gone home, my father took me again into the mansion and told me to place one hand on Joseph's breast and to raise my other arm and swear with hand uplifted that I would never make a compromise with any of the sons of Hell. Which vow I took with a determination to fulfill to the very letter. I took the same vow with Hyrum. (*Mosiah Hancock Journal,* typescript, BYU Special Collections Archives, 28)

One can imagine the impact such an incident would have on a young man. Studying the great events associated with the Restoration can have a similar impact on us. As we hold these eyewitness accounts in our hands and read them, it can be as if, spiritually speaking, we are placing our hands over the hearts of those who participated in the Restoration. As we read their narratives, we too can vow with a renewed determination to avoid making compromises with the wickedness of this world and recommit to sustaining the living prophets as they seek to establish Zion in these latter days.

Speaking of the early Saints' experiences, the Prophet Joseph Smith said:

> The building up of Zion is a cause that has interested the people of God in every age; it is a theme upon which prophets, priests and kings have dwelt with peculiar delight; they have looked forward with joyful anticipation to the day in which we live; and fired with heavenly and joyful anticipations they have sung and written and prophesied of this our day; but they died without the sight; *we are the favored people that God has made choice of to bring about the Latter-day glory.* (*History of the Church,* 4:609–10)

Through *The Eyewitness History of the Church* you will vicariously experience the events of early Church history precisely as those who were privileged to take part in this ongoing adventure. Within these pages, you will relive the moments which "interested the people of God" in every previous age and fired their souls with "joyful anticipations" for the marvelous work and wonder of the latter days, which we are privileged to experience.

The Prophet Joseph Smith further recognized and described the great effort it would take to fully establish this marvelous, latter-day Zion. For those of us now living, there will yet be historical drama and high adventures to look forward to:

> The work of the Lord in these last days, is one of vast magnitude and almost beyond the comprehension of mortals. Its glories are past description, and its grandeur unsurpassable. It is the theme which has animated the bosom of prophets and righteous men from the creation of the world down through every succeeding generation to the present time; and it is truly the dispensation of the fulness of times . . . when all things shall be restored, as spoken of by all the holy prophets since the world began. . . . The work which has to be accomplished in the last days is one of vast importance, and will call into action the energy, skill, talent, and ability of the Saints, so that it may roll forth with that glory and majesty described by the prophet; and will consequently require the concentration of the Saints, to accomplish works of such magnitude and grandeur. (*History of the Church* 4:185–86)

There is spiritual power to be found in studying these first-person accounts of the Restoration. What is it that first plants the desire in people's hearts to want to see and know the truth for themselves? The Prophet Joseph answered, "Human testimony and human testimony only [is what] excite[s] this inquiry, in the first instance, in their minds" (*Lectures on Faith*, [Salt Lake City: Deseret Book, 1985], 2:56).

The *Eyewitness History of the Church* will allow you to see and know for yourself the truthfulness of the Restoration as you walk with those who were there and see what they saw through the prism of their experiences—the eyewitness accounts they left for us.

Note: Whenever a citation is attributed to the Prophet Joseph Smith from the *History of the Church* or from the *Teachings of the Prophet Joseph Smith* (which was compiled using the *History of the Church* as its source), it should be remembered that the volumes contained in that history were compiled from a variety of journals, diaries, and accounts by a committee called by the Prophet Joseph Smith to help him write his history. Most of the *History of the Church* was completed after the Prophet Joseph Smith's death, but it was compiled from the journals of those who were themselves eyewitnesses to the events being described.

ᐳᠬᠬ 1 ᠬᠬᐸ

MEETING THE PROPHET JOSEPH SMITH

Perhaps one of the most memorable events the early Saints experienced was meeting the Prophet Joseph Smith for the first time and hearing him speak. Numerous accounts describe the overwhelming feeling and testimony the Saints received as they learned for themselves of the divinity of Joseph's calling as the Lord's servant. The following are selected statements that allow us to view the Prophet just as his closest associates and friends knew him.

Lorenzo Snow

The first time I saw Joseph Smith. . . . I was seventeen years of age. It was in 1831, in the fall of the year. It was rumored that he was going to hold a meeting in Hiram, Portage County, Ohio, about four miles from my father's home. . . . Having heard many stories about him, my curiosity was considerably aroused and I thought I would take advantage of this opportunity to see and hear him. . . .

When we reached there the people were already assembled in a small bowery; there were about two hundred and fifty or two hundred people present. . . . The meeting had already commenced and Joseph Smith was standing in the door of Father Johnson's house, looking into the bowery and addressing the people.

I made a critical examination as to his appearance, his dress, and his manner as I heard him speak. He was only twenty-five years of age and was not, at that time, what would be called a fluent speaker. His remarks were confined principally to his own experiences, especially the visitation of the angel, giving a strong and powerful testimony in regard to these marvelous manifestations. He simply bore his testimony to what the Lord had manifested to him, to the dispensation of the

Gospel which had been committed to him, and to the authority that he possessed. At first he seemed a little diffident and spoke in rather a low voice, but as he proceeded he became very strong and powerful, and seemed to affect the whole audience with the feeling that he was honest and sincere. It certainly influenced me in this way and made impressions upon me that remain until the present day.

As I looked upon him and listened, I thought to myself that a man bearing such a wonderful testimony as he did, and having such a countenance as he possessed, could hardly be a false prophet. He certainly could not have been deceived, it seemed to me, and if he was a deceiver he was deceiving the people knowingly; for when he testified that he had had a conversation with Jesus, the Son of God, and had talked with Him personally, as Moses talked with God upon Mount Sinai, and that he had also heard the voice of the Father, he was telling something that he either knew to be false or to be positively true (LeRoi C. Snow, "How Lorenzo Snow Found God," *Improvement Era* 40 [February 1937]: 82–83).

Lorenzo Snow

(Observing Joseph Smith several years later.)

Soon after arriving in Kirtland I was on the street with my sister, Eliza. Joseph Smith came along. He was in a great hurry and stopped just long enough to be introduced and shake hands. He turned to my sister and said: "Eliza, bring your brother over to the house to dinner." She was then boarding at his home and teaching his private school. As he left us I watched him just as far as I could see him and then I turned to my sister and said: "Joseph Smith is a most remarkable man; I want to get better acquainted with him. Perhaps, after all, there is something more to Joseph Smith and to Mormonism than I have ever dreamed."

Accordingly, the next time I saw the Prophet was at his own house in Kirtland . . . He sat down at one end of the table and I sat next to him. . . . He seemed to have changed considerably in his appearance since I first saw him at Hiram, four and a half years before. He was very ready in conversation, and had apparently lost that reserve and diffident feeling that he seemed to have before. He was free and easy in his conversation with me, making me feel perfectly at home in his presence. In fact, I felt as free with him as if we had been special friends for years ("How Lorenzo Snow Found God," 83).

Orson Pratt

I . . . became intimately acquainted with the Prophet Joseph Smith, and continued intimately acquainted with him until the day of his death. I had the great privilege . . . of boarding . . . at his house, so that I not only knew him as a public teacher, but as a private citizen, as a husband and father. I witnessed his earnest and humble devotions both morning and evening in his family. I heard the words of eternal life flowing from his mouth, nourishing, soothing, and comforting his family, neighbors, and friends. I saw his countenance lighted up as the inspiration of the Holy Ghost rested upon him, dictating the great and most precious revelations now printed for our guide. I saw him translating, by inspiration, the Old and New Testaments, and the inspired book of Abraham from Egyptian papyrus. . . .

I knew that he was a man of God. It was not a matter of opinion with me, for I received a testimony from the heavens concerning that matter (in *Journal of Discourses*, 26 vols. [London: Latter-day Saints' Book Depot, 1854–86], 7:176–77; spelling standardized).

Jane Snyder Richards

I first saw the Prophet Joseph Smith and shook hands with him, in a dream, about eighteen months before my removal to Nauvoo. Later, at Nauvoo, from the recollections of my dream, I recognized him at first sight, while he was preaching to the people. His was one of the most engaging personalities it has ever been my good fortune to meet (Jane Snyder Richards, "Joseph Smith the Prophet," *Young Woman's Journal* 16 [December 1905]: 550).

Jane Snyder Richards
(Courtesy of the Daughters of the Utah Pioneers)

Amasa Lyman

Of the impressions produced I will here say, although there was nothing strange or different from other men in his personal appearance, yet when he grasped my hand in that cordial way (known to those who have met him in the honest simplicity of truth), I felt as one of old in the presence of the Lord (Joseph Smith, *History of The Church of Jesus Christ of Latter-day Saints*, 7 vols., ed. B. H. Roberts [Salt Lake

City: Deseret Book, 1964], 1:332).

Gilbert Belnap

After arriving in Nauvoo, June 1, 1844, I went to the residence of the Prophet, where a friend had agreed to meet me. I was introduced to the Prophet, whose mild and penetrating glance denoted great depth of thought and extensive forethought. While I was standing before his penetrating gaze, he seemed to read the very recesses of my heart. A thousand thoughts passed through my mind. I seemed to be transfigured before him. I gazed with wonder at his person and listened with delight to the sound of his voice. My very destiny seemed to be interwoven with his (Gilbert Belnap, *Autobiography of Gilbert Belnap* [L. Tom Perry Special Collections, Harold B. Lee Library, Brigham Young University, Provo, Utah], 30–37; as cited in *They Knew the Prophet*, ed. Hyrum L. Andrus and Helen Mae Andrus [Salt Lake City: Deseret Book, 1999], 202–3).

Mary Alice Cannon Lambert

At Nauvoo, several of the leading brethren were there to meet the company [at the dock on the Mississippi River] . . . Among those brethren was the Prophet Joseph Smith. I knew him the instant my eyes rested upon him, and at that moment I received my testimony that he was a Prophet of God, for I never had such a feeling for mortal man as thrilled my being . . . He was not pointed out to me. I knew him from all the other men, and, child that I was (I was only fourteen) I knew that I saw a Prophet of God ("Joseph Smith, the Prophet," *Young Woman's Journal* 16 [December 1905]: 554).

Robert Crookston

As we approached the landing place to our great joy we saw the Prophet Joseph Smith there to welcome his people who had come so far. We were all so glad to see him and set our feet upon the promised land so to speak. It was the most thrilling experience of my life for I know he was a Prophet of the Lord (Robert Crookston, *Autobiography of Robert Crookston* [LDS Church Archives, Church Historical Department, The Church of Jesus Christ of Latter-day Saints, Salt Lake City], 65).

Mary Ann Winters

In April, 1843, when we returned from England to Nauvoo, Brother Joseph came down to the landing at the foot of Main street to meet the company. He came in the cabin, shook hands with our family, took my two little brothers on his knees, and said, "Well, well, Brother Parley, you have come home, bringing your sheaves with you," and the tears rolled down his cheeks.

Brother Pratt answered,

"Why Brother Joseph, if you feel so bad about our coming, I guess we will have to go back again."

Then a smile went all around. Brother Joseph arose and said,

"Come, bring your folks right up to my house" ("Joseph Smith, the Prophet," *Young Woman's Journal* 16 [December 1905]: 557).

Emmeline Blanche Wells

Journeying from my home in Massachusetts to Nauvoo, Illinois, with a company of Latter-day Saints . . . Among them was the late Jacob Gates, who was accompanied by his wife. . . . Sister Gates talked a great deal about the Prophet Joseph . . . and when she saw that I was specially interested in him, promised me that she would introduce me to him on our arrival in Nauvoo. . . .

As we neared our destination in sailing up the Mississippi, the elders . . . were full of enthusiasm at the thought of seeing the Prophet again. But not once in all the conversation did I hear a description of his personal appearance. . . . I had not formed any idea of him except of his wonderful power. . . .

At last the boat reached the upper landing, and a crowd of people were coming toward the bank of the river. As we stepped ashore . . . I could see one person who towered away and above all the others around him; in fact I did not see distinctly any others. His majestic bearing, so entirely different from any one I had ever seen (and I had seen many superior men) was more than a surprise. It was as if I beheld a vision; I seemed to be lifted off my feet, to be as it were walking in the air, and paying no heed whatever to those around me. I made my way through the crowd, then I saw this man whom I had noticed, because of his lofty appearance, shaking hands with all the people, men, women and children. Before I was aware of it he came to me, and when he took my hand, I was simply electrified,—thrilled through and through to the tips of my fingers, and every part of my body, as if some magic elixir had given me new life and vitality. I am sure that for a few minutes I was not conscious of motion. I think I stood still, I did not want to speak, or be spoken to. I was overwhelmed with indefinable emotion.

Sister Gates came to me and said, "I'll introduce you to the Prophet Joseph now, he is here."

I replied,

"I don't want to be introduced to him."

She was astonished, and said curtly,

"Why you told me how desirous you were of meeting him."

I answered,

"Yes, but I've seen him and he spoke to me."

"But he didn't know who you were!"

I replied,

"I know that but it don't matter," and Sister Gates walked away without another word of explanation. I was in reality too full for utterance. I think had I been formally presented to the Prophet, I should have fallen down at his feet. . . . The one thought that filled my soul was, I have seen the Prophet of God, he has taken me by the hand, and this testimony has never left me in all the "perils by the way." For many years, I felt it too sacred an experience even to mention ("Joseph Smith, The Prophet," *Young Woman's Journal* 16 [December 1905]: 554–55).

Mary Isabella Hales

In the latter part of the summer of 1837 I had the great pleasure of being introduced to, and entertaining, the beloved prophet, Joseph Smith, with Sidney Rigdon and T. B. Marsh. . . . On shaking hands with Joseph Smith, I received the Holy Spirit in such great abundance that I felt it thrill my whole system, from the crown of my head to the soles of my feet. I thought I had never beheld so lovely a countenance. Nobility and goodness were in every feature (Mary Isabella Hales, "Autobiography, Kenneth Hales," in *Writings of Early Latter-day Saints and Their Contemporaries, A Database Collection*, comp. Milton V. Backman [Provo, Utah: BYU Religious Studies Center, 1996], 30–31).

Wilford Woodruff

My first introduction to him was rather singular. I saw him out in the field with his brother Hyrum: he had on a very old hat, and was engaged shooting at a mark. I was introduced to him, and he invited me home with him.

I accepted the invitation, and I watched him pretty closely, to see what I could learn. He remarked, while passing to his house, that this was the first hour he had spent in recreation for a long time.

Shortly after we arrived at his house, he went into an adjoining room, and brought out a wolf-skin, and said, "Brother Woodruff, I want you to help me to tan this;" so I pulled off my coat, went to work and helped him, and felt honored in so doing. He was about going up with the brethren to redeem Zion [to march in Zion's Camp], and he wanted this wolf-skin to put upon his wagon seat, as he had no buffalo robe. . . .

I have felt to rejoice exceedingly in what I saw of brother Joseph, for in his public and private career he carried with him the Spirit of the Almighty, and he manifested a greatness of soul which I had never seen in any other man (*Journal of Discourses*, 7:101; spelling standardized).

DESCRIPTIONS OF JOSEPH SMITH BY HIS NON-LDS CONTEMPORARIES

Mayor Josiah Quincy

(Son of the president of Harvard University and later mayor of Boston.)

It is by no means improbable that some future text-book, for the use of generations yet unborn, will contain a question something like this: What historical American of the nineteenth century has exerted the most powerful influence upon the destinies of his countrymen? And it is by no means impossible that the answer to that interrogatory may be thus written: Joseph Smith, the Mormon Prophet. And the reply, absurd as it doubtless seems to most men now living, may be an obvious commonplace to their descendants. . . . The man who established a religion in this age of free debate, who was and is to-day accepted by hundreds of thousands as a direct emissary from the Most High,—such a rare human being is not to be disposed of by pelting his memory with unsavory epithets (Josiah Quincy, *Figures of the Past* [Boston: Roberts Brothers, 1883], 376–400; as cited in Hyrum L. Andrus, *Joseph Smith the Man and the Seer* [Salt Lake City: Deseret Book, 1979], 2).

The New York Sun
(4 September 1843)

This Joe Smith must be set down as an extraordinary character, a prophet-hero, as Carlyle might call him. He is one of the great men of this age, and in future history will rank with those who, in one way or another, have stamped their impress strongly on society (*History of the Church*, 6:3).

John Greenleaf Whittier
(Poet)

Once in the world's history we were to have a Yankee prophet, and we have had him in Joe Smith. For good or for evil, he has left his track on the great pathway of life; or, to use the words of Horne, "knocked out for himself a window in the wall of the nineteenth century," whence his rude, bold, good-humored face will peer out upon the generations to come (John G. Whitier, "A Mormon Conventicle," *Millennial Star* 10 [October 1848]: 303).

PHYSICAL DESCRIPTIONS OF THE PROPHET JOSEPH SMITH

Edward Stevenson

In 1834, we had the pleasure of having a visit from the Prophet Joseph Smith: a plain but noble looking man, of large frame and about 6 feet high (Edward Stevenson, *The Life and History, Elder Edward Stevenson* [LDS Church Archives], 19–23; as cited in Milton V. Backman, *Joseph Smith's First Vision* [Salt Lake City: Bookcraft, 1980], 178).

Lydia Bailey Knight

[He was] a tall, well built form, with the carriage of an Apollo, brown hair, handsome blue eyes, which seemed to dive down to the innermost thoughts with their sharp, penetrating gaze, a striking countenance, and with manners at once majestic yet gentle, dignified yet exceedingly pleasant.

Elder Rigdon was a middle-aged man of medium height, stout and quite good-looking, but without the noble grandeur that was so distinguishing a mark of the prophet (Lydia Knight, "Lydia Knight's History," *Journal History* [LDS Church Archives], 17; as cited in Roy W. Doxey, *The Doctrine and Covenants Speaks*, 2 vols. [Salt Lake City: Deseret Book, 1970], 2:246).

Bathsheba W. Smith

The Prophet was a handsome man,—splendid looking, a large man, tall and fair and his hair was light. He had a very nice complexion, his eyes were blue, and his hair a golden brown and very pretty (Bathsheba W. Smith, "Joseph Smith, the Prophet," *Young Woman's Journal* 16 [December 1905]: 549).

Angus M. Cannon

He was one of the grandest samples of manhood that I ever saw walk or ride at the head of a legion of men. In listening to him as he has addressed the Saints his words have so affected me that I would rise upon my feet in the agitation that would take hold of my mind (Angus M. Cannon, "Joseph Smith, The Prophet," *Young Woman's Journal* 17 [December 1906]: 546).

Thomas Ford

He was full six feet high, strongly built, and uncommonly well muscled. No doubt he was as much indebted for his influence over an ignorant people, to the superiority of his physical vigor, as to his greater cunning and intellect (*History of the Church*, 7:36).

Thomas Ford
(Courtesy of the Church Archives, The Church of Jesus Christ of Latter-day Saints)

Bathsheba W. Smith

My first impressions were that he was an extraordinary man—a man of great penetration; was different from any other man I ever saw: had the most heavenly countenance, was genial, affable and kind, and looked the soul of honor and integrity (Bathsheba W. Smith, "Recollections of the Prophet Joseph Smith," *The Juvenile Instructor* 27 [June 1892]: 344–45).

William Fawcett

His appearance was that of a fine, portly gentleman, six feet high, weighing about two hundred pounds. He was pleasant and kind. His character was unimpeachable among the Saints. They loved him and he loved them (William Fawcett, "Recollections of the Prophet Joseph Smith," *The Juvenile Instructor* 27 [15 January 1892]: 66).

HEARING THE PROPHET
JOSEPH SMITH PREACH

Joseph Smith Jr.

I do not calculate or intend to please your ears with superfluity of words or oratory, or with much learning; but I calculate to edify you with the simple truths from heaven (*History of the Church*, 6:303).

Lorenzo Snow

The Prophet Joseph Smith was not a natural orator, but his sentiments were so sublime and far-reaching that every body was eager to hear his discourses (Ray Evans, "Y.L.M.I.A. Quarterly Conference," *Young Woman's Journal* 2 [September 1891]: 574).

Mary C. Westover

I was very small when we lived in Nauvoo, but . . . I always attended the meetings. The most striking thing I remember of him was a prophecy [Joseph Smith] made, which I saw fulfilled immediately. I was at the funeral service of King Follett, which was held in the Nauvoo

Grove. There was a heavy thunder storm arose and as it increased the people became frightened and started to go home; but . . . the Prophet arose and told the multitude if they would remain still and pray in their hearts the storm would not molest them in their services.

They did as they were bidden, the storm divided over the grove. I well remember how it was storming on all sides of the grove, yet it was as calm around us as if there was no sign of a storm so near by.

I thought as I sat there that the Lord was speaking through Joseph (Mary C. Westover, "Joseph Smith, The Prophet," *Young Women's Journal* 17 [December 1906]: 545).

Daniel Tyler

I attended a meeting "on the flats," [in Kirtland, Ohio] where Joseph presided. Entering the school-house a little before meeting opened, and gazing upon the man of God, I perceived sadness in his countenance and tears trickling down his cheeks. . . . A few moments later a hymn was sung and he opened the meeting by prayer. Instead, however, of facing the audience, he turned his back and bowed upon his knees, facing the wall. This, I suppose, was done to hide his sorrow and tears.

I had heard men and women pray—especially the former—from the most ignorant, both as to letters and intellect, to the most learned and eloquent, but never until then had I heard a man address his Maker as though He was present listening as a kind father would listen to the sorrows of a dutiful child. Joseph was at that time unlearned, but that prayer, which was to a considerable extent in behalf of those who accused him of having gone astray and fallen into sin, that the Lord would forgive them and open their eyes that they might see aright—that prayer, I say, to my humble mind, partook of the learning and eloquence of heaven. There was no ostentation, no raising of the voice as by enthusiasm, but a plain conversational tone, as a man would address a present friend. It appeared to me as though, in case the veil were taken away, I could see the Lord standing facing His humblest of all servants I had ever seen. . . . it was the crowning, so to speak, of all the prayers I ever heard (Daniel Tyler, "Recollections of the Prophet Joseph Smith," *Juvenile Instructor* 27 [February 1892]: 127–28; spelling standardized).

William I. Appleby

His deportment is calm and dignified . . . no ostentation, no affectation of address or manners (William I. Appleby, *Journal of William I. Appleby, Journal History* [LDS Church Archives, 1841] February 19, 1837; as cited in Truman G. Madsen, *Joseph Smith the Prophet* [Salt Lake City: Bookcraft, 1989], 166).

George Q. Cannon

In 1842 or 1843, a Methodist preacher by the name of Prior visited Nauvoo and on the Sabbath day attended religious services for the purpose of hearing a sermon by the Prophet. He published the following description of Joseph's appearance and words:

"I will not attempt to describe the various feelings of my bosom as I took my seat in a conspicuous place in the congregation, who were waiting in breathless silence for his appearance. While he tarried, I had plenty of time to revolve in my mind the character and common report of that truly singular personage. I fancied that I should behold a countenance sad and sorrowful, yet containing the fiery marks of rage and exasperation. I supposed that I should be enabled to discover in him some of those thoughtful and reserved features, those mystic and sarcastic glances, which I had fancied the ancient sages to possess. I expected to see that fearful, faltering look of conscious shame which, from what I had heard of him, he might be expected to evince. He appeared at last; but how was I disappointed when instead of the heads and horns of the beast and false prophet, I beheld only the appearance of a common man, of tolerably large proportions. I was sadly disappointed, and thought that, although his appearance could not be wrested to indicate anything against him, yet he would manifest all I had heard of him when he began to preach. I sat uneasily, and watched him closely. He commenced preaching, not from the Book of Mormon, however, but from the Bible; the first chapter of the first of Peter was his text. He commenced calmly, and continued dispassionately to pursue his subject, while I sat in breathless silence, waiting to hear that foul aspersion of the other sect, that diabolical disposition of revenge, and to hear rancorous denunciation of every individual but a Mormon; I waited in vain; I listened with surprise; I sat uneasy in my seat, and could hardly persuade myself but that he had been apprised of my presence, and so ordered his discourse on my account, that I might not be able to find fault with it; for instead of a jumbled jargon of half-connected sentences, and a volley of imprecations, and diabolical and malignant denunciations, heaped upon the heads of all who differed from him, and the dreadful twisting and wresting of the Scriptures to suit his own peculiar views, and attempt to weave a web of dark and mystic sophistry around the gospel truths, which I had anticipated, he glided along through a very interesting and elaborate discourse with all the care and happy facility of one who was well aware of his important station, and his duty to God and man" (George Q. Cannon, *Life of Joseph Smith the Prophet,* [Salt Lake City: Deseret Book, 1986], 353–54).

George W. Taggart

The information which comes out of His mouth . . . is not in big words . . . but that which anyone can understand (George W. Taggart, "George W. Taggart to Henry Taggart, September 6–10, 1843," *Albert Taggart Correspondence,* LDS Church Archives; as cited in Ronald O. Barney, "A Man That You Could Not Help Liking," *BYU Studies* 40 [Spring 2001]: 173; spelling standardized).

Brigham Young

[President Smith] took heaven, figuratively speaking, and brought it down . . . and opened up, in plainness and simplicity, the things of God (*Journal of Discourses,* 5:332).

Brigham Young

The excellency of the glory of the character of brother Joseph Smith was that he could reduce heavenly things to the understanding of the finite. When he preached to the people—revealed the things of God, the will of God, the plan of salvation, the purposes of Jehovah, the relation in which we stand to him and all the heavenly beings, he reduced his teachings to the capacity of every man, woman, and child, making them as plain as a well-defined pathway. This should have convinced every person that ever heard of him of his divine authority and power, for no other man was able to teach as he could, and no person can reveal the things of God, but by the revelations of Jesus Christ (*Journal of Discourses,* 8:206).

Bathsheba W. Smith

Father sold his farm in West Virginia and we moved to Missouri in 1838. We went to Illinois in February, 1839, but did not see the Prophet Joseph until the spring, when he got out of prison and came to Illinois. A conference was called soon after Joseph and his brethren arrived at Quincy. My brother took my sisters and me and went to that conference, and there I saw Joseph for the first time and heard him preach. I knew he was a Prophet of God, when I joined the Church before I saw him; my testimony was strengthened when I heard him preach, though at this time I did not get to speak to him. I do not remember just when I did first speak to him and shake hands with him. . . .

I have heard the Prophet Joseph preach many a time. I have heard him prophesy, and I never knew but that everything came to pass that he said. . . .

My testimony today is, I know Joseph Smith was and is a Prophet, as well as I know anything. I know that he was just what he professed to be. I am the only one now living who had her endowments while he was alive, and I received them in Nauvoo before the Temple was built. I have seen very many good men, but they had not the gift and blessing that Joseph had. He was truly a Prophet of God (Bathsheba W. Smith, "Joseph Smith, the Prophet," *Young Women's Journal* 16 [December 1905], 549–50).

Elizabeth H. B. Hyde

(Recalling her first meeting in one of the groves surrounding the Nauvoo Temple on her first sabbath in Nauvoo.)

His words thrilled my whole being, and I knew he was a prophet of God (Flora B. Horne, "Daughters of the Utah Pioneers," *Utah Genealogical and Historical Magazine* 3 [October 1912]: 207).

Alfred Cordon

In the morning of Sunday when the weather was favorable we attended meeting ground. [That was the ground area where they were building the temple.] And with what eagerness did the people assemble to hear the words of the Prophet. One lecture from his mouth well repaid me for all my troubles and journeyings to this land, which were not a few (Alfred Cordon, *Journal of Alfred Cordon* [LDS Church Archives, 1841–44]; as cited in *Joseph Smith the Prophet*, 90–91).

Brigham Young

In my experience I never did let an opportunity pass of getting with the Prophet Joseph and of hearing him speak in public or in private, so that I might draw understanding from the fountain from which he spoke, that I might have it and bring it forth when it was needed.... In the days of the Prophet Joseph, such moments were more precious to me than all the wealth of the world. No matter how great my poverty—if I had to borrow meal to feed my wife and children, I never let an opportunity pass of learning what the Prophet had to impart (*Journal of Discourses*, 12:269–70).

John Taylor

Many a time have I listened to the voice of our beloved prophet, while in council ... his eyes sparkling with animation, and his soul fired with the inspiration of the spirit of the living God. It was a theme that caused the bosoms of all who were privileged to listen, to thrill with delight; intimately connected with this were themes upon which prophets, patriarchs, priests, and kings dwelt with pleasure and delight; ... My spirit glows with sacred fire while I reflect upon these scenes, and I say, O Lord, hasten the day! Let Zion be established! Let the mountain of the Lord's house be established in the tops of the mountains! Let deliverance be proclaimed unto Zion! Let redemption echo from mountain to mountain, from hill to hill, from nation to nation! Let the world hear! Let the law go forth from Zion, and the word of the Lord from Jerusalem! ("Address to the Saints in Great Britain," *Millennial Star* 8 [1 November 1846]: 97–98).

OBSERVATIONS ABOUT JOSEPH SMITH'S CHARACTER, POSITIVE ATTITUDE, AND CHEERFUL DISPOSITION

Joseph Smith Jr.

No one need suppose me guilty of any great or malignant sins. A disposition to commit such was never in my nature. But I was guilty [in my youth] of levity, and sometimes associated with jovial company, etc., not consistent with that character which ought to be maintained by one who was called of God as I had been. But this will not seem very strange to any one who recollects my youth, and is acquainted with my native cheery temperament (*Joseph Smith–History* 1:28).

Aroet Hale

(He lived in Nauvoo as a child and knew the family of the Prophet Joseph Smith.)

The Prophet was fond of children and frequently used to come out of the Mansion and play ball with us boys. Joseph would always conform to the rules. He would catch till it came his turn to take the club. Then, being a very stout man, he would knock the ball so far that we used to holler to the boy that was going for the ball to take his dinner. This used to make the Prophet laugh. Joseph was always good natured and full of fun. I have seen him sit down on the carpet in his office in the Mansion and pull sticks with the Nauvoo Police.... The Prophet would ... pull the stoutest man up with one hand (Aroet L. Hale, *First Book or Journal of the Life and Travels of Aroet L. Hale* [Salt Lake City: The Church of Jesus Christ of Latter-day Saints] 24; spelling and punctuation standardized).

Benjamin F. Johnson

The Prophet often came to our town, but after my arrival, he lodged in no house but mine, and I was proud of his partiality and took great delight in his society and friendship. When with us, there was no lack of amusement; for with jokes, games, etc., he was always ready to provoke merriment, one phase of which was matching couplets in rhyme, by which we were at times in rivalry; and his fraternal feeling, in great degree did away with the disparity of age or greatness of his calling (Benjamin F. Johnson, *My Life's Review* [Mesa, Arizona: 21st Century Printing, 1992], 92–93).

George Q. Cannon

He was a great hater of sham. He disliked long-faced hypocrisy, and numerous stories are told of his peculiar manner of rebuking it. He knew that what many people call sin is not sin, and he did many things to break down superstition. He would wrestle, play ball, and enjoy himself in physical exercises, and he knew that he was not committing sin in so doing. The religion of heaven is not to make men sorrowful, to curtail their enjoyment and to make them groan and sigh and wear long faces, but to make them happy. This Joseph desired to teach the people, but in doing so, he, like our Savior, when he was on the earth, was a stumbling block to bigots and hypocrites. They could not understand him; he shocked their prejudices and traditions ("Joseph Smith, the Prophet," *The Historical Record* 7 [January 1888]: 489).

Jane Manning James

(Jane Manning James was a freeborn black woman from Connecticut who walked a thousand miles with eight members of her extended family to Nauvoo, Illinois, in 1843. She lived and worked in the Prophet's house.)

Yes, indeed, I guess I did know the Prophet Joseph. That lovely hand! He used to put it out to me. Never passed me without shaking hands with me wherever he was. Oh, he was the finest man I ever saw on earth. . . .

I used to read in the Bible so much and in the Book of Mormon and Revelations [Doctrine and Covenants], and now I have to sit and can't see to read, and I think over them things, and I tell you I do wake up in the middle of the night, and I just think about Brother Joseph and Sister Emma and how good they was to me. When I went there [to Nauvoo] I only had two things on me, no shoes nor stockings, wore them all out on the road. I had a trunk full of beautiful clothes, which I had sent around by water, and I was thinking of having them when I got to Nauvoo, and they stole them at St. Louis, and I did not have a rag of them. . . . Sister

Emma she come to the door first and she says, "Walk in, come in all of you," and she went up stairs, and down he comes and goes into the sitting room and told the girls that they had there, he wanted to have the room this evening, for we have got company come. I knew it was Brother Joseph because I had seen him in a dream. He went and brought Dr. Bernhisel down and Sister Emma, and introduced him to everyone of

us, and said, "Now, I want you to tell me about some of your hard trials. I want to hear of some of those hard trials." And we told him. He slapped his hands.

"Dr. Bernhisel," he said, "what do you think of that?" And he said, "I think if I had had it to do I should not have come; would not have had faith enough."

[The family stayed with the Smith's for a week until they were all settled in places to stay.]

Jane Manning James

... He [Joseph Smith] came in every morning to see us and shake hands and know how we all were. One morning, before he came in, I had been up to the landing and found all my clothes were gone. Well, I sat there crying. He came in and looked around.

"Why where's all the folks?"

"Why Brother," I says, "they have all got themselves places; but," I says, "I haint got any place," and I burst out a-crying.

"We won't have tears here," he says.

"But," I says, "I have got no home."

"Well you've got a home here," he says, "Have you seen Sister Emma this morning[?]"

"No, sir," I says.

So he started out and went upstairs and brought Sister Emma down and says, "Here's a girl who says she's got no home. Don't you think she's got a home here?"

And she says, "If she wants to stay here."

And he says, "[D]o you want to stay here?"

"Yes, sir," says I. "Well, now," he says, "Sister Emma you just talk to her and see how she is." He says, "Good morning," and he went. . . .

I did not talk much to him, but every time he saw me he would say, "God bless you," and pat me on the shoulder. To Sister Emma, he said, "go and clothe her up, go down to the store and clothe her up." Sister Emma did. She got me clothes by the bolt. I had everything (Jane Manning James, "Joseph Smith, the Prophet," *Young Woman's Journal* 16 [December 1905]: 551–52).

Mary Frost Adams

While he was acting as mayor of the city, a colored man called Anthony was arrested for selling liquor on Sunday, contrary to law. He pleaded that the reason he had done so was that he might raise the money to purchase the freedom of a dear child held as a slave in a Southern State. He had been able to purchase the liberty of himself and wife and now wished to bring his little child to their new home. Joseph said,

"I am sorry, Anthony, but the law must be observed, and we will have to impose a fine."

The next day Brother Joseph presented Anthony with a fine horse, directing him to sell it, and use the money obtained for the purchase of the child (Mary Frost Adams, "Joseph Smith, the Prophet," *Young Woman's Journal* 17 [December 1906]: 538).

Emma Smith

(This comes from a letter to one of her sons after the Prophet's death.)

I do not expect you can do much more in the garden than your father could, and I never wanted him to go into the garden to work for if he did it would not be fifteen minutes before there would be three or four, or sometimes a dozen men round him and they would tramp the ground faster than he would hoe it up (Emma Smith, "Emma Smith to Joseph Smith III, 1 August, n.d., but after 1847," *The Emma Bidamon Papers* [RLDS Church Archives, Independence, Missouri]; as cited in Marvin S. Hill, "Joseph Smith the Man: Some Reflections on a Subject of Controversy," *BYU Studies* 21 [Spring 1981]: 179).

William Fawcett

My heart has been made glad by the sayings of the Prophet many times, in fact whenever I heard him. When Joseph was kidnapped in Dixon, his brother Hyrum called for volunteers, and I volunteered to go to rescue Joseph. I felt willing to lay down my life for him. I loved him, and have ever believed that that offering of mine was acceptable to the Lord. I recollect Joseph was preaching one day out doors to a large congregation. When he said, "I understand that a man in the meeting has offered a thousand dollars for my head. I wonder if he will get it!" and then he kept on preaching (William Fawcett, "Recollections of the Prophet Joseph Smith," *The Juvenile Instructor* 27 [January 1892]: 66–67).

Helen Mar Whitney

Near the first of June 1843 ... the Prophet called and invited [my father, Heber C. Kimball,] to ride with him ... to give invitations to his friend[s], to take a pleasure trip with him down to Quincy ... I was invited to go along. ...

We had a most enjoyable trip ... But on our return trip a heavy thunder storm came up, and Judge Elias Higbee being taken very ill we were obliged to stop over night at Keokirk [KeoKuk]. The cabin was small and the Judge being so sick the majority stayed on deck, where we sat all night; umbrellas being our only protection from the beating storm. The heat had been very excessive, and being thinly clad, many were made sick, and I was among that number. ...

The Prophet, who was noted for his tender sympathies towards the afflicted, could not rest until he went around and informed himself of the condition of each one who had accompanied him to Quincy, and offered advice and some he administered to (Helen Mar Whitney, "Scenes and Incidents in Nauvoo," *Women's Exponent* 10 [15 September 1882]: 58; spelling standardized).

Sarah M. Pomeroy

My father, Thomas Colborn, a member of Zion's Camp, and well acquainted with the Prophet Joseph, moved from the State of New York to Nauvoo with his family in the spring of 1843. I was then in my ninth year. Upon arriving there, we camped down by the river in a little log cabin, near the Hilbert stone house. The day after our arrival, I was out in the yard, when a gentleman rode up and inquired for Thomas Colborn. Of course I did not know who it was, but there was something so noble and dignified in his appearance that it struck me forcibly.

My father soon came out and shook him cordially by the hand, and called him Brother Joseph. I knew then it was the Prophet. Father invited him in and he alighted and followed him into the house. He soon told his errand.

It was quite an exciting time just then. The Prophet had been falsely accused of an attempt to murder Governor Boggs of Missouri. The mobbers had tried every means to take him, and had made their boast that if they got him, he never should return alive. Porter Rockwell, a firm friend of Joseph's, had been kidnapped and taken to Missouri as an accomplice, and was about to have his trial, but money was scarce wherewith to pay the lawyers' fees. Joseph requested my father to lend him $100.00 to pay the lawyer who defended Porter Rockwell. He explained the situation, and father freely counted out the money.

"This shall be returned within three days, if I am alive," said the Prophet, and departed.

My aunt, father's sister, who was camped with us, was quite wrathy, and called my father very foolish and unwise.

"Don't you know, Thomas," said she, "you will never see a cent of that money again. Here [is] your family without a home, and you throw your money away."

"Don't worry, Katie," father replied, "if he cannot pay it, he is welcome to it."

This conversation was held before us children, and I thought seriously about it. Would he pay it, or would he not? But I had strong faith that he would.

The day came when it was to be paid. A cold, wet, rainy day. The day passed. Night came; 9 o'clock, 10 o'clock, and we all retired for the night. Shortly after there was a knock at the door. Father arose and went to it, and there in the driving rain stood the Prophet Joseph.

"Here, Brother Thomas, is the money." A light was struck, and seated at the table, he counted out the $100.00 in gold.

He said, "Brother Thomas, I have been trying all day to raise this sum, for my honor was at stake. God bless you."

My aunt had nothing to say. She afterwards left the Church.

My testimony is that Joseph Smith was truly a Prophet of God. This incident I have related strengthened my testimony (Sarah M. Pomeroy, "Joseph Smith, the Prophet," *Young Woman's Journal* 17 [December 1906]: 538–39).

THE PROPHET'S LOVE FOR LITTLE CHILDREN

James W. Phippen

I have seen him on the playground with "the boys," as he called them, ball playing, wrestling, jumping, and helping to roll up logs on buildings for the widows. I have seen him in public and in private talking with the Saints on various occasions, so kind, so charitable, a Prophet in very deed, so noble in appearance. He loved the Saints. He was willing to suffer for them and die if necessary. Old members of the Church never tire of talking of Joseph, what he said and did. May his memory be fresh in their minds forever and with the children of the Saints (James W. Phippen, "Joseph Smith, the Prophet," *Young Woman's Journal* 17 [December 1906]: 540).

Jane Snyder Richards

As an instance of his humility and faith in prayer, I recall that upon one occasion when his enemies were threatening him with violence, he was told that quite a number of little children were then gathered together praying for his safety. Upon hearing of that he replied:

"Then I need have no fear; I am safe" (Jane Snyder Richards, "Joseph Smith, the Prophet," *Young Woman's Journal* 16 [December 1905]: 550).

William Somerville

William Somerville served as a bodyguard to the Prophet Joseph Smith, and, with side arms in hand, lay on the floor of the bedroom in the Nauvoo House in which Joseph slept, placing his feet against the door, which opened inwards toward the bedroom, so that anyone entering would have to waken him before being able to reach the Prophet.

On one occasion, while on a guard duty assignment, the Prophet came to him and told him that on that particular night his guard service would not be needed, as it had been revealed to him that the little children had been praying for his welfare and the Lord had heard their prayers and would honor their faith by protecting him (Mark L. McConkie, *Remembering Joseph* [Salt Lake City: Deseret Book, 2003], 116–17).

Margarette McIntire Burgess

The Prophet Joseph was often at my father's house. Some incidents which I recollect of him made deep impressions on my child-mind. One morning when he called at our house, I had a very sore throat. It was much swollen and gave me great pain. He took me up in his lap, and gently anointed my throat with consecrated oil and administered to me, and I was healed. I had no more pain nor soreness (Margarette McIntire Burgess, "Recollections of the Prophet Joseph Smith," *Juvenile Instructor* 27 [January 1892]: 66).

Margarette McIntire Burgess

Another time my older brother and I were going to school, near to the building which was known as Joseph's brick store. It had been raining the previous day, causing the ground to be very muddy, especially along that street. My brother Wallace and I both got fast in the mud, and could not get out, and of course, child-like, we began to cry, for we thought we would have to stay there. But looking up, I beheld the loving friend of children, the Prophet Joseph, coming to us. He soon had us on higher and drier ground. Then he stooped down and cleaned the mud from our little, heavy-laden shoes, took his handkerchief from his pocket and wiped our tear-stained faces. He spoke kind and cheering words to us, and sent us on our way to school rejoicing (Margarette McIntire Burgess, "Recollections of the Prophet Joseph Smith," *Juvenile Instructor* 27 [January 1892]: 66–67).

Sariah A. Workman

The Prophet used to come to [the home of my father, Joel H. Johnson,] before I can remember. . . .

[He] was a great lover of children and made a great impression upon me from my earliest recollection. . . .

But what I remember best is that I always felt a divine influence whenever I was in his presence. The Holy Ghost testified to me then, though I was only 12 years of age at the time of his martyrdom, and that testimony has still remained with me, that he is a prophet of the true and living God (Sariah A. Workman, "Joseph Smith, the Prophet," *Young Woman's Journal* 17 [December 1906]: 542).

Jesse N. Smith

Passing the Prophet's house one morning, he called me to him and asked what book I read in at my school. I replied, "The Book of Mormon." He seemed pleased, and taking me into the house he gave me a copy of the Book of Mormon to read in at school, a gift greatly prized by me (Jesse N. Smith, "Recollections of the Prophet Joseph Smith," *The Juvenile Instructor* 27 [January 1892]: 24).

Edwin Holden

In 1838 Joseph and some of the young men were playing various out-door games, among which was a game of ball. By and by they began to get weary. He saw it, and calling them together he said: 'Let us build a log cabin.' So off they went, Joseph and the young men, to build a log cabin for a widow woman. Such was Joseph's way, always assisting in whatever he could (Edwin Holden, "Recollections of the Prophet Joseph Smith," *Juvenile Instructor* 27 [March 1892]: 153).

Evaline Burdick Johnson

(She relates an encounter with the Prophet from her childhood.)

When he saw me, he came and picked me up and sat me on his left arm and crossed the room to a large mirror. We both looked into the glass. He then turned and sat me down and asked me where father was. When he went out of the room, mother called me to her and told me he was the Prophet of the Lord, and what a good man he was (*The Presidents of the Church*, ed. Leonard J. Arrington [Salt Lake City: Deseret Book, 1986], 25–26).

Louisa Y. Littlefield

In Kirtland, when wagon loads of grown people and children came in from the country to meeting, Joseph would make his way to as many of the wagons as he well could and cordially shake the hand of each person. Every child and young babe in the company were especially noticed by him and tenderly taken by the hand, with his kind words and blessings. He loved innocence and purity, and he seemed to find it in the greatest perfection with the prattling child (Louisa Y. Littlefield, "Recollections of the Prophet Joseph Smith," *Juvenile Instructor* 27 [January 1892]: 24).

Mary Ann Winters

As we were going home on the little boat, Brother Joseph sat on the upper deck with the company gathered around him listening to his wonderful words. My father sat opposite him, so near that their knees almost touched. I, a little girl, being tired and sleepy, my Pa took me in his arms to rest. Brother Joseph stopped speaking, stooped and took my feet on his knees and when I would have drawn them away, he said, "No, let me hold them; you will rest better" (Mary Ann Winters, "Joseph Smith, the Prophet," *Young Woman's Journal* 16 [December 1905]: 558).

Schuyler Everett

(As a small boy, Everett called his sister a fool for failing to catch an escaped calf. Joseph overheard him, caught the calf, and consoled Everett's sister.)

At Nauvoo he saw the Prophet Joseph Smith many times on a beautiful white horse. They were staying with an aunt, (Mrs. Redfield), and saw a little calf for the first time. They went out to pet and examine the animal, but it became frightened and broke the rope. Time and again Schuyler got it into a corner, but each time it came near Adelaide [his younger sister], she became frightened and ran in the opposite direction. Finally Schuyler lost his temper and shouted:

"You darn fool! Why don't you head it?" At that moment Joseph Smith happened to be riding by. He got off his horse, tied up the calf, and then petting Adelaide on the head, said, "You are not a little fool, are you sissy?" He never even looked at Schuyler. This was a lesson the boy never forgot. Often in his later years, he related the story to his grandchildren, and his eyes always filled with tears ("Biography of Schuyler Everett," Holograph on microfilm, *Utah Historic Records Survey, Federal Writers' Project (WPA)*, [BYU Special Collections]; as cited in *Remembering Joseph*, 55).

IMPACT ON HIS HEARERS

Peter Hardeman Burnett

He had great influence over others. As an evidence of this I will state that after he had been taken a prisoner in Missouri, I saw him out among the crowd conversing freely with everyone and seeming to be perfectly at ease. In the short space of five days he had managed so to mollify his enemies that he could go unprotected among them without the slightest danger.

Among the Mormons he had much greater influence than Sidney Rigdon. The latter was a man of superior education, an eloquent speaker, of fine appearance and dignified manners; but he did not possess the native intellect of Smith, and lacked his determined will (Peter Hardeman Burnett, *An Old California Pioneer* [Oakland, California: Biobooks, 1946], 40–41; as cited in *They Knew the Prophet*, 126–27).

William Taylor

(William was President John Taylor's brother.)

Much has been said of his geniality and personal magnetism. I was a witness of this—people, old or young, loved him and trusted him instinctively. . . .

My devotion to the Prophet was akin to that felt by all who came under his influence (William Taylor, "Joseph Smith, the Prophet," *Young Woman's Journal* 17 [December 1906]: 548).

Parley P. Pratt

He possessed a noble boldness and independence of character; his manner was easy and familiar; his rebuke terrible as the lion; his benevolence unbounded as the ocean; his intelligence universal, and his language abounding in original eloquence peculiar to himself—not polished—not studied—not smoothed and softened by education and refined by art; but flowing forth in its own native simplicity, and profusely abounding in variety of subject and manner. He interested and edified, while, at the same time, he amused and entertained his audience; and none listened to him that were ever weary with his discourse. I have even known him to retain a congregation of willing and anxious listeners for many hours together, in the midst of cold or sunshine, rain or wind, while they were laughing at one moment and weeping the next. Even his most bitter enemies were generally overcome, if he could once get their ears (Parley P. Pratt, *Autobiography of Parley P. Pratt*, ed. Scot Facer Proctor and Maurine Jensen Proctor [Salt Lake City: Deseret Book, 2000], 45).

Lucy Mack Smith

(Lucy illustrates Joseph's effect on some of his enemies.)

We, who were living at Far West, heard nothing of this [a series of false reports accusing Joseph Smith of plotting a violent uprising] until a few days after when Joseph was at our house writing a letter. I was standing at the door of the room where he was sitting, and upon casting my eyes toward the prairie, I saw a large company of armed men advancing toward the city, but, supposing it to be a training day, I said nothing about it to anyone.

I soon observed that the main body of men came to a halt. The officers dismounted and eight of them came up to the house. Thinking that they wanted refreshment or something of that sort, I set chairs. But instead, they entered and placed themselves in a menacing line like a rank of soldiers across the room. When I requested them to sit down they replied, "We do not choose to sit. We have come here to kill Joe Smith and all the Mormons."

"Oh," said I, "what has Joseph Smith done that you should want to kill him?"

"He has killed seven men in Daviess County," replied the foremost, "and we have come to kill him, and all his church."

"He has not been in Daviess County," I answered, "consequently the report must be false. Furthermore, if you should see him, you would not want to kill him."

"There is no doubt that the report is perfectly correct," rejoined the officer; "it came straight to us, and I believe it; and we were sent to kill the Prophet and all who believe him, and I'll be d—d if I don't execute my orders."

"Then you are going to kill me with the rest, I suppose," said I.

"Yes, we will," he replied.

"Very well," I answered, "but I want you to act like a gentleman about it and do the job quick. Just shoot me down at once, for then it will be but a moment till I shall be perfectly happy. But I would hate to be murdered by any slow process, and I do not see the need of it either, for you can just as well dispatch the work at once as for it to be ever so long a time."

"There it is again," said he. "That is always their plea. You tell a Mormon that you'll shoot him, and all the good it does is to hear them answer, 'Well, that's nothing. If you kill me, we shall be happy.' D—, seems that's all the satisfaction you can get from them anyway."

Joseph had continued writing till now, but having finished his letter, he asked me for a wafer to seal it. Seeing that he was at liberty, I said, "Gentlemen, suffer me to make you acquainted with Joseph Smith the Prophet." He looked upon them with a very pleasant smile and, stepping up to them, gave each of them his hand in a manner which convinced them that he was neither a guilty criminal nor yet a cowering hypocrite. They stopped and stared as though a specter had crossed their path.

Joseph sat down and entered into conversation with them and explained the views and feelings of the people called "Mormons," what their course had been, and the treatment which they had received from their enemies since the first. He told them that malice and detraction had pursued them ever since they entered Missouri, but they were a people who had never broken the laws to his knowledge. They stood ready to be tried by the law—and if anything contrary to the law had been done by any of the brethren at Daviess, it would certainly be just to call them to an account, before molesting or murdering others that knew nothing of these transactions at Gallatin.

After this he rose and said, "Mother, I believe I will go home.

Emma will be expecting me." At this, two of the men sprang to their feet, saying, "You shall not go alone, for it is not safe. We will go with you and guard you." Joseph thanked them and they left with him.

While they were absent, the remainder of the officers stood by the door, and I overheard the following conversation between them:

First Officer: "Did you not feel something strange when Smith took you by the hand? I never felt so in my life."

Second Officer: "I felt as though I could not move. I would not harm one hair of that man's head for the whole world."

Third Officer: "This is the last time you will ever catch me coming to kill Joe Smith or the Mormons either."

First Officer: "I guess this is my last expedition against this place. I never saw a more harmless, innocent-appearing man than the Mormon Prophet."

Second Officer: "That story about his killing them men is all a d—d lie. There is no doubt of that, and we have had all this trouble for nothing. It's the last time I'll be fooled in this way."

Those men who went home with my son promised to disband the militia under them and go home. They said that if Joseph had any use for them, they would come back and follow him anywhere. Thus, we considered that hostilities were no longer to be feared from the citizens. Joseph and Hyrum thought it proper, however, to go to Daviess County and ascertain the cause of the difficulty. They did so, and after receiving the strongest assurance of the future good attentions of the civil officers to administer equal rights and privileges among all the citizens, Mormons and anti-Mormons alike, they returned, hoping all would be well (Lucy Mack Smith, *The Revised and Enhanced History of Joseph Smith by His Mother,* ed. Scot Facer Proctor and Maurine Jensen Proctor [Salt Lake City: Bookcraft, 1996], 361–63).

DESCRIPTIONS BY THOSE WHO WITNESSED JOSEPH RECEIVING REVELATION OR BEARING HIS TESTIMONY

While in vision, the Prophet's physical features would at times undergo a transformation that apparently was visible to those who were observing him.

Brigham Young

Those who were acquainted with him knew when the Spirit of revelation was upon him, for his countenance wore an expression peculiar to himself while under that influence. He preached by the Spirit of revelation, and taught in his council by it, and those who were acquainted with him could discover it at once, for at such times there was a peculiar clearness and transparency in his face (*Journal of Discourses*, 9:89).

Mary Ann Winters

I stood close by the Prophet while he was preaching to the Indians in the Grove by the Temple. The Holy Spirit lighted up his countenance till it glowed like a halo around him, and his words penetrated the hearts of all who heard him and the Indians looked as solemn as Eternity. I saw him on parade at the head of the Nauvoo Legion, looking noble and grand as a leader could do. His commanding presence could be discerned above all others, and all eyes were centered on him, as he rode back and forth giving the commands of his office (Mary Ann Winters, "Joseph Smith, the Prophet," *Young Woman's Journal* 16 [December 1905]: 558).

Wilford Woodruff

I went up to the House of the Lord and heard the Prophet Joseph address the people for several hours. He had been absent from Kirtland on business for the Church. Though he had not been away half as long as Moses was in the Mount, yet many were stirred up in their hearts, and some were against him as the Israelites were against Moses; but when he arose in the power of God in the midst of them, they were put to silence, for the murmurers saw that he stood in the power of a Prophet of the Lord God (*Journal of William I. Appleby*, 19 February 1837; as cited in *Joseph Smith the Prophet*, 89).

Isabella Horne

I heard him relate his first vision when the Father and Son appeared to him; also his receiving the gold plates from the Angel Moroni. This recital was given in compliance with a special request of a few particular friends in the home of Sister Walton, whose house was ever open to the

Saints. While he was relating the circumstance the Prophet's countenance lighted up, and so wonderful a power accompanied his words that
everybody who heard them felt his influence and power, and none could
doubt the truth of his narration (Isabella Horne, "Joseph Smith a True
Prophet," *Young Woman's Journal* 31 [April 1920]: 212).

Emmeline Blanche Wells

In the Prophet Joseph Smith, I believed I recognized the great
spiritual power that brought joy and comfort to the Saints; . . . and
in which he reached men's souls, and appealed most forcibly to their
friendship and loyalty. He possessed too the innate refinement that one
finds in the born poet, or in the most highly cultivated intellectual and
poetical nature; this extraordinary temperament and force combined
is something of a miracle and can scarcely
be accounted for except as a "heavenly mystery" of the "higher sort."

. . . He was beyond my comprehension.
The power of God rested upon him to such
a degree that on many occasions he seemed
transfigured. His expression was mild
and almost childlike in repose; and when
addressing the people, who loved him it
seemed to adoration, the glory of his countenance was beyond description. At other
times the great power of his manner, more
than of his voice (which was sublimely eloquent to me) seemed to shake the place on

Emmeline B. Wells
*(Courtesy of the Church Archives,
The Church of Jesus Christ of Lat-
ter-day Saints)*

which we stood and penetrate the inmost soul of his hearers, and I am
sure that then they would have laid down their lives to defend him. I
always listened spell-bound to his every utterance—the chosen of God
in this last dispensation" (Emmeline Blanche Wells, "Joseph Smith, the
Prophet," *Young Women's Journal* 16 [December 1905]: 556).

Mercy Thompson

I have seen him as if carried away by the power of God beyond all mortal conception, when speaking to the Saints in their public gatherings; and in less public places I have heard him explaining to the brethren and sisters the glorious principles of the gospel, as no man could, except by prophetic power (Mercy Thompson, "Recollections of the Prophet Joseph Smith," *Juvenile Instructor* 27 [July 1892]: 398–99).

Mary Alice Lambert

Many, many times between the time I reached Nauvoo and his martyrdom, I heard him preach. The love the saints had for him was inexpressible. They would willingly have laid down their lives for him. If he was to talk, every task would be laid aside that they might listen to his words. He was not an ordinary man. Saints and sinners alike felt and recognized a power and influence which he carried with him. It was impossible to meet him and not be impressed by the strength of his personality and influence (Mary Alice Lambert, "Joseph Smith, the Prophet," *Young Women's Journal* 16 [December 1905]: 554).

Lyman O. Littlefield

I was a mere boy, between thirteen and fourteen years old, when I first met the Prophet. His appearance as a man won my reverence for him; but his conversation and public teaching—all attended by a power truly Godlike—established me in the faith and knowledge of his prophetic mission which strengthened with the lapse of years until he sealed his testimony with his blood in the jail at Carthage, in 1844. . . .

The Spirit of the Lord had previously testified to me, in the State of Michigan, that Joseph Smith was a Prophet of God, and when I beheld him at Salt River, where Zion's Camp was resting near Brother Burget's house, the spirit of truth furnished me with an additional evidence of his divine mission (Lyman O. Littlefield, "Recollections of the Prophet Joseph Smith," *The Juvenile Instructor* 27 [January 1892]: 64–65).

Mary E. Rollins Lightner

I joined the Church in the year 1830, in Kirtland, Ohio, just six months after it was first organized. I was then twelve years old.

The Smith family came to Kirtland early in the spring of 1831. After they were settled in their house, mother and I went to see them. We had heard so much about the Golden Bible, as it was then called, that we were very anxious to hear more. The whole Smith family, excepting Joseph, was there. As we stood talking to them, Brother Joseph and Martin Harris came in with two or three others. When the greetings were over, Brother Joseph looked around very solemnly (it was the first time some of them had ever seen him) and said, "There are enough here to hold a little meeting."

A board was put across two chairs to make seats. Martin Harris sat on a little box at Joseph's feet. They sang and prayed, then Joseph got up to speak. He began very solemnly and very earnestly; all at once his countenance changed and he stood mute. He turned so white, he seemed perfectly transparent. Those who looked at him that night said he looked like he had a searchlight within him. I never saw anything like it on earth. I could not take my eyes away from him. I remember I thought we could almost see the bones through the flesh of his face.

I shall remember him as he looked then as long as I live.

He stood some moments looking over the congregation, as if to pierce each heart, then said, "Do you know who has been in your midst this night?"

One of the Smiths said, "An angel of the Lord."

Martin Harris said, "It was our Lord and Savior, Jesus Christ."

Joseph put his hand down on Martin's head and said,

"The Spirit of God revealed that to thee. Yes, brothers and sisters, the Savior has been in your midst this night, and I want you all to remember it. There is a veil over your eyes, for you could not endure to look upon him. You must be fed with milk not with strong meat. I want you all to remember this as if it were the last thing that escapes my lips" (Mary E. Rollins Lightner, "Joseph Smith, the Prophet," *Young Woman's Journal* 16 [December 1905]: 556–57; spelling standardized).

William Henrie

You could not be in [the Prophet's] presence without feeling the influence and Spirit of God, which seemed to flow from him almost as heat does from a stove. You could not see it, but you felt it (Callie O. Morley, *History of William and Myra Mayall Henrie, Pioneers of 1847* [LDS Church Archives], 4–5).

Wilford Woodruff

The last speech that Joseph Smith ever made to the quorum of the Apostles was in a building in Nauvoo, and it was such a speech as I never heard from mortal man before or since. He was clothed upon with the Spirit and power of God. His face was clear as amber. The room was filled as with consuming fire. He stood three hours upon his feet. Said he: "You Apostles of the Lamb of God have been chosen to carry out the purposes of the Lord on the earth. Now, I have received, as the Prophet, seer and revelator, standing at the head of this dispensation, every key, every ordinance, every principle and every Priesthood that belongs to the last dispensation and fullness of times. And I have sealed all these things upon your head" (Wilford Woodruff, in Conference Report, April 1898, 89).

Edward Stevenson

We very often went to Nauvoo to meetings. I have never heard or seen a man so filled with inspiration as the Prophet. He was full of light. I began to believe that he possessed an infinity of knowledge. I looked upon him as upon no other man. I have often heard him speak under divine influence, and I have felt as though I have been lifted in spirit beyond mortality, and that I was looking upon a simile of God, and at times I found myself in tears of joy. Others have I seen in the same condition, and at times even those not members of our church (Edward Stevenson, *Autobiography of Edward Stevenson* [LDS Church Archives]; as cited in *They Knew the Prophet*, 98).

Wilford Woodruff

The Prophet Joseph then arose and addressed the congregation for the space of three hours, clothed with the power, spirit, and image of God. He presented many things of vast importance to the Elders of Israel. O! That the record could be written as with an iron pen, of the light, principles and virtue that came forth out of the mouth and heart of the Prophet Joseph, whose soul, like Enoch's, seems wide as eternity. That day showed strikingly that he is in very deed a prophet of God, raised up for the deliverance of Israel (Wilford Woodruff, *Journal History*, 6 April 1837; punctuation standardized).

Wilford Woodruff

(After hearing Joseph speak at two different meetings.)

Joseph then arose and, like the Lion of the Tribe of Judah, poured out his soul in the midst of the congregation of Saints. While listening, I thought "Who can find language to write his words and teaching, as with an iron pen in a rock, that they might stand for future generations to look upon." He seemed a fountain of Knowledge, from whose mouth streams of eternal wisdom flowed; and as he stood before the people, he showed that the authority of God was upon him (Wilford Woodruff, *Journal History*, 9 April 1837; punctuation standardized).

Wilford Woodruff

His mind was opened by the visions of the Almighty, and the Lord taught him many things by vision and revelation that were never taught publicly in his days; for the people could not bear the flood of intelligence which God poured into his mind (*Journal of Discourses*, 5:83–84).

Sarah N. Williams Reynolds

I was a close neighbor of Philo Dibble who visited me very often. He had been very familiar and intimately acquainted with the Prophet Joseph Smith, and took great delight in rehearsing his wealth of information concerning this acquaintance. Brother Dibble stated to me that the Prophet Joseph told him in connection with the others who were present in Father Johnson's home at the time the Vision was given to the Prophet Joseph and Sidney Rigdon, that (the Prophet speaking): "My whole body was full of light and I could see even out at the ends of my fingers and toes" (N. B. Lundwall, *The Visions of the Degrees of Glory* [Kaysville, Utah: Bookcraft, 1951], 11).

Howard Coray

One morning, I went as usual into the Office to go to work: I found Joseph sitting on one side of a table and Robert B. Thompson on the opposite side, and the understanding I got was that they were examining or hunting in the manuscript of the new translation of the Bible [the Joseph Smith Translation] for something on Priesthood, which Joseph wished to present, or have read to the people the next Conference: Well, they could not find what they wanted and Joseph said to Thompson, "put the manuscript [to] one side and take some paper and I will tell you what to write." Bro. Thompson took some foolscap paper that was at his elbow and made himself ready for the business. I was seated probably 6 or 8 feet on Joseph's left side, so that I could look almost squarely into Joseph's left eye—I mean the side of his eye. Well, the Spirit of God descended upon him, and a measure of it upon me, insomuch that I could fully realize that God, or the Holy Ghost, was talking through him. I never, neither before or since, have felt as I did on that occasion. I felt so small and humble I could have freely kissed his feet (*The Words of Joseph Smith. The Contemporary Accounts of the Nauvoo Discourses of the Prophet Joseph*, ed. Andrew F. Ehat and Lyndon W. Cook [Provo, Utah: Brigham Young University, 1980], 51).

Parley P. Pratt

(Observing Joseph Smith receive the revelation that became Doctrine and Covenants, section 50.)

After we had joined in prayer in his translating room, he dictated in our presence the following revelation:—(Each sentence was uttered slowly and very distinctly, and with a pause between each, sufficiently long for it to be recorded, by an ordinary writer, in long hand).

This was the manner in which all his written revelations were dictated and written. There was never any hesitation, reviewing, or reading back, in order to keep the run of the subject; neither did any of these communications undergo revisions, interlinings, or corrections. As he dictated them so they stood, so far as I have witnessed; and I was present to witness the dictation of several communications of several pages each (Parley P. Pratt, *Autobiography of Parley Parker Pratt*, ed. Parley P. Pratt Jr. [Salt Lake City: Deseret Book, 1964], 62).

Orson Pratt

I was present when Joseph received revelations. I particularly remember the one on the United Order. There was no great noise or physical manifestation. Joseph was as calm as the morning sun. But I noticed a change in his countenance that I had never noticed before, when a revelation was given to him. His face was exceedingly white, and seemed to shine.

I had been present many times when the Prophet was revising the [N]ew Testament, and wondered why he did not use the urim and thummim, as in translating the *Book of Mormon*. While this thought passed through my mind, Joseph, as if he had read my thoughts, looked up and explained that the Lord gave him the urim and thummim when he was inexperienced in the Spirit of inspiration. But now that he had advanced so far as to understand the operations of that Spirit, he did not need the assistance of that instrument ("Two Days' Meeting at Brigham City, June 27 and 28, 1874," *Millennial Star* 36 [11 August 1874]: 498–99).

PRAISE TO THE MAN WHO COMMUNED WITH JEHOVAH

Daniel H. Wells

Though I did not at first believe that he [Joseph Smith] was inspired or that he was more than a man of great natural ability, I soon learned that he knew more about religion and the things of God and eternity than any man I had ever heard talk. I read the Book of Mormon and the Book of Doctrine and Covenants without their having any particular effect on my mind. I did not get the principles from either of these sources, but I obtained them from Joseph, and it seemed to me that he advanced principles that neither he nor any other man could have obtained except from the Source of all wisdom—the Lord himself. I soon discovered that he was not what the world termed a well-read or an educated man; then where could he have got this knowledge and understanding, that so far surpassed all I had ever witnessed, unless it had come from Heaven? (*Journal of Discourses*, 12:72).

Brigham Young

I feel like shouting hallelujah, all the time, when I think that I ever knew Joseph Smith, the Prophet whom the Lord raised up and ordained, and to whom He gave keys and power to build up the kingdom of God on earth and sustain it. These keys are committed to this people, and we have power to continue the work that Joseph commenced, until everything is prepared for the coming of the Son of Man.

. . . Who can justly say aught against Joseph Smith? I was as well acquainted with him, as any man. I do not believe that his father and mother knew him any better than I did. I do not think that a man lives on the earth that knew him any better than I did; and I am bold to say that, Jesus Christ excepted, no better man ever lived or does live upon this earth. I am his witness (*Journal of Discourses*, 3:51; 9:332).

John Taylor

Joseph Smith, in the first place, was set apart by the Almighty according to the councils of the gods in the eternal worlds, to introduce the principles of life among the people, of which the Gospel is the grand power and influence, and through which salvation can extend to all peoples, all nations, all kindreds, all tongues and all worlds. It is the principle that brings life and immortality to light, and places us in communication with God. God selected him for that purpose, and he fulfilled his mission and lived honorably and died honorably. I know of what I speak for I was very well acquainted with him, and was with him a great deal during his life, and was with him when he died. . . .

Who was Joseph Smith? . . . God chose this young man. He was ignorant of letters as the world has it, but the most profoundly learned and intelligent man that I ever met in my life, and I have traveled hundreds of thousands of miles, been on different continents and mingled among all classes and creeds of people, yet I have never met a man so intelligent as he was. And where did he get his intelligence from? Not from books, not from the logic or science or philosophy of the day, but he obtained it through the revelation of God made known to him through the medium of the everlasting Gospel (*Journal of Discourses*, 21:94, 163; punctuation standardized).

John Taylor

I was acquainted with Joseph Smith for years. I have traveled with him; I have been with him in private and in public; I have associated with him in councils of all kinds; I have listened hundreds of times to his public teachings, and his advice to his friends and associates of a more private nature. I have been at his house and seen his deportment in his family. I have seen him arraigned before the courts of his country, and seen him honorably acquitted, and delivered from the pernicious breath of slander, and the machinations and falsehoods of wicked and corrupt men. I was with him living, and with him when he died; when he was murdered in Carthage jail by a ruthless mob with their faces painted . . . I have seen him under all these various circumstances, and I testify before God, angels and men that he was a good, honorable, virtuous man—that his doctrines were good, scriptural and wholesome—that his precepts were such as became a man of God—that his private and public character was unimpeachable—and that he lived and died as a man of God, and a gentleman (*A Comprehensive History of the Church of Jesus Christ of Latter-day Saints*, 6 vols., ed. B. H. Roberts [Provo, Utah: Brigham Young University Press, 1965], 2:352–53).

Wilford Woodruff

Those who have been acquainted with the Prophet Joseph, who laid the foundation of this Church and kingdom, who was an instrument in the hand of God in bringing to light the Gospel in this last dispensation, know well that every feeling of his soul, every sentiment of his mind, and every act of his life, proved that he was determined to maintain the principle of truth, even to the sacrificing of his life. His soul swelled wide as eternity for the welfare of the human family. He began entirely alone, as far as the influence of the children of men was concerned upon the earth, to endeavor to establish a religion and order of things diverse from anything then existing among men, a religion that was unpopular and contrary to the feelings, and views, and traditions of the whole human family (*Journal of Discourses*, 2:192).

Brigham Young

What I have received from the Lord, I have received by Joseph Smith; he was the instrument made use of. If I drop him, I must drop these principles; they have not been revealed, declared, or explained by any other man since the days of the Apostles (*Discourses of Brigham Young*, ed. John A. Widtsoe [Salt Lake City: Deseret Book, 1977], 458).

John Taylor

He learned by communication from the heavens, from time to time, of the great events that should transpire in the latter days. He understood things that were past, and comprehended the various dispensations and the designs of those dispensations. He not only had the principles developed, but he was conversant with the parties who officiated as the leading men of those dispensations, and from a number of them he received authority and keys and priesthood and power for the carrying out of the great purposes of the Lord in the last days, who were sent and commissioned specially by the Almighty to confer upon him those keys and this authority, and hence he introduced what was spoken of by all the prophets since the world was; the dispensation in which we live, which differs from all other dispensations in that it is the dispensation of the fullness of times, embracing all other dispensations, all other powers, all other keys and all other privileges and immunities that ever existed upon the face of the earth (*Journal of Discourses*, 20:174–75; spelling standardized).

Howard Coray

Among other great men who called to see him was Cyrus Walker, a lawyer of much note; he tried to sound the Prophet, and see how deep he was. Well, it was with Walker as it had been with all the others. He soon got enough, found Joseph too deep for his lead and line, and gave up the enterprise. Thus it was in every instance that came under my observation: How could we expect it to be otherwise, for any man who had never peered into heaven and seen heavenly things, [to] be a match for one who had had a half a score or more heavenly messengers for teachers (Howard Coray, *Howard Coray's Autobiography* [LDS Church Archives], 3–4; as cited in Charles D. Tate Jr., "Howard and Martha Jane Knowlton Coray of Nauvoo," *Regional Studies in Latter-day Saint Church History: Illinois*, ed. H. Dean Garrett [Provo, Utah: Brigham Young University, 1995], 334).

The Savior

The ends of the earth shall inquire after thy name, and fools shall have thee in derision, and hell shall rage against thee;

While the pure in heart, and the wise, and the noble, and the virtuous, shall seek counsel, and authority, and blessings constantly from under thy hand.

And thy people shall never be turned against thee by the testimony of traitors (D&C 122:1–3).

John Taylor

Joseph Smith, the Prophet and Seer of the Lord, has done more, save Jesus only, for the salvation of men in this world, than any other man that ever lived in it. In the short space of twenty years, he has brought forth the Book of Mormon, which he translated by the gift and power of God, and has been the means of publishing it on two continents; has sent the fulness of the everlasting gospel, which it contained, to the four quarters of the earth; has brought forth the revelations and commandments which compose this book of Doctrine and Covenants, and many other wise documents and instructions for the benefit of the children of men; gathered many thousands of the Latter-day Saints, founded a great city, and left a fame and name that cannot be slain. He lived great, and he died great in the eyes of God and his people; and like most of the Lord's anointed in ancient times, has sealed his mission and his works with his own blood; and so has his brother Hyrum. In life they were not divided, and in death they were not separated! (D&C 135:3).

☞ 2 ☜

JOSEPH SMITH'S FAMILY
AND HIS EARLY YEARS

Joseph Smith Sr. and Lucy Mack were married in January 1796. Together, they formed a hardworking, loyal family that offered Joseph Smith Jr. unending support that sustained him in his divine calling during the trials and hardships he endured to bring forth the gospel. Following are observations about this unique family.

LUCY MACK SMITH

William Smith

My mother who was a very pious woman and much interested in the welfare of her children, both here and hereafter, made use of every means which her parental love could suggest, to get us engaged in seeking for our souls' salvation (William Smith, *William Smith on Mormonism* [Lamoni, Iowa: Herald Steam Book and Job Office, 1883], 6; as cited in *Church History in the Fulness of Times*, prepared by the Church Educational System [Salt Lake City: The Church of Jesus Christ of Latter-day Saints, 1993], 21–22).

Lucy Mack Smith

(Relating an experience she had while recovering from illness.)

I made a solemn covenant with God that if He would let me live I would endeavor to serve him according to the best of my abilities. Shortly after this I heard a voice say to me, "Seek, and ye shall find;

knock, and it shall be opened unto you. Let your heart be comforted; ye believe in God, believe also in me."

. . . As soon as I was able I made all diligence in endeavoring to find someone who was capable of instructing me more perfectly in the way of life and salvation.

. . . I went from place to place for the purpose of getting information and finding, if it were possible, some congenial spirit who could enter into my feelings and thus be able to strengthen and assist me in carrying out my resolutions.

. . . I said in my heart that there was not then upon earth the religion which I sought. I therefore determined to examine my Bible and, taking Jesus and His disciples for my guide, to endeavor to obtain from God that which man could neither give nor take away. . . .

At length I considered it my duty to be baptized and, finding a minister who was willing to baptize me and leave me free in regard to joining any religious denomination, I stepped forward and yielded obedience to this ordinance (Lucy Mack Smith, *History of Joseph Smith by His Mother*, ed. Preston Nibley [Salt Lake City: Bookcraft, 1958], 34–36).

Lucy Mack Smith

(relating a conversation she had with a minister)

"And you," said Mr. Ruggles, upon shaking hands with me, "are the mother of that poor, foolish, silly boy, Joe Smith, who pretended to translate the Book of Mormon."

I looked him steadily in the face, and replied, "I am, sir, the mother of Joseph Smith; but why do you apply to him such epithets as those?"

"Because," said his reverence, "that he should imagine he was going to break down all other churches with that simple 'Mormon' book."

"Did you ever read that book?" I inquired.

"No," said he, "it is beneath my notice."

"But," rejoined I, "the Scriptures say, 'prove all things'; and, now, sir, let me tell you boldly, that that book contains the everlasting gospel, and it was written for the salvation of your soul, by the gift and power of the Holy Ghost."

"Pooh," said the minister, "nonsense—I am not afraid of any member of my church being led astray by such stuff; they have too much intelligence."

"Now, Mr. Ruggles," said I, and I spoke with emphasis, for the Spirit of God was upon me, "mark my words—as true as God lives, before three years we will have more than one-third of your church; and, sir, whether you believe it or not, we will take the very deacon, too."

This produced a hearty laugh at the expense of the minister.

Not to be tedious, I will say that I remained in this section of country about four weeks, during which time I labored incessantly for the truth's sake, and succeeded in gaining the hearts of many, among who were David Dort and his wife. Many desired me to use my influence to have an elder sent into that region of country, which I agreed to do. As I was about starting home, Mr. Cooper observed that our ministers would have more influence if they dressed in broadcloth.

When I returned, I made known to Joseph the situation of things where I had been, so he dispatched Brother Jared Carter to that country. And in order that he might not lack influence, he was dressed in a suit of superfine broadcloth. He went immediately into the midst of Mr. Ruggles' church, and, in a short time, brought away seventy of his best members, among whom was the deacon, just as I told the minister. This deacon was Brother Samuel Bent, who now presides over the High Council (*History of Joseph Smith*, 215–17).

JOSEPH SMITH SR.

William Smith

My father's religious habits [were] strictly pious and moral (*Church History in the Fulness of Times*, 22).

Joseph Smith Jr.
(on the occasion of his father's baptism)

Praise to my God! that I lived to see my own father baptized into the true Church of Jesus Christ! (*History of Joseph Smith*, 168).

Lorenzo Snow

Lorenzo Snow
(Courtesy of the Church Archives, The Church of Jesus Christ of Latter-day Saints)

Anyone seeing Father Smith as he then appeared and having read of old Father Abraham in the scriptures, would be apt to think that Father Smith looked a good deal like Abraham must have looked; at least, that is what I thought. I do not know that any man among the Saints was more loved than Father Smith; and when any one was seriously sick Father Smith would be called for, whether it was night or day. He was as noble and generous a man as I have ever known (LeRoi C. Snow, "How Lorenzo Snow Found God," *The Improvement Era* 40 [February 1937]: 84).

Eliza R. Snow

The old gentleman's [Joseph Smith Sr.'s] prediction, that I should ere long be baptized, was strange to me, for I had not cherished a thought of becoming a member of the 'Mormon' Church. . . . I looked at Father Smith, and silently asked myself the question: Can that man be a deceiver? His every appearance answered in the negative. At first sight, his presence impressed me with feelings of love and reverence. I had never seen age so prepossessing. Father Joseph Smith, the Patriarch, was indeed a noble specimen of aged manhood (Eliza R. Snow, *Biography and Family Record of Lorenzo Snow*, 1884, 10; as cited in Karl Ricks Anderson, *Joseph Smith's Kirtland* [Salt Lake City: Deseret Book, 1989], 52).

Eliza R. Snow
(Courtesy of the Church Archives, The Church of Jesus Christ of Latter-day Saints)

Joseph Smith Sr.

I have never denied the Lord. . . . The Lord has often visited me in visions and dreams, and has brought me, with my family, through many afflictions, and I this day thank his holy name (*Book of Patriarchal Blessings* [LDS Church Archives, Church Historical Department, The

Church of Jesus Christ of Latter-day Saints, Salt Lake City], index 1:1; as cited in Susan Easton Black, *Who's Who in the Doctrine and Covenants* [Salt Lake City: Bookcraft, 1997], 290).

Lucy Mack Smith

(Commenting on the first of her husband's dreams.)

One night my husband retired to his bed in a very thoughtful state of mind, contemplating the situation of the Christian religion, or the confusion and discord that were extant. He soon fell into a sleep, and before waking had the following vision, which I shall relate in his own words, just as he told it to me the next morning:

"I seemed to be traveling in an open, barren field, and as I was traveling, I turned my eyes towards the east, the west, the north and the south, but could see nothing save dead, fallen timber. Not a vestige of life, either animal or vegetable, could be seen; besides, to render the scene still more dreary, the most death-like silence prevailed, no sound of anything animate could be heard in all the field. I was alone in this gloomy desert, with the exception of an attendant spirit, who kept constantly by my side. Of him I inquired the meaning of what I saw, and why I was thus traveling in such a dismal place. He answered thus: 'This field is the world, which now lieth inanimate and dumb, in regard to the true religion, or plan of salvation; but travel on, and by the wayside you will find on a certain log a box, the contents of which, if you eat thereof, will make you wise, and give unto you wisdom and understanding.' I carefully observed what was told me by my guide, and proceeding a short distance, I came to the box. I immediately took it up, and placed it under my left arm; then with eagerness I raised the lid, and began to taste of its contents; upon which all manner of beasts, horned cattle, and roaring animals, rose up on every side in the most threatening manner possible, tearing the earth, tossing their horns, and bellowing most terrifically all around me, and they finally came so close upon me, that I was compelled to drop the box and fly for my life. Yet, in the midst of all this I was perfectly happy, though I awoke trembling" (*History of Joseph Smith*, 46–47).

Lucy Mack Smith

(Commenting on a dream her husband had.)

In 1811, we moved from Royalton, Vermont, to the town of Lebanon, New Hampshire. Soon after arriving here, my husband received another very singular vision, which I will relate:

"I thought," said he, "I was traveling in an open, desolate field, which appeared to be very barren. As I was thus traveling, the thought suddenly came into my mind that I had better stop and reflect upon what I was doing, before I went any farther. So I asked myself, 'What motive can I have in traveling here, and what place can this be?' My guide, who was by my side, as before, said, 'This is the desolate world; but travel on.' The road was so broad and barren that I wondered why I should travel in it; for, said I to myself, 'Broad is the road, and wide is the gate that leads to death, and many there be that walk therein; but narrow is the way, and strait is the gate that leads to everlasting life, and few there be that go in thereat.' Traveling a short distance further, I came to a narrow path. This path I entered, and, when I had traveled a little way in it, I beheld a beautiful stream of water, which ran from the east to the west. Of this stream, I could see neither the source nor yet the mouth; but as far as my eyes could extend I could see a rope, running along the bank of it, about as high as a man could reach, and beyond me was a low, but very pleasant valley, in which stood a tree such as I had never seen before. It was exceedingly handsome, insomuch that I looked upon it with wonder and admiration. Its beautiful branches spread themselves somewhat like an umbrella, and it bore a kind of fruit, in shape much like a chestnut bur, and as white as snow, or, if possible, whiter. I gazed upon the same with considerable interest, and as I was doing so, the burs or shells commenced opening and shedding their particles, or the fruit which they contained, which was of dazzling whiteness. I drew near and began to eat of it, and I found it delicious beyond description. As I was eating, I said in my heart, 'I cannot eat this alone, I must bring my wife and children, that they may partake with me.' Accordingly, I went and brought my family, which consisted of a wife and seven children, and we all commenced eating and praising God for this blessing. We were exceedingly happy, insomuch that our joy could not easily be expressed. While thus engaged, I beheld a spacious building standing opposite the valley which we were in, and it appeared to reach to the very heavens. It was full of doors and windows, and they were all filled with people, who were very finely dressed. When these people observed us in the low valley, under the tree, they pointed the finger of scorn at us, and treated us with all manner of disrespect and contempt. But their contumely we utterly disregarded. I presently turned to my guide and inquired of him the meaning of the fruit that was so delicious. He told me it was the pure love of God, shed abroad in the hearts of all those who love him, and keep his commandments. He then commanded me to go and bring the rest of my children. I told him that we were all there. 'No,' he replied, 'look yonder, you have two more, and you must bring them also.' Upon raising my eyes, I saw two small children, standing some distance off. I immediately went to them, and brought them to the tree; upon which they commenced eating with the rest, and we all rejoiced together. The more we ate, the more we seemed to desire, until we even got down upon our knees and scooped it up, eating it by double handfuls. After feasting in this manner a short time, I asked my guide what was the meaning of the spacious building which I saw. He replied, 'It is Babylon, it is Babylon, and it must fall. The people in the doors and windows are the inhabitants thereof, who scorn and despise the Saints of God because of their humility.' I soon awoke, clapping my hands together for joy" (*History of Joseph Smith*, 48–50).

Lucy Mack Smith

(Commenting on her husband's final dream.)

I shall here insert the seventh vision that my husband had, which vision was received in the year 1819. It was as follows:

"I dreamed," said he, "that a man with a peddler's budget on his back, came in and thus addressed me: 'Sir, will you trade with me today? I have now called upon you seven times, I have traded with you each time, and have always found you strictly honest in all your dealings. Your measures are always heaped and your weights over-balance; and I have now come to tell you that this is the last time I shall ever call on you, and that there is but one thing which you lack in order to secure your salvation.' As I earnestly desired to know what it was I still lacked, I requested him to write the same upon paper. He said he would do so. I then sprang to get some paper, but in my excitement, I awoke." [He later indicated that membership in the true church was what he was found wanting] (*History of Joseph Smith*, 68).

CHILDREN OF JOSEPH SMITH SR. AND LUCY MACK SMITH

Name	Birth Date	Place of Birth	Death Date
child	about 1797	Tunbridge, Vermont	about 1797
Alvin	11 Feb. 1798	Tunbridge, Vermont	19 Nov. 1823
Hyrum	9 Feb. 1800	Tunbridge, Vermont	27 June 1844
Sophronia	16 May 1803	Tunbridge, Vermont	1876
Joseph Jr.	23 Dec. 1805	Sharon, Vermont	27 June 1844
Samuel Harrison	13 Mar. 1808	Tunbridge, Vermont	30 July 1844
Ephraim	13 Mar. 1810	Royalton, Vermont	24 Mar. 1810
William	13 Mar. 1811	Royalton, Vermont	13 Nov. 1893
Catherine	28 July 1812	Lebanon, New Hampshire	1 Feb. 1900
Don Carlos	25 Mar. 1816	Norwich, Vermont	7 Aug. 1841
Lucy	18 July 1821	Palmyra, New York	9 Dec. 1882

THE PROPHET'S BROTHERS AND SISTERS

Joseph Smith Jr.

(About Hyrum)

There was Brother Hyrum who next took me by the hand—a natural brother. Thought I to myself, Brother Hyrum, what a faithful heart you have got! Oh may the Eternal Jehovah crown eternal blessings upon your head, as a reward for the care you have had for my soul! (Joseph Smith, *The History of The Church of Jesus Christ of Latter-day Saints*, 7 vols., ed. B. H. Roberts [Salt Lake City: Deseret Book, 1978], 5:107–8).

Joseph Smith Jr.

(About Hyrum)

I could pray in my heart that all my brethren were like unto my beloved brother Hyrum, who possess[es] the mildness of a lamb, and the integrity of a Job, and in short, the meekness and humility of Christ; and I love him with that love that is stronger than death, for I never had occasion to rebuke him, nor he me (Joseph Smith, *History of the Church*, 2:338).

Hyrum Smith
(Courtesy of the Church Archives, The Church of Jesus Christ of Latter-day Saints)

Joseph Smith Jr.

(About Alvin)

He [Alvin] was the oldest and noblest of my father's family. He was one of the noblest of the sons of men. . . . In him there was no guile. He lived without spot from the time he was a child. From the time of his birth he never knew mirth. He was candid and sober and never would play; and minded his father and mother in toiling all day. He was one of the soberest of men, and when he died the angel of the Lord visited him in his last moments (*History of the Church*, 5:126–27).

Joseph Smith Jr.

(About Alvin)

[Alvin] was a very handsome man, surpassed by none but Adam and Seth (*History of the Church*, 5:247).

Joseph Smith Jr.

(About William)

[William] was six feet four inches high, was very straight and well made, had light hair, and was very strong and active. His usual weight when in health was two hundred pounds. He was universally beloved by the Saints (*History of the Church*, 4:399).

William Smith

(About Joseph)

We all had the most implicit confidence in what he [Joseph Smith Jr.] said. He was a truthful boy. Father and mother believed him, why should not the children? (J. W. Peterson, "Another Testimony," *Deseret Evening News* [20 January 1894]: 11).

Hyrum Smith

(About Joseph)

I have been acquainted with him ever since he was born, which was thirty-seven years in December last; and I have not been absent from him at any one time not even for the space of six months, since his birth, to my recollection (Pearson H. Corbett, *Hyrum Smith Patriarch* [Salt Lake City: Deseret Book, 1963], 194).

BIRTH OF JOSEPH SMITH

Joseph Smith Jr.

I was born in the year of our Lord one thousand eight hundred and five, on the twenty-third day of December, in the town of Sharon, Windsor County, State of Vermont (Joseph Smith–History 1:3).

Joseph Smith Jr.

(Original spelling preserved)

We were deprived of the bennifit of an education suffice it to say I was mearly instructed in reading writing and the ground rules of Arithmatic which constuted my whole literary acquirements (Joseph Smith Jr., *History of Joseph Smith by Himself* [LDS Church Archives, 1832], 1; as cited in Dean C. Jessee, "The Early Accounts of Joseph Smith's First Vision," *BYU Studies* 4 [Spring 1969]: 279).

Impressions of Joseph's Mission

Joseph of Egypt

(Prophesying that from his descendants in the latter days, God would raise up a "choice seer" whose name would be Joseph.)

A seer will I raise up out of the fruit of thy loins; and unto him will I give power to bring forth my word unto the seed of thy loins . . .

And thus prophesied Joseph, saying: Behold, that seer will the Lord bless; . . .

And his name shall be called after me [Joseph]; and it shall be after the name of his father. And he shall be like unto me; for the thing, which the Lord shall bring forth by his hand, by the power of the Lord shall bring my people unto salvation.

And the words which he shall write shall be the words which are expedient in my wisdom should go forth unto the fruit of thy loins (2 Nephi 3:11, 14–15, 19).

Asael Smith

(Joseph's grandfather had this spiritual impression)

It has been borne in upon my soul that one of my descendants will promulgate a work to revolutionize the world of religious faith (Joseph Fielding Smith, *Church History and Modern Revelation* [Salt Lake City: The Council of the Twelve Apostles of the Church of Jesus Christ of Latter-day Saints, 1953], 1:4; as cited in Susan Easton Black, "Joseph Smith stands at head of Lord's work in last dispensation," *Church News* [4 January 1997]: 4).

Joseph Smith Jr.

My grandfather, Asael Smith, long ago predicted that there would be a prophet raised up in his family, and my grandmother was fully satisfied that it was fulfilled in me. My grandfather Asael died in East Stockholm, St. Lawrence county, New York, after having received the Book of Mormon, and read it nearly through; and he declared that I was the very Prophet that he had long known would come in his family (*History of the Church*, 2:443).

Joseph Smith Jr.

I calculate to be one of the instruments of setting up the kingdom of Daniel by the word of the Lord, and I intend to lay a foundation that will revolutionize the whole world. . . . It will not be by sword or gun that this kingdom will roll on: the power of truth is such that all nations will be under the necessity of obeying the Gospel (*History of the Church*, 6:365).

Daniel H. Wells

Daniel H. Wells
(Courtesy of the Church Archives, The Church of Jesus Christ of Latter-day Saints)

It seemed to me that he advanced principles that neither he nor any other man could have obtained except from the Source of all wisdom—the Lord himself. . . . Where could he have gotten this knowledge and understanding, that so far surpassed all I had ever witnessed, unless it had come from Heaven? (in *Journal of Discourses*, 26 vols. [London: Latter-day Saints' Book Depot, 1854–86], 12:72).

JOSEPH SMITH'S EARLY YEARS
(1805–1820)

Lucy Mack Smith

I now come to the history of Joseph. . . . I shall say nothing respecting him until he arrived at the age of fourteen. However, in this I am aware that some of my readers will be disappointed, for I suppose, from questions which are frequently asked me, that it is thought by some that I shall be likely to tell many very remarkable incidents which attended his childhood; but, as nothing occurred during his early life except those trivial circumstances which are common to that state of human existence, I pass them in silence (*History of Joseph Smith*, 67).

Mrs. Palmer

I remember the excitement stirred up among some of the people over Joseph's First Vision, and of hearing my father contend that it was only the sweet dream of a pure minded boy. One of our church leaders came to my father to remonstrate against his allowing such close friendship between his family and the "Smith Boy," as he called him. My father defended his own position by saying that Joseph was the best help he had ever found. He told the churchman that he always fixed the time of hoeing his large field to that when he could secure the services of Joseph Smith, because of the influence that boy had over the wild boys of the neighborhood, and explained that when these boys, or young men, worked by themselves much time would be spent in arguing and quarreling, which often ended in a ring fight. But when Joseph Smith worked with them, the work went steadily forward, and he got the full worth of the wages he paid (Martha Cox, *Stories from the Notebook of Martha Cox, Grandmother of Fern Cox Anderson*, LDS Church Archives, as cited in *They Knew the Prophet*, ed. Hyrum L. Andrus and Helen Mae Andrus [Salt Lake City: Deseret Book, 1999], 1; see also Mark L. McConkie, *Remembering Joseph* [Salt Lake City: Deseret Book 2003], 27–28).

JOSEPH'S LEG OPERATION

In 1812, typhoid fever raged throughout the upper Connecticut valley, and soon afflicted the Smith family. Nine-year-old Sophronia Smith came dangerously close to death after battling the disease for nearly three months. Joseph Jr. was himself fever-stricken for two weeks when complications requiring surgery began to set in.

Lucy Mack Smith

As our children had, in a great measure, been debarred from the privilege of schools, we began to make every arrangement to attend to this important duty. We established our second son Hyrum in an academy at Hanover; and the rest, that were of sufficient age, we were sending to a common school that was quite convenient. Meanwhile, myself and companion were doing all that our abilities would admit of for the future welfare and advantage of the family, and were greatly blessed in our labours.

But this state of things did not long continue. The typhus fever came into Lebanon, and raged tremendously (Lucy Mack Smith, *Biographical Sketches of Joseph Smith, the Prophet and his Progenitors for Many Generations* [Liverpool: published for Orson Pratt and S. W. Richards, 1853], 58; as cited in Milton V. Backman Jr., *Eyewitness Accounts of the Restoration* [Salt Lake City: Deseret Book, 1986], 7).

Joseph Smith Jr.

When I was five years old or thereabouts I was attacked with the Typhus Fever, and at one time, during my sickness, my father despaired of my life. The doctor broke the fever, after which it settled under my shoulder, and Dr. Parker called it a sprained shoulder and anointed it with bone ointment, and freely applied the hot shove, when it proved to be a swelling under the arm which was opened, and discharged freely, after which the disease removed and descended into my left leg and ankle and terminated in a fever sore of the worst kind, and I endured the most acute suffering for a long time under the care of Drs. Smith, Stone and Perkins of Hanover. At one time eleven doctors came from Dartmouth Medical College, at Hanover, New Hampshire, for the purpose of amputation, but, young as I was, I utterly refused to give my assent to the operation, but consented to their trying an experiment by removing a large portion of the bone from my left leg, which they did, and fourteen additional pieces of bone afterwards worked out before my leg healed, during which time I was reduced so very low that my mother could carry me with ease

After I began to get about I went on crutches till I started for the state of New York (Joseph Smith, "1839 History of the Church," *Book A-1* [LDS Church Archives], 131–32; as cited in Reed C. Durham Jr., "Joseph Smith's Own Story of a Serious Childhood Illness," *BYU Studies*, ed. James B. Allen [Summer 1970]: 481; capitalization standardized).

Lucy Mack Smith

Joseph, our third son, having recovered from the typhus fever, after something like two weeks' sickness, one day screamed out while sitting in a chair, with a pain in his shoulder, and, in a very short time he appeared to be in such agony that we feared the consequence would prove to be something very serious. We immediately sent for a doctor. When he arrived and had examined the patient, he said that it was his opinion that this pain was occasioned by a sprain. But the child declared this could not be the case as he had received no injury in any way whatever, but that a severe pain had seized him all at once, of the cause of which he was entirely ignorant.

Notwithstanding the child's protestations, still the physician insisted that it must be a sprain, and consequently he anointed his shoulder with some bone liniment, but this was of no advantage to him, for the pain continued the same after the anointing as before.

When two weeks of extreme suffering had elapsed, the attendant physician concluded to make closer examination, whereupon he found that a large fever sore had gathered between his breast and shoulder. He immediately lanced it, upon which it discharged fully a quart of matter.

As soon as the sore had discharged itself, the pain left it, and shot like lightning (using his own terms) down his side into the marrow of the bone of his leg and soon became very severe. My poor boy, at this, was almost in despair, and he cried out "Oh, father! the pain is so severe, how can I bear it!"

His leg soon began to swell and he continued to suffer the greatest agony for the space of two weeks longer. During this period I carried him much of the time in my arms in order to mitigate his suffering as much as possible; in consequence of which I was taken very ill myself. The anxiety of my mind that I experienced, together with physical overexertion, was too much for my constitution and my nature sunk under it.

Hyrum, who was rather remarkable for his tenderness and sympathy, now desired that he might take my place. As he was a good, trusty boy, we let him do so, and, in order to make the task easy for him as possible, we laid Joseph upon a low bed and Hyrum sat beside him, almost day and night for some considerable length of time, holding the affected part of his leg in his hands and pressing it between them, so that his afflicted brother might be enabled to endure the pain which was so excruciating that he was scarcely able to bear it.

At the end of three weeks, we thought it advisable to send again for the surgeon. When he came he made an incision of eight inches, on the front side of the leg, between the knee and ankle. This relieved the pain in a great measure, and the patient was quite comfortable until the wound began to heal, when the pain became as violent as ever.

The surgeon was called again, and he this time enlarged the wound, cutting the leg even to the bone. It commenced healing the second time, and as soon as it began to heal it also began to swell again, which swelling continued to rise till we deemed it wisdom to call a council of surgeons; and when they met in consultation they decided that amputation was the only remedy.

Soon after coming to this conclusion, they rode up to the door and were invited into a room apart from the one in which Joseph lay. They being seated, I addressed them thus: "Gentlemen, what can you do to save my boy's leg?" They answered, "We can do nothing; we have cut it open to the bone and find it so affected that we consider his leg incurable and that amputation is absolutely necessary in order to save his life."

This was like a thunderbolt to me. I appealed to the principal surgeon, saying, "Dr. Stone, can you not make another trial? Can you not, by cutting around the bone, take out the diseased part, and perhaps that which is sound will heal over, and by this means you will save his leg? You will not, you must not, take off his leg, until you try once more. I will not consent to let you enter his room until you make me this promise."

After consulting a short time with each other, they agreed to do as I had requested, then went to see my suffering son. One of the doctors, on approaching his bed, said, "My poor boy, we have come again." "Yes," said Joseph, "I see you have; but you have not come to take off my leg, have you, sir?" "No," replied the surgeon, "it is your mother's request that we make one more effort, and that is what we have now come for."

The principal surgeon, after a moment's conversation, ordered cords to be brought to bind Joseph fast to the bedstead; but to this Joseph objected. The doctor, however, insisted that he must be confined, upon which Joseph said very decidedly, "No, doctor, I will not be bound, for I can bear the operation much better if I have my liberty." "Then," said Dr. Stone, "will you drink some brandy?"

"No," said Joseph, "not one drop."

"Will you take some wine?" rejoined the doctor. "You must take something, or you can never endure the severe operation to which you must be subjected."

"No," exclaimed Joseph, "I will not touch one particle of liquor, neither will I be tied down; but I will tell you what I will do—I will have my father sit on the bed and hold me in his arms, and then I will do whatever is necessary in order to have the bone taken out." Looking at me, he said, "Mother, I want you to leave the room, for I know you cannot bear to see me suffer so; father can stand it, but you have carried me so much, and watched over me so long, you are almost worn out." Then looking up into my face, his eyes swimming in tears, he continued[,] "Now, mother, promise me you will not stay, will you? The Lord will help me, and I shall get through with it."

To this request I consented, and getting a number of folded sheets, and laying them under his leg, I retired, going several hundred yards from the house in order to be out of hearing.

The surgeons commenced operating by boring into the bone of his leg, first on one side of the bone where it was affected, then on the other side, after which they broke it off with a pair of forceps or pincers. They thus took away large pieces of the bone. When they broke off the first piece, Joseph screamed out so loudly, that I could not forbear running to him. On my entering his room, he cried out, "Oh, mother, go back, go back; I do not want you to come in—I will try to tough it out, if you will go away."

When the third piece was taken away, I burst into the room again—and oh, my God! What a spectacle for a mother's eye! The wound torn open, the blood still gushing from it, and the bed literally covered with blood. Joseph was pale as a corpse, and large drops of sweat were rolling down his face, whilst upon every feature was depicted the utmost agony!

I was immediately forced from the room, and detained until the operation was completed; but when the act was accomplished, Joseph put upon a clean bed, the room cleared of every appearance of blood, and the instruments which were used in the operation removed, I was permitted again to enter.

Joseph immediately commenced getting better, and from this onward, continued to mend until he became strong and healthy. When he had so far recovered as to be able to travel, he went with his uncle, Jesse Smith, to Salem, for the benefit of his health, hoping the sea-breezes would be of service to him, and in this he was not disappointed.

Having passed through about a year of sickness and distress, health again returned to our family, and we most assuredly realized the blessing; and indeed, we felt to acknowledge the hand of God, more in preserving our lives through such a tremendous scene of affliction, than if we had, during this time, seen nothing but health and prosperity (*History of Joseph Smith*, 54–58; spelling standardized).

~ 3 ~

PALMYRA REVIVALS

During a nineteenth century period of fervent and enthusiastic religious revivals, upstate New York became known as the "burned-over district." Itinerant preachers and ministers flooded the area, attempting to entice residents into joining their religious sects. Historians of religion have termed these periods of religious revival as "Great Awakenings." With the popularity of religious fervor on the rise, nearly all churches held revivals.

Milton V. Backman Jr.

(On the nature of camp meetings during this period.)

One of the most effective missionary programs adopted by the Methodists to promulgate their faith was the camp meeting. Although Baptists, Presbyterians, and members of other religious societies also sponsored such meetings and while Christians of various faiths participated in these gatherings, the Methodists in western New York conducted more camp meetings in the early nineteenth century than did members of any other denomination. These meetings were usually held on the edge of a beautiful grove of trees or in a small clearing in the midst of a forest. After traveling many miles along dusty or water-logged roads, the settlers would locate their wagons and pitch their tents on the outskirts of the encampment. Farmers' markets and grog or liquor shops often sprung up near the camp grounds, thereby providing some farmers with unusual economic opportunities. The meetings frequently continued for several days, and sometimes one session would last nearly all day and into the night. Ministers would rotate preaching assignments so that one minister would immediately be followed by another, and at times two or three ministers would preach simultaneously in

A typical camp meeting about 1830–35, by A. Rider
(Courtesy of Church Archives, The Church of Jesus Christ of Latter-day Saints)

different parts of the camp ground. Ministers not only preached lengthy sermons but devoted much of their time in counseling and directing prayer circles and group singing.

The numbers who attended camp meetings held in New York about 1820 varied considerably. There were times when only a few hundred gathered, and on other occasions thousands witnessed the proceedings. In a camp meeting held in Palmyra in 1826 one reporter estimated that 10,000 people gathered on the grounds to behold the spiritual drama.

In some sections of early America, camp meetings frequently erupted into exciting spectacles in which enthusiasts demonstrated their emotional aspirations with a variety of physical demonstrations. During these exuberant meetings, people went into trances, jerked, rolled and crawled on the ground, barked like dogs, and fell to the ground as though they had been hit by a piercing cannon ball, remaining unconscious for minutes or even sometimes for hours. In western New York, however, at the time of the First Vision, physical demonstrations were rarely manifest, except for the occasional practice of falling to the ground and crying out for mercy. Nevertheless, some settlers who were attending these New York meetings for the first time were alarmed by the piercing, dissonant commotions that would occasionally erupt. Some viewed with mixed emotions the weeping, the crying, the mourning, and the sighing which created loud noises in the encampment (Milton V. Backman Jr., "Awakenings in the Burned-Over District: New Light on the Historical Setting of the First Vision," *BYU Studies* 9 [Spring 1969]: 306–7).

Lucy Mack Smith

In the anxiety of my soul to abide by the covenant which I had entered into with the Almighty, I went from place to place to seek information or find, if possible, some congenial spirit who might enter into my feelings and sympathize with me.

At last I heard that one noted for his piety would preach the ensuing Sabbath in the Presbyterian church. Thither I went in expectation of obtaining that which alone could satisfy my soul—the bread of eternal life. When the minister commenced, I fixed my mind with breathless attention upon the spirit and matter of the discourse, but all was emptiness, vanity, vexation of spirit, and fell upon my heart like the chill, untimely blast upon the starting ear ripening in a summer sun. It did not fill the aching void within nor satisfy the craving hunger of my soul. I was almost in total despair, and with a grieved and troubled spirit I returned home, saying in my heart, there is not on earth the religion which I seek (Lucy Mack Smith, *The Revised and Enhanced History of Joseph Smith by His Mother*, ed. Scot Facer Proctor and Maurine Jensen Proctor [Salt Lake City: Bookcraft, 1996], 49–50).

Lucy Mack Smith

There was a great revival in religion, which extended to all the denominations of Christians in the surrounding country in which we resided. Many of the world's people, becoming concerned about the salvation of their souls, came forward and presented themselves as seekers after religion. Most of them were desirous of uniting with some church but were not decided as to the particular faith which they would adopt. When the numerous meetings were about breaking up, and the candidates and the various leading church members began to consult upon the subject of adopting the candidates into some church or churches, as the case may be, a dispute arose, and there was a great contention among them (*The Revised and Enhanced History of Joseph Smith*, 94).

Peter Cartwright

(Commenting on the emergence and rise of this religious fervor, he describes a typical camp meeting.)

From this camp-meeting . . . the news spread through all the Churches, and through all the land, and it excited great wonder and surprise; but it kindled a religious flame that spread all over Kentucky and through many other states. And I may here be permitted to say, that this was the first camp-meeting ever held in the United States, and here our camp-meetings took their rise.

. . . Just in the midst of our controversies on the subject of the powerful exercises among the people under preaching, a new exercise broke out among us, called the *jerks*, which was overwhelming in its effects upon the bodies and minds of the people. No matter whether they were saints or sinners, they would be taken under a warm song or sermon, and seized with a convulsive jerking all over, which they could not by any possibility avoid, and the more they resisted the more they jerked. If they would not strive against it and pray in good earnest, the jerking would usually abate. I have seen more than five hundred persons jerking at one time in my large congregations. Most usually persons taken with the jerks, to obtain relief, as they said, would rise up and dance. Some would run, but could not get away. Some would resist; on such the jerks were generally very severe.

The Reverend George Lane, the circuit rider who preached from James 1:5 at a meeting Joseph Smith attended *(Courtesy of the Church Archives, The Church of Jesus Christ of Latter-day Saints)*

To see those proud young gentlemen and young ladies, dressed in their silks, jewelry, and prunella, from top to toe, take the *jerks*, would often excite my risibilities. The first jerk or so, you would see their fine bonnets, caps, and combs fly; and so sudden would be the jerking of the head that their long loose hair would crack almost as loud as a wagoner's whip.

. . . Somewhere between 1800 and 1801, in the upper part of Kentucky, at a memorable place called "Cane Ridge," there was appointed a sacramental meeting by some of the Presbyterian ministers, at which meeting, seemingly unexpected by ministers or people, the mighty power of God was displayed in a very extraordinary manner; many were moved to tears, and bitter and loud crying for mercy. The meeting was protracted for weeks. Ministers of almost all denominations flocked in from far and near. The meeting was kept up by night and day. Thousands heard of the mighty work, and came on foot, on horseback, in carriages and wagons. It was supposed that there were in attendance at times during the meeting from twelve to twenty-five thousand people. Hundreds fell prostrate under the mighty power of God, as men slain in battle. Stands were erected in the woods from which preachers of different Churches proclaimed repentance toward God and faith in our Lord Jesus Christ, and it was supposed, by eye and ear witnesses, that between one and two thousand souls were happily and powerfully converted to God during the meeting. It was not unusual for one, two, three, and four to seven preachers to be addressing the listening thousands at the same time from the different stands erected for the purpose. The heavenly fire spread in almost every direction. It was said, by truthful witnesses, that at times more than one thousand persons broke out into loud shouting all at once, and that the shouts could be heard for miles around (Peter Cartwright, *Autobiography of Peter Cartwright, the Backwoods Preacher* [New York: Carlton and Porter, 1856], 30–31, 48–49).

Mark Twain

(This description of a camp meeting comes from Huckleberry Finn.*)*

So me and the king lit out for the camp-meeting.

We got there in about a half an hour fairly dripping, for it was a most awful hot day. There was as much as a thousand people there, from twenty mile around. The woods was full of teams and wagons, hitched everywheres, feeding out of the wagon troughs and stomping to keep off the flies. There was sheds made out of poles and roofed over with branches, where they had lemonade and gingerbread to sell, and piles of watermelons and green corn and such-like truck.

The preaching was going on under the same kinds of sheds, only they was bigger and held crowds of people. The benches was made out of outside slabs of logs, with holes bored in the round side to drive sticks into for legs. They didn't have no backs. The preachers had high platforms to stand on, at one end of the sheds. The women had on sun-bonnets; and some had linsey-woolsey frocks, some gingham ones, and a few of the young ones had on calico. Some of the young men was barefooted, and some of the children didn't have on any clothes but just a tow-linen shirt. Some of the old women was knitting, and some of the young folks was courting on the sly.

The first shed we come to, the preacher was lining out a hymn. He lined out two lines, everybody sung it, and it was kind of grand to hear it, there was so many of them and they done it in such a rousing way; then he lined out two more for them to sing—and so on. The people woke up more and more, and sung louder and louder; and towards the end, some begun to groan, and some begun to shout. Then the preacher begun to preach; and begun in earnest, too; and went weaving first to one side of the platform and then the other, and then a leaning down over the front of it, with his arms and his body going all the time, and shouting his words out with all his might; and every now and then he would hold up his Bible and spread it open, and kind of pass it around this way and that, shouting, "It's the brazen serpent in the wilderness! Look upon it and live!" And people would shout out, "Glory!—A-a-men!" And so he went on, and the people groaning and crying and saying amen:

"Oh, come to the mourners' bench! come, black with sin! (amen!) come, sick and sore! (amen!) come, lame and halt, and blind! (amen!) come, pore and needy, sunk in shame! (a-a-men!) come all that's worn, and soiled, and suffering!—come with a broken spirit! come with a con-trite heart! come in your rags and sin and dirt! the waters that cleanse is free, the door of heaven stands open—oh, enter in and be at rest!" (a-a-men! glory, glory hallelujah!)

And so on. You couldn't make out what the preacher said, any more, on account of the shouting and crying. Folks got up everywheres in the crowd, and worked their way, just by main strength, to the mourn-ers' bench, with the tears running down their faces; and when all the mourners had got up there to the front benches in a crowd, they sung, and shouted, and flung themselves down on the straw, just crazy and wild.

Well, the first I knowed, the king got agoing; and you could hear him over everybody; and next he went a-charging up on to the platform and the preacher he begged him to speak to the people, and he done it. He told them he was a pirate—been a pirate for thirty years out, out in the Indian Ocean, and his crew was thinned out considerable, last spring, in a fight, and he was home now, to take out some fresh men, and thanks to goodness he'd been robbed last night, and put ashore off of a steamboat without a cent, and he was glad of it, it was the blessedest thing that ever happened to him, because he was a changed man now, and happy for the first time in his life; and poor as he was, he was going to start right off and work his way back to the Indian Ocean and put in the rest of his life trying to turn the pirates into the true path; for he could do it better than anybody else, being acquainted with all pirate crews in that ocean; and though it would take him a long time to get there, without money, he would get there anyway, and every time he convinced a pirate he would say to him, "Don't you thank me, don't you give me no credit, it all belongs to them dear people in Pokeville campmeeting, natural brothers and benefactors of the race, and that dear preacher there, the truest friend a pirate ever had!"

And then he busted into tears, and so did everybody. Then somebody sings out, "Take up a collection for him, take up a collection!" Well, a half a dozen made a jump to do it, but somebody sings out, "Let *him* pass the hat around!" Then everybody said it, the preacher too.

So the king went all through the crowd with his hat, swabbing his eyes, and blessing the people and praising them and thanking them for being so good to the poor pirates away off there; and every little while the prettiest kind of girls, with the tears running down their cheeks, would up and ask him would he let them kiss him, for to remember him by; and he always done it; and some of them he hugged and kissed as many as five or six times—and he was invited to stay a week; and everybody wanted him to live in their houses, and said they'd think it was an honor; but he said as this was the last day of the camp-meeting he couldn't do no good, and besides he was in a sweat to get to the Indian Ocean right off and go to work on the pirates.

When we got back to the raft and he come to count up, he found he had collected eighty-seven dollars and seventy-five cents. And then he had fetched away a three-gallon jug of whisky, too, that he found under a wagon when we was starting home through the woods. The king said, take it all around, it laid over any day he'd ever put in in the missionarying line. He said it warn't no use talking, heathens don't amount to shucks, alongside of pirates, to work a camp-meeting with (Mark Twain, *Huckleberry Finn* [New York: W. W. Norton, 1977], 106–8).

~4~

THE RESTORATION

After years of spiritual darkness, the light of the Restoration burst upon the earth in the spring of 1820 beginning with the First Vision and the restoration of the gospel of Jesus Christ.

The Restoration came at a pivotal moment in American history. There is great significance to the Lord's timing in restoring His eternal truth to the earth when and where He did. The necessary precursors of the restoration of the gospel of Jesus Christ include such important milestones as the Protestant Reformation, the English translation and dissemination of the Holy Bible, the discovery and colonization of the New World, the American Revolution, the founding of America with its constitutionally guaranteed freedom of religion, the restoration of the priesthood, and the coming forth of the Book of Mormon.

In this chapter we will site several modern statements describing past events. We do this to provide perspective and to show just how seamlessly such events fit together in the grand panorama of the Restoration.

THE TIMING OF THE RESTORATION WAS PROVIDENTIAL

Bruce R. McConkie

Beginning in the 14th century, the Lord began to prepare those social, educational, religious, economic, and governmental conditions under which he could more easily restore the gospel for the last time (Bruce R. McConkie, *Mormon Doctrine* [Salt Lake City: Bookcraft, 1989], 717).

James E. Talmage

[The Renaissance and Reformation were not chance occurrences, but rather] a development predetermined in the Mind of God to illumine the benighted minds of men in preparation for the restoration of the gospel of Jesus Christ, which was appointed to be accomplished some centuries later (James E. Talmage, *Jesus the Christ* [Salt Lake City: The Church of Jesus Christ of Latter-day Saints, 1981], 749).

Joseph Fielding Smith

In preparation for this restoration the Lord raised up noble men, such as Luther, Calvin, Knox and others whom we call reformers, and gave them power to break the shackles which bound the people and denied them the sacred right to worship God according to the dictates of conscience. The Almighty gave men their agency, or the power to act for themselves in choosing good or evil, before the foundation of the earth was laid; but the dragon, from the beginning when he was cast out of heaven, has endeavored to deprive men of this great gift of God.

In the days of greatest spiritual darkness, when evil raged, the Lord raised up honorable men, who rebelled against the tyranny of the dragon and his emissaries who held dominion on the earth, and had subdued in abject slavery the consciences of men.

Latter-day Saints pay all honor to these great and fearless reformers, who shattered the fetters which bound the religious world. The Lord was their Protector in this mission, which was fraught with many perils. In that day, however, the time had not come for the restoration of the fulness of the gospel. The work of the reformers was of great importance, but it was a preparatory work, and they shall in no wise lose their well earned reward.

It was not until the close of the first quarter of the nineteenth century that the time fully came for the restoration of light and truth in its primitive fulness. At that time the world had been prepared sufficiently, both by the establishment of political and religious liberty, for the Church of Jesus Christ and the holy priesthood to be again returned safely to the earth (*Doctrines of Salvation*, 3 vols., ed. Bruce R. McConkie [Salt Lake City: Bookcraft, 1954], 1:174–75).

Spencer W. Kimball
N. Eldon Tanner
Marion G. Romney

Based upon ancient and modern revelation, The Church of Jesus Christ of Latter-day Saints gladly teaches and declares the Christian doctrine that all men and women are brothers and sisters, not only by blood relationship from mortal progenitors, but also as literal spirit children of an Eternal Father.

Spencer W. Kimball
(Courtesy of the Church Archives, The Church of Jesus Christ of Latter-day Saints)

The great religious leaders of the world such as Mohammed, Confucius, and the Reformers, as well as philosophers including Socrates, Plato, and others, received a portion of God's light. Moral truths were given to them by God to enlighten whole nations and to bring a higher level of understanding to individuals.

The Hebrew prophets prepared the way for the coming of Jesus Christ, the promised Messiah, who should provide salvation for all mankind who believe in the gospel.

Consistent with these truths, we believe that God has given and will give to all people sufficient knowledge to help them on their way to eternal salvation, either in this life or in the life to come.

We also declare that the gospel of Jesus Christ, restored to his Church in our day, provides the only way to a mortal life of happiness and a fullness of joy forever. For those who have not received this gospel, the opportunity will come to them in the life hereafter if not in this life.

Our message therefore is one of special love and concern for the eternal welfare of all men and women, regardless of religious belief, race, or nationality, knowing that we are truly brothers and sisters because we are the sons and daughters of the same Eternal Father (*First Presidency Statement*, [Salt Lake City: The Church of Jesus Christ of Latter-day Saints], February 1978).

Joseph Fielding Smith

The discovery [of America] was one of the most important factors in bringing to pass the purpose of the Almighty in the restoration of his Gospel in its fulness for the salvation of men in the latter days (Joseph Fielding Smith, *The Progress of Man* [Salt Lake City: Deseret Book, 1964], 258).

Neal A. Maxwell

Recall the new star that announced the birth at Bethlehem? It was in its precise orbit long before it so shone. . . . Divine correlation functions not only in the cosmos but on this planet too. After all, the Book of Mormon plates were not buried in Belgium, only to have Joseph Smith born centuries later in distant Bombay.

The raising up of that constellation of "wise" Founding Fathers to produce America's remarkable Constitution, whose rights and protection belong to "every man," was not a random thing either (D&C 101:77–78, 80). One historian called our Founding Fathers "the most remarkable generation of public men in the history of the United States or perhaps of any other nation" (Arthur M. Schlesinger, *The Birth of the Nation* [1968], 245). Another historian added, "It would be invaluable if we could know what produced this burst of talent from a base of only two and a half million inhabitants" (Barbara W. Tuchman, *The March of Folly: From Troy to Vietnam* [1984], 18) (Neal A. Maxwell, "Encircled in the Arms of His Love," *Ensign*, November 2002, 17).

Gordon S. Wood

Its [the Restoration of the Church's] timing in 1830 was providential. It appeared at precisely the right moment in American history; much earlier or later and the Church might not have taken hold. The Book of Mormon would probably not have been published in the eighteenth century, in that still largely oral world of folk beliefs prior to the great democratic revolution that underlay the religious tumult of the early Republic. In the eighteenth century, Mormonism might have been too easily stifled and dismissed by the dominant enlightened gentry culture as just another enthusiastic folk superstition. Yet if Mormonism had emerged later, after the consolidation of authority and the spread of science in the middle decades of the nineteenth century, it might have had problems of verifying its texts and revelations (Gordon S. Wood, "Evangelical America and Early Mormonism," *New York History* [October 1980]: 381; as cited in *Church History in the Fulness of Times*, Prepared by the Church Educational System [Salt Lake City: The Church of Jesus Christ of Latter-day Saints, 1989], 12).

JOSEPH SMITH INAUGURATED THE DISPENSATION OF THE FULNESS OF TIMES

Brigham Young

Joseph Smith, junior, was ordained to this great calling before the worlds were. . . . It was decreed in the counsels of eternity, long before the foundations of the earth were laid, that he should be the man, in the last dispensation of this world, to bring forth the word of God to the people, and receive the fullness of the keys and power of the Priesthood of the Son of God. The Lord had his eye upon him, and upon his father, and upon his father's father, and upon their progenitors clear back to Abraham, and from Abraham to the flood, from the flood to Enoch, and from Enoch to Adam. He has watched that family and that blood as it has circulated from its fountain to the birth of that man. He was foreordained in eternity to preside over this last dispensation . . . Joseph Smith, junior, was foreordained to come through the loins of Abraham, Isaac, Jacob, Joseph, and so on down through the Prophets and Apostles; and thus he came forth in the last days to be a minister of salvation, and to hold the keys of the last dispensation of the fullness of times (in *Journal of Discourses*, 26 vols. [London: Latter-day Saints' Book Depot, 1854-86], 7:289–90; spelling standardized).

J. Reuben Clark Jr.

To assist men in their efforts fully to return to him, our Heavenly Father has provided from time to time, beginning with Adam, organizations of his Priesthood, to bring to men principles they had abandoned and sometimes forgotten, and to reemphasize and where necessary restore, the Priesthood, with its duties and divine powers. These occasions are called dispensations in Holy Writ, and we speak of the dispensations of Adam, Enoch, Noah, Abraham, Moses, the Messiah, and now of the Dispensation of the Fullness of Times. In each pre-Messianic dispensation God gave to the men who established it, special authority and commandments with particular missions (J. Reuben Clark Jr., *On the Way to Immortality and Eternal Life* [Salt Lake City: Deseret Book, 1961], 33).

JOSEPH SMITH RECOGNIZED THE SIGNIFICANCE OF THE EVENTS OF THE RESTORATION

Joseph Smith Jr.

The building up of Zion is a cause that has interested the people of God in every age; it is a theme upon which prophets, priests and kings have dwelt with peculiar delight; they have looked forward with joyful anticipation to the day in which we live; and fired with heavenly and joyful anticipations they have sung and written and prophesied of this our day; but they died without the sight; we are the favored people that God has made choice of to bring about the Latter-day glory; it is left for us to see, participate in and help to roll forward the Latter-day glory, "the dispensation of the fullness of times, when God will gather together all things that are in heaven, and all things that are upon the earth,["] "even in one," when the Saints of God will be gathered in one from every nation, and kindred and people, and tongue, when the Jews will be gathered together into one ... [Which prophecy is being fulfilled in modern Israel today.] the Spirit of God will also dwell with His people, and be withdrawn from the rest of the nations, and all things whether in heaven or on earth will be in one, even in Christ. The heavenly Priesthood will unite with the earthly, to bring about those great purposes; and whilst we are thus united in the one common cause, to roll forth the kingdom of God, the heavenly Priesthood are not idle spectators, the Spirit of God will be showered down from above, and will dwell in our midst. The blessings of the Most High will rest upon our tabernacles, and our name will be handed down to future ages; our children will rise up and call us blessed; and generations yet unborn will dwell with peculiar delight upon the scenes that we have passed through, the privations that we have endured; the untiring zeal that we have manifested; the all but insurmountable difficulties that we have overcome in laying the foundation of a work that brought about the glory and blessing which they [our children] will realize; a work that God and angels have contemplated with delight for generations past; that fired the souls of the ancient patriarchs and prophets; a work that is destined to bring about the destruction of the powers of darkness, the renovation of the earth, the glory of God, and the salvation of the human family (Joseph Smith, *History of The Church of Jesus Christ of Latter-day Saints*, 7 vols., ed. B. H. Roberts [Salt Lake City: Deseret Book, 1978], 4:609–10).

Joseph Smith Jr.

It is in the order of heavenly things that God should always send a new dispensation into the world when men have apostatized from the truth and lost the priesthood; but when men come out and build upon other men's foundations, they do it on their own responsibility, without authority from God; and when the floods come and the winds blow, their foundations will be found to be sand, and their whole fabric will crumble to dust.

Did I build on any other man's foundation? I have got all the truth which the Christian world possessed, and an independent revelation in the bargain, and God will bear me off triumphant (*History of the Church*, 6:478–79).

Wilford Woodruff
(Courtesy of the Church Archives, The Church of Jesus Christ of Latter-day Saints)

Wilford Woodruff

There never was a dispensation on the earth when prophets and apostles, the inspiration, revelation and power of God, the holy priesthood and the keys of the kingdom were needed more than they are in this generation. There never has been a dispensation when the friends of God and righteousness among the children of men needed more faith in the promises and prophecies than they do today; and there certainly never has been a generation of people on the earth that has had a greater work to perform than the inhabitants of the earth in the latter days (*Journal of Discourses*, 15:8).

Wilford Woodruff

It is no light thing for any people in any age in the world to have a dispensation of the Gospel of Jesus Christ committed into their hands, and when a dispensation has been given, those receiving it are held responsible before high heaven for the use they make of it (*Journal of Discourses*, 22:205).

THE STONE CUT OUT OF THE MOUNTAIN

The Prophet Daniel saw in vision that, in the latter days, God would establish His kingdom upon this earth in preparation for the Second Coming of Jesus Christ. This kingdom would be "cut out without hands." In other words, it would be a work of God, not of man. It would "become a great mountain and fill the whole earth," it would "never be destroyed," "not be left to other people," and "stand forever" (Daniel 2:34, 35, 44).

The Church of Jesus Christ of Latter-day Saints is this prophesied Kingdom of God. In October 1831, the Lord revealed: "The keys of the kingdom of God are committed unto man on the earth, and from thence shall the gospel roll forth unto the ends of the earth, as the stone which is cut out of the mountain without hands shall roll forth, until it has filled the whole earth" (D&C 65:2).

George Albert Smith

The preparation for the ushering in of the Gospel of Jesus Christ in this latter dispensation was indicated in the reign of Nebuchadnezzar, and repeated again in the days of the Apostles, and then the foundation was laid for the organization of the government of the United States by men and women who believed in the divine mission of Jesus Christ.

George Albert Smith
*(Courtesy of the Church Archives,
The Church of Jesus Christ of
Latter-day Saints)*

The stage was not set hastily; it was preparing through hundreds of years. . . . Our Heavenly Father prepared the way for the coming of the Gospel of Jesus Christ, which was to precede the second coming of our Lord (George Albert Smith, in Conference Report, April 1930, 65).

Joseph Smith Jr.

The ancient prophets declared that in the last days the God of heaven should set up a kingdom which should never be destroyed, nor left to other people; and the very time that was calculated on, this people were struggling to bring it out. . . .

I calculate to be one of the instruments of setting up the kingdom of Daniel by the word of the Lord, and I intend to lay a foundation that will revolutionize the whole world. . . . It will not be by sword or gun that this kingdom will roll on: the power of truth is such that all nations will be under the necessity of obeying the Gospel (*History of the Church*, 6:364–65).

Heber J. Grant

I bear my witness to you here today that Joseph Smith was a prophet of the true and the living God, that he was the instrument in the hands of God of establishing again upon the earth the plan of life and salvation, not only for the living but for the dead, and that this gospel, commonly called "Mormonism," by the people of the world, is in very deed the plan of life and salvation, the gospel of the Lord Jesus Christ, that the little stone has been cut out of the mountain, and that it shall roll forth until it fills the whole earth (Heber J. Grant, in Conference Report, October 1919, 15).

The Gospel Will Roll Forward Until It Fills the Earth

Joseph Smith Jr.

No unhallowed hand can stop the work from progressing; persecutions may rage, mobs may combine, armies may assemble, calumny may defame, but the truth of God will go forth boldly, nobly, and independent, till it has penetrated every continent, visited every clime, swept every country, and sounded in every ear, till the purposes of God shall be accomplished, and the Great Jehovah shall say the work is done (*History of the Church*, 4:540).

Brigham Young

The powers of earth and hell have striven to destroy this kingdom from the earth. The wicked have succeeded in doing so in former ages; but this kingdom they cannot destroy, because it is the last dispensation—because it is the fullness of times. It is the dispensation of all dispensations, and will excel in magnificence and glory every dispensation that has ever been committed to the children of men upon this earth. The Lord will bring again Zion, redeem his Israel, plant his standard upon the earth, and establish the laws of his kingdom, and those laws will prevail (*Journal of Discourses*, 8:36).

Wilford Woodruff

This is the only dispensation that God has ever established that was foreordained, before the world was made, not to be overcome by wicked men and devils (*Journal of Discourses*, 17:245).

Heber J. Grant

Any Latter-day Saint that thinks for one minute that this Church is going to fail is not a really converted Latter-day Saint. There will be no failure in this Church. It has been established for the last time, never to be given to another people and never to be thrown down (Heber J. Grant, "Teach That Which Encourages Faith," *Church News* [8 September 1934]: 1).

Ezra Taft Benson

With all my soul I testify that this work will go forward till every land and people have had opportunity to accept our message. Barriers will come down for us to accomplish this mission, and some of us will see this done. Our Heavenly Father will cause conditions in the world to change so that His gospel can penetrate every border (*The Teachings of Ezra Taft Benson* [Salt Lake City: Bookcraft, 1988], 174).

Ezra Taft Benson

I testify that wickedness is rapidly expanding in every segment of our society. (See D&C 1:14–16; 84:49–53.) It is more highly organized, more cleverly disguised, and more powerfully promoted than ever before. Secret combinations lusting for power, gain, and glory are flourishing. A secret combination that seeks to overthrow the freedom of all lands, nations, and countries is increasing its evil influence and control over America and the entire world. (See Ether 8:18–25.)

Ezra Taft Benson
(Courtesy of the Church Archives, The Church of Jesus Christ of Latter-day Saints)

I testify that the church and kingdom of God is increasing in strength. Its numbers are growing, as is the faithfulness of its faithful members. It has never been better organized or equipped to perform its divine mission.

I testify that as the forces of evil increase under Lucifer's leadership and as the forces of good increase under the leadership of Jesus Christ, there will be growing battles between the two until the final confrontation. As the issues become clearer and more obvious, all mankind will eventually be required to align themselves either for the kingdom of God or for the kingdom of the devil. As these conflicts rage, either secretly or openly, the righteous will be tested. God's wrath will soon shake the nations of the earth and will be poured out on the wicked without measure (see Joseph Smith–History 1:45; D&C 1:9). But God will provide strength for the righteous and the means of escape; and eventually and finally truth will triumph. (1 Nephi 22:15–23) (Ezra Taft Benson, "I Testify," *Ensign*, November 1988, 87).

John Taylor

We have got this kingdom to build up; and it is not a phantom, but a reality. We have to do it, God expects it at our hands. . . . We have got to establish a government upon the principles of righteousness, justice, truth and equality and not according to the many false notions that exist among men. And then the day is not far distant when this nation will be shaken from centre to circumference. And now, you may write it down, any of you, and I will prophesy it in the name of God. And then will be fulfilled that prediction to be found in one of the revelations given through the Prophet Joseph Smith. Those who will not take up their sword to fight against their neighbor must needs flee to Zion for safety. And they will come, saying, we do not know anything of the principles of your religion, but we perceive that you are an honest community; you administer justice and righteousness, and we want to live with you and receive the protection of your laws, but as for your religion we will talk about that some other time. Will we protect such people? Yes, all honorable men (*Journal of Discourses*, 21:8).

Gordon B. Hinckley

Now, what of the future? What of the years that lie ahead? It looks promising indeed. People are beginning to see us for what we are and for the values we espouse. The media generally treat us well. We enjoy a good reputation, for which we are grateful.

If we will go forward, never losing sight of our goal, speaking ill of no one, living the great principles we know to be true, this cause will roll on in majesty and power to fill the earth. Doors now closed to the preaching of the gospel will be opened. The Almighty, if necessary, may have to shake the nations to humble them and cause them to listen to the servants of the living God. Whatever is needed will come to pass (Gordon B. Hinckley, "Look to the Future," *Ensign*, November 1997, 68).

⟨5⟩

THE FIRST VISION

The most significant event not only in latter-day Church History but also in world history, since the resurrection of the Lord Jesus Christ, occurred in the spring of 1820 in a small grove of trees just outside the Smith family home in Palmyra, New York. God the Eternal Father and His Son, Jesus Christ, appeared to fourteen-year-old Joseph Smith. This "First Vision" became the pivotal moment in modern history, marking a new day for all mankind. What took place in the sacred grove changed the world because it introduced the dispensation of the fulness of times. As President Gordon B. Hinckley noted, the truthfulness of the Restoration rests on the validity of the First Vision:

> Our entire case as members of The Church of Jesus Christ of Latter-day Saints rests on the validity of this glorious First Vision. It was the parting of the curtain to open this, the dispensation of the fulness of times. Nothing on which we base our doctrine, nothing we teach, nothing we live by is of greater importance than this initial declaration. I submit that if Joseph Smith talked with God the Father and His Beloved Son, then all else of which he spoke is true. This is the hinge on which turns the gate that leads to the path of salvation and eternal life. (Gordon B. Hinckley, "What Are People Asking about Us," *Ensign*, November 1998, 71)

If Joseph Smith did see the Father and the Son, and they did indeed tell him that he was chosen and called of God to restore the Church of Jesus Christ to the Earth, then the message and work of the Restoration is the most wonderful work on Earth.

This message has had and will continue to have a great impact on its hearers. While traveling with Joseph Smith and Sidney Rigdon through Pennsylvania, Parley P. Pratt described the impression Joseph Smith's testimony of his experiences left on those who heard it. He wrote:

> While visiting with brother Joseph in Philadelphia, a very large church was opened for him to preach in, and about three thousand people assembled to hear him. Brother [Sidney] Rigdon spoke first, and dwelt on the Gospel, illustrating his doctrine by the Bible. When he was through, brother Joseph arose like a lion about to roar; and being full of the Holy Ghost, spoke in great power, bearing testimony of the visions he had seen, the ministering of angels which he had enjoyed; and how he had found the plates of the Book of Mormon, and translated them by the gift and power of God. He commenced by saying: "If nobody else had the courage to testify of so glorious a message from Heaven, and of the finding of so glorious a record, he felt to do it in justice to the people, and leave the event with God." The entire congregation were astounded; electrified, as it were, and overwhelmed with the sense of the truth and power by which he spoke, and the wonders which he related. A lasting impression was made; many souls were gathered into the fold. And I bear witness, that he, by his faithful and powerful testimony, cleared his garments of their blood. (Parley P. Pratt, *Autobiography of Parley Parker Pratt*, ed. Parley P. Pratt Jr. [Salt Lake City: Deseret Book, 1964], 298–99)

Accounts of the First Vision

Only a small number of first-hand accounts of the First Vision exist. Of the ten described below, four were penned by the Prophet Joseph himself or dictated to a scribe (the 1832, 1835, 1838, and 1842 accounts). The other six were written by those who heard him relate his experience, either in a sermon or in a private interview (two accounts from Orson Pratt and one each from Orson Hyde, Levi Richards, David Nye White, and Alexander Neibaur). The most famous of these accounts was written in 1838 by the Prophet. It is the most beautifully written of the accounts. A portion of it reads as follows:

While I was laboring under the extreme difficulties caused by the contests of these parties of religionists, I was one day reading the Epistle of James, first chapter and fifth verse, which reads: *If any of you lack wisdom, let him ask of God, that giveth to all men liberally, and upbraideth not; and it shall be given him.*

Never did any passage of scripture come with more power to the heart of man than this did at this time to mine. It seemed to enter with great force into every feeling of my heart. I reflected on it again and again, knowing that if any person needed wisdom from God, I did; for how to act I did not know, and unless I could get more wisdom than I then had, I would never know; for the teachers of religion of the different sects understood the same passages of scripture so differently as to destroy all confidence in settling the question by an appeal to the Bible.

At length I came to the conclusion that I must either remain in darkness and confusion, or else I must do as James directs, that is, ask of God. I at length came to the determination to "ask of God," concluding that if he gave wisdom to them that lacked wisdom, and would give liberally, and not upbraid, I might venture.

So, in accordance with this, my determination to ask of God, I retired to the woods to make the attempt. It was on the morning of a beautiful, clear day, early in the spring of eighteen hundred and twenty. It was the first time in my life that I had made such an attempt, for amidst all my anxieties I had never as yet made the attempt to pray vocally.

After I had retired to the place where I had previously designed to go, having looked around me, and finding myself alone, I kneeled down and began to offer up the desires of my heart to God. I had scarcely done so, when immediately I was seized upon by some power which entirely overcame me, and had such an astonishing influence over me as to bind my tongue so that I could not speak. Thick darkness gathered around me, and it seemed to me for a time as if I were doomed to sudden destruction.

But, exerting all my powers to call upon God to deliver me out of the power of this enemy which had seized upon me, and at the very moment when I was ready to sink into despair and abandon myself to destruction—not to an imaginary ruin, but to the power of some actual being from the unseen world, who had such marvelous power as I had never before felt in any being—just at this moment of great alarm, I saw a pillar of light exactly over my head, above the brightness of the sun, which descended gradually until it fell upon me.

It no sooner appeared than I found myself delivered from the enemy which held me bound. When the light rested upon me I saw two Personages, whose brightness and glory defy all description, standing above me in the air. One of them spake unto me, calling me by name and said, pointing to the other—*This is My Beloved Son. Hear Him!* (Joseph Smith–History 1:11–17)

The ten accounts of the First Vision listed below are given in the order in which they were written. A brief description of each account is followed by a few important highlights mentioned in the narrative. (To see the full account of each recital, see *Encyclopedia of Joseph Smith's Teachings*, ed. Larry E. Dahl and Donald Q. Cannon [Salt Lake City: Bookcraft, 1997], 252–69.

Joseph Smith Jr. (1832)

This autobiographical account was prepared between 20 July 1832 and 1 Dec. 1832, and was the first time Joseph Smith made an attempt to record his history and the "rise of the church of Christ." Frederick G. Williams, Joseph's scribe, penned the introduction, but Joseph himself wrote the portion dealing with the First Vision. The original copy is currently in the Church Historian's Office in Salt Lake City. Some of the unique teachings found in this account include the following:

"I was born . . . of goodly Parents who spared no pains to instructing me in the christian religion."

Joseph Smith stated that for two or three years he had been engaged in a quest for religious truth: "At about the age of twelve years my mind became seriously impressed with regard to the all important concerns for the welfare of my immortal Soul which led me to Searching the Scriptures believing as I was taught, that they contained the word of God."

"My intimate acquaintance with those of different

denominations led me to marvel exceedingly for I discovered that they did not ~~adorn instead of~~ adorning their profession by a holy walk and Godly conversation agreeable to what I found contained in that Sacred depository this was a grief to my Soul thus from the age of twelve years to fifteen."

"I pondered many things in my heart concerning the situation of the world of mankind the contentions and divisions the wickedness and abominations and the darkness which pervaded the ~~of the~~ minds of mankind"

"I felt to mourn for my own Sins and for the Sins of the world."

"A pillar of ~~fire~~ light above the brightness of the Sun at noon day come down from above and rested upon me and I was filled with the Spirit of God and the Lord opened the heavens upon me and I Saw the Lord and he Spake unto me Saying Joseph my Son thy Sins are forgiven thee. Go thy way walk in my Statutes and keep my commandments behold I am the Lord of glory I was crucified for the world that all those who believe on my name may have Eternal life."

He learned of the immanency of the second coming of Christ. He recorded the following statement made by the Savior: "Mine anger is kindling against the inhabitants of the earth to visit them according to this ungodliness and to bring to pass that which hath been spoken by the mouth of the prophets and Apostles behold and lo I come quickly as it written of me in the cloud clothed in the glory of my Father."

"My Soul was filled with love and for many days I could rejoice with great joy and the Lord was with me but could find none that would believe the heavenly vision." (In *Encyclopedia of Joseph Smith's Teachings*, ed. Larry E. Dahl and Donald Q. Cannon [Salt Lake City: Deseret Book, 2000], 252–54; spelling and grammar standardized)

Joseph Smith Jr. (1835)

In November 1835, Joseph related his vision to a visiting Jewish minister who introduced himself as Robert Matthias, but said his priestly name was Joshua. This account was recorded by Warren Parrish, a scribe to the Prophet, and later re-recorded in Joseph's Kirtland diary by another of his scribes, Warren A. Cowdery. Later this account was copied from Joseph's journal and placed in the manuscript history of the Church, which Joseph began in 1838 (see *Teachings*, 103–5). This is the shortest account of the First Vision. Some of the unique teachings found in this account include the following:

The Sacred Grove
(Courtesy of the Church Archives, The Church of Jesus Christ of Latter-day Saints)

"I knew not who was right or who was wrong, but considered it of the first importance to me that I should be right, in matters of so much moment, matter[s] involving eternal consequences."

"My tongue seemed to be swollen in my mouth, so that I could not utter, I heard a noise behind me like some one walking towards me. I strove again to pray, but could not; the noise of walking seemed to draw nearer, I sprang upon my feet and looked round, but saw no person or thing that was calculated to produce the noise of walking. I kneeled again, my mouth was opened and my tongue loosed; I called on the Lord in mighty prayer."

"A pillar of fire appeared above my head, which presently rested down upon me, and filled me with unspeakable joy. A personage appeared in the midst of this pillar of flame, which was spread all around and yet nothing consumed."

"Another personage soon appeared like unto the first: he said unto me thy sins are forgiven thee. He testified also unto me that Jesus Christ is the son of God."

"I saw many angels in this vision." (In *Encyclopedia of*

Joseph Smith's Teachings, 254–55; spelling and grammar standardized)

Joseph Smith Jr. (1838)

This account of the First Vision is the most commonly known, and is found in *Joseph Smith–History* in the *Pearl of Great Price.* Dictated by Joseph Smith, it is in the handwriting of Joseph's scribe James Mulholland. The account was first published in the *Times and Seasons* in 1842, and in the *Pearl of Great Price* by Franklin D. Richards in 1851, for the Saints in England. It was written to replace the account that was lost with John Whitmer's apostasy in 1838. Whitmer had been the Church historian and when he left he took his history of the Church with him (see D&C 47:1). The manuscript copy of this account is in the Church Historian's Office (Salt Lake City). Of all the accounts, this is the most comprehensive; some of its unique teachings include the following:

Franklin D. Richards
(Courtesy of the Church Archives, The Church of Jesus Christ of Latter-day Saints)

"Owing to the many reports which have been put in circulation by evil disposed and designing persons in relation to the rise and progress of the Church of Jesus Christ of Latter day Saints, all of which have been designed by the authors thereof to militate against its Character as a Church, and its progress in the world I have been induced to write this history so as to disabuse the public mind, and put all enquirers after truth into possession of the facts."

"There was in the place where we lived an unusual excitement on the subject of religion. It commenced with the Methodists, but soon became general among all the sects in that region of country, indeed the whole district of Country seemed affected by it and great multitudes united themselves to the different religious parties, which Created no Small stir and division among the people."

"Notwithstanding the great love which the Converts to these different faiths expressed at the time of their conversion, and the great Zeal manifested by the respective Clergy who were active in getting up and promoting this extraordinary scene of religious feeling, in order to have everybody converted as they were pleased to Call it, let them join what sect they pleased. Yet when the Converts began to file off some to one party and some to another, it was seen that the seemingly good feelings of both the Priests and the Converts were more pretended than real, for a scene of great confusion and bad feeling ensued, Priest contending against priest, and convert against convert So that all their good feelings one for another (if they ever had any) were entirely lost in a strife of words and a contest about opinions."

"During this time of great excitement my mind was called up to serious reflection and great uneasiness, but though my feelings were deep and often poignant, still I kept myself aloof from all these parties though I attended their several meetings as often as occasion would permit."

"In the midst of this war of words, and tumult of opinions, I often said to myself, what is to be done? Who of all these parties are right? Or are they all wrong together? And if any one of them be right which is it? And how shall 1 know it? While I was laboring under the extreme difficulties caused by the contests of these parties of religionists, I was one day reading the Epistle of James, First Chapter and fifth verse which reads, 'If any of you lack wisdom, let him ask of God, that giveth to all men liberally and upbraideth not, and it shall be given him.' Never did any passage of scripture come with more power to the heart of man tha[n] this did at this time to mine. It seemed to enter with great force into every feeling of my heart. I reflected on it again and again, knowing that if any person needed wisdom from God, I did, for how to act I did not know and unless I could get more wisdom than I then had, would never know."

"So in accordance with this my determination to ask of God, I retired to the woods to make the attempt. It was on the morning of a beautiful clear day early in the spring of Eighteen hundred and twenty. It was the first time in my life that I had made such an attempt, for amidst all my anxieties

I had never as yet made the attempt to pray vocally."

"Having looked around me and finding myself alone, I kneeled down and began to offer up the desires of my heart to God, I had scarcely done so, when immediately I was seized upon by some power which entirely overcame me and had such astonishing influence over me as to bind my tongue so that I could not speak. Thick darkness gathered around me and it seemed to me for a time as if I were doomed to sudden destruction. But exerting all my powers to call upon God to deliver me out of the power of this enemy which had seized upon me, and at the very moment when I was ready to sink into despair and abandon myself to destruction, not to an imaginary ruin but to the power of some actual being from the unseen world who had such a marvelous power as I had never before felt in any being. Just at this moment of great alarm I saw a pillar of light exactly over my head above the brightness of the sun, which descended grace~ fully gradually until it fell upon me. It no sooner appeared than I found myself delivered from the enemy which held me bound. When the light rested upon me I saw two personages (whose brightness and glory defy all description) standing above me in the air. One of them spake unto me calling me by name and said (pointing to the other) 'This is my beloved Son, Hear him.'"

Through this vision, Joseph learned many other important truths: "And many other things did he say unto me which I cannot write at this time."

"Some few days after I had this vision I happened to be in company with one of the Methodist Preachers who was very active in the before mentioned religious excitement and conversing with him on the subject of religion I took occasion to give him an account of the vision which I had had. I was greatly surprised at his behavior, he treated my communication not only lightly but with great contempt, Saying it was all of the Devil, that there was no such thing as visions or revelations in these days, that all such things had ceased with the Apostles and that there never would be any more of them."

"I soon found however that my telling the story had

excited a great deal of prejudice against me among professors of religion and was the Cause of great persecution which
continued to increase and though I was an obscure boy only
between fourteen and fifteen years of age or thereabouts and
my circumstances in life such as to make a boy of no consequence in the world, Yet men of high standing would take
notice sufficiently to excite the public mind against me and
create a hot persecution, and this was common among all
the Sects: all united to persecute me. It has often caused me
serious reflection both then and since, how very strange it
was that an obscure boy of a little over fourteen years of age
and one too who was doomed to the necessity of obtaining
a scanty maintenance by his daily labor should be thought a
character of sufficient importance to attract the attention of
the great ones of the most popular sects of the day so as to
create in them a spirit of the bitterest persecution and reviling. But strange or not, so it was, and was often [the] cause
of great sorrow to myself. However it was nevertheless a
fact, that I had had a Vision. I have thought since that I felt
much like Paul did when he made his defence before King
Aggrippa and related the account of the vision he had when
he saw a light and heard a voice, but still there were but few
who believed him, Some Said he was dishonest, others said
he was mad, and he was ridiculed and reviled, But all this
did not destroy the reality of his vision. He had seen a vision
he knew he had, and all the persecution under Heaven could
not make it otherwise, and though they should persecute
him unto death Yet he knew and would know to his latest
breath that he had both seen a light and heard a voice speaking unto him and all the world could not make him think or
believe otherwise."

"So it was with me, I had actually seen a light and in
the midst of that light I saw two personages, and they did
in reality speak unto me, or one of them did, And though I
was hated and persecuted for saying that I had seen a vision,
Yet it was true and while they were persecuting me reviling
me and speaking all manner of evil against me falsely for so
saying, I was led to say in my heart why persecute me for
telling the truth? I have actually seen a vision, "and who am
I that I can withstand God" or why does the world think
to make me deny what I have actually seen, for I had seen a
vision, I knew it, and I knew that God knew it, and I could

not deny it, neither dare I do it, at least I knew that by so doing I would offend God and come under condemnation."

"When the light had departed I had no strength, but soon recovering in some degree, I went home. & as I leaned up to the fire piece, Mother enquired what the matter was. I replied never mind all is well.—I am well enough off. I then told my Mother I have learned for myself that Presbyterianism is not True. It seems as though the adversary was aware at a very early period of my Life that I was destined to prove a disturbance & annoyer of his kingdom, or else why should the powers of Darkness combine against me, why the oppression & persecution that arose against me, almost in my infancy?" (As cited in *Encyclopedia of Joseph Smith's Teachings*, 256–60)

Orson Pratt (1840)

This account comes from a missionary tract Elder Pratt published while serving as a missionary in the British Isles. It was published in Edinburgh, Scotland in the September of 1840 under the title, *An Interesting Account of Several Remarkable Visions*. This is the first known publication of the First Vision and the first time the Fist Vision was used as a printed missionary tool. Some of the unique teachings found in this account include the following:

"He began seriously to reflect upon the necessity of being prepared for a future state of existence; but how, or in what way, to prepare himself, was a question, as yet, undetermined in his own mind. He perceived that it was a question of infinite importance, and that the salvation of his soul depended upon a correct understanding of the same. He saw, that if he understood not the way, it would be impossible to walk in it, except by chance; and the thought of resting his hopes of eternal life upon chance, or uncertainties, was more than he could endure. If he went to the religious denominations to seek information, each one pointed to its particular tenets, saying—'This is the way, walk ye in it;' while, at the same time, the doctrines of each were in many respects, in direct opposition to one another. It also occurred to his mind that God was the author of but one doctrine, and therefore could acknowledge but one denomination as his church, and that such denomination must be a people who believe and teach that one doctrine, (whatever it may be,) and build upon the same."

"His mind soon caught hold of the following passage:— 'If any of you lack wisdom let him ask of God, that giveth to all men liberally, and upbraideth not; and it shall be given him.'—James 1:5. From this promise he learned, that it was the privilege of all men to ask God for wisdom, with the sure and certain expectation of receiving liberally; without being upbraided for so doing. This was cheering information to him; tidings that gave him great joy. It was like a light shining forth in a dark place, to guide him to the path in which he should walk. He now saw that if he inquired of God, there was not only a possibility, but a probability; yea, more, a certainty, that he should obtain a knowledge, which, of all the doctrines, was the doctrine of Christ; and, which, of all the churches, was the church of Christ."

The whole wilderness was illuminated for a considerable distance around and Joseph noticed the leaves on the trees did not burn. "And while thus pouring out his soul, anxiously desiring an answer from God, he at length, saw a very bright and glorious light in the heavens above; which, at first, seemed to be a considerable distance. He continued praying, while the light appeared to be gradually descending towards him; and as it drew nearer, it increased in brightness and magnitude, so that, by the time that it reached the tops of the trees, the whole wilderness, for some distance around was illuminated in a most glorious and brilliant manner. He expected to have seen the leaves and boughs of the trees consumed, as soon as the light came in contact with them; but perceiving that it did not produce that effect, he was encouraged with the hope of being able to endure its presence."

"He was enwrapped in a heavenly vision, and saw two glorious personages, who exactly resembled each other in their features or likeness."

"He received a promise that the true doctrine—the fullness of the gospel, should, at some future time, be made known to him; after which, the vision withdrew, leaving his mind in a state of calmness and peace, indescribable." (As cited in *Encyclopedia of Joseph Smith's Teachings*, 262–64; spelling and punctuation standardized)

Orson Hyde (1842)

This account was a missionary tract and was published in Frankfurt, Germany in 1842 under the title, *Ein Ruf aus der Wüste, eine Stimme aus dem Schoose der Erde* ["A Cry from the Wilderness, a Voice from the Dust of the Earth"]. Orson Hyde's account is very similar to Orson Pratt's account, and may have been copied somewhat. Some of the unique teachings found in this account include the following:

Orson Hyde
(Courtesy of the Church Archives, The Church of Jesus Christ of Latter-day Saints)

"When ten years old, his parents with their family, moved to Palmyra, New York, in the vicinity of which he resided for about eleven years, the latter part in the town of Manchester. His only activity was to plow and cultivate the fields. As his parents were poor and had to take care of a large family, his education was very limited. He could read without much difficulty, and write a very imperfect hand; and had a very limited understanding of the elementary rules of arithmetic. These were his highest and only attainments; while the rest of those branches, so universally taught in the common schools throughout the United States, were entirely unknown to him."

"He began seriously to reflect upon the necessity of being prepared for a future state of existence; but how, or in what way to prepare himself, was a question, as yet, undetermined in his own mind; he perceived that it was a question of infinite importance. He saw, that if he understood not the way, it would be impossible to walk in it, except by chance; and the thought of resting his hopes of eternal life upon chance or uncertainties, was more than he could endure."

"He discovered a religious world working under numerous errors, which through their contradicting nature and principles, gave cause to the organization of so many different sects and parties, and whose feelings against each other were poisoned through hate, envy, malice and rage."

"Nature had gifted him with a strong, discerning mind and so he looked through the glass of soberness and good sense upon these religious systems which all were so different."

"He, therefore, retired to a secret place, in a grove, but a short distance from his father's house, and knelt down and began to call upon the Lord. At first, he was severely tempted by the powers of darkness, which endeavored to overcome him. The adversary benighted his mind with doubts, and brought to his soul all kinds of improper pictures and tried to hinder him in his efforts and the accomplishment of his goal. However, the overflowing mercy of God came to buoy him up, and gave new impulse and momentum to his dwindling strength."

"He was enwrapped in a heavenly vision, and saw two glorious personages, who exactly resembled each other in their features or likeness. They told him that his prayers had been answered, and that the Lord had decided to grant him a special blessing."

"He received a promise that the true doctrine—the fulness of the gospel—should, at some future time, be made known to him; after which, the vision withdrew, leaving his mind in a state of calmness and peace indescribable." (As cited in *Encyclopedia of Joseph Smith's Teachings*, 265–66)

Joseph Smith Jr. (1842)

The Articles of Faith and a brief history of the Church were published in the 15 March 1842 issue of the *Times and Seasons*. Joseph Smith Jr. said of this account: "At the request of Mr. John Wentworth, Editor and Proprietor of the *Chicago Democrat*, I have written the following sketch of the rise, progress, persecution, and faith of the Latter-Day Saints, of which I have the honor, under God, of being the founder . . . all that I ask at his hands is that he publish the account entire, ungarnished, and without misrepresentation" ("Church History," *Times and Seasons* 3 [1 March 1842]: 706). The text of the Wentworth Letter appears also to have been published by I. Daniel Rupp in 1843. Rupp inquired about an account of Mormonism from Joseph Smith that he desired to include in a book about religions that he was compiling for publication. The wording of Rupp's version is identical to the letter Joseph Smith sent to John Wentworth. Some of the unique teachings found in this account include the following:

> "When about fourteen years of age, I began to reflect upon the importance of being prepared for a future state, and upon inquiring [about] the plan of salvation, I found that there was a great clash in religious sentiment; if I went to one society they referred me to one plan, and another to another; each one pointing to his own particular creed as the summum bonum of perfection. Considering that all could not be right, and that God could not be the author of so much confusion, I determined to investigate the subject more fully, believing that if God had a Church it would not be split up into factions, and that if He taught one society to worship one way, and administer in one set of ordinances, He would not teach another, principles which were diametrically opposed."

> The Prophet Joseph learned that the fulness of the Gospel would be revealed to him: "I was enwrapped in a heavenly vision, and saw two glorious personages, who exactly resembled each other in features and likeness, surrounded with a brilliant light which eclipsed the sun at noon day. They told me that all religious denominations were believing in incorrect doctrines, and that none of them was acknowledged of God as His Church and kingdom: and I was expressly commanded "to go not after them," at the same time receiving a promise that the fullness of the Gospel should at some future time be made known unto me." (As cited in *Encyclopedia of Joseph Smith's Teachings*, 266–67)

Levi Richards (1843)

This account was taken from an entry in Levi Richards journal, dated 11 June 1843. Richards was a member of the church and this entry was supposedly written shortly after he heard the Prophet share his experience in the sacred grove. Some of the unique teachings found in this account include the following:

Levi Richards

(Courtesy of the Church Archives, The Church of Jesus Christ of Latter-day Saints)

"Pres. J. Smith bore testimony to the same saying that when he was a youth he began to think about these things but could not find out which of all the sects were right he went into the grove & enquired of the Lord which of all the sects were right he received for answer that none of them were right, that they were all wrong, & that the Everlasting Covenant was broken."

"He said he understood the fulness of the Gospel from beginning to end—& could Teach it & also the order of the priesthood in all its ramifications."

"Earth & hell had opposed him & tried to destroy him, but they had not done it . . . and they never would." (As cited in *Encyclopedia of Joseph Smith's Teachings,* 268; spelling standardized)

David Nye White (1843)

The first account of the First Vision by a non-Latter-day Saint comes from a newspaper article by David Nye White, senior editor of the *Pittsburgh Weekly Gazette.* It was based on an interview with Joseph Smith when White visited Nauvoo in 1843. The article first appeared in the 15 September 1843 issue of the *Gazette,* and was reprinted the following week (23 September 1843) in the *New York Spectator.* His account reads as follows:

"He [Joseph Smith] said: '. . . The Lord does reveal himself to me. I know it. He revealed himself first to me when I was about fourteen years old, a mere boy. I will tell you about it. There was a reformation among the different religious denominations in the neighborhood where I lived, and I became serious, and was desirous to know what Church to join. While thinking of this matter, I opened the Testament promiscuously on these words, in James, 'Ask of the Lord who giveth to all men liberally and upbraideth not.' I just determined I'd ask him. I immediately went out into the woods where my father had a clearing, and went to the stump where I had stuck my axe when I had quit work, and I kneeled down, and prayed, saying, 'O Lord, what Church shall I join?' Directly I saw a light, and then a glorious personage in the light, and then another personage, and the first personage said to the second, 'Behold my beloved Son, hear him.' I then, addressed this second person, saying, 'O Lord, what Church shall I join.' He replied, 'don't join any of them, they are all corrupt.' The vision then vanished, and when I came to myself, I was sprawling on my back; and it was some time before my strength returned. When I went home and told the people that I had a revelation, and that all the churches were corrupt, they persecuted me, and they have persecuted me ever since." (As cited in *Encyclopedia of Joseph Smith's Teachings*, 268)

Alexander Neibaur (1844)

Shortly before the death of the Prophet, Niebaur, a Jewish German convert and immigrant, heard Joseph relate his experience in the sacred grove and recorded in his journal his impressions of what Joseph said on that occasion. His account reads as follows:

"After Dinner ... at BR. J.S. [I] met Mr. Bonnie. Br. Joseph told us the first call he had a Revival Meeting, his Mother, Br. and Sisters got Religion. He wanted to get Religion too, wanted to feel and shout like the rest but could feel nothing, opened his Bible of the first Passage that struck him was if any man lack wisdom let him ask of God who giveth to all men liberally & upbraideth not. [He] went into the wood[s] to pray, kneels himself Down, his tongue was closet cleaveth to his roof—could utter not a word, felt easier after a while—saw a fire toward heaven came near[er] and nearer; saw a personage in the fire, light complexion, blue eyes, a piece of white cloth Drawn over his shoulders his right arm bear after a while a other person came to the side of the first. Mr. Smith then asked, 'Must I join the Methodist Church?' 'No, they are not my People, have gone astray. There is none that Doeth good, not one, but this is my Beloved Son harken ye him.' The fire drew nigher, Rested upon the tree, enveloped him comforted I endeavored to arise but felt uncommon feeble—got into the house told the Methodist priest, said this was not a age for God to Reveal himself in Vision Revelation has ceased with the New Testament." (As cited in *Encyclopedia of Joseph Smith's Teachings*, 269)

Orson Pratt (1869)

What were the circumstances that enabled him [Joseph Smith] to have manifestations from Heaven at that early period of his life? He was very anxious, as most of mankind are, to be saved; and he was also very anxious to understand how to be saved. . . . He was a farmer's boy; he was not brought up and educated in high schools, academies or colleges . . . First one and then another of the different persuasions would come and converse with him and try to influence him to join his lot with them; and seeing so much confusion, each sect claiming that they were the true people of God, he became at a loss what to do. He occasionally devoted an hour, when his labors on the farm would permit, to reading the Bible, and while doing so his eyes happened to fall on a certain passage of scripture, recorded in the epistle of James, which says that if any man lack wisdom let him ask of God who giveth liberally to all men and upbraideth not. Now this youth . . . was just simple enough to believe that that passage really meant what it said. He went out into a little grove near his father's house, . . . and there he knelt down in all the simplicity of a child and prayed to the Father in the name of Jesus that He would show him which, among all the churches, was the true one. . . .

He had now come to a Person who was able to teach him. All his inquiries previously had been futile and vain, but he now applied to the right source. Did the Lord hear him? Yes. But he had to exercise faith. . . . The Lord hearkened. Being the same God who lived in ancient times, He was able to hear and answer prayers that were offered up in this sincere manner, and He answered the prayers of this youth. The heavens, as it were, were opened to him . . . and he was filled with the visions of the Almighty, and he saw, in the midst of this glorious pillar of fire, two glorious personages, whose countenances shown with an exceeding great luster. One of them spoke to him, saying, while pointing to the other, "This is my beloved Son in whom I am well pleased, hear ye him."

Now here was a certainty; here was something that he saw and heard; here were personages capable of instructing him, and of telling him which was the true religion. How different this from going to an uninspired man professing to be a minister! One minute's instruction from personages clothed with the glory of God coming down from the eternal worlds is worth more than all the volumes that ever were written by uninspired men. . . .

He was told there was no Christian church on the face of the earth according to the ancient pattern, as recorded in the New Testament; but they had all strayed from the ancient faith and had lost the gifts and power of the Holy Ghost; they had lost the spirit of revelation and prophecy, [and] the power to heal the sick . . . "Go not after them," was the command given to this young man; and he was told that if he would be faithful in serving the true and living God, it should be made manifest to him, in a time to come, the true church that God intended to establish.

Now we can see the wisdom of God in not revealing everything to him on that occasion. He revealed as much as Joseph was capacitated to receive (in *Journal of Discourses*, 26 vols. [London: Latter-day Saints' Book Depot, 1854–86], 12:353–55).

～6 ～

EARLY TRIALS AND PERSECUTIONS
OF THE PROPHET JOSEPH SMITH

Even prior to the persecution that followed his First Vision, Joseph Smith Jr. faced life-threatening ordeals. Daunting challenges, oppressive trials, and onerous persecutions were common occurrences throughout the Prophet's brief life, beginning at a very early age.

Joseph Smith Jr.

It seems as though the adversary was aware, at a very early period of my life, that I was destined to prove a disturber and an annoyer of his kingdom; else why should the powers of darkness combine against me? Why the opposition and persecution that arose against me, almost in my infancy? (*Joseph Smith–History* 1:20).

Lucy Mack Smith

At the age of fourteen an incident occurred which alarmed us much, as we knew not the cause of it. Joseph being a remarkably quiet, well-disposed child, we did not suspect that anyone had aught against him. He was out on an errand one evening about twilight. When he was returning through the dooryard, a gun was fired across his pathway with evident intention of killing him. He sprang to the door, threw it open, and fell upon the floor with fright.

We went in search of the person who fired the gun, but found no trace of him until the next morning when we found his tracks under a wagon where he lay when he fired. We found the balls that were discharged from his piece the next day in the head and neck of a cow that stood opposite the wagon in a dark corner, but we never found out the man, nor ever suspected the cause of the act (Lucy Mack Smith, *The Revised and Enhanced History of Joseph Smith by His Mother*, ed. Scot Facer Proctor and Maurine Jensen Proctor [Salt Lake City: Bookcraft, 1996], 93–94).

PROPHETIC WARNINGS GIVEN TO THE PROPHET

Beginning with the angel Moroni's appearance to the seventeen-year-old Joseph Smith, Joseph was repeatedly warned by revelation and by the Spirit that opposition loomed on the horizon. While translating the Book of Mormon and receiving the revelations now included in the Doctrine and Covenants, Joseph was further warned of the dangers that lay ahead.

The Lord Jesus Christ

(When Christ appeared to the Nephites and Lamanites after His resurrection, He prophesied to them of Joseph Smith's life and mission.)

For in that day, for my sake shall the Father work a work, which shall be a great and a marvelous work among them; and there shall be among them those who will not believe it, although a man shall declare it unto them.

But behold, the life of my servant shall be in my hand; therefore they shall not hurt him, although he shall be marred because of them. Yet I will heal him, for I will show unto them that my wisdom is greater than the cunning of the devil (3 Nephi 21:9–10).

Joseph Smith Jr.

(Regarding the angel Moroni's appearance on 21 September 1823.)

He [the angel Moroni] called me by name, and said unto me that he was a messenger sent from the presence of God to me, and that his name was Moroni; that God had a work for me to do; and that my name should be had for good and evil among all nations, kindreds, and tongues, or that it should be both good and evil spoken of among all people. . . .

After telling me these things, he commenced quoting the prophecies of the Old Testament [prophecies about the last days]. . . . Saying that [they were about] to be [fulfilled] (*Joseph Smith–History* 1:33, 36, 41).

The Angel Moroni

(Moroni added an additional warning, which was recorded by Oliver Cowdery in a letter he wrote to the Church. Joseph Smith said that Moroni told him the following.)

The workers of iniquity will seek your overthrow: they will circulate falsehoods to destroy your reputation, and also will seek to take your life . . . But, notwithstanding the workers of iniquity shall seek your destruction the arm of the Lord will be extended, and you will be borne off conqueror (Oliver Cowdery, "Letter No. 11," *Messenger and Advocate* 2 [October 1835]: 199).

The Lord Jesus Christ

(To Joseph Smith and Oliver Cowdery, 7 April 1829)

Verily, verily, I say unto you, if they reject my words, and this part of my gospel and ministry, blessed are ye, for they can do no more unto you than unto me.

And even if they do unto you even as they have done unto me, blessed are ye, for you shall dwell with me in glory (D&C 6:29–30).

PERSECUTED FOR RECEIVING REVELATION

The persecution Joseph Smith experienced at the time of his First Vision in 1820 intensified over time, culminating in his death in 1844.

Brigham Young

If a thousand hounds were on this Temple Block [Temple Square in Salt Lake City], let loose on one rabbit, it would not be a bad illustration of the situation at times of the Prophet Joseph. He was hunted unremittingly" (Discourses of Brigham Young, ed. John A. Widtsoe [Salt Lake City: Deseret Book, 1966], 464).

Brigham Young

Why was he hunted from neighborhood to neighborhood, from city to city, and from State to State, and at last suffered death? Because he received revelations from the Father, from the Son, and was ministered to by holy angels, and published to the world the direct will of the Lord concerning his children on the earth (in *Journal of Discourses*, 26 vols. [London: Latter-day Saints' Book Depot, 1854-86], 18:231).

Joseph Smith Jr.

When I went home and told the people that I had a revelation, and that all the churches were corrupt, they persecuted me, and they have persecuted me ever since (David Nye White, "Editor's Account of the First Vision," *New York Spectator* [23 September 1843]; as cited in Milton V. Backman Jr., *Joseph Smith's First Vision*, 2d ed. [Salt Lake City: Bookcraft, 1980], 176).

William Smith

(In an interview, responding to the statement, "It is said that Joseph and the rest of the family were lazy and indolent.")

We never heard of such a thing until after Joseph told his vision, and not then, by our friends. Whenever the neighbors wanted a good day's work done they knew where they could get a good hand and they were not particular to take any of the other boys before Joseph either. We cleared sixty acres of the heaviest timber I ever saw. We had a good

William Smith
(Courtesy of the Church Archives, The Church of Jesus Christ of Latter-day Saints)

place. We also had on it from twelve to fifteen hundred sugar trees, and to gather the sap and make sugar molasses from that number of trees was no lazy job. We worked hard to clear our place and the neighbors were a little jealous. If you will figure up how much work it would take to clear sixty acres of heavy timber land, heavier than any here, trees you could not conveniently cut down, you can tell whether we were lazy or not, and Joseph did his share of the work with the rest of the boys. We never knew we were bad folks until Joseph told his vision. We were considered respectable till then, but at once people began to circulate falsehoods and stories in a wonderful way (*A Comprehensive History of the Church of Jesus Christ of Latter-day Saints*, 6 vols., ed. B. H. Roberts [Provo, Utah: Brigham Young University Press, 1965], 1:40).

ARRESTS AND TRIALS

After Joseph Smith saw the Father and the Son in the First Vision and received the Book of Mormon plates from the angel Moroni, he and those associated with him experienced "growing opposition in the form of harassment, social ostracism, threats of attack on persons and property, arrests . . . and a constant flood of libelous charges aimed at disrupting the missionary activities of the Prophet in the area of Colesville, New York" (Milton V. Backman Jr., *The Heavens Resound: A History of the Latter-day Saints in Ohio, 1830–1838* [Salt Lake City: Deseret Book, 1983], 44).

Following the June 1830 conference of the Church in Fayette, New York, Joseph Smith, Oliver Cowdery, John Whitmer, and David Whitmer held a meeting in Colesville. They were harassed by a mob but proceeded to baptize thirteen people, including Emma Smith, Joseph Knight, and Polly Knight, among others. Joseph was arrested on charges of setting the country in an uproar with his preaching. He was tried and acquitted in South Bainbridge, New York, but was immediately arrested again and then tried and acquitted in Colesville.

Joseph Knight Jr.

(He describes his family's relationship with the Prophet Joseph Smith and the persecution that accompanied the baptisms at Colesville.)

My father bought three farms on the Susquehanna River, in Broome County, New York. In 1827, he hired Joseph Smith Jr. Joseph and I worked and slept together. My father said that Joseph was the best hand he ever hired. We found him a boy of truth. He was about twenty-one years of age.

I think it was in November, 1827, he made known to my father and me that he had seen a vision, that a personage had appeared to him and told him where there was a gold book of ancient date buried, and if he would follow the directions of the angel he could get it. We were told it in secret. My father and I believed what he told us. I think we were the first after his father's family.

At last he got the plates, and rode in my father's wagon and carried them home.

Joseph then commenced to translate the plates. Father and I often went to see him, to carry him some things to live upon. After many trials and troubles, he got the plates translated. By this time, my mother and many of my relations believed.

Joseph and Oliver came to Colesville, in May, 1830, where we lived, and Oliver baptized my father's family, and a few of my relatives. When we were going from the water, we were met by many of our neighbors, who pointed at us and asked if we had been washing our sheep. Before Joseph could confirm us, he was taken by the officers to Chenango County for trial, for saying that the Book of Mormon was a revelation from God.

My father employed two lawyers to plead for him, and they cleared him. That night our wagons were turned over and wood piled on them, and some sunk in the water. Rails were piled against our doors, and chains sunk in the stream, and a great deal of mischief done. Before Joseph got to my father's house, he was taken again to be tried in Broome County. Father employed the same lawyers, who cleared him there.

Four weeks passed before Joseph could get a chance to confirm us. Then we had the greatest time I ever saw. The house was filled with the Holy Ghost, which rested upon us (Joseph Knight Jr., *Folder* [LDS Church Archives, Church Historical Department, The Church of Jesus

Christ of Latter-day Saints, Salt Lake City]; as cited in *They Knew the Prophet,* ed. Hyrum L. Andrus and Helen Mae Andrus [Salt Lake City: Deseret Book, 1999], 6).

Joseph Fielding Smith

(Though not an eyewitness himself to these events, President Joseph Fielding Smith provided the following description of the persecution at Colesville.)

They found a number of persons [in Colesville] anxiously awaiting them and desiring baptism. A meeting was appointed for the Sabbath; on Saturday a dam was constructed across a stream in preparation for the ordinance on the following day. During the night the dam was maliciously destroyed. It was later learned that this was the work of a mob, at the instigation of sectarian priests. On Sunday the meeting was held as contemplated. Oliver Cowdery was the principal speaker, but others also spoke. The first principles of the Gospel were presented and witness to the divine message of the Book of Mormon was borne. In the meeting were many who had helped to form the mob, who, at the close, endeavored to destroy the influence of the meeting, but were unsuccessful. Extreme bitterness was manifested on the part of those who opposed. The sister of Newel Knight's wife was violently treated because she was kindly disposed, and against her will was forced by a Rev. Shearer, to return to her father's home, some distance from her sister's where she was stopping. This man, a Presbyterian minister, on false pretenses, obtained from the father a power of attorney, by which he dragged her off. His labor was all in vain, for she also was baptized.

Early Monday morning the dam was replaced and thirteen persons were baptized by Oliver Cowdery. They were: Emma, wife of Joseph Smith; Hezekiah Peck and wife, Joseph Knight, Sen., and wife, William Stringham and wife, Joseph Knight Jr., Aaron Culver and wife, Levi Hale, Polly Knight and Julia Stringham.

Arrest of Joseph Smith. Before they were through with the ordinance the mob began to gather. They surrounded the house of Joseph Knight, Sen., prepared to do violence, but through the blessings of the Lord the Saints were protected, but were subjected to numerous insults and threatenings. A meeting was called for that evening for the purpose of attending to the confirmation of those baptized in the morning.

When they met at the appointed hour, they were all surprised at the appearance of a constable, who with a warrant, arrested Joseph on the charge of being "a disorderly person, setting the country in an uproar by preaching the Book of Mormon." The constable frankly informed him that the arrest was for the purpose of getting him into the hands of a mob, then lying in ambush for him, but he would save him from their hands as he, the constable, had discovered that Joseph was not the sort of person he had been led to believe. As Joseph accompanied the constable in a wagon, they encountered the mob, not far from the home of Joseph Knight. The mobbers waited for the prearranged signal from the constable, but he, whipping up his horse, obtained a lead. The mobbers followed as best they could. In the flight one of the wagon wheels came off, and before it could be replaced the mobbers were again in sight. However, the wheel was replaced in time and with renewed energy Joseph was able to escape.

The constable took Joseph to South Bainbridge, Chenango County, and lodged him in a tavern, where he kept guard all night. The following day a court convened to investigate the charges. Great excitement prevailed because of falsehoods which had been circulated freely among the people. Joseph Knight, Sen., engaged the services of two respectable farmers who were versed in the law, namely, James Davidson and John Reid, and brought them to South Bainbridge to defend the Prophet.

The Trial of South Bainbridge. The enemies of Joseph Smith scoured the country for witnesses who would testify against him. The justice of the peace who heard the case, Joseph Chamberlain, was a man of fair mind and a lover of justice. Many witnesses were heard, but among those who testified were Josiah Stowel, Jonathan Thompson and the two daughters of Mr. Stowel, all of whom gave evidence of his good character. Other testimony was proved to be false. The trial lasted from ten o'clock in the morning until midnight, when a verdict of "not guilty" was rendered.

The Second Arrest. No sooner was Joseph freed by the court than he was again arrested on a second warrant from Broome County, a distance of about fifteen miles. The constable who came for him forced him to leave that night without permitting him to eat, although he had been in the court room all day without nourishment. He took him to Colesville and lodged him in a tavern. Then, calling in a number of rowdies, he began to abuse his prisoner with the assistance of his rabble.

Spitting upon him and pointing their fingers at him they cried in fiendish glee, "Prophesy! prophesy!" Being near his home, Joseph requested the constable to take him there for the remainder of the night, but this was denied him. He asked for something to eat and was given some crusts of bread and water.

The Trial at Colesville. The next day the trial began before three justices. The most able help had been secured to prosecute the case while the defense was again represented by Esquires Reid and Davidson. Many witnesses were called who bore false and contradictory testimony. Newel Knight was placed upon the stand and questioned in ridicule by one of the lawyers, named Seymour, in relation to the casting out of a devil from his person, but the testimony turned to the discomfiture of the prosecution.

At the close of the testimony the court deliberated for about thirty minutes, although it was then nearly two o'clock a.m. and they had been in session since the morning of the previous day. The prisoner was brought before the court and the presiding justice said: "Mr. Smith, we have had your case under consideration, examined the testimony and find nothing to condemn you, and therefore you are discharged." The judges then proceeded to reprimand him severely, "Not because anything derogatory to his character in any shape had been proved against him by the host of witnesses that had testified during the trial," said Mr. Reid, "but merely to please those fiends in human shape who were engaged in the unhallowed persecution of an innocent man, sheerly on account of his religious opinions."

Statement of Mr. Reid. Several years later, Mr. Reid visited Nauvoo, and in the course of an address said, speaking of these trials:

"But, alas! the devil, not satisfied with his defeat (at the first trial) stirred up a man not unlike himself, who was more fit to dwell among the fiends of hell than to belong to the human family, to go to Colesville and get another writ, and take him to Broome County for another trial. They were sure they could send that boy to hell, or to Texas, they did not care which; and in half an hour after he was discharged by the court he was arrested again, and on the way to Colesville for another trial. I was again called upon by his friends to defend him against his malignant persecutors, and clear him from the false charges they had preferred against him. I made every reasonable excuse I could, as I was nearly worn down through fatigue and want of sleep, as I had been engaged in law suits for two days, and nearly the whole of two nights. But I saw the persecution was great against him; and here, let me say, Mr. Chairman, singular as it may seem, while Mr. Knight was pleading with me to go, a peculiar impression, or thought struck my mind, that I must go and defend him, for he was the Lord's anointed. I did not know what it meant, but thought I must go and clear the Lord's anointed. I said I would go, and started with as much faith as the apostles had when they could remove mountains, accompanied by Father Knight, who was like the old patriarchs that followed the ark of God to the city of David. * * * We got him away that night from the midst of three hundred people without his receiving any injury; but I am well aware that we were assisted by some higher power than man; for to look back on the scene, I cannot tell how we succeeded in getting him away. I take no glory to myself; it was the Lord's work and marvelous in our eyes" (John S. Reid, "Some of the Remarks of John S. Reid, Esq., as Delivered Before the State Convention," *Times and Seasons* 5 [1 June 1884]: 549–52).

Inspiration of the Attorneys. At the trial the Prophet's lawyers, who were not members of the Church, spoke with an inspiration that caused their enemies to quake before them. So powerful were their words that many of the assembled multitude were pricked in their hearts. The constable who had been so vicious came forward and apologized for his illtreatment and misbehavior, and revealed the plans of the mob who were then prepared to tar and feather the Prophet and ride him on a rail. By the aid of the constable, Joseph was able to escape and make his way in safety to his sister's home, where he found his wife awaiting him.

The Mob Threatens Joseph and Oliver. A few days later Joseph Smith and Oliver Cowdery returned to Colesville to confirm those whom they had been forced to leave, at the time of Joseph's arrest. Their presence was the signal for the mobbers to again assemble. So sinister were their movements that Joseph and Oliver departed from the town without waiting for refreshments. Their enemies pursued them but through extreme diligence they were able to make their escape. All night they traveled, except for a short period when they sought some rest in sleep, each taking turn in watching. The next day they arrived home, footsore and weary.

The spirit of opposition which took such decided form, was the result of agitation on the part of professors of religion. The Rev. Shearer, Cyrus McMaster, Dr. Boyington and a Mr. Benton, pillars in the Presbyterian Church, incited the mobbers to do their work. Benton was the man who signed the first warrant for Joseph Smith's arrest as a "disorderly person" for preaching the Book of Mormon. In this manner Satan stirred up the hearts of the people to try and overthrow the work (Joseph Fielding Smith, *Essentials in Church History* [Salt Lake City: Deseret Book, 1979], 84–88).

B. H. Roberts

(He provides the transcription of Newel Knight's testimony during the first trial at Colesville.)

[Shortly after the first miracle occurred (when Joseph Smith cast an evil spirit out of Newel Knight during a meeting), Newel Knight was called to testify in court concerning this incident. Joseph Smith had been arrested in Colesville, New York, probably for disturbing the peace, and Newel Knight recorded in his autobiography his response to questions he was asked during this trial by one of the attorneys.]

Question.—"Did the prisoner, Joseph Smith, Jun., cast the devil out of you?"

Answer.—"No, sir."

Question.—"Why, have you not had the devil cast out of you?"

A.—"Yes, sir."

Q.—"And had not Joseph Smith some hand in it being done?"

A.—"Yes, sir."

Q.—"And did he not cast him out of you?"

A.—"No, sir, it was done by the power of God, and Joseph Smith was the instrument in the hands of God on this occasion. He commanded him to come out of me in the name of Jesus Christ."

Q.—"And are you sure it was the devil?"

A.—"Yes, sir."

Q.—"Did you see him after he was cast out of you?"

A.—"Yes, sir, I saw him."

Q.—"Pray, what did he look like?"

(Here one of the lawyers on the part of the defense told me I need not answer that question). I replied:

"I believe, I need not answer you that question, but I will do it if I am allowed to ask you one, and you can answer it. Do you, Mr. Seymour, understand the things of the Spirit?"

"No," answered Mr. Seymour, "I do not pretend to such big things."

"Well, then," I replied, "it will be of no use for me to tell you what the devil looked like, for it was a spiritual sight and spiritually discerned, and, of course, you would not understand it were I to tell you of it."

The lawyer dropped his head, while the loud laugh of the audience proclaimed his discomfiture (as cited in Milton V. Backman Jr., *Eyewitness Accounts of the Restoration* [Salt Lake City: Deseret Book, 1983], 193).

Testimony of Josiah Stoal, John Anderson, and the Stoal daughters

Joseph Knight Sen., engaged the services of two of his neighbors, well versed in the law, although not practicing attorneys. They were respectable farmers, James Davidson and John Reid, by name and both widely known for their integrity and honor. These gentlemen and a number of the Prophet's friends arrived at South Bainbridge before the opening of the trial.

The main charge apparently, was soon abandoned, as it could not possibly be entertained by the court; but a number of other charges utterly irrelevant were investigated, the nature of which is disclosed by the questions put to the witnesses. And here let it be said, that although these matters are insignificant in themselves, yet they disclose the nature of the charges made against the Prophet, and the untruthfulness of such accusations made against him as involve the employment of his prophetic gifts, or the use of his official position, for material gain. For example, his friend Josiah Stoal was put upon the stand and questioned as follows:

"Did not he [Joseph Smith] go to you and tell you that an angel had appeared unto him and authorized him to get the horse from you?"

"No, he told me no such story."

"Well, how had he the horse of you?"

"He bought him of me as any other man would."

"Have you had your pay?"

"That is none of your business."

"The question being put again the witness replied:"

"I hold his note for the price of the horse, which I consider as good as the pay; for I am well acquainted with Joseph Smith, Jun., and know him to be an honest man; and if he wishes, I am ready to let him have another horse on the same terms."

Mr. Jonathan Thompson was next called up and examined:

"Has not the prisoner, Joseph Smith, Jun., had a yoke of oxen of you?"

"Yes."

"Did he not obtain them of you by telling you that he had a revelation to the effect that he was to have them?"

"No, he did not mention a word of the kind concerning the oxen; he purchased them the same as any other man would."

The court was detained until two daughters of Mr. Stoal could be sent for and questioned. These were two young ladies with whom the Prophet had kept company before his marriage. They were examined as to his conduct generally, but especially as to his behavior towards them, both in public and in private. They both gave such answers as left the young Prophet's enemies without pretext of action on their account.

Incidents alleged to have taken place in Broome county were introduced, but these the court, being held in Chenango county, would not entertain; and after the court had been in session from ten in the morning until midnight, the trial closed, by the justice declaring the prisoner "not guilty."

During the day a successful application had been made for a warrant against the Prophet in Broome county; and no sooner was he discharged by Justice Chamberlain than he was arrested under the warrant from Broome county, and dragged off to Colesville some fifteen miles distant. He was taken to a tavern where a number of men gathered and for some time, in the presence of the constable, they ridiculed and insulted the helpless prisoner.

The next day the trial began, and the Prophet found his faithful friends and his counsel of the day before, Messrs. Davidson and Reid, by his side. Many witnesses were called, but their testimony was so palpably false and contradictory that it could not be admitted by the court. A lawyer by the name of Seymour assisted by a Mr. Burch conducted the case for the prosecution. They called Newel Knight as a witness against the prisoner, to detail the account of the Prophet's ministration to him when possessed of an evil spirit, as already related—such were the matters of inquiry in a court of justice in an early decade of the nineteenth century, in the state of New York! In the plea for the state, prosecutor Seymour dragged in the matter of the Prophet having been "a money digger," and in every way that occurred to his ingenuity sought to influence the court against him (*A Comprehensive History of the Church,* 1:206–8; punctuation standardized).

John Reid

(Years after the fact, attorney John Reid described his experiences defending the Prophet Joseph Smith.)

Those bigots soon made up a false accusation against him and had him arraigned before Joseph Chamberlain, a justice of the peace, a man that was always ready to deal justice to all, and a man of great discernment of mind. The case came on about 10 o'clock a. m. I was called upon to defend the prisoner. The prosecutors employed the best counsel they could get, and ransacked the town of Bainbridge and county of Chenango for witnesses that would swear hard enough to convict the prisoner; but they entirely failed. *Yes, sir, let me say to you that not one blemish nor spot was found against his character, he came from that trial, notwithstanding the mighty efforts that were made to convict him of crime by his vigilant persecutors, with his character unstained by even the appearance of guilt.* The trial closed about 12 o'clock at night. After a few moments' deliberation, the court pronounced the words "not guilty," and the prisoner was discharged. But alas! the devil, not satisfied with his defeat, stirred up a man not unlike himself, who was more fit to dwell among the fiends of hell than to belong to the human family, to go to Colesville and get another writ, and take him to Broome county for another trial. They were sure they could send that boy to hell, or to Texas, they did not care which; and in half an hour after he was discharged by the court, he was arrested again, and on the way to Colesville for another trial. I was again called upon by his friends to defend him against his malignant persecutors, and clear him from the false charges they had preferred against him. I made every reasonable excuse I could, as I was nearly worn down through fatigue and want of sleep; as I had been engaged in lawsuits for two days, and nearly the whole of two nights. But I saw the persecution was great against him; and here let me say, Mr. Chairman, singular as it may seem, while Mr. Knight was pleading with me to go, a peculiar impression or thought struck my mind, that I must go and defend him, for he was the Lord's anointed. I did not know what it meant, but thought I must go and clear the Lord's anointed. I said I would go, and started with as much faith as the Apostles had when they could remove mountains, accompanied by Father Knight, who was like the old patriarchs that followed the ark of God to the city of David. * * *

The next morning about 10 o'clock the court was organized. The prisoner was to be tried by three justices of the peace, that his departure out of the county might be made sure. Neither talents nor money were wanting to insure them success. They employed the ablest lawyer in that county, and introduced twenty or thirty witnesses before dark, but proved nothing. They then sent out runners and ransacked the hills and vales, grog shops and ditches, and gathered together a company that looked as if they had come from hell and had been whipped by the soot boy thereof; which they brought forward to testify one after the other, but with no better success than before, although they wrung and twisted into every shape, in trying to tell something that would criminate the prisoner. Nothing was proven against him whatever. Having got through with the examination of their witnesses about 2 o'clock in the morning, the case was argued about two hours. There was not one particle of testimony against the prisoner. No, sir, he came out like the three [Hebrew] children from the fiery furnace, without the smell of fire upon his garments. The court deliberated upon the case for half an hour with closed doors, and then we were called in. The court arraigned the prisoner and said: "Mr. Smith, we have had your case under consideration, examined the testimony and find nothing to condemn you, and therefore you are discharged." They then proceeded to reprimand him severely; not because anything derogatory to his character in any shape had been proven against him by the host of witnesses that had testified during the trial, but merely to please those fiends in human shape who were engaged in the unhallowed persecution of an innocent man, sheerly on account of his religious opinions.

After they had got through, I arose and said: "This court puts me in mind of a certain trial held before Felix of old, when the enemies of Paul arraigned him before the venerable judge for some alleged crime, and nothing was found in him worthy of death or of bonds. Yet, to please the Jews, who were his accusers, he was left bound contrary to law; and this court has served Mr. Smith in the same way, by their unlawful and uncalled for reprimand after his discharge, to please his accusers." We got him away that night from the midst of three hundred people without his receiving any injury; but I am well aware that we were assisted by some higher power than man; for to look back on the scene, I cannot tell how we succeeded in getting him away. I take no glory to myself; it was the Lord's work and marvelous in our eyes (Joseph Smith, *History of The Church of Jesus Christ of Latter-day Saints*, 7 vols., ed. B. H. Roberts [Salt Lake City: Deseret Book, 1932–51], 1:95–96; Mr. Reid's speech is published in full in the *Times and Seasons* 5 [1 June 1884]: 549–52; spelling standardized).

✎ 7 ✎

VISITATIONS OF MORONI

Following his vision of the Father and the Son in the spring of 1820, Joseph was visited by other heavenly beings. These angelic ministrants gave him revelation, counsel, and instruction regarding the restoration of the gospel and concerning his role as the prophet of the final gospel dispensation. Beginning with the evening of 21 September 1823, the angel Moroni would appear to the Prophet Joseph Smith more than twenty times over the next seven years to tutor him and give him direction.

Joseph Smith Jr.

(The Prophet recites his experience with the angel Moroni. Milton V. Backman has combined various recitals written by Joseph Smith to create the following narrative.)

On the evening of September 21, 1823, when I was seventeen years of age, I retired to my bed for the night and while praying unto God asked for forgiveness of all my sins and follies and for a manifestation to me, that I might know of my state and standing before him. I had not been asleep, but was meditating upon my past life and experience. I was very conscious that I had not kept the commandments and I repented heartily of all my sins and transgressions and humbled myself before Him whose eyes are in all things. I had full confidence in obtaining a divine manifestation, as I had previously had one.

While I was thus in the act of calling upon God, I discovered a light appearing in my room which continued to increase until the room was lighter than at noonday. Indeed the first sight was as though the house was filled with consuming fire; the appearance produced a shock that affected my whole body. In a moment a personage stood before me, surrounded with a glory yet greater than that with which I was already surrounded. An angel appeared at my bedside and stood in the air, for his feet did not touch the floor.

He had on a loose robe of most exquisite whiteness. It was a whiteness beyond anything earthly I had ever seen, nor do I believe that any earthly thing could be made to appear so exceedingly white and brilliant. His hands were naked, pure and white, and his arms also, a little above the wrist; so, also, were his feet naked, as were his legs, a little above the ankles. His head and neck were also bare. I could discover that he had no other clothing on but this robe, as it was open so that I could see into his bosom.

Not only was his robe exceedingly white, but his whole person was glorious beyond description and his countenance truly like lightning. When I first looked upon him, I was afraid; but the fear soon left me. He called me by name and said unto me that he was a messenger sent from the presence of God to me to bring joyful tidings and that his name was Moroni. He told me that the Lord had forgiven me of my sins and said, "Be faithful and keep His commandments in all things." I was informed that I was a chosen instrument in the hands of God to bring about some of his purposes in this glorious dispensation (Milton V. Backman Jr., *Eyewitness Accounts of the Restoration* [Salt Lake City: Deseret Book, 1986], 38–40; see also Joseph Smith–History 1:27–32).

Oliver Cowdery

Oliver Cowdery
(Courtesy of the Church Archives, The Church of Jesus Christ of Latter-day Saints)

The messenger also informed Joseph Smith that the Lord had chosen him to be an instrument in His hand to bring to light that which shall perform his act, His strange act, and bring to pass a marvelous work and a wonder. He further said that Joseph Smith's prayers were heard that the scriptures might be fulfilled, which say—"God has chosen the foolish things of the world to confound the things which are mighty; and base things of the world, and things which are despised, has God chosen; yea, and things which are not, to bring to naught things which are, that no flesh should glory in his presence. Therefore, says the

Lord, I will proceed to do a marvelous work among this people, even a marvelous work and a wonder; the wisdom of their wise shall perish, and the understanding of their prudent shall be hid;" [Isaiah 29:14] for according to this covenant which he made with his ancient saints, his people, the house of Israel, must come to a knowledge of the gospel, and own that Messiah whom their fathers rejected, and with them the fullness of the Gentiles be gathered in, to rejoice in one fold under one Shepherd (*Eyewitness Accounts of the Restoration*, 40–41; see also *Messenger & Advocate* 1 [April 1835]: 79).

Joseph Smith Jr.

(Milton V. Backman has combined various recitals written by Joseph Smith to create the following narrative.)

He further told me that my name should be had for good and evil among all nations, kindreds and tongues, or that it should be both good and evil spoken among all people.

He said there was a book deposited, written upon gold plates by Moroni and his father, containing an abridgment of the records of the ancient prophets who had lived on this continent, giving an account of these people; and I was shown who they were and from whence they came, learning that the Indians were literal descendants of Abraham. He also said that the fullness of the everlasting gospel was contained in it, as delivered by the Savior to the ancient inhabitants. A brief sketch of their origin, progress, civilization, laws, governments, of their righteousness and iniquity, and the blessings of God being finally withdrawn from them as a people was [made] known unto me (*Eyewitness Accounts of the Restoration*, 41; see also Joseph Smith–History 1:33–34).

Orson Pratt

It was also made manifest to him, that the "American Indians" were a remnant of Israel; that when they first emigrated to America, they were an enlightened people, possessing a knowledge of the true God, enjoying his favor, and peculiar blessings from his hand; that the prophets, and inspired writers among them, were required to keep a sacred history of the most important events transpiring among them: which history was handed down for many generations, till at length they fell into great wickedness: the most part of them were destroyed, and the records, (by commandment of God, to one of the last prophets among them,) were safely deposited, to preserve them from the hands of the wicked, who sought to destroy them. He was informed, that these records contained many sacred revelations pertaining to the gospel of the kingdom, as well as prophecies relating to the great events of the last days; and that to fulfill his [God's] promises to the ancients, who wrote the records, and to accomplish his purposes, in the restitution of their children, etc., they were to come forth to the knowledge of the people. If faithful, he [Joseph] was to be the instrument, who should be thus highly favored in bringing these sacred things to light (Orson Pratt, *An Interesting Account of Several Remarkable Visions* [Edinburgh: Ballantyne and Hughes, 1840], 7; spelling standardized).

Joseph Smith Jr.

(Milton V. Backman has combined various recitals written by Joseph Smith to create the following narrative.)

The messenger further told me that two transparent stones in silver bows were deposited with the plates; and these stones, which were fastened to a breastplate, constituted what is called the Urim and Thummim. The angel said that possession and use of these stones was what constituted seers in ancient or former times, and that God had prepared them for the purpose of translating the book.

After telling me these things, he commenced quoting the prophecies of the Old Testament. He first quoted part of the third chapter of Malachi; and he quoted also the fourth or last chapter of the same prophecy, though with a little variation from the way it reads in our Bibles. Instead of quoting the first verse of chapter four as it reads in our books, he quoted it thus: "For behold, the day cometh that shall burn as an oven, and all the proud, yea, and all who do wickedly shall burn as stubble; for they that cometh shall burn them, saith the Lord of Hosts, that it shall leave them neither root nor branch."

And again, he quoted the fifth verse thus: "Behold I will reveal unto you the Priesthood, by the hand of Elijah the prophet, before the coming of the great and dreadful day of the Lord."

He also quoted the next verse differently: "And he shall plant in the hearts of the children the promises made to the fathers, and the hearts of the children shall turn to their fathers. If it were not so, the whole earth would be utterly wasted at his coming."

In addition to these, he quoted the eleventh chapter of Isaiah, saying that it was about to be fulfilled. He quoted also the third chapter of Acts, twenty-second and twenty-third verses, precisely as they stand in our New Testament. He said that that prophet was Christ; but the day had not yet come when "they who would not hear His voice should be cut off from among the people," but soon would come.

He also quoted the second chapter of Joel, from the twenty-eighth verse to the last. He also said that this was not yet fulfilled, but was soon to be. And he further stated that the fullness of the Gentiles was soon to come in. He quoted many other passages of scripture, and offered many explanations which cannot be mentioned here.

The messenger, therefore, told me that the covenant which God made with ancient Israel was at hand to be fulfilled; that the prepara-tory work for the second coming of the Messiah was speedily to com-mence; that the time was at hand for the gospel, in all its fullness to be preached in power, unto all nations that a people might be prepared for the millennial reign (*Eyewitness Accounts of the Restoration*, 42–43; see also Joseph Smith–History 1:35–41; punctuation standardized).

Oliver Cowdery

Moreover, the messenger declared that before the history of the aborigines of the country is translated, the scripture must be fulfilled which says that the words of a book which were sealed were presented to the learned; [Isaiah 29:11] for thus has God determined to leave men without excuse, and show to the meek that his arm is not shortened that it cannot save.

The angel instructed Joseph concerning the blessings, promises and covenants to Israel, and the great manifestations of favor to the world in the ushering in of the fullness of the gospel to prepare the way for the second advent of the Messiah. Most clearly was it shown to the prophet that the righteous should be gathered from all the earth before the great and dreadful day of the Lord and be taught the fullness of the gospel (A combination of Oliver Cowdery, "Letter IV to W. W. Phelps," *Mes-senger & Advocate* 1 [February 1835]: 79; Oliver Cowdery, "Letter VII to W. W. Phelps," *Messenger & Advocate* 1 [July 1835]: 155; and Oliver Cowdery, "Letter VI to W. W. Phelps," *Messenger & Advocate* 1 [April 1835]: 109; as cited in *Eyewitness Accounts of the Restoration*, 43–44).

Joseph Smith Jr.

*(Milton V. Backman has combined various recitals written by
Joseph Smith to create the following narrative.)*

Again, he told me that when I got those plates of which he had
spoken [for the time that they should be obtained was not yet fulfilled]
I should not show them to any person, neither the breastplate with the
Urim and Thummim, only to those to whom I should be commanded
to show them; if I did, I should be destroyed. While he was conversing
with me about the plates, the vision was opened to my mind that I could
see the place where the plates were deposited, and that so clearly and
distinctly that I knew the place again when I visited it.

After this communication, I saw the light in the room begin to
gather immediately around the person of him who had been speaking to
me, and it continued to do so until the room was again left dark, except
just around him; when, instantly I saw, as it were, a conduit open right
up into heaven, and he ascended up till he entirely disappeared. After
the messenger gradually vanished out of my sight or the vision closed,
the room was left as it had been before this heavenly light had made its
appearance.

I lay musing on the singularity of the scene, and marveling greatly
at what had been told to me by this extraordinary messenger; when, in
the midst of my meditation, I suddenly discovered that my room was
again beginning to get lighted, and in an instant, as it were, the same
heavenly messenger was again by my bedside.

He commenced, and again stated the very same things which he
had done at his first visit, without the least variation, and much more;
which having done, he informed me of great judgments which were
coming upon the earth, with great desolations by famine, sword, and
pestilence; and that these grievous judgments would come on the earth
in this generation. Having related these things he again ascended as he
had done before.

By this time, so deep were the impressions made on my mind, that
sleep had fled from my eyes, and I lay overwhelmed in astonishment at
what I had both seen and heard. But what was my surprise when again
I beheld the same messenger at my bedside, and heard him rehearse or
repeat over again to me the same things as before; and added a caution
to me, telling me that Satan would try to tempt me (in consequence of
the indigent circumstances of my father's family), to get the plates for

the purpose of getting rich. This he forbade me, saying that I must have no other object in view in getting the plates but to glorify God, and must not be influenced by any other motive than that of building his kingdom; otherwise I could not get them.

After the third visit he again ascended into heaven as before, and I was again left to ponder on the strangeness of what I had just experienced; when almost immediately after the heavenly messenger had ascended from me for the third time, the cock crowed, and I found that day was approaching, so that our interviews must have occupied the whole of that night (*Eyewitness Accounts of the Restoration*, 44–45; see also *Joseph Smith–History* 1:42–47; spelling standardized).

Joseph Smith Jr.

(Milton V. Backman has combined various recitals written by Joseph Smith to create the following narrative.)

I shortly after arose from my bed, and, as usual, went to the necessary labors of the day; but, in attempting to labor as at other times, I found my strength so exhausted as rendered me entirely unable. My father, who was laboring along with me, discovered something to be wrong with me, and told me to go home. I started with the intention of going to the house; but, in attempting to cross the fence out of the field where we were, my strength entirely failed me, and I fell helpless on the ground, and for a time was quite unconscious of anything.

The first thing that I can recollect was a voice speaking unto me, calling me by name. I looked up, and beheld the same messenger standing over my head, surrounded by light as before. He then again related unto me all that he had related to me the previous night, and commanded me to go to my father and tell him of the vision and commandments which I had received.

I obeyed; I returned to my father in the field, and rehearsed the whole matter to him. He replied to me that it was of God, and [told me] to go and do as commanded by the messenger. I left the field, and went to the place where the messenger had told me that the plates were deposited; and owing to the distinctness of the vision which I had had concerning it, I knew the place the instant that I arrived there (*Eyewitness Accounts of the Restoration*, 45–47; see also Joseph Smith–History 1:48–50).

Joseph Smith Jr.

[The angel Moroni] informed [me] that the time for bringing [the plates] forth had not yet arrived, neither would it, until four years from that time; but he told me that I should come to that place precisely in one year from that time, and that he would there meet with me, and that I should continue to do so until the time should come for obtaining the plates (Joseph Smith–History 1:53).

Lucy Mack Smith

The ensuing evening [September 22, 1823], when the family were all together, Joseph made known to them all that he had communicated to his father in the field, and also of his finding the Record, as well as what passed between him and the angel while he was at the place where the plates were deposited.

Sitting up late that evening, in order to converse upon these things, together with over-exertion of mind, had much fatigued Joseph; and when Alvin observed it, he said, "Now, brother, let us go to bed, and rise early in the morning, in order to finish our day's work at an hour before sunset, then, if mother will get our suppers early, we will have a fine long evening, and we will all sit down for the purpose of listening to you while you tell us the great things which God has revealed to you."

Accordingly, by sunset the next day we were all seated, and Joseph commenced telling us the great and glorious things which God had manifested to him; but, before proceeding, he charged us not to mention out of the family that which he was about to say to us, as the world was so wicked that when they came to a knowledge of these things they would try to take our lives; and that when we should obtain the plates, our names would be cast out as evil by all people. Hence the necessity of suppressing these things as much as possible, until the time should come for them to go forth to the world.

After giving us this charge, he proceeded to relate further particulars concerning the work which he was appointed to do, and we received them joyfully, never mentioning them except among ourselves, agreeable to the instructions which we had received from him.

From this time forth, Joseph continued to receive instructions from the Lord, and we continued to get the children together every evening, for the purpose of listening while he gave us a relation of the same. I presume our family presented an aspect as singular as any that ever lived upon the face of the earth—all seated in a circle, father, mother, sons, and daughters, and giving the most profound attention to a boy, eighteen years of age, who had never read the Bible through in his life: he seemed much less inclined to the perusal of books than any of the rest of our children, but far more given to meditation and deep study.

We were now confirmed in the opinion that God was about to bring to light something upon which we could stay our minds, or that would give us a more perfect knowledge of the plan of salvation and the redemption of the human family. This caused us greatly to rejoice, the sweetest union and happiness pervaded our house, and tranquility reigned in our midst.

During our evening conversations, Joseph would occasionally give us some of the most amusing recitals that could be imagined. He would describe the ancient inhabitants of this continent, their dress, mode of traveling, and the animals upon which they rode; their cities, their buildings, with every particular; their mode of warfare; and also their religious worship. This he would do with as much ease, seemingly, as if he had spent his whole life with them (Lucy Mack Smith, *Biographical Sketches of Joseph Smith, the Prophet and his Progenitors for Many Generations* [Liverpool: published for Orson Pratt and S. W. Richards, 1853], 83–85; spelling standardized).

Moroni's Known Appearances to Joseph Smith (1823–1829)

Date—Circumstance—References

1. September 21–22, 1823—Joseph's bedroom—Message repeated three times, Manchester, New York (Joseph Smith–History 1:30–47).
2. September 22, 1823—Field outside Joseph's home—Initial message repeated, Manchester, New York (Joseph Smith–History 1:48–49).
3. September 22, 1823—At the Hill Cumorah—Plates, Urim and Thummim, and breastplate shown in addition to an open vision, Hill Cumorah, New York (Joseph Smith–History 1:51–53 and

Messenger & Advocate [July and October 1835]).

4. September 22, 1824, 1825, and 1826—Yearly at Cumorah, instructions were given to aid Joseph in preparation for the restoration, Hill Cumorah, New York (Joseph Smith–History 1:53–54).

5. Winter 1827—Moroni met Joseph by the Hill Cumorah and said that the time had come for the record to be brought forth. He told Joseph to be up and doing the things that he had been commanded, Hill Cumorah, New York (*Biographical Sketches*, 99).

6. September 22, 1827—Joseph receives the plates, Hill Cumorah, New York (Joseph Smith–History 1:59).

7. June-July 1828—Urim and Thummim taken by Moroni over the Martin Harris incident, Harmony, Pennsylvania (*History of the Church*, 1:21–22).

8. July 1828—Urim and Thummim returned, Harmony, Pennsylvania (*History of the Church*, 1:21–22, and *Biographical Sketches*, 126).

9. July 1828—Plates and Urim and Thummim taken, Harmony, Pennsylvania (*History of the Church*, 1:23).

10. July–August 1828—Plates and Urim and Thummim returned, Harmony, Pennsylvania (*History of the Church*, 1:23, and *Biographical Sketches*, 126).

11. June 1829—Angel obtained the plates at Harmony, Pennsylvania, to transport them to Fayette township, New York, because Joseph was apprehensive about their safety en route, Harmony, Pennsylvania (*Biographical Sketches*, 126).

12. June 1829—Joseph, Emma, Oliver, and David Whitmer saw Moroni carrying the plates en route to Cumorah—Moroni appeared and disappeared instantly on the road between Harmony, Pennsylvania, and the Hill Cumorah (Joseph F. Smith Journal, "The Three Witnesses," Andrew Jensen, *The Historical Record* [5 January 1886]: 209).

13. June 1829—Joseph had the plates once again in his possession in Fayette township. Moroni met Joseph in the garden and gave the plates to him, Fayette township, New York (*Biographical Sketches*, 137).

14. June 1829—Joseph finished the translation and Moroni took the record, Fayette township, New York (*History of the Church*, 1:60).

15. June 1829—Oliver [Cowdery], David Whitmer, and Joseph Smith

(Book of Mormon witnesses) were shown the plates by Moroni, Fayette township, New York (*History of the Church*, 1:60).

16. June 1829—Martin Harris and Joseph Smith (Book of Mormon witnesses) saw Moroni and the plates, Fayette township, New York (*History of the Church*, 1:55).

17. June 1829—Moroni gave the plates to Joseph and he showed them to the Eight Witnesses. Moroni then called for them and kept them, Manchester township, New York (*Biographical Sketches*, 140–41; H. Donl Peterson, *Moroni—Ancient Prophet, Modern Messenger* [Salt Lake City: Deseret Book, 2000], 132–35).

ADDITIONAL HEAVENLY PERSONAGES WHO APPEARED TO THE PROPHET JOSEPH SMITH OR WERE SEEN BY HIM IN VISION

John Taylor
(Courtesy of the Church Archives, The Church of Jesus Christ of Latter-day Saints)

John Taylor

If you were to ask Joseph what sort of a looking man Adam was, he would tell you at once; he would tell you his size and appearance and all about him. You might have asked him what sort of men Peter, James, and John were, and he could have told you. Why? Because he had seen them (in *Journal of Discourses*, 26 vols. [London: Latter-day Saints' Book Depot, 1854-86], 18:326).

John Taylor

And when Joseph Smith was raised up as a Prophet of God, Mormon, Moroni, Nephi and others of the ancient Prophets who formerly lived on this Continent, and Peter and John and others who lived on the Asiatic Continent, came to him and communicated to him certain principles pertaining to the Gospel of the Son of God (*Journal of Discourses*, 17:374).

John Taylor

The principles which he had, placed him in communication with the Lord, and not only with the Lord, but with the ancient apostles and prophets; such men, for instance, as Abraham, Isaac, Jacob, Noah, Adam, Seth, Enoch, and Jesus and the Father, and the apostles that lived on this continent, as well as those who lived on the Asiatic continent. He seemed to be as familiar with these people as we are with one another. Why? Because he had to introduce a dispensation which was called the dispensation of the fulness of times, and it was known as such by the ancient servants of God (*Journal of Discourse*, 21:94).

OTHER ANGELIC MINISTERS THAT APPEARED TO JOSEPH SMITH

Personage—References

1. God the Father (Joseph Smith–History 1:17; *History of the Church,* 1:5; D&C 76:20)
2. Jesus Christ (Joseph Smith–History 1:17; *History of the Church,* 1:5–6; D&C 76:20–24; D&C 110:2–10)
3. Moroni (see chart above; Joseph Smith–History 1:30–49; *Journal of Discourses,* 17:374)
4. Elijah (D&C 110:13–16; *Journal of Discourses,* 23:48)
5. John the Baptist (D&C 13; *History of the Church,* 1:39–40)
6–8. Peter, James, John (D&C 27:12; D&C 128:20; *History of the Church,* 1:40–42; *Journal of Discourses,* 18:326)
9. Adam (Michael) (*History of the Church,* 2:380; 3:388; D&C 128:21; *Journal of Discourses,* 18:326)
10. Noah (Gabriel) (D&C 128:21; *Journal of Discourses,* 21:94)
11. Raphael (D&C 128:21)
12. Moses (D&C 110:11; *Journal of Discourses,* 21:65)
13. Elias (D&C 110:12; D&C 27:6; *Journal of Discourses,* 23:48)
14. Joseph, son of Jacob (D&C 27:10)
15. Abraham (D&C 27:10; *Journal of Discourses,* 21:94)
16. Isaac (D&C 27:10; *Journal of Discourses,* 21:94)
17. Jacob (D&C 27:10; *Journal of Discourses,* 21:94)
18. Enoch (*Journal of Discourses,* 21:65)

19–27. Twelve Jewish Apostles (*Journal of Discourses*, 21:94) (Peter, James, and John already counted above; names are in Matthew 10:1–4 and Luke 6:13–16)

28–39. Twelve Nephite Apostles (*Journal of Discourses*, 21:94; including Three Nephites; names are recorded in 3 Nephi 19:4)

40. Nephi (*Journal of Discourses*, 21:161; Orson Pratt Letter, Box 3/11/1876 CHO)

41. Seth (*Journal of Discourses*, 21:94; *History of the Church*, 3:388; D&C 107:53–57)

42. Methuselah (*Journal of Discourses*, 21:94; *History of the Church*, 3:388; D&C 107:53–57)

43. Enos (*Journal of Discourses*, 21:94; *History of the Church*, 3:388; D&C 107:53–57)

44. Mahalaleel (*Journal of Discourses*, 21:94; *History of the Church*, 3:388; D&C 107:53–57)

45. Jared (Bible) (*History of the Church*, 3:388; D&C 107:53–57)

46. Lamech (*Journal of Discourses*, 18:235)

47. Abel (*Journal of Discourses*, 18:325; *History of the Church*, 3:388)

48. Cainan (*History of the Church*, 3:388; D&C 107:53–57)

49. Zelph the Lamanite (*Times and Seasons* 6:788)

50. Alvin Smith, Joseph's deceased brother (*History of the Church*, 2:380)

51. Mormon (*Journal of Discourses*, 17:374)

52. Paul (*Teachings of the Prophet Joseph Smith*, 180)

53. Eve (Oliver B. Huntington Diary, Part 2, 214, L. Tom Perry Special Collections, Harold B. Lee Library, Brigham Young University, Provo, Utah)

54. Alma (*Journal of Discourses*, 13:47)

55. Unnamed angel (D&C 27, Concerning wine in Sacrament; *History of the Church*, 1:106)

56. Unnamed angel sent to accept dedication of temple (*Life of Heber C. Kimball*, 106; *Temples of the Most High*, 159)

57. Unnamed angel (visited Joseph Smith three different times and commanded him to practice polygamy—Eliza R. Snow, Biography and Family Records of Lorenzo Snow, 69–70).

58. "I saw many angels" (Warren Cowdery's Account of the First Vision, in *Joseph Smith's First Vision*, 159)

59. Satan, as an angel of light (and his associates) (D&C 128:20;

Journal of Discourses, 3:229–30; Peterson, *Moroni—Ancient Prophet, Modern Messenger*, 148–50).

⚛ 8 ⚛

THE COMING FORTH OF
THE BOOK OF MORMON

In September 1823, Joseph Smith walked to the Hill Cumorah to see the plates the angel Moroni had described to him in vision the previous night. More than fourteen hundred years earlier, Moroni had chosen the hill as the repository for the sacred record.

DESCRIPTIONS OF THE HILL CUMORAH
AND THE PLATES

Oliver Cowdery

You are acquainted with the mail-road from Palmyra, Wayne Co., to Canandaigua, Ontario Co., N.Y., . . . as you pass from the former to the later place, before arriving at the little village of Manchester, say from three to four . . . miles from Palmyra, you pass a large hill on the east side of the road. Why I say large, is because it is as large, perhaps, as any in that country. . . . The north end rises quite sudden, until it assumes a level with the more southerly extremity, and, I think I may say, an elevation higher than at the south a short distance, say half, or three-fourths of a mile. As you pass toward Canandaigua it lessens gradually, until the surface assumes its common level, or is broken by other smaller hills or ridges, water courses and ravines. I think I am justified in saying, that this is the highest hill for some distance round, and I am certain that its appearance, as it rises so suddenly from a plain on the north, must attract the notice of the traveler as he passes by. . . .

The north end rose suddenly from the plain, forming a promontory

The Hill Cumorah *(Courtesy of the Church Archives, The Church of Jesus Christ of Latter-day Saints)*

without timber, but covered with grass. As you pass to the south you soon come to scattered timber, the surface having been cleared by art or by wind; and a short distance further left, you are surrounded with the common forest of the country. It is necessary to observe that even the part cleared was only occupied for pasturage, its steep ascent and narrow summit not admitting the plough of the husbandman, with any degree of ease or profit (Oliver Cowdery, "Letter IV to W. W. Phelps," *Messenger & Advocate* 1 [July 1835]: 152, 174; spelling standardized).

Joseph Smith Jr.

On the west side of this hill, not far from the top . . . a hole of sufficient depth, (how deep I know not,) was dug. At the bottom of this was laid a stone of suitable size, the upper surface being smooth. At each edge was placed a large quantity of cement, and into this cement, at the four edges of this stone, were placed, erect, four others, *their* bottom edges resting *in* the cement at the outer edges of the first stone. The four last named, when placed erect, formed a box, the corners, or where the edges of the four came in contact, were also cemented so firmly that the moisture from without was prevented from entering. It is to be observed, also, that the inner surface of the four erect, or side stones was smooth. This box was sufficiently large to admit a breast-plate, such as was used by the ancients to defend the chest, &c. from the arrows and weapons of their enemy. From the bottom of the box, or from the breast-plate, arose three small pillars composed of the same description of cement used on the edges; and upon these three pillars was placed the record of the children of Joseph (Oliver Cowdery, "Letter IV to W. W. Phelps," *Messenger & Advocate* 2 [October 1835]: 196).

FIRST ATTEMPT TO OBTAIN THE BOOK OF MORMON PLATES
(22 September 1823)

After arriving at the Hill Cumorah and locating the stone box that held the ancient plates, the Prophet Joseph Smith tried to remove the record from the box, but was unable to.

Joseph Smith Jr.

(Milton V. Backman has combined various recitals written by Joseph Smith to create the following narrative.)

[I] made three attempts to get [take] them but was forbidden by the messenger. I cried unto the Lord in the agony of my soul, [asking] why I could not obtain them, and the angel said unto me that I had not kept the commandments of the Lord ... for ... I had been tempted ... [by] the adversary and sought the plates to obtain riches and kept not the commandment that I should have an eye single to the glory of God. Therefore, I was chastened (A combination of Joseph Smith Jr., *1832 History, 1835 History,* and *1838 History;* as cited in Milton V. Backman, *Eyewitness Accounts of the Restoration* [Salt Lake City: Deseret Book, 1986], 48).

Lucy Mack Smith

(Commenting on a vision the angel Moroni showed Joseph Smith while he was at the Hill Cumorah.)

While Joseph remained here, the angel showed him, by contrast, the difference between good and evil, and likewise the consequences of both obedience and disobedience to the commandments of God, in such a striking manner, that the impression was always vivid in his memory until the very end of his days; and in giving a relation of this circumstance, not long prior to his death, he remarked, that "ever afterwards he was willing to keep the commandments of God" (Lucy Mack Smith, *Biographical Sketches of Joseph Smith, the Prophet and his Progenitors for Many Generations* [Liverpool: published for Orson Pratt and S. W. Richards, 1853], 83).

Oliver Cowdery

[After making three attempts to secure the plates, Joseph Smith saw] the angel who had previously given him the directions concerning this matter. In an instant, all the former instructions, the great intelligence concerning Israel and the last days, were brought to his mind: . . . He had come, to be sure, and found the word of the angel fulfilled concerning the reality of the record, but he had failed to remember the great end for which they had been kept, and in consequence could not have power to take them into his possession and bear them away.

At that instant he looked to the Lord in prayer, and as he prayed darkness began to disperse from his mind and his soul was lit up as it was the evening before, and he was filled with the Holy Spirit; and again did the Lord manifest his condescension and mercy: the heavens were opened and the glory of the Lord shone round about and rested upon him. While he thus stood gazing and admiring, the angel said, "Look!" and as he thus spake he beheld the prince of darkness, surrounded by his innumerable train of associates. All this passed before him, and the heavenly messenger said, "All this is shown, the good and the evil, the holy and impure, the glory of God and the power of darkness, that you may know hereafter the two powers and never be influenced or overcome by that wicked one. . . . You now see why you could not obtain this record. . . . They [the plates] are not deposited here for the sake of accumulating gain and wealth for the glory of the world" (Oliver Cowdery, "Letter VIII to W. W. Phelps," *Messenger & Advocate* 2 [October 1835]: 198).

ANNUAL VISITS TO THE HILL CUMORAH
(1824–1827)

Before Joseph was able to obtain the plates, he was commanded by the angel Moroni to return to the Hill Cumorah each year, at the same time, for four years (see Joseph Smith–History 1:53–54). On each of these visits, Joseph was instructed in the building up of the kingdom of God and in the history of the Book of Mormon people. These yearly visits acted as preparatory courses for the role he would play in the restoration of the gospel and in the translation of the Book of Mormon.

Joseph Smith Jr.

Accordingly, as I had been commanded, I went at the end of each year, and at each time I found the same messenger there, and received instruction and intelligence from him at each of our interviews, respecting what the Lord was going to do, and how and in what manner his kingdom was to be conducted in the last days (*Joseph Smith–History* 1:54).

Catherine Salisbury

(Joseph Smith's sister)

I well remember the trials my brother had, before he obtained the records. After he had the vision, he went frequently to the hill, and upon returning would tell us, "I have seen the records, also the brass plates and the sword of Laban with the breast plate and interpreters." He would ask father why he could not get them. The time had not yet come (Catherine Salisbury, "Dear Sisters," *The Saint's Herald* 33 [1 May 1886]: 260; as cited in *Eyewitness Accounts of the Restoration*, 53).

Lucy Mack Smith

On the 22d of September, 1824, Joseph again visited the place where he found the plates the year previous; and supposing at this time that the only thing required, in order to possess them until the time for their translation, was to be able to keep the commandments of God—and he firmly believed he could keep every commandment which had been given him—he fully expected to carry them home with him. Therefore, having arrived at the place, and uncovering the plates, he put forth his hand and took them up, but, as he was taking them hence, the unhappy thought darted through his mind that probably there was something else in the box besides the plates, which would be of some pecuniary advantage to him. So, in the moment of excitement, he laid them down very carefully, for the purpose of covering the box, lest some one might happen to pass that way and get whatever there might be remaining in it. After covering it, he turned round to take the record again, but behold it was gone, and where he knew not, neither did he know the means by which it had been taken from him.

At this, as a natural consequence, he was much alarmed. He kneeled down and asked the Lord why the record had been taken from him; upon which the angel of the Lord appeared to him, and told him that he had not done as he had been commanded, for in a former revelation he had been commanded not to lay the plates down, or put them for a moment out of his hands, until he got into the house and deposited them in a chest or trunk, having a good lock and key, and contrary to this, he had laid them down with the view of securing some fancied or imaginary treasure that remained.

In the moment of excitement, Joseph was overcome by the powers of darkness, and forgot the injunction that was laid upon him.

Having some further conversation with the angel on this occasion, Joseph was permitted to raise the stone again, when he beheld the plates as he had done before. He immediately reached forth his hand to take them, but instead of getting them, as he anticipated, he was hurled back upon the ground with great violence. When he recovered, the angel was gone, and he arose and returned to the house, weeping for grief and disappointment.

As he was aware that we would expect him to bring the plates home with him, he was greatly troubled, fearing that we might doubt his having seen them . . .

Joseph then related the circumstance in full, which gave us much uneasiness, as we were afraid that he might utterly fail of obtaining the record through some neglect on his part. We, therefore, doubled our diligence in prayer and supplication to God, in order that he might be more fully instructed in his duty, and be preserved from all the wiles and machinations of him "'who lieth in wait to deceive" (*Biographical Sketches*, 92–95).

Orson Pratt

The Prophets who deposited these plates in the hill Cumorah were commanded of the Lord to deposit the Urim and Thummim with them, so that when the time came for them to be brought forth, the individual who was entrusted with them might be able to translate them by the gift and power of God. Joseph put forth his hands to take the plates, but upon doing so the angel immediately appeared to him and said, "Joseph, the time has not yet come for you to take the plates; you must be taught and instructed, and you must give heed to my commandments and to the commandments of the Lord until you are fully prepared to be entrusted with them, for the Lord promised his ancient servants on this land that no one should have them for the purpose of speculation, and that they should be brought forth with an eye single to the glory of God; and now, if you will keep the commandments of God in all things, and prepare yourself, you will in due time be permitted to take these plates from their place of deposit." He would not suffer him to take them at that time. Four years from that day—on the morning of the 22nd of September, 1827—having been commanded of the Lord to come to that place at that special time, he went and was met by the angel. I will state, however, that during these four years he was often ministered to by the angels of God, and received instruction concerning the work that was to be performed in the later days. But when the time had fully arrived he went to the hill Cumorah, according to appointment, and took the plates, and the Urim and Thummim with them, and took them to his father's house in a wagon, which he had brought near to the hill for that purpose. He was then nearly twenty-two years old—twenty-two the following December (in *Journal of Discourses*, 26 vols. [London: Latter-day Saints' Book Depot, 1854–86], 15:184–85).

Lucy Mack Smith

Furthermore, the angel told him at the interview mentioned last that the time had not yet come for the plates to be brought forth to the world; that he could not take them from the place wherein they were deposited until he had learned to keep the commandments of God—not only till he was willing, but able to do it. The angel bade Joseph come to this place every year, at the same time of the year, and he would meet him there and give him further instructions. . . .

From this time forth Joseph continued to receive instructions from time to time, and every evening we gathered our children together and gave our time up to the discussion of those things which he instructed to us. I think that we presented the most peculiar aspect of any family that ever lived upon the earth, all seated in a circle, father, mother, sons and daughters, listening in breathless anxiety to the religious teachings of a boy eighteen years of age who had never read the Bible through by course in his life.

. . . He would describe the ancient inhabitants of this continent, their dress, their manner of traveling, the animals which they rode, the cities that they built, and the structure of their buildings with every particular, their mode of warfare, and their religious worship as specifically as though he had spent his life with them (Lucy Mack Smith, *The Revised and Enhanced History of Joseph Smith by His Mother*, ed. Scot Facer Proctor and Maurine Jensen Proctor [Salt Lake City: Bookcraft, 1996], 110–12).

Lucy Mack Smith

(Describing in 1826 how Moroni chastened the Prophet Joseph and warned him to prepare himself to receive the plates.)

Mr. Smith had occasion to send Joseph to Manchester on business. He set out in good time, and we expected him to be home as soon as six o'clock in the evening, but he did not arrive. We had always had a peculiar anxiety about this child, for it seemed as though something was always occurring to place his life in jeopardy, and if he was absent one-half an hour longer than expected, we were apprehensive of some evil befalling him.

It is true he was now a man, grown and capable of using sufficient judgment to keep out of common difficulties. But we were now aware that God intended him for a good and an important work; consequently we expected that the powers of darkness would strive against him more than any other, on this account, to overthrow him.

But to return to the circumstances which I commenced relating. He did not return home until the night was considerably advanced. When he entered the house, he threw himself into a chair, seemingly much exhausted. He was pale as ashes. His father exclaimed, "Joseph, why have you stayed so late? Has anything happened to you? We have been in distress about you these three hours."

As Joseph made no answer, he continued his interrogations, until finally I said, "Now, Father, let him rest a moment—don't trouble him now—you see he is home safe, and he is very tired, so pray wait a little."

The fact was, I had learned to be a little cautious about matters with regard to Joseph, for I was accustomed to see him look as he did on that occasion, and I could not easily mistake the cause thereof.

After Joseph recovered himself a little, he said, "Father, I have had the severest chastisement that I ever had in my life."

My husband, supposing that it was from some of the neighbors, was quite angry and observed, "Chastisement indeed! Well, upon my word, I would like to know who has been taking you to task and what their pretext was. I would like to know what business anybody has to find fault with you."

Joseph smiled to see his father so hasty and indignant. "Father," said he, "it was the angel of the Lord. He says I have been negligent, that the time has now come when the record should be brought forth, and that I must be up and doing, that I must set myself about the things which God has commanded me to do. But, Father, give yourself no uneasiness as to this reprimand, for I know what course I am to pursue, and all will be well."

It was also made known to him, at this interview, that he should make another effort to obtain the plates, on the twenty-second of the following September, but this he did not mention to us at that time (*The Revised and Enhanced History of Joseph Smith*, 134–35).

JOSEPH RECEIVES THE PLATES
(22 September 1827)

Heber C. Kimball

(Commenting about the unusual display in the heavens the night of 21–22 September 1827. At this time, Heber and his wife, Vilate, were living in Mendon, New York, several miles from the Hill Cumorah, where Joseph Smith received the Book of Mormon

plates from the angel Moroni that very night. Brigham Young and his wife, who were living at Port Byron, also witnessed this heavenly manifestation that same night. Brigham and Heber were both impressed that God was marshaling his forces on earth and that they each had a role to play in the dramatic events about to occur. None of the aforementioned had yet met the Smiths, and none was aware that the Restoration was underway.)

Heber C. Kimball
(Courtesy of the Church Archives, The Church of Jesus Christ of Latter-day Saints)

I had retired to bed, when John P. Greene, who was living within a hundred steps of my house, came and waked me up, calling upon me to come out and behold the scenery in the heavens. I woke up and called my wife [Vilate] and Sister Fanny Young (sister to Brigham Young), who was living with us, and we went out-of-doors.

It was one of the most beautiful starlight nights, so clear that we could see to pick up a pin. We looked to the eastern horizon, and beheld a white smoke arise toward the heavens; as it ascended it formed itself into a belt, and made a noise like the sound of a mighty wind, and continued southwest, forming a regular bow dipping in the western horizon. After the bow had formed, it began to widen out and grow clear and transparent, of a bluish cast; it grew wide enough to contain twelve men abreast.

In this bow an army moved, commencing from the east and marching to the west; they continued marching until they reached the western horizon. They moved in platoons, and walked so close that the rear ranks trod in the steps of their file leaders, until the whole bow was literally crowded with soldiers. We could distinctly see the muskets, bayonets and knapsacks of the men, who wore caps and feathers like those used by the American soldiers in the last war with Britain; and also saw their officers with their swords and equipage, and the clashing and jingling of their implements of war, and could discover the forms and features of the men. The most profound order existed throughout the entire army; when the foremost man stepped, every man stepped at the same time; I could hear the steps. When the front rank reached the western horizon a battle ensued, as we could distinctly hear the report of arms and the rush.

No man could judge of my feelings when I beheld that army of men, as plainly as ever I saw armies of men in the flesh; it seemed as though every hair of my head was alive. This scenery we gazed upon for hours, until it began to disappear (Orson F. Whitney, *The Life of Heber C. Kimball* [Salt Lake City: Bookcraft, 1996], 15–16).

Joseph Smith Jr.

At length the time arrived for obtaining the plates, the Urim and Thummim, and the breastplate; on the twenty-second day of September, one thousand eight hundred and twenty-seven, having went as usual at the end of another year to the place where they were deposited, the same heavenly messenger delivered them up to me, with this charge that I should be responsible for them: that if I should let them go carelessly or through any neglect of mine I should be cut off; but that if I would use all my endeavors to preserve them, until he the messenger should call for them, they should be protected ("History of Joseph Smith," *Times & Seasons* 3 [2 May 1842]: 772).

Lucy Mack Smith

On the twentieth of September, Mr. Knight and his friend Stoal [Josiah Stowell], came to see how we were managing matters with Stoddard and Co.; and they tarried with us until the twenty-second. On the night of the twenty-first, I sat up very late, as my work rather pressed upon my hands. I did not retire until after twelve o'clock at night. About twelve o'clock, Joseph came to me, and asked me if I had a chest with a lock and key. I knew in an instant what he wanted it for, and not having one, I was greatly alarmed, as I thought it might be a matter of considerable moment. But Joseph, discovering my anxiety, said, "Never mind, I can do very well for the present without it—be calm—all is right."

Shortly after this, Joseph's wife passed through the room with her bonnet and riding dress; and in a few minutes they left together, taking Mr. Knight's horse and wagon. I spent the night in prayer and supplication to God, for the anxiety of my mind would not permit me to sleep. At the usual hour, I commenced preparing breakfast. My heart fluttered at every footstep, as I now expected Joseph and Emma momentarily, and feared lest Joseph might meet with a second disappointment.

When the male portion of the family were seated at the breakfast table, Mr. Smith enquired for Joseph, for he was not aware that he had left home. I requested my husband not to call him, for I would like to have him take breakfast with his wife that morning.

"No, no;" said my husband, "I must have Joseph sit down here and eat with me."

"Well, now, Mr. Smith," continued I, "*do* let him eat with his wife *this* morning; he almost always takes breakfast with you."

His father finally consented, and [ate] without him, and no further inquiries were made concerning his absence, but in a few minutes Mr. Knight came in quite disturbed.

"Why, Mr. Smith," exclaimed he, "my horse is gone, and I can't find him on the premises, and I wish to start for home in half an hour."

"Never mind the horse," said I. "Mr. Knight does not know all the nooks and corners in the pastures; I will call William, he will bring the horse immediately."

This satisfied him for the time being; but he soon made another discovery. His wagon also was gone. He then concluded, that a rogue had stolen them both.

"Mr. Knight," said I, "do be quiet; I would be ashamed to have you go about, waiting upon yourself—just go out and talk with Mr. Smith until William comes, and if you really must go home, your horse shall be brought, and you shall be waited upon like a gentleman. "He accordingly went out, and while he was absent Joseph returned.

I trembled so with fear, lest all might be lost in consequence of some failure in keeping the commandments of God, that I was under the necessity of leaving the room in order to conceal my feelings. Joseph saw this, and said, "Do not be uneasy mother, all is right" (*Biographical Sketches*, 99–101).

DESCRIPTIONS OF THE PLATES

William Smith

(Milton V. Backman has combined various recitals written by William Smith, brother of Joseph Smith Jr., to create the following narrative.)

After my father's family moved to New York State, in about five years they cleared sixty acres of land, and fenced it. The timber on this land was very heavy. Some of the elms were so large that we had to [struggle to get] them off. They were too large to be cut with a cross-cut saw. We built a frame dwelling house and out buildings. My brothers Joseph and Hyrum had to work. Joseph did not have time to make gold plates.

The time to receive the plates came at last. When Joseph received them, he came in and said: "Father, I have got the plates." All believed it was true, father, mother, brothers and sisters. You can tell what a child is. Parents know whether their children are truthful or not. . . . Father knew his child was telling the truth. When the plates were brought in they were wrapped up in a tow frock. My father then put them into a pillow case. Father said, "What, Joseph, can we not see them?"

"No, I was disobedient the first time, but I intend to be faithful this time; for I was forbidden to show them until they are translated, but you can feel them. . . ."

I was permitted to lift them as they laid in a pillow case; but not to see them, as it was contrary to the commands he had received. They weighed about sixty pounds according to the best of my judgment. . . . They were not quite as large as this Bible. . . . One could easily tell that they were not stone, hewn out to deceive, or even a block of wood. Being a mixture of gold and copper, they were much heavier than stone, and very much heavier than wood (*Eyewitness Accounts of the Restoration*, 69–70).

Catherine Salisbury

(Sister of Joseph Smith Jr.)

When [the time to secure the plates had] arrived, he [Joseph Smith] was commanded to go on the 22nd day of September 1827 at 2 o'clock. We had supposed that when he should bring them home, the whole family would be allowed to see them, but he said it was forbidden of the Lord. They could be seen only by those who were chosen to bear their testimony to the world. We had therefore to be content until they were translated and we could have the book to read (Catherine Salisbury, "Letter of Katherine Salisbury, March 10, 1886," *Saints' Herald* 33 [1886]: 260; as cited in *Eyewitness Accounts of the Restoration*, 70).

Joseph Knight

[In] the forepart of September [1827], I went to Rochester on business and returned by Palmyra to be there by the 22nd of September. I was there several days. . . . That night we went to bed and in the morning I got up and my horse and carriage were gone. . . . After a while he [Joseph Smith] came home [with] the horse. All came into the house to breakfast but nothing [was] said about where they had been. After breakfast Joseph called me into the other room. . . . He set his foot on the bed, leaned his head on his hand and said, . . . "It is ten times better than I expected." Then he went on to tell length and width and thickness of the plates; and said he, "They appear to be gold." But he seemed to think more of the glasses or the Urim and Thummim than he did of the plates, for, said he, "I can see anything; they are marvelous. Now they are written in characters and I want them translated" (Joseph Knight, *Reminiscences of Joseph Knight* [LDS Church Archives, Church Historical Department, The Church of Jesus Christ of Latter-day Saints, Salt Lake City]; as cited in *Eyewitness Accounts of the Restoration*, 72; spelling and punctuation standardized).

Joseph Smith Jr.

These records were engraven on plates which had the appearance of gold, each plate was six inches wide and eight inches long and not quite so thick as common tin. They were filled with engravings, in Egyptian characters and bound together in a volume, as the leaves of a book with three rings running through the whole. The volume was something near six inches in thickness, a part of which was sealed. The characters on the unsealed part were small and beautifully engraved. The whole book exhibited many marks of antiquity in its construction and much skill in the art of engraving. With the records was found a curious instrument which the ancients called "Urim and Thummim," which consisted of two transparent stones set in the rim of a bow fastened to a breast-plate (Joseph Smith Jr., "Church History," *Times & Seasons* 3 [1 March 1842]: 707; original spelling preserved).

Lucy Mack Smith

[On the morning of September 22, after Joseph had returned from the hill, he placed] the article [the Urim and Thummim] of which he spoke into my hands, and, upon examination, [I] found that it consisted of two smooth three-cornered diamonds set in glass, and the glasses were set in silver bows, which were connected with each other in much the same way as old fashioned spectacles. . . .

That of which I spoke, which Joseph termed a key, was indeed, nothing more nor less than the Urim and Thummim, and it was by this that the angel showed him many things which he saw in vision; by which he could also ascertain, at any time, the approach of danger, either to himself or the record, and on account of which he always kept the Urim and Thummim about his person.

After bringing home the plates, Joseph commenced working with his father and brothers on the farm, in order to be as near as possible to the treasure which was confided to his care.

Soon after this, he came in from work, one afternoon, and . . . handed me the breastplate spoken of in his history.

It was wrapped in a thin muslin handkerchief, so thin that I could see the glistening metal, and ascertain its proportions without any difficulty.

It was concave on one side and convex on the other, and extended from the neck downwards as far as the center of the stomach of a man of extraordinary size. It had four straps of the same material for the purpose of fastening it to the breast, two of which ran back to go over the shoulders, and the other two were designed to fasten to the hips. They were just the width of two of my fingers, (for I measured them,) and they had holes in the ends of them, to be convenient in fastening.

The whole plate was worth at least five hundred dollars. After I had examined it, Joseph placed it in the chest with the Urim and Thummim (*Biographical Sketches*, 116, 123–24).

PERSECUTION AND ATTEMPTS TO STEAL THE PLATES

Joseph Smith Jr.

I soon found out the reason why I had received such strict charges to keep them safe, and why it was that the messenger had said that when I had done what was required at my hand, he would call for them. For no sooner was it known that I had them, than the most strenuous exertions were used to get them from me, and false reports, misrepresentations and slander flew as on the wings of the wind in every direction. Rumor with her thousand tongues was all the time employed in circulating tales about my father's family, and about myself. If I were to relate a thousandth part of them, it would fill up volumes. The house was frequently beset by mobs and evil designing persons. Several times I was shot at and very narrowly escaped. The persecution became more bitter and severe than before, and multitudes were on the alert continually to get them [the plates] from me if possible. But by the wisdom of God, they remained safe in my hands until I had accomplished by them what was required (A combination of *Joseph Smith–History* 1:60–61 and "History of Joseph Smith," *Times and Seasons* 3 [2 May 1842]: 772; as cited in *Eyewitness Accounts of the Restoration*, 74).

Joseph Knight

Now he [Joseph Smith] was Commanded not to let [anybody] see those things [plates and the Urim and Thimmim] except for a few witnesses at a given time. Now it soon got about that Joseph had found the plates and people came to see them, but he told them that they could not, for he must not show them. But many insisted and offered money and property to see them. [And] for keeping them from the people, they [others] persecuted and abused them him. The Smiths were obliged to hide them [the plates], and they hid them under a brick hearth in the west room (*Reminiscences of Joseph Knight;* as cited in *Eyewitness Accounts of the Restoration,* 74–75).

Lucy Mack Smith

[A few days after Joseph obtained the Record], one of the neighbors asked Mr. Smith many questions concerning the plates. I will here observe, that no one ever heard anything from us respecting them, except a confidential friend, whom my husband had spoken to about them some two or three years previous. It appeared that Satan had now stirred up the hearts of those who had gotten a hint of the matter from our friend, to search into it, and make every possible move towards thwarting the purposes of the Almighty. . . .

[One day Joseph] sent Carlos, my youngest son, to his brother Hyrum's, to have him come up immediately, as he desired to see him. When he came, Joseph requested him to get a chest, having a good lock and key, and to have it there by the time he (Joseph) should return. And, after giving these instructions, Joseph started for the plates.

The plates were secreted about three miles from home, in the following manner. Finding an old birch log much decayed, excepting the bark, which was in a measure sound, he took his pocket-knife and cut the bark with some care, then turned it back, and made a hole of sufficient size to receive the plates, and laying them in the cavity thus formed, he replaced the bark; after which he laid across the log, in several places, some old stuff that happened to lay near, in order to conceal, as much as possible, the place in which they were deposited.

Joseph, on coming to them, took them from their secret place, and, wrapping them in his linen frock, placed them under his arm and started for home.

After proceeding a short distance, he thought it would be more safe to leave the road and go through the woods. Traveling some distance after he left the road, he came to a large windfall, and as he was jumping over a log, a man sprang up from behind it, and gave him a heavy blow with a gun. Joseph turned around and knocked him down, then ran at the top of his speed. About half a mile further he was attacked again in the same manner as before; he knocked this man down in like manner as the former, then ran on again; and before he reached home he was assaulted the third time. In striking the last one, he dislocated his thumb, which, however, he did not notice until he came within sight of the house, when he threw himself down in the corner of the fence in order to recover his breath. As soon as he was able, he arose and came to the house. He was still altogether speechless from fright and the fatigue of running.

After resting a few moments, he desired me to send Carlos . . . to Hyrum's, to tell him to bring the chest.

I did as I was requested, and when Carlos arrived at Hyrum's, he found him at tea, with two of his wife's sisters. Just as Hyrum was raising a cup to his mouth Carlos touched his shoulder. Without waiting to hear one word from the child, he dropped the cup, sprang from the table, caught the chest, turned it upside down, and emptying its contents on the floor, left the house instantly with the chest on his shoulder.

The young ladies were greatly astonished at his singular behavior, and declared to his wife—who was then confined to her bed, her oldest daughter, Lovina, being but four days old—that he was certainly crazy.

His wife laughed heartily, and replied, "Oh, not in the least; he has just thought of something which he has neglected, and it is just like him to fly off in a tangent when he thinks of anything in that way."

When the chest came, Joseph locked up the record, then threw himself upon the bed, and after resting a little, so that he could converse freely, he arose and went into the kitchen, where he related his recent adventure to his father, Mr. Knight, and Mr. Stoal [Stowell], besides many others, who had by this time collected, with the view of hearing something in regard to the strange circumstance which had taken place. He showed them his thumb, saying, "I must stop talking, father, and get you to put my thumb in place, for it is very painful. . . ."

Shortly after this circumstance, Joseph . . . determined that a portion of the hearth should be taken up, and that the record and breastplate should be buried under the same, and then the hearth be re-laid, to prevent suspicion.

This was done as speedily as possible, but the hearth was scarcely re-laid when a large company of men, well armed, came rushing up to the house. Joseph threw open the doors, and taking a hint from the stratagem of his grandfather Mack, hallooed as if he had a legion at hand, in the meanwhile giving the word of command with great emphasis; while all the male portion of the family, from the father down to little Carlos, ran out of the house with such fury upon the mob, that it struck them with terror and dismay, and they fled before the little Spartan band into the woods, when they dispersed themselves to their several homes.

In a short time Joseph received another intimation of the approach of a mob, also of the necessity of removing the Record and breastplate from the place wherein they were secreted; consequently he took them out of the box in which they were placed, and wrapping them in clothes, carried them across the road to a cooper's shop, and laid them in a quantity of flax, which was stowed in the shop loft. After which he nailed up the box again, then tore up the floor of the shop, and put it under the same.

As soon as night came, the mob came also, and commenced ransacking the place. They rummaged round the house, and all over the premises, but did not come into the house. After making satisfactory search they went away.

The next morning we found the floor of the cooper's shop torn up, and the box which was laid under it shivered in pieces (*Biographical Sketches*, 116–22, 124–26; spelling standardized).

JOSEPH AND EMMA MOVE TO PENNSYLVANIA (1827)

Joseph Smith Jr.

Persecution became so intolerable [in Palmyra] that I was under the necessity of leaving Manchester, and going with my wife to Susquehanna County, in the State of Pennsylvania. While preparing to start—being very poor, and the persecution so heavy upon us that there was no probability that we would ever be otherwise—in the midst of our afflictions we found a friend in a gentleman by the name of Martin Harris, who came to us and gave me fifty dollars [to bear my expenses]. Mr. Harris was a resident of Palmyra Township, Wayne County, in the state of New York, and a farmer of respectability. By this timely aid, I was enabled to reach the place of my destination in Pennsylvania (A combination of *Joseph Smith–History* 1:61–62 and "History of Joseph Smith," *Times and Seasons* 3 [2 May 1842]: 772; as cited in *Eyewitness Accounts of the Restoration*, 77).

Lucy Mack Smith

Soon afterwards, Alva Hale, Joseph's brother-in-law, came to our house, from Pennsylvania, for the purpose of moving Joseph to his father-in-law's, as word had been sent to them, that Joseph desired to move there as soon as he could settle up his business. During the short interval of Alva's stay with us, he and Joseph were one day in Palmyra, at a public-house, transacting some business. As they were thus engaged, Mr. Harris came in: he stepped immediately up to my son, and taking him by the hand, said, "How do you do, Mr. Smith." After which, he took a bag of silver from his pocket, and said again, "Here, Mr. Smith, is fifty dollars; I give this to you to do the Lord's work with; no, I give it to the Lord for his own work."

"No," said Joseph, "we will give you a note, Mr. Hale, I presume, will sign it with me."

"Yes," said Alva, "I will sign it."

Mr. Harris, however, insisted that he would give the money to the Lord, and called those present to witness the fact that he gave it freely, and did not demand any compensation, that it was for the purpose of helping Mr. Smith to do the Lord's work. And as I have been informed, many were present on that occasion, who witnessed the same circumstance.

Joseph, in a short time, arranged his affairs, and was ready for the journey. [He placed] the Record and breast-plate . . . [in a box and] nailed up . . . (the) box and then put . . . [the box] into a strong cask; and after filling the cask with beans, headed it up again.

When it became generally known that Joseph was about moving to Pennsylvania, a mob of fifty men collected themselves together, and they went to one Dr. Mc. Intyre, and requested him to take the command of the company, stating, that they were resolved on following "Joe Smith," and taking his "gold bible" from him. The doctor's ideas and feelings did not altogether harmonize with theirs, and he told them they were a pack of devilish fools, and to go home and mind their own business; that, if Joseph Smith had any business of that sort to attend to, he was capable of doing it, and that it would be better for them to busy themselves about that which more concerned them.

After this, a quarrel arose among them respecting who should be captain, and it ran so high that it broke up the expedition (*Biographical Sketches*, 112–13; original spelling has been preserved).

Orson Pratt

[After packing] his goods, [and] putting the plates into a barrel of beans, [Joseph] proceeded upon his journey. He had not gone far, before he was overtaken by an officer with a search-warrant, who flattered himself with the idea, that he should surely obtain the plates; after searching very diligently, he was sadly disappointed at not finding them. Mr. Smith then drove on; but before he got to his journey's end, he was again overtaken by an officer on the same business, and after ransacking the wagon very carefully, he went his way, as much chagrined as the first, at not being able to discover the object of his research. Without any further molestation, he [Joseph] pursued his journey until he came into the northern part of Pennsylvania, near the Susquehanna river, in which part his father-in-law resided (Orson Pratt, *An Interesting Account of Several Remarkable Visions* [Edinburgh: Ballantyne and Hughes, 1840], 13–14; spelling standardized).

William Smith

We were all very much scoffed at and persecuted during all this time, while Joseph was receiving his visions and translating the plates. . . . In consequence of his vision, and his having the golden plates and refusing to show them [to others], a great persecution arose against the whole family, and he was compelled to remove to Pennsylvania with the plates, where he translated them by means of the Urim and Thummim, which he obtained with the plates (William Smith, *William Smith on Mormonism* [Lamoni, Iowa: Herald Steam Book and Job Office, 1883], 11–12; as cited in *Eyewitness Accounts of the Restoration*, 79).

MARTIN HARRIS AND CHARLES ANTHON
(1828)

Isaiah

And the vision of all is become unto you as the words of a book that is sealed, which *men* deliver to one that is learned, saying, Read this, I pray thee: and he saith, I cannot; for it *is* sealed:

And the book is delivered to him that is not learned, saying, Read this, I pray thee: and he saith, I am not learned (Isaiah 29:11–12).

Joseph Smith Jr.

Immediately after my arrival there, I commenced copying the characters off the plates. I copied a considerable number of them, and by means of the Urim and Thummim, I translated some of them, between the time I arrived at the house of my wife's father, in the month of December, and the following February. [Meanwhile,] because of [the] faith and righteous deed of Martin Harris [in giving financial assistance for the move to Pennsylvania], the Lord appeared to him in a vision and shewed him the marvelous work which he [the Lord] was about to do. He immediately came to Susquehanna sometime in the month of February, and said that the Lord had shown him that he must go to New York City with some of the characters. [After I had given him]the characters which I had drawn off the plates, he started with them to the city of New York.

While in New York City, Martin Harris showed the manuscript to the learned, saying, "Read this, I pray thee." The learned replied, "I cannot," but said that if Martin Harris would bring the plates to him, he would read it. But the Lord forbade it. After Martin Harris' return to Pennsylvania, I told the Lord that I was not learned and could not translate the record, but the Lord [had] prepared spectacles (the Urim and Thummim) for me to read the book by, therefore I commenced translating the characters. Thus, the prophecy of Isaiah which is written in the 29th chapter of that book was fulfilled.

For [a description of] what took place [in New York City,] I refer to his [Martin Harris'] own account of the circumstances, as he related them to me after his return:

"I went to the city of New York, and presented the characters which had been translated, with the translation thereof, to Professor Anthon, a gentleman celebrated for his literary attainments. Professor Anthon stated that the translation was correct, more so than any he had before seen translated from the Egyptian. I then showed him those which were not yet translated, and he said that they were Egyptian, Chaldaic, Assyriac, and Arabic; and he said they were true characters. He gave me a certificate, certifying to the people of Palmyra that they were true characters, and that the translation of such of them as had been translated was also correct. I took the certificate and put it into my pocket, and was just leaving the house when Mr. Anthon called me back and asked me how the young man found that there were gold plates in the place where he found them. I answered that an angel of God had revealed it unto him. He then said to me, 'Let me see the certificate.' I accordingly took it out of my pocket and gave it to him, when he took it and tore it to pieces, saying that there was no such thing now as ministering of angels, and that if I would bring the plates to him he would translate them. I informed him that part of the plates were sealed, and that I was forbidden to bring them. He replied, 'I cannot read a sealed book.' I left him and went to Dr. Mitchell, who sanctioned what Professor Anthon had said respecting both the characters and the translation" (A combination of *Joseph Smith–History* 1:64–65 and "History of Joseph Smith," *Times and Seasons* 3 [2 May 1842]: 772–73; as cited in *Eyewitness Accounts of the Restoration,* 79–80).

Charles Anthon
(Courtesy of the Church Archives, The Church of Jesus Christ of Latter-day Saints)

Nephi

Wherefore, the Lord God will proceed to bring forth the words of the book; and in the mouth of as many witnesses as seemeth him good will he establish his word; and wo be unto him that rejecteth the word of God!

But behold, it shall come to pass that the Lord God shall say unto him to whom he shall deliver the book: Take these words which are not sealed and deliver them to another, that he may show them unto the learned, saying: Read this, I pray thee. And the learned shall say: Bring hither the book, and I will read them.

And now, because of the glory of the world and to get gain will they say this, and not for the glory of God.

And the man shall say: I cannot bring the book, for it is sealed.

Then shall the learned say: I cannot read it.

Wherefore it shall come to pass, that the Lord God will deliver again the book and the words thereof to him that is not learned; and the man that is not learned shall say: I am not learned.

Then shall the Lord God say unto him: The learned shall not read them, for they have rejected them, and I am able to do mine own work; wherefore thou shalt read the words which I shall give unto thee (2 Nephi 27:14–20).

Lucy Mack Smith

Not long after the circumstance of the mob's going into the cooper's shop, and splitting in pieces the box, Joseph began to make arrangements to accomplish the translation of the record. The first step that he was instructed to take in regard to this work, was to make a facsimile of some of the characters, which were called reformed Egyptian, and to send them to some of the most learned men of this generation, and ask them for the translation thereof.

The reader will here observe, that on a preceding page of this volume, I spoke of a confidential friend to whom my husband merely mentioned the existence of the plates, some two or three years prior to their coming forth. This was no other than Martin Harris, one of the witnesses to the book subsequent to its being translated. . . .

When Joseph had had a sufficient time to accomplish the journey [from Palmyra to Harmony], and transcribe some of the Egyptian characters, it was agreed that Martin Harris should follow him—and that he (Martin) should take the characters to the East, and, on his way, he was to call on all the professed linguists, in order to give them an opportunity to display their talents in giving a translation of the characters (*Biographical Sketches*, 126–27, 132).

Martin Harris

(Milton V. Backman has combined various recitals written by Martin Harris to create the following narrative.)

I took a transcript of the characters of the plates to Dr. Anthon, of New York. When I arrived at the home of Professor Anthon, I found him in his office and alone, and [I] presented the transcript to him and asked him to read it. . . . Professor Anthon . . . pronounced them [the characters copied from the golden plates] correct Egyptian characters, but somewhat changed and gave me a certificate, . . . certifying that the characters were Arabic, Chaldaic and Egyptian. . . . he said if I would bring [him] the plates, he would assist in the translation. I told him I could not, for they were sealed. . . . I then [was preparing to leave] . . . and was near the door, when he said, "How did the young man know the plates were there?" I said an angel had shown them to him. Professor Anthon then said, "Let me see the certificate."—upon which I took it from my waistcoat pocket and unsuspectingly gave it to him. He then tore it up in anger, saying there was no such things as angels now—it was all a hoax. I then went to Dr. Mitchell with the transcript, and he confirmed what Professor Anthon had said. . . .

[David Whitmer has] a transcript of a portion of the characters as found on the golden plates taken or copied on a small piece of paper, perhaps about six or seven inches by four or five. Seven or eight lines of them were very carefully transmitted to this paper as the words of this book which were taken [by me] to Professor Charles Anthon of New York. . . . Oliver Cowdery . . . left this relic with David Whitmer . . . shortly before his demise [death] (*Eyewitness Accounts of the Restoration*, 81–82).

Martin Harris
(Courtesy of the Church Archives, The Church of Jesus Christ of Latter-day Saints)

Orson Pratt

(Milton V. Backman has combined various recitals written by Orson Pratt to create the following narrative.)

The perfect agreement between the prediction of Isaiah (Chap. 29) and Mr. Smith's account of the finding and translation of the Book of Mormon is another collateral proof that he was divinely commissioned. Mr. Smith testifies that the plates from which that book was translated were *taken out of the ground*, from where they were originally deposited by the prophet Moroni; that the box containing them was composed of stone, so constructed as to exclude, in a great degree, the moisture of the soil; that with the plates he discovered a Urim and Thummim, through the aid of which he afterward was enabled to translate the book into the English language. Soon after obtaining the plates, a few of the original characters were accurately transcribed and translated by Mr. Smith, which, with the translation, were taken by a gentleman by the name of Martin Harris to the city of New York, where they were presented to some of the most learned individuals in the United States to see if they could translate them. Among the rest, they were presented to Professor Anthon of New York City, who professed to be extensively acquainted with many languages, both ancient and modern. He examined them but was unable to decipher them correctly, but he presumed that if the original records could be brought, he could assist in translating them. No man was found able to read them by his own learning or wisdom. Mr. Smith, though an unlearned man, testifies that he was commanded to translate them, through the inspiration of the Holy Ghost, by the aid of the Urim and Thummim and that the Book of Mormon is that translation. Now, Isaiah says to Israel, "Thou shalt be brought down, and shalt speak out of the ground, and thy speech shall be low out of the dust, and thy voice shall be as of one that hath a familiar spirit, out of the ground, and thy speech shall whisper out of the dust" (Isaiah 29:4) (*Eyewitness Accounts of the Restoration*, 82–83).

THE LOST 116 PAGES

When the Book of Mormon was published, Martin Harris was nearly forty-seven years old, more than twenty years older than Joseph Smith and the other two witnesses. He was a prosperous and respected citizen of Palmyra, New York. He owned a farm of over two hundred and forty acres, large for the time and place. He was an honored veteran of two battles in the War of 1812. His fellow citizens entrusted him with many elective offices and responsibilities in the community. He was universally respected for his industry and integrity. Assessments by contemporaries described him as "an industrious, hard-working farmer, shrewd in his business calculations, frugal in his habits," and "strictly upright in his business dealings" (as quoted in Richard Lloyd Anderson, *Investigating the Book of Mormon Witnesses* [Salt Lake City: Deseret Book, 1981], 96–98).

Dallin H. Oaks

This prosperous and upright older man befriended the young and penniless Joseph Smith, giving him the $50 that permitted him to pay his debts in Palmyra and move to northeastern Pennsylvania about a hundred and fifty miles away. There, in April 1828, Joseph Smith began his first persistent translation of the Book of Mormon. He dictated, and Martin Harris wrote, until there were one hundred and sixteen pages of manuscript.

Martin's persistent requests to show this manuscript to his family wearied Joseph into letting him take it to Palmyra, where its pages were stolen from him, lost and probably burned. For this the Lord rebuked Martin and Joseph. Joseph had his gift of translation suspended for a season, and Martin was rebuked as "a wicked man" who had "set at naught the counsels of God, and . . . broken the most sacred promises which were made before God" (D&C 3:12–13; see also D&C 10). Fortunately, both Joseph and Martin were later forgiven by the Lord, and the work of translation resumed with other scribes (Dallin H. Oaks, "The Witness: Martin Harris," *Ensign,* May 1999, 36).

Joseph Smith Jr.

Mr. Harris having returned from this tour he left me and went home to Palmyra, arranged his affairs and returned again to my house about the twelfth of April, eighteen hundred and twenty eight ("History of Joseph Smith," *Times & Seasons* 3 [16 May 1842], 785).

Lucy Mack Smith

[After Martin Harris returned from his journey to New York City, Mrs. Harris] endeavored to dissuade her husband from taking any further part in the publication of the record; however, Mr. Harris paid no attention to her, but returned [to Harmony] and continued writing.

Immediately after Martin Harris left home for Pennsylvania, his wife went from place to place, and from house to house, telling her grievances, and declaring that Joseph Smith was practicing a deception upon the people, which was about to strip her of all that she possessed, and that she was compelled to deposit a few things away from home in order to secure them. So she carried away her furniture, linen, and bedding; also other moveable articles, until she nearly stripped the premises of everything that could conduce either to comfort or convenience, depositing them with those of her friends and acquaintances, in whom she reposed sufficient confidence to assure her of their future safety (*Biographical Sketches,* 135–36).

Lucy Mack Smith

As soon as [Mrs. Harris] arrived there [at Joseph Smith's home at Harmony, Pennsylvania], she informed him that her object in coming, was to see the plates, and that she would never leave until she had accomplished it. Accordingly, without delay, she commenced ransacking every nook and corner about the house—chests, trunks, cupboards, etc.; consequently, Joseph was under the necessity of removing both the breast-plate and the Record from the house, and secreting them elsewhere. Not finding them in the house, she concluded that Joseph had buried them, and the next day she commenced searching out of doors, which she continued to do until about two o'clock P.M. She then came in rather ill-natured; after warming herself a little, she asked Joseph's wife if there were snakes in that country in the winter. She replied in the negative. Mrs. Harris then said, "I have been walking round in the woods to look at the situation of your place, and as I turned round to come home, a tremendous black snake stuck up his head before me, and commenced hissing at me."

The woman was so perplexed and disappointed in all her undertakings, that she left the house and took lodgings during her stay in Pennsylvania with a near neighbor, to whom she stated that the day previous she had been hunting for the plates, and that, after a tedious search, she at length came to a spot where she judged, from the appearance of things, they must be buried; but upon stooping down to scrape away the snow and leaves, in order to ascertain the fact, she encountered a horrible black snake which gave her a terrible fright, and she ran with all possible speed to the house.

While this woman remained in the neighborhood, she did all that lay in her power to injure Joseph in the estimation of his neighbors— telling them that he was a grand imposter, and, that by his specious pretensions, he had seduced her husband into the belief that he (Joseph Smith) was some great one, merely through a design upon her husband's property.

When she returned home [to Palmyra], being about two weeks after her arrival in Harmony, the place where Joseph resided, she endeavored to dissuade her husband from taking any further part in the publication of the Record; however, Mr. Harris paid no attention to her, but returned and continued writing.

[In 1831, Martin and Lucy divorced. Martin moved to Kirtland

and later married a daughter of John Young] (Lucy Mack Smith, *History of Joseph Smith by His Mother*, ed. Preston Nibley [Salt Lake City: Bookcraft, 1958], 122–23; spelling standardized).

Lucy Mack Smith

Martin Harris, having written some one hundred and sixteen pages for Joseph, asked permission of my son to carry the manuscript home with him in order to let his wife read it, as he hoped it might have a salutary effect upon her feelings. He also wanted to show his family what he had been employed in during his absence from them. Joseph was very partial to Mr. Harris, on account of the friendship which he had manifested in an hour when there seemed to be no earthly friend to succor or to sympathize. Still, Joseph, for a long time, resisted every entreaty of this kind.

At last, however, since Joseph felt a great desire to gratify the man's feelings as far as it was justifiable to do so, he inquired of the Lord to know if he might do as Martin Harris had requested, but was refused. With this, Mr. Harris was not altogether satisfied, and, at his urgent request, Joseph inquired again, but received a second refusal. Still, Martin Harris persisted as before, and Joseph applied again, but the last answer was not like the two former ones. In this, the Lord permitted Martin Harris to take the manuscript home with him, on the condition that my son was responsible for its safety. This my son was willing to do, as he could not conceive it possible for so kind a friend to betray the trust reposed in him. But there is no doubt of this indulgence being given to Joseph in order to show him by another lesson of bitter experience how vain are all human calculations, and also that he might learn not to put his trust in man, nor make flesh his arm.

Mr. Harris now took the most solemn oath that he would not show the manuscript to any save five individuals who belonged to his household. His anxious desires were now gratified, for he hoped that this might be the means of carrying the truth home to their hearts. The idea of affecting a union of sentiment in his family animated him very much.

He was now fully prepared to set out for home, which he did, carrying with him one hundred and sixteen pages of the record in manuscript. Immediately after Mr. Harris's departure, Emma became the mother of a son, but she had but small comfort from the society of the dear little stranger, for he was very soon snatched from her arms and borne aloft to the world of spirits before he had time to learn good or evil. For some time, the mother seemed to tremble upon the verge of the silent home of her infant. So uncertain seemed her fate for a season that, in the space of two weeks, Joseph never slept one hour in undisturbed quiet. At the expiration of this time she began to recover, but as Joseph's anxiety about her began to subside, another cause of trouble forced itself upon his mind. Mr. Harris had been absent nearly three weeks, and Joseph had received no intelligence whatever from him, which was altogether aside of the arrangement when they separated. He determined that as soon as his wife gained a little more strength, he would make a trip to New York and see after the manuscript. He did not mention the subject to Emma for fear of agitating her mind in her delicate health.

In a few days, however, she soon manifested that she was not without her thoughts upon the subject. She called Joseph to her and asked him what he thought about the manuscript. "I feel so uneasy," said she, "that I cannot rest and shall not be at ease until I know something about what Mr. Harris is doing with it. Do you not think it would be advisable for you to go and inquire into the reason of his not writing or sending any word back to you since he left us?"

Joseph begged her to be quiet and not worry herself, as he could not leave her just then, as he should not dare to be absent from her one hour while her situation was so precarious. "I will," said Emma, "send for my mother and she shall stay with me while you are gone."

After much persuasion, he concluded to leave his wife in the care of her mother for a few days, and set out on the before-mentioned journey. Only one other passenger was in the stage besides himself, and since this individual did not seem inclined to urge conversation, Joseph was left to the solitude of his own imagination. But the sensations which he experienced when he found himself well seated in the stagecoach cannot be imagined by anyone who reads this, for they have not been in like circumstances, and, of course, they cannot be correctly described.

There were various causes acting upon his mind which were calculated to have a very peculiar effect upon him. In the first place was the consideration of the calling which he had received at the hand of God. . . .

He had not now that feeling of justification which assured him of the especial favor of God, for he feared awfully that he had ventured too far in vouching for the safety of the manuscript after it was out of his possession. . . .

Whilst these thoughts, accompanied by ten thousand others, pulsed in rapid succession through his brain, there was but small opportunity of rest and little relish for refreshment. Consequently, Joseph neither ate nor slept while on the route.

This was observed by his fellow traveler, insomuch that when Joseph remarked, as he descended from the stage, that he had still twenty miles to travel on foot, the stranger objected, saying, "I have watched you since you first entered the stage, and I know that you have not slept nor eaten since you commenced your journey. You shall not go on foot twenty miles alone this night, for if you must go, I will be your company. And now tell me what can be the trouble which makes you thus desperate and also weighs down your spirits to such an extent that you refuse every proffered comfort and convenience."

Joseph told the gentleman that he had left his wife in so low a state of health that he had reason to fear that he would not find her alive when he returned; also he had buried his first and only child but a few days previous to leaving home. The explanation was given in truth and sincerity, although there was heavy trouble lying at his heart that he did not dare to mention.

"I feel," said the kind stranger, "to sympathize with you, and I will go with you, for I fear that your constitution, which is evidently not strong, will be insufficient to support you. You will be in danger of falling asleep in the forest, and some accident befall you."

Joseph thanked him for his kindness, and they proceeded together. When they arrived at our house, it was nearly daylight. The last four miles of the distance, the stranger was under the necessity of leading Joseph by his arm, for nature was too much exhausted to support him any longer, and he would fall asleep as he stood upon his feet every few minutes. . . .

Joseph requested us to send with all possible speed for Martin Harris. We did so, and after the stranger left (whose name we never knew), we prepared breakfast for the family, as soon as we conveniently could—for Martin Harris always came in such haste, when sent for, that we supposed he would be there and ready to take breakfast with us before we were ready.

It was now nearly six o'clock, and he lived three miles distant. At eight o'clock, we set the victuals on the table, looking for him every moment. We waited till nine, and he came not; till ten, and he was not there; till eleven, still he did not make his appearance. At half past twelve we saw him walking with a slow and measured tread toward the house, his eyes fixed thoughtfully upon the ground. When he came to the gate, he did not open it but got upon the fence and sat some time with his hat drawn over his eyes. At last he entered the house. After we sat down and were ready to commence eating, Martin took up his knife and fork as if to use them but dropped them from his hands. Hyrum said, "Martin, why do you not eat? Are you sick?" Martin pressed his hands upon his temples and cried out in a tone of anguish, "Oh! I have lost my soul. I have lost my soul."

Joseph, who had smothered his fears till now, sprang from the table, exclaiming, "Oh! Martin, have you lost that manuscript? Have you broken your oath and brought down condemnation upon my head as well as your own?"

"Yes," replied Martin, "it is gone and I know not where."

"Oh, my God, my God," said Joseph, clinching his hands together. "All is lost, is lost! What shall I do? I have sinned. It is I who tempted the wrath of God by asking him for that which I had no right to ask, as I was differently instructed by the angel." And he wept and groaned, walking the floor continually.

At last he told Martin to go back to his house and search again. "No," said Mr. Harris, "it is all in vain, for I have looked in every place in the house. I have even ripped open beds and pillows, and I know it is not there."

"Then must I," said Joseph, "return to my wife with such a tale as this? I dare not do it lest I should kill her at once. And how shall I appear before the Lord? Of what rebuke am I not worthy from the angel of the Most High?"

I besought him not to mourn so, for it might be that the Lord would forgive him, after a short season of humiliation and repentance on his part. But what could I say to comfort him when he saw all the family in the same state of mind that he was? Our sobs and groans and the most bitter lamentations filled the house. Joseph, in particular, was more distressed than the rest, for he knew definitely and by sorrowful experience the consequence of what would seem to others to be a very trifling neglect of duty. He continued walking backwards and forwards, weeping and grieving like a tender infant until about sunset, when we persuaded him to take a little nourishment.

The next morning he went home. We parted with heavy hearts, for it seemed as though all our fond anticipations, that which we had fed upon and which had been the source of so much secret gratification to us, had in a moment fled, and fled forever (*The Revised and Enhanced History of Joseph Smith by His Mother*, 160–66; spelling standardized).

Doctrine and Covenants 10:1–23

(Several months after losing the one hundred and sixteen pages, the angel Moroni appeared to Joseph Smith and returned the Urim and Thummim and the plates. The Lord revealed to Joseph what had happened to the one hundred and sixteen pages of manuscript. The introduction to D&C 10 states: "The evil design was to await the expected retranslation of the matter covered by the stolen pages, and then to discredit the translator by showing discrepancies created by the alterations. The Book of Mormon makes clear that this wicked purpose had been conceived by the evil one, and was known to the Lord even while Mormon, the ancient Nephite historian, was making his abridgment of the accumulated plates [The Words of Mormon 1:3–7].")

Now, behold, I say unto you, that because you delivered up those writings which you had power given unto you to translate by the means of the Urim and Thummim, into the hands of a wicked man, you have lost them.

And you also lost your gift at the same time, and your mind became darkened.

Nevertheless, it is now restored unto you again; therefore see that you are faithful and continue on unto the finishing of the remainder of the work of translation as you have begun.

Do not run faster or labor more than you have strength and means provided to enable you to translate; but be diligent unto the end.

Pray always, that you may come off conqueror; yea, that you may conquer Satan, and that you may escape the hands of the servants of Satan that do uphold his work.

Behold, they have sought to destroy you; yea, even the man in whom you have trusted has sought to destroy you. And for this cause I said that he is a wicked man, for he has sought to take away the things wherewith you have been entrusted; and he has also sought to destroy your gift.

And because you have delivered the writings into his hands, behold, wicked men have taken them from you.

Therefore, you have delivered them up, yea, that which was sacred, unto wickedness.

And, behold, Satan hath put it into their hearts to alter the words which you have caused to be written, or which you have translated, which have gone out of your hands.

And behold, I say unto you, that because they have altered the words, they read contrary from that which you translated and caused to be written;

And, on this wise, the devil has sought to lay a cunning plan, that he may destroy this work;

For he hath put into their hearts to do this, that by lying they may say they have caught you in the words which you have pretended to translate.

Verily, I say unto you, that I will not suffer that Satan shall accomplish his evil design in this thing.

For behold, he has put it into their hearts to get thee to tempt the Lord thy God, in asking to translate it over again.

And then, behold, they say and think in their hearts—We will see if God has given him power to translate; if so, he will also give him power again;

And if God giveth him power again, or if he translates again, or, in other words, if he bringeth forth the same words, behold, we have the same with us, and we have altered them;

Therefore they will not agree, and we will say that he has lied in his words, and that he has no gift, and that he has no power;

Therefore we will destroy him, and also the work; and we will do this that we may not be ashamed in the end, and that we may get glory of the world.

Verily, verily, I say unto you, that Satan has great hold upon their hearts; he stirreth them up to iniquity against that which is good;

And their hearts are corrupt, and full of wickedness and abominations; and they love darkness rather than light, because their deeds are evil; therefore they will not ask of me. Satan stirreth them up, that he may lead their souls to destruction.

And thus he has laid a cunning plan, thinking to destroy the work of God; but I will require this at their hands, and it shall turn to their shame and condemnation in the day of judgment.

Oliver Cowdery serves as Joseph's scribe
(April 1829)

After Joseph was able to translate again, the Lord commanded him to continue the translation where he had left off rather than retranslating the lost portion. He was informed that the Lord had prepared the record in such a way that the loss of pages would not hinder the coming forth of the Book of Mormon. Joseph and Emma struggled to continue translating the Book of Mormon, and before long, Joseph realized that he and Emma would need help in order to complete the translation. Joseph then asked the Lord to send him help.

Joseph Smith Jr.

The Lord appeared to a young man by the name of Oliver Cowdery and showed [the plates] to him in a vision and also the truth of the work and what the Lord was about to do through me, his unworthy servant. Therefore, he was desirous to come and write for me [as I translated.] Now, my wife had written some for me and also my brother, Samuel H. Smith, but we had become reduced in property and my wife's father was about to turn me out of doors. . . . I had nowhere to go . . . I cried unto the Lord that he would provide for me to accomplish the work whereunto he had commanded me.

On the fifth day of April, 1829, Oliver Cowdery [whom I had never previously seen] came to my house [Harmony, Pennsylvania]. . . . He stated to me that having been teaching school in the neighborhood where my father resided, and my father being one of those who sent to the school, he went to board for a season at his [my father's] house, and while there the family related to him the circumstance of my having received the plates. . . . Accordingly he had come to make enquires of me (a combination of *Joseph Smith–History* 1:66 and "History of Joseph Smith," *Times and Seasons* 3 [1 July 1842]: 832; as cited in *Eyewitness Accounts of the Restoration*, 101).

Lucy Mack Smith

Soon after we returned from Harmony, a man by the name of Lyman Cowdery came into the neighborhood, and applied to Hyrum, (as he was one of the trustees,) for the district school. A meeting [of the trustees] was called, and Mr. Cowdery was employed. But the following day, this Mr. Cowdery brought his brother Oliver to the trustees, and requested them to receive him instead of himself, as circumstances had transpired which rendered it necessary for him to disappoint them, or which would not allow of his attending to the school himself; and he would warrant the good conduct of the school under his brother's supervision. All parties being satisfied, Oliver commenced his school, boarding for the time being at our house. He had been in the school but a short time, when he began to hear from all quarters concerning the plates, and as soon began to importune Mr. Smith upon the subject, but for a considerable length of time did not succeed in eliciting any information. At last, however, he gained my husband's confidence, so far as to obtain a sketch of the facts relative to the plates.

Shortly after receiving this information, he told Mr. Smith that he was highly delighted with what he had heard; that he had been in a deep study upon the subject all day, and that it was impressed upon his mind, that he should yet have the privilege of writing for Joseph. Furthermore, that he had determined to pay him a visit at the close of the school which he was then teaching.

On coming in on the following day, he said, "The subject upon which we were yesterday conversing seems working in my very bones, and I cannot, for a moment, get it out of my mind; finally, I have resolved on what I will do. Samuel, I understand, is going down to Pennsylvania to spend the spring with Joseph; I shall make my arrangements to be ready to accompany him thither, by the time he recovers his health; for I have made it a subject of prayer, and I firmly believe it is the will of the Lord that I should go. If there is a work for me to do in this thing, I am determined to attend to it."

... In April Samuel and Mr. Cowdery set out for Pennsylvania. The weather, for some time previous, had been very wet and disagreeable—raining, freezing, and thawing alternately, which had rendered the roads almost impassable, particularly in the middle of the day. Notwithstanding, Mr. Cowdery was not to be detained, either by wind or weather, and they persevered until they arrived at Joseph's.

Joseph had been so hurried with his secular affairs, that he could not proceed with his spiritual concerns so fast as was necessary for the speedy completion of the work; there was also another disadvantage under which he labored, his wife had so much of her time taken up with the care of her house, that she could write for him but a small portion of the time. On account of these embarrassments, Joseph called upon the Lord, three days prior to the arrival of Samuel and Oliver, to send him a scribe, according to the promise of the angel; and he was informed that the same should be forthcoming in a few days. Accordingly, when Mr. Cowdery told him the business that he had come upon, Joseph was not at all surprised (*Biographical Sketches*, 151–52, 154–55).

Oliver Cowdery

Near the time of the setting of the sun, sabbath evening, April 5th, 1829, my natural eyes, for the first time beheld this brother [Joseph Smith]. . . . On Monday, the 6th, I assisted him in arranging some business of a temporal nature, and on Tuesday, the 7th, commenced to write the book of Mormon. These were days never to be forgotten—to sit under the sound of a voice dictated by the *inspiration* of heaven, awakened the utmost gratitude of this bosom! Day after day I continued, uninterrupted, to write from his mouth, as he translated with the Urim and Thummim, or, as the Nephites would have said, "Interpreters," the history or record called, "The Book of Mormon" (Oliver Cowdery, "Norton, Medina Co. Ohio, Sabbath evening, September 7, 1834," *Messenger & Advocate* 1 [January 1843]: 14).

Joseph Smith Jr.

(Milton V. Backman has combined various recitals written by Joseph Smith to create the following narrative.)

Two days after the arrival of Mr. Cowdery (being the 17th of April), [7th] I commenced to translate the Book of Mormon, and he commenced to write for me. [This] having continued for some time, I enquired of the Lord, through the Urim and Thummim, and obtained the following revelation: . . . Behold thou [Oliver Cowdery] hast a gift, and blessed art thou because of thy gift. Remember it is sacred and cometh from above.

And if thou wilt inquire, thou shalt know mysteries which are great and marvelous: therefore thou shalt exercise thy gift, that thou mayest find out mysteries, that thou mayest bring many to the knowledge of the truth, yea, convince them of the error of their ways.

Make not thy gift known unto any save it be those who are of thy faith. Trifle not with sacred things.

If thou wilt do good, yea, and hold out faithful to the end, thou shalt be saved in the kingdom of God, which is the greatest of all the gifts of God; for there is no gift greater than the gift of salvation. . . .

Therefore be diligent; stand by my servant Joseph, faithfully, in whatsoever difficult circumstances he may be, for the word's sake.

Admonish him in his faults, and also receive admonition of him. . . .

Verily, verily, I say unto you, if you desire a further witness, cast your mind upon the night that you cried unto me in your heart, that you might know concerning the truth of these things.

Did I not speak peace to your mind concerning the matter? What greater witness can you have than from God?

And now, behold, you have received a witness; for if I have told you things which no man knoweth have you not received a witness?

And, behold, I grant unto you a gift, if you desire of me, to translate, even as my servant Joseph. [See D&C Section 6:10–13, 18–19, 22–25.]

After we had received this revelation, he [Oliver Cowdery], stated to me that after he had gone to my father's to board, and after the family communicated to him concerning my having got the plates, that one night, after he had retired to bed he called upon the Lord to know if these things were so and the Lord manifested to him that they were true, but he had kept the circumstance entirely secret and had mentioned it to no being, so that after this revelation having been given, he knew that the work was true, because no being living knew of the thing alluded to in the revelation but God and himself.

During the month of April, I continued to translate and he to write with little cessation. . . . While continuing the work of translation . . . Oliver Cowdery became exceedingly anxious to have the power to translate bestowed upon him, and in relation to this desire, the following revelations were obtained. . . .

Oliver Cowdery, verily, verily, I say unto you, that assuredly as the Lord liveth, who is your God and your Redeemer, even so surely shall you receive a knowledge of whatsoever things you shall ask in faith, with an honest heart, believing that you shall receive a knowledge concerning the engravings of old records, which are ancient, which contain those parts of my scripture of which has been spoken by the manifestation of my Spirit.

Yea, behold, I will tell you in your mind and in your heart, by the Holy Ghost, which shall come upon you and which shall dwell in your heart. . . .

Oh, remember these words, and keep my commandments. Remember, this is your gift.

Now this is not all thy gift; for you have another gift, which is the gift of Aaron; behold, it has told you many things;

Behold, there is no other power, save the power of God, that can cause this gift of Aaron to be with you.

Therefore, doubt not, for it is the gift of God; and you shall hold it in your hands, and do marvelous works; and no power shall be able to take it away out of your hands, for it is the work of God. . . .

Ask that you may know the mysteries of God, and that you may translate and receive knowledge from all those ancient records which have been hid up, that are sacred; and according to your faith shall it be done unto you. [See D&C 8:1–2, 5–8, 11.]

Behold, I say unto you, my son, that because you did not translate according to that which you desired of me, and did commence again to write for my servant, Joseph Smith, Jun., even so I would that ye should continue until you have finished this record, which I have entrusted unto him.

And then, behold, other records have I, that I will give unto you power that you may assist to translate. . . .

Behold, the work which you are called to do is to write for my servant Joseph.

And, behold, it is because that you did not continue as you commenced, when you began to translate, that I have taken away this privilege from you. . . .

Behold, you have not understood; you have supposed that I would give it unto you, when you took no thought save it was to ask me.

But, behold, I say unto you, that you must study it out in your mind; then you must ask me if it be right, and if it is right I will cause that your bosom shall burn within you; therefore, you shall feel that it is right.

But if it be not right you shall have no such feelings, but you shall have a stupor of thought that shall cause you to forget the thing which is wrong; therefore, you cannot write that which is sacred save it be given you from me.

Now, if you had known this you could have translated; nevertheless, it is not expedient that you should translate now.

Behold, it was expedient when you commenced; but you feared, and the time is past, and it is not expedient now (see D&C 9:1–2, 4–5, 7–11; *Eyewitness Accounts of the Restoration*, 103–6).

Emma Smith

(In an 1879 interview.)

[During the translation] the plates often lay on the [table in our home], without any attempt at concealment, wrapped in a small linen tablecloth, which I had given him [Joseph Smith] to fold them in. I once felt . . . the plates, as they thus lay on the table, tracing their outline and shape. They seemed to be pliable like thick paper, and would rustle with a metallic sound when the edges were moved by the thumb, as one does sometimes thumb the edges of the book. . . . I did not attempt to handle the plates, other than [through the linen cloth] . . . I was satisfied that it was the work of God, and therefore did not feel it to be necessary to do so. I knew that he [Joseph Smith] had them, and was not especially curious about them. I moved them from place to place on the table, as it was necessary in doing my work. . . . Oliver Cowdery and . . . [Joseph Smith] wrote in the room where I was at work (Emma Smith, "Statement of Emma Smith to her son, Joseph Smith III, Feb. 1–10, 1879," cited in *The Saints' Herald* 26 [1 October 1879]: 289–90; as cited in *Eyewitness Accounts of the Restoration*, 107; spelling standardized).

The Move to Fayette and Miraculous Events with the Whitmer Family

As persecution began to emerge in Harmony, Joseph was divinely directed to move to Fayette, New York, to live with Oliver Cowdery's friends, the Whitmers.

Joseph Smith Jr.

(Original capitalization and punctuation have been preserved.)

Shortly after commencing to translate, I became acquainted with Mr. Peter Whitmer of Fayette, Seneca co. New York, and also with some of his family. In the beginning of the month of June, his son David Whitmer came to the place where we were residing, and brought with him a two horse wagon, for the purpose of having us accompany him to his father's place and there remain until we should finish the work. He proposed that we should have our board free of charge, and the assistance of one of his brothers to write for me, as also his own assistance when convenient.

Having much need of such timely aid in an undertaking so arduous, and being informed that the people of the neighborhood were anxiously awaiting the opportunity to enquire into these things, we accepted the invitation and accompanied Mr. Whitmer to his father's house ("History of Joseph Smith," *Times & Seasons* 3 [15 August 1842]: 884–85).

David Whitmer

(Milton V. Backman has combined various recitals written by David Whitmer to create the following narrative of an interview.)

After thinking over the matter for a long time [the story of Joseph Smith securing the golden plates that he had heard from people in the area of Palmyra], and talking with [Oliver] Cowdery, who also gave me a history of the finding of the plates, I went home; and after several months, Cowdery told me he was going to Harmony, Pennsylvania, where Joseph Smith had gone with the plates on account of the persecutions of the neighbors, . . . [to] see him [Joseph Smith] about the matter. He did go, and on the way stopped at my father's house and told me that as soon as he found out anything, either truth or untruth, he would let me know. After he got there he became acquainted with Joseph Smith, and shortly after, wrote to me telling me that . . . Joseph had told him his [Oliver's] secret thoughts, and all he had meditated about going to see him, which no man on earth knew, as he supposed, but himself . . . [He also told me that] he was convinced that Smith had the records, and that he [Joseph Smith] had told him that it was the will of heaven that he [Oliver Cowdery] should be his scribe to assist in the translation of the plates. He went on and Joseph translated from the plates and he wrote it down. Shortly after this, Cowdery wrote me another letter, in which he gave me a few lines of what they translated, and he assured me that he knew of a certainty that he had a record of a people that inhabited this continent, and that the plates they were translating gave a complete history of these people. When Cowdery wrote me these things and told me that he had revealed knowledge concerning the truth of them, I showed these letters to my parents and my brothers and sisters. Soon after I received another letter from Cowdery, telling me to come down into Pennsylvania, and bring him and Joseph to my father's house, giving as a reason therefore that they had received a commandment from God to that effect. . . .

I did not know what to do, I was pressed with my work. I had some twenty acres to plow, so I concluded I would finish plowing and then go. I got up one morning to go to work as usual, and on going to the field, found between five and seven acres of my ground had been plowed during the night.

I don't know who did it; but it was done just as I would have done it myself, and the plow was left standing in the furrow.

This enabled me to start sooner. When I arrived at Harmony, Joseph and Oliver were coming toward me, and met me some distance from the house. Oliver told me that Joseph had informed him when I started from home, where I had stopped the first night, how I read the sign at the tavern, where I stopped the next night, etc., and that I would be there that day before dinner, and this was why they had come out to meet me; all of which was exactly as Joseph had told Oliver, at which I was greatly astonished. . . .

The next day after I got there they packed up the plates, and we proceeded on our journey to my father's house. . . .

When I was returning to Fayette, with Joseph and Oliver, all of us riding in the wagon, Oliver and I on an old fashioned wooded spring seat and Joseph behind us; while traveling along in a clear open place, a very pleasant, nice-looking old man suddenly appeared by the side of our wagon and saluted us with, "good morning, it is very warm," at the same time wiping his face or forehead with his hand. We returned the salutation, and, by a sign from Joseph, I invited him to ride if he was going our way. But he said very pleasantly, "No, I am going to Cumorah." This name was something new to me, I did not know what Cumorah meant. We all gazed at him and at each other, and as I looked around enquiringly again. . . . He [the stranger] was about 5 feet 8 or 9 inches tall and heavy set. . . . He was dressed in a suit of brown woolen clothes, his hair and beard were white. I also remember that he had on his back sort of a knapsack with something, shaped like a book. It was the messenger who had the plates, who had taken them from Joseph just prior to our starting from Harmony . . .

Joseph . . . said that . . . he had the plates of the Book of Mormon in the knapsack (*Eyewitness Accounts of the Restoration,* 119–20).

B. H. Roberts

With the coming forth of the *Book of Mormon* there are associated superhuman events. What men usually call miraculous events. The book's existence was revealed by Moroni, an ancient American Prophet, now raised from the dead, and co-operating with Joseph Smith to bring forth to the world this record of an ancient people. The integrity of the whole story unfolding in the text of these pages depends upon the reality of these things. Was the Christ raised from the dead? Were ancient saints at the time of the Christ's resurrection also raised from the dead? The *New Testament* answers both questions in the affirmative. And now, if the resurrection be a reality, and the times and the power thereof rest with God, then it is not incredible that the blessings of that resurrection should extend to the inhabitants of the western world as well as to those of the eastern hemisphere. And if men are raised from the dead and made co-laborers with men in bringing to pass the purposes of God, then there is nothing incredible in the co-operation of Moroni, and other resurrected personages, with Joseph Smith and his associates in bringing to pass the great events of this New Dispensation of the gospel. Hence the repeated visitations and aid of the resurrected man, Moroni; hence the apparent superhuman aid given to David Whitmer in his preparations to bring the Prophet and Oliver Cowdery to the Whitmer home. The incidents of seeming superhuman aid given to David Whitmer as related by himself are as follows: The request of Oliver and the Prophet to come and remove them from Harmony, where they were threatened with mob violence, to the home of his father, found David in the midst of his spring work. He had some twenty acres of land to plow and concluded to do that and then go. "I got up one morning to go to work as usual," he says, "and on going to the field, found that between five and seven acres of my land had been plowed under during the night. I don't know who did it; but it was done just as I would have done it myself, and the plow was left standing in the furrow. This enabled me to start sooner."

Nor was this the only assistance of like character given to him. While harrowing in a field of wheat before starting on his journey he found to his surprise that he had accomplished more in a few hours than was usual to do in two or three days. The day following this circumstance he went out to spread plaster over a field, according to the custom of the farmers in that locality, when, to his surprise, he found the work had been done, and well done. David Whitmer's sister, who lived near the field, told him that three strangers had appeared in the field the day before and spread the plaster with remarkable skill. She at the time presumed that they were men whom David had hired to do the work.

"When I was returning to Fayette, with Joseph and Oliver," he says again, "all of us riding in the wagon, Oliver and I on an old fashioned, wooden spring seat, and Joseph behind us, when traveling along in a clear, open place, a very pleasant, nice looking old man suddenly appeared by the side of our wagon and saluted us with, 'Good morning; it is very warm;' at the same time wiping his face or forehead with his hand. We returned the salutation, and by a sign from Joseph, I invited him to ride if he was going our way. But he said very pleasantly, 'No, I am going to Cumorah.' This name was somewhat new to me, and I did not know what 'Cumorah' meant. We all gazed at him and at each other, and as I looked round inquiringly of Joseph, the old man instantly disappeared, so that I did not see him again. * * * It was the messenger who had the plates, who had taken them from Joseph just prior to our starting from Harmony."

David Whitmer says that soon after the installment of Joseph, his wife, and Oliver Cowdery in the Whitmer household, he saw something which led him to believe that the plates were concealed in his father's barn, and frankly asked the Prophet if it were so. Joseph replied that it was. "Some time after this," David adds: "My mother was going to milk the cows, when she was met out near the yard by the same old man [meaning the one who had saluted his party on the way from Harmony; at least, David Whitmer judged him to be the same, doubtless from his mother's description of him], who said to her: 'You have been very faithful and diligent in your labors, but you are tired because of the increase of your toil; it is proper, therefore, that you should receive a witness, that your faith may be strengthened.' Thereupon he showed her the plates. My father and mother had a large family of their own, the addition to it, therefore, of Joseph, his wife Emma, and Oliver, very greatly increased the toil and anxiety of my mother. And although she had never complained she had sometimes felt that her labor was too much, or, at least, she was perhaps beginning to feel so. This circumstance, however, completely removed all such feelings, and nerved her up for her increased responsibilities" (*A Comprehensive History of the Church of Jesus Christ of Latter-day Saints.* 6 vols. ed. B. H. Roberts [Provo, Utah: Brigham Young University Press, 1965], 1:125–27).

Joseph Smith Jr.

Upon our arrival [in Fayette], we found Mr. Whitmer's family very anxious concerning the work, and very friendly towards ourselves. They continued so, boarded and lodged us according to proposal, and John Whitmer, in particular, assisted us very much in writing during the remainder of the work ("History of Joseph Smith," *Times & Seasons* 3 [15 August 1842]: 885).

TRANSLATION OF THE BOOK OF MORMON
(September 1827–June 1829)

On 22 September 1827 Joseph Smith received from the angel Moroni the plates used in the translation of the Book of Mormon. Approximately twenty-one months later, after completing the translation, he returned the plates to Moroni. Although Joseph Smith had the plates for nearly two years, almost all the work of translation of the current text of the Book of Mormon was accomplished in the equivalent of about two months of actual working days, nearly all of it being done between April 7 and June 30, 1829 ("Book of Mormon, Translation of," *Book of Mormon Reference Companion*, ed. Dennis L. Largey [Salt Lake City: Deseret Book, 2003], 157).

David Whitmer

Something went wrong about the house and he [Joseph Smith] was put out about it. Something that Emma, his wife, had done. Oliver and I went upstairs and Joseph came up soon after to continue the translation but he could not do anything. He could not translate a single syllable. He went downstairs, out into the orchard, and made supplication to the Lord; was gone about an hour—came back to the house, and asked Emma's forgiveness and then came upstairs where we were and then the translation went on all right. He could do nothing save he was humble and faithful (*A Comprehensive History of the Church*, 1:131).

JOSEPH KNIGHT ASSISTS JOSEPH SMITH
(May 1829)

Joseph Smith Jr.

(Milton V. Backman has combined various recitals written by Joseph Smith to create the following narrative.)

Our minds being now enlightened, we began to have the scriptures laid open to our understandings, and the true meaning and intention of their more mysterious passages revealed unto us in a manner which we never could attain to previously, nor ever before had thought of. In the meantime, we were forced to keep secret the circumstances of our having received the Priesthood and our having been baptized, owing to a spirit of persecution which had already manifested itself in the neighborhood. We had been threatened with being mobbed, from time to time, and this, too by professors of religion. And their intentions of mobbing us were only counteracted by the influence of my wife's father's family (under Divine providence), who had become very friendly to me, and who were opposed to mobs, and were willing that I should be allowed to continue the work of translation without interruption; and therefore [they] offered and promised us protection from all unlawful proceedings as far as in them [protection] lay.

After a few days, however, feeling it to be our duty, we commenced to reason out of the scriptures with our acquaintances and friends, as we happened to meet with them. About this time, my brother Samuel H. Smith came to visit us. We informed him of what the Lord was about to do for the children of men, and [we reasoned] with him out of the Bible. We also showed him that part of the work which we had translated and labored to persuade him concerning the gospel of Jesus Christ, which was now about to be revealed in its fullness. He was not, however, very easily persuaded of these things, but after much enquiry and explanation he retired to the woods in order that by secret and fervent prayer he might obtain of a merciful God wisdom to enable him to judge for himself. The result was that he obtained revelations for himself sufficient to convince him of the truth of our assertions to him, and, on the fifteenth day [twenty-fifth] of that same month in which we had been baptized and ordained, Oliver Cowdery baptized him; and he returned to his father's house greatly glorifying and praising God, being filled with the Holy Spirit.

[While Oliver and I were working on the translation of the Book of Mormon,] an old gentleman, came to visit us of whose name I wish to make honorable mention: Mr. Joseph Knight, Sen. of Colesville, Broome County, New York, who, having heard of the manner in which we were occupying our time, very kindly and considerately brought us a quantity of provisions in order that we might not be interrupted in the work of translation by the want of such necessaries of life; and I would just mention here (as in duty bound) that he several times brought us supplies (a distance of at least thirty miles), which enabled us to continue work which otherwise we must have relinquished for a season.

Being very anxious to know his duty as to this work, I enquired of the Lord for him and obtained as follows: . . .

A great and marvelous work is about to come fourth among the children of men . . .

Behold, the field is white already to harvest; therefore, whoso desireth to reap let him thrust in his sickle with his might, and reap while the day lasts . . .

Now, as you have asked, behold, I say unto you, keep my commandments, and seek to bring forth and establish the cause of Zion.

Behold, I speak unto you, and also to all those who have desires to bring forth and establish this work;

And no one can assist in this work except he shall be humble and full of love, having faith, hope, charity, being temperate in all things, whatsoever shall be entrusted to his care [see D&C Section 12:1, 3, 6–8] (*Eyewitness Accounts of the Restoration*, 115–17).

Joseph Knight

When Joseph began to translate he was poor . . . and had no one to write for him but his wife, and, in the winter, her brother wrote a little for him. Even though his wife, Emma, did write for him she could not do much because she had to take care of the house. His wife's father and family were all against him [Joseph] and would not help him. He and his wife came up to see me [in Colesville, New York,] the first winter of 1828 and told me his case. But I was not in easy circumstances and I did not know what it might amount to, and my wife and family were all against me helping him. But I did give him a few provisions and a few things out of the store: a pair of shoes and three dollars in money to help him a little . . .

The last of March [1828] I told my wife that I must go down and see Joseph again. She asked, "Why do you go so soon?"

I said, "Come, go and see."

And she went with me. Next morning we went down and found them well and they were glad to see us. Joseph talked to us about his translating and some revelations he had received. From that time my wife began to believe . . .

In the spring of 1829 Oliver Cowdery [traveled to Pennsylvania where] he received a revelation concerning the work. Oliver was convinced of the truth of the work and agreed to write for Joseph until the work was finished. Now Joseph and Oliver came up to see me and asked if I could help them buy some provisions, they having no way to buy them. When they arrived I was not there. I was in the Catskills. But when I came home my folks told me what Joseph wanted. I had engaged to go to the Catskills again the next day and I went, but I did buy a barrel of mackerel and some lined paper for writing. When I returned home, I bought some nine or ten bushels of grain and five or six bushels of taters and a pound of tea. I left to see them and they were in want. Joseph and Oliver were gone seeking employment for provisions, but they found none. They returned home and found me there with the provisions and they were glad for they were out. Their family consisted of four, Joseph, and his wife, Oliver, and Samuel Smith. They went back to work and had provisions enough to last until the translation was finished (*Reminiscences of Joseph Knight*; as cited in *Eyewitness Accounts of the Restoration*, 117–18).

COMPLETION OF THE BOOK OF MORMON TRANSLATION
(June–July 1829)

After two long years of enduring physical persecution, moving from house to house and attempting to complete the sacred responsibility the Lord had given him, Joseph finally completed the translation of the Book of Mormon in June 1829.

Joseph Smith Jr.

[We (Joseph, his wife, and Oliver)] resided [in Peter Whitmer's home] until the translation was finished, and the copy-right secured ("History of Joseph Smith," *Times & Seasons* 3 [15 August 1842]: 885).

David Whitmer

(In an interview.)

I, as well as all of my father's family, Smith's wife, Oliver Cowdery, and Martin Harris, were present during the translation. . . . The translation at my father's occupied about one month, that is from June 1 to July 1, 1829 (as cited in Albert Carrington, "Mormonism," *Millennial Star* 43 [4 July 1881]: 423).

Lucy Mack Smith

[After arriving at the Whitmer home, Joseph and Oliver] continued without further interruption until the whole work [of translation] was accomplished.

Lucy Mack Smith
(Courtesy of the Church Archives, The Church of Jesus Christ of Latter-day Saints)

As soon as the Book of Mormon was translated, Joseph dispatched a messenger to Mr. Smith, bearing intelligence of the completion of the work, and a request that Mr. Smith and myself should come immediately to Waterloo [a community located near the Whitmer farm]. . . .

Accordingly, the next morning, we all set off together, and before sunset met Joseph and Oliver at Mr. Whitmer's.

The evening was spent in reading the manuscript, and it would be superfluous for me to say, to one who has read the foregoing pages, that we rejoiced exceedingly. It then appeared to those of us who did not realize the magnitude of the work, as if the greatest difficulty was then surmounted (*Biographical Sketches*, 137–38).

Diedrich Willers

(Willers was a German Reformed Church minister from Fayette. This account was included in a letter dated 18 June 1830 and was designed to warn the people about an uprising religious movement known as Mormonism. He was concerned because many of his congregation, including the Whitmers, had embraced Mormonism.)

In the month of July [in 1829], Joseph Smith made his appearance in Seneca County, in the neighborhood of Waterloo, about 6 miles from my hometown. There a certain David Whitmer claimed to have seen an angel of the Lord, so Smith proceeded to his house, in order to complete the translation of the above work [Book of Mormon] himself. According to the reports, only there could he work—where men who have had association with the other world also reside. . . .

He [Joseph Smith] asserted that the Angel of the Lord appeared to him and made it known that in the neighborhood of Palmyra there were golden plates in the earth, upon which was described the doings of a Jewish prophet's family, associated with many not yet fulfilled prophecies. The Angel indicated that the Lord destined him to translate these things into English from the ancient language, that under these plates were hidden spectacles, without which he could not translate these plates, that by using these spectacles, he (Smith) would be in a position to read these ancient languages, which he had never studied, and that the Holy Ghost would reveal to him the translation in the English language. Therefore, he (Smith) proceeded to Manchester township, Ontario County, and found everything as described, the plates buried next to the spectacles in the earth, and soon he completed the translation of this work.

Upon receiving this report, I hurried immediately to Whitmer's house to see this man, in order to learn the actual source of this story and to find out how it might be possible to nip this work in the bud. However, I received the reply from Whitmer's father that Smith had already departed to take his translation to press (Diedrich Willers, "The First Months of Mormonism: A Contemporary View by Rev. Diedrich Willers," *New York History* 54 [July 1973]: 326–27).

Lucy Mack Smith

The evening was spent in reading the manuscript, and it would be superfluous for me to say, to one who has read the foregoing pages, that we rejoiced exceedingly. It then appeared to those of us who did not realize the magnitude of the work, as if the greatest difficulty was then surmounted; but Joseph better understood the nature of the dispensation of the Gospel which was committed unto him.

The next morning, after attending to the usual services, namely, reading, singing and praying, Joseph arose from his knees, and approaching Martin Harris with a solemnity that thrills through my veins to this day, when it occurs to my recollection, said, "Martin Harris, you have got to humble yourself before God this day, that you may obtain a forgiveness of your sins. If you do, it is the will of God that you should look upon the plates, in company with Oliver Cowdery and David Whitmer."

In a few minutes after this, Joseph, Martin, Oliver and David, retired to a grove, a short distance from the house, where they commenced calling upon the Lord, and continued in earnest supplication, until he permitted an angel to come down from his presence, and declare to them, that all which Joseph had testified of concerning the plates was true.

When they returned to the house it was between three and four o'clock P.M. Mrs. Whitmer, Mr. Smith and myself, were sitting in a bedroom at the time. On coming in, Joseph threw himself down beside me, and exclaimed, "Father, mother, you do not know how happy I am: the Lord has now caused the plates to be shown to three more besides myself. They have seen an angel, who has testified to them, and they will have to bear witness to the truth of what I have said, for now they know for themselves, that I do not go about to deceive the people, and I feel as if I was relieved of a burden which was almost too heavy for me to bear, and it rejoices my soul, that I am not any longer to be entirely alone in the world." Upon this, Martin Harris came in: he seemed almost overcome with joy, and testified boldly to what he had both seen and heard. And so did David and Oliver, adding that no tongue could express the joy of their hearts, and the greatness of the things which they had both seen and heard (Lucy Mack Smith, *History of Joseph Smith by His Mother*, ed. Preston Nibley [Salt Lake City: Bookcraft, 1958], 151–53).

The Plates are Returned to Moroni

Joseph Smith Jr.

By the wisdom of God they [the plates] remained safe in my hands until I had accomplished by them what was required at my hand, when according to arrangements the messenger called for them, I delivered them up to him and he has them in his charge until this day, being the second day of May, one thousand eight hundred and thirty-eight ("History of Joseph Smith," *Times & Seasons* 3 [2 May 1842]: 772).

Martin Harris

The plates from which the Book of Mormon was translated ... were returned to the angel, Moroni, from whom they were received, to be brought forth again in the due time of the Lord; for they contain many things pertaining to the gathering of Israel, which gathering will take place in this generation and shall be testified of among all nations, according to the old Prophets; as the Lord will set his ensign to the people, and gather the outcasts of Israel (Martin Harris, *Martin Harris to H. B. Emerson, January 1871,* LDS Church Archives; as cited in *Eyewitness Accounts of the Restoration,* 166).

Brigham Young

When Joseph got the plates, the angel instructed him to carry them back to the hill Cumorah, which he did. Oliver says that when Joseph and Oliver went there, the hill opened, and they walked into a cave, in which there was a large and spacious room. He says he did not think, at the time, whether they had the light of the sun or artificial light; but that it was just as light as day. They laid the plates on a table; it was a large table that stood in the room. Under this table there was a pile of plates as much as two feet high, and there were altogether in this room more plates than probably many wagon loads; they were piled up in the corners and along the walls. The first time they went there the sword of Laban hung upon the wall; but when they went again it had been taken down and laid upon the table across the gold plates; it was unsheathed, and on it was written these words: "This sword will never be sheathed again until the kingdoms of this world become the kingdom of our God and his Christ." I tell you this as coming not only from Oliver Cowdery, but others who were familiar with it (*Journal of Discourses,* 19:38).

WITNESSES TO THE
BOOK OF MORMON

2 Corinthians 13:1

In the mouth of two or three witnesses shall every word be established.

Ether 5:3–4

And unto three shall [the plates] be shown by the power of God; wherefore they shall know of a surety that these things are true.

And in the mouth of three witnesses shall these things be established; and the testimony of three, and this work . . . shall stand as a testimony against the world at the last day.

2 Nephi 27:12

Wherefore, at that day when the book shall be delivered unto the man of whom I have spoken, the book shall be hid from the eyes of the world, that the eyes of none shall behold it save it be that three witnesses shall behold it, by the power of God, besides him to whom the book shall be delivered; and they shall testify to the truth of the book and the things therein.

THREE WITNESSES
(June 1829)

Joseph Smith Jr.

In the course of the work of translation, we ascertained that three special witnesses were to be provided by the Lord, to whom He would grant that they should see the plates from which this work (the Book of Mormon) should be translated, and that these witnesses should bear record of the same; as will be found [in the] Book of Mormon . . . [which reads as follows:]

> Wherefore, at that day when the book shall be delivered unto the man of whom I have spoken, the book shall be hid from the eyes of the world, that the eyes of none shall behold it save it be that three witnesses shall behold it, by the power of God, besides him to whom the book shall be delivered; and they shall testify to the truth of the book and the things therein.
>
> And there is none other which shall view it, save it be a few according to the will of God, to bear testimony of this word unto the children of men; . . .
>
> Wherefore, the Lord will proceed to bring forth the words of the book; and in the mouth of as many witnesses as seemeth him good will he establish his word. (See 2 Nephi 27: 12–14; "History of Joseph Smith," *Times & Seasons* 3 [September 1842]: 897; punctuation standardized)

REVELATION GIVEN TO JOSEPH SMITH JR.
(March 1829)

Behold, I say unto you, that as my servant Martin Harris has desired a witness at my hand, that you, my servant Joseph Smith, Jun., have got the plates of which you have testified and borne record that you have received of me;

And now, behold, this shall you say unto him—he who spake unto you, said unto you: I, the Lord, am God, and have given these things unto you, my servant Joseph Smith, Jun., and have commanded you that you should stand as a witness of these things; . . .

And the testimony of three witnesses will I send forth of my word. And behold, whosoever believeth on my words, them will I visit with the manifestation of my Spirit. . . . And their testimony shall also go forth unto the condemnation of this generation if they harden their hearts against them (D&C 5:1–2, 15–16, 18).

Joseph Smith Jr.

Almost immediately after we had made this discovery [that three special witnesses would view the plates by the power of God], it occurred to Oliver Cowdery, David Whitmer and the aforementioned Martin Harris (who had come to inquire after our progress in the work) that they would have me inquire of the Lord to know if they might not obtain of him the privilege to be these three special witnesses; and finally they became so very solicitous, and urged me so much to inquire that at length I complied; and through the Urim and Thummim, I obtained of the Lord for them the following: [D&C 5] (Joseph Smith, *History of the Church of Jesus Christ of Latter-day Saints*, 7 vols., ed. B. H. Roberts [Salt Lake City: Deseret Book, 1964], 52–53).

REVELATION TO OLIVER COWDERY, DAVID WHITMER, AND MARTIN HARRIS:

Behold, I say unto you, that you must rely upon my word, which if you do with full purpose of heart, you shall have a view of the plates, and also of the breastplate, the sword of Laban, the Urim and Thummim, which were given to the brother of Jared upon the mount, when he talked with the Lord face to face, and the miraculous directors which were given to Lehi while in the wilderness, on the borders of the Red Sea. And it is by your faith that you shall obtain a view of them, even by that faith which was had by the prophets of old.

And after that you have obtained faith, and have seen them with your eyes, you shall testify of them, by the power of God;

And this you shall do that my servant Joseph Smith Jr., may not be destroyed, that I may bring about my righteous purposes unto the children of men in this work.

And ye shall testify that you have seen them, even as my servant Joseph Smith Jr., has seen them; for it is by my power that he has seen them, and it is because he had faith.

And he has translated the book, even that part which I have commanded him, and as your Lord and your God liveth it is true (see D&C 17: 1–6; see also Milton V. Backman Jr., *Eyewitness Accounts of the Restoration* [Salt Lake City: Deseret Book, 1986], 148–50).

Lucy Mack Smith

The next morning [the morning following the arrival of Joseph's father and mother and his friend, Martin Harris, at the Whitmer home], after attending to the usual services, namely, reading, singing, and praying, Joseph arose from his knees, and approaching Martin Harris with a solemnity that thrills through my veins to this day, when it occurs to my recollection, said, "Martin Harris, you have got to humble yourself before your God this day, that you may obtain a forgiveness of your sins. If you do, it is the will of God that you should look upon the plates, in company with Oliver Cowdery and David Whitmer" (Lucy Mack Smith, *Biographical Sketches of Joseph Smith the Prophet and His Progenitors for Many Generations* [Independence, Missouri: Herald Publishing House, 1969], 164).

Joseph Smith Jr.

Not many days after the above commandment was given [D&C 17], we four viz: Martin Harris, David Whitmer, Oliver Cowdery and myself agreed to retire into the woods, and try to obtain by fervent and humble prayer, the fulfillment of the promises given in the revelation: that they should have a view of the plates & etc. we accordingly made choice of a piece of woods convenient to Mr. Whitmer's house, to which we retired, and having knelt down we began to pray in much faith, to Almighty God to bestow upon us a realization of these promises. According to previous arrangements I commenced, by vocal prayer to our heavenly Father and was followed by each of the rest in succession; we did not yet however obtain any answer, or manifestation of the divine favor in our behalf. We again observed the same order of prayer each calling on, and praying fervently to God in rotation; but with the same result as before. Upon this our second failure, Martin Harris proposed that he would withdraw himself from us, believing as he expressed himself that his presence was the cause of our not obtaining what we wished for; he accordingly withdrew from us, and we knelt down again, and had not been many minutes engaged in prayer when presently we beheld a light above us in the air of exceeding brightness, and behold an angel stood before us; in his hands he held the plates which we had been praying for these [Cowdery and Whitmer] to have a view of: he turned over the leaves one by one, so that we could see them, and discover the engravings thereon distinctly. He addressed himself to David Whitmer, and said, "David, blessed is the Lord, and he that keeps his commandments." When immediately afterwards, we heard a voice from out of the bright light above us saying, "These plates have been revealed by the power of God, and they have been translated by the power of God; the translation of them which you have seen is correct, and I command you to bear record of what you now see and hear."

I now left David and Oliver, and went in pursuit of Martin Harris, who I found at a considerable distance, fervently engaged in prayer, he soon told me however that he had not yet prevailed with the Lord, and earnestly requested me to join him in prayer, that he also might realize the same blessings which we had just received. We accordingly joined in prayer, and ultimately obtained our desires, for before we had yet finished, the same vision was opened to our view; at least it was again to me, and I once more beheld, and heard the same things; whilst at the same moment, Martin Harris cried out, apparently in ecstasy of joy, "'Tis enough; mine eyes have beheld," and jumping up he shouted, hosanna, blessing God, and otherwise rejoiced exceedingly.

Having thus through the mercy of God, obtained these manifestations, it now remained for these three individuals to fulfill the commandment which they had received, viz: to bear record of these things, in order to accomplish which, they drew up and subscribed the following document.

The Testimony of Three Witnesses

Be it known unto all nations, kindreds, tongues, and people, unto whom this work shall come, that we, through the grace of God the Father, and our Lord Jesus Christ, have seen the plates which contain this record, which is a record of the people of Nephi, and also of the

Lamanites, their brethren, and also of the people of Jared, who came from the tower of which hath been spoken; and we also know that they have been translated by the gift and power of God, for his voice hath declared it unto us: wherefore we know of a surety, that the work is true. And we also testify that we have seen the engravings which are upon the plates; and we know that it is by the grace of God the Father, and our Lord Jesus Christ, that we beheld and bear record that these things are true; and it is marvelous in our eyes, nevertheless, the voice of the Lord commanded us that we should bear record of it; wherefore, to be obedient unto the commandments of God, we bear testimony of these things. And we know that if we are faithful in Christ we shall rid our garments of the blood of all men, and be found spotless before the judgment seat of Christ, and shall dwell with him eternally in the heavens. And the honor be to the Father, and to the Son, and to the Holy Ghost, which is one God. Amen.

OLIVER COWDERY
DAVID WHITMER
MARTIN HARRIS

("History of Joseph Smith," *Times & Seasons* 3 [1 September 1842]: 897–98; spelling standardized)

David Whitmer

(Milton V. Backman has combined various recitals written by David Whitmer to create the following narrative.)

Joseph and Oliver and I were sitting on a log, when we were overshadowed by a light more glorious than that of the sun . . . It extended away round us, I cannot tell how far, but in the midst of this light . . . there appeared as it were, a table with many records or plates upon it, besides the plates of the Book of Mormon, also the Sword of Laban, the directors—i.e., the ball which Lehi had, and the Interpreters. The Interpreters . . . which I saw . . . in the holy vision . . . looked like whitish stones put in the rim of a bow . . . like spectacles, only much larger. The heavenly messenger brought the several plates and laid them on the table before our eyes. I saw them just as plain as I see this bed . . . and the angel told us we must bear testimony to the world. . . . I [also] heard the voice of the Lord, distinctly as I ever heard anything in my life, declaring that the records of the plates of the Book of Mormon were translated by the gift and power of God. Our testimony as recorded in the Book of Mormon is absolutely true, just as it is there written.

It is recorded in the American Cyclopaedia and the Encyclopaedia Britannica, that I, David Whitmer, have denied my testimony as one of the three witnesses to the divinity of the Book of Mormon; and that the other two witnesses, Oliver Cowdery and Martin Harris, denied their testimony to that Book. I will say once more to all mankind, that I have never at any time denied that testimony or any part thereof. I also testify to the world, that neither Oliver Cowdery or Martin Harris ever at any time denied their testimony. They both died reaffirming the truth of the divine authenticity of the Book of Mormon.

I wish now, standing as it were, in the very sunset of life, and in the fear of God, once [and] for all to make this public statement:

That I have never at any time denied that testimony or any part thereof, which has so long since been published with that Book, as one of the three witnesses. Those who know me best, well know that I have always adhered to that testimony. And that no man may be misled or doubt my present views in regard to the same, I do again affirm the truth of all my statements, as then made and published.

"He that hath an ear to hear, let him hear;" it was no delusion! What is written is written, and he that readeth let him understand.

Beware how you hastily condemn that book which I know to be the word of God; for his own voice and an angel from heaven declared the truth of it unto me, and to two other witnesses who testified on their death-bed that it was true.

And if these things are not true, then there is no truth; and if there is no truth, there is no God; and if there is no God, there is no existence. But I know there is a God, for I have heard His voice and witnessed the manifestation of his power (*Eyewitness Accounts of the Restoration*, 154–56).

Oliver Cowdery

(In an interview)

In company with the Prophet Joseph Smith and David Whitmer, [I] . . . beheld the plates, the leaves being turned over by the angel, whose voice I heard, and . . . we were commanded as witnesses to bear a faithful testimony to the world of the vision that we were favored to behold, and that the translation from the plates in the Book of Mormon was accepted of the Lord, and that it should go forth to the world and no power on earth should stop its progress (Edward Stevenson, "The Three Witnesses to the Book of Mormon," *Millennial Star* 48 [5 July 1886]: 420; as cited in *Eyewitness Accounts of the Restoration*, 156; this quote has been changed from the third to the first person).

Martin Harris

(Milton V. Backman has combined various recitals given in an interview by Martin Harris to create the following narrative.)

The Prophet Joseph Smith, Oliver Cowdery, and David Whitmer and myself went into the woods to pray that we might have the privilege of seeing the golden plates. We bowed our heads in prayer, but we seemed to be praying with no results. The Prophet was the spokesman. He prayed with no results twice, then I withdrew from them, telling them that it was on my account that their prayer was not answered. After they had been visited by the angel, the Prophet then came over to me where I was praying, and I asked the Prophet to pray with me so that I might have the privilege also of seeing the golden plates; and after praying, I saw the angel descend from heaven. The angel stood on the opposite side of the table on which were the plates . . . took the plates in his hand and turned them over . . . one by one. I [also] saw the Urim and Thummim, the Breastplate, and the Sword of Laban. The angel declared that the Book of Mormon was correctly translated by the power of God and not of man, and that it contained the fullness of the gospel of Jesus Christ to the Nephites, who were a branch of the lost sheep of the House of Israel and had come from the land of Jerusalem to America. When he [the angel] had finished his message, I saw him ascend up into heaven. Then . . . I heard the voice of God declare that everything the angel had told us was true and that the Book of Mormon was translated correctly. I was [then] commanded by God's voice to testify to the whole world what I had seen and heard. Following the vision, I cried out in . . . ecstasy.

[I have] never failed to bear testimony to the divine authenticity of the Book of Mormon. I know of a surety that the work is true. It is not a matter of belief . . . but of knowledge. Just as surely as the sun is shining on us and gives us light, and the sun and stars give us light by night, just as surely as the breath of life sustains us, so surely do I know that Joseph Smith was a true prophet of God, chosen of God to open the last dispensation of the fullness of times; so surely do I know that the Book of Mormon was divinely translated. I saw the plates; I saw the angel; I heard the voice of God. I know that the Book of Mormon is true, and that Joseph Smith was a true prophet of God. I might as well doubt my own existence as to doubt the divine authenticity of the Book of Mormon or the divine calling of Joseph Smith.

[My] testimony [which] has accompanied every copy of the Book [of Mormon], that an angel of God came down from heaven, and he brought and laid before our eyes, that we beheld and saw the plates, and the engravings thereon . . . has not varied . . . in 41 years (*Eyewitness Accounts of the Restoration*, 157–59; spelling standardized).

Lucy Mack Smith

Joseph, Martin, Oliver, and David, repaired to a grove, a short distance from the house, where they commenced calling upon the Lord, and continued in earnest supplication, until he permitted an angel to come down from his presence, and declare to them, that all which Joseph had testified of concerning the plates was true.

When they returned to the house, it was between three and four o'clock in the afternoon. Mrs. [Mary] Whitmer, Mr. Smith, and myself, were sitting in a bedroom at the time. On coming in, Joseph threw himself down besides me, and exclaimed, "Father, mother, you do not know how happy I am; the Lord has now caused the plates to be shown to three more besides myself. They have seen an angel, who has testified to them, and they will have to bear witness to the truth of what I have said, for now they know for themselves, that I do not go about to deceive the people, and I feel as if I was relieved of a burden which was almost too heavy for me to bear, and it rejoices my soul, that I am not any longer to be entirely alone in the world." Upon this, Martin Harris came in: he seemed almost overcome with joy, and testified boldly to what he had both seen and heard. And so did David and Oliver, adding, that no tongue could express the joy of their hearts, and the greatness of the things which they had both seen and heard.

Their written testimony . . . is contained in the Book of Mormon (*Biographical Sketches*, 164–65).

ADDITIONAL TESTIMONIES OF THE THREE WITNESSES

Elder Dallin H. Oaks

The testimony of the Three Witnesses to the Book of Mormon stands forth in great strength. Each of the three had ample reason and opportunity to renounce his testimony if it had been false or to equivocate on details if any had been inaccurate. As is well known, because of disagreements or jealousies involving other leaders of the Church, each one of these three witnesses was excommunicated from The Church of Jesus Christ of Latter-day Saints about eight years after the publication of their testimony. All three went their separate ways, with no common interest to support a collusive effort. Yet to the end of their lives—periods ranging from 12 to 50 years after their excommunications—not one of these witnesses deviated from his published testimony or said anything that cast any shadow on its truthfulness (Dallin H. Oaks, "The Witness: Martin Harris," *Ensign*, May 1999, 46).

Oliver Cowdery

(Later in his life, Oliver was elected as prosecuting attorney in Michigan. During one trial, the defense attorney stood and demanded that Oliver say something about "that golden Bible that Joe Smith dug out of that hill; something about the great fraud he perpetrated upon the American people whereby he gained thousands of dollars." Oliver's reply follows.)

May it please the court, and gentlemen of the jury, my brother attorney on the other side has charged me with connection with Joseph Smith and the golden Bible. The responsibility has been placed upon me, and I cannot escape reply. Before God and man I dare not deny what I have said, and what my testimony contains as written and printed on the front page of the Book of Mormon. May it please your honor and gentlemen of the jury, this I say, I saw the angel and heard his voice—how can I deny it? It happened in the daytime when the sun was shining bright in the firmament; not in the night when I was asleep. That glorious messenger from heaven, dressed in white, standing above the ground, in a glory I have never seen anything to compare with, the sun insignificant in comparison, and this personage told us if we denied that testimony there is no forgiveness in this life nor in the world to come. Now, how can I deny it—I dare not; I will not! (C. M. Nielsen, "Oliver Cowdery for the Defense," *The Improvement Era* 46 [August 1943]: 464).

Oliver Cowdery

Friends and Brethren:—My name is Cowdery, Oliver Cowdery. In the early history of this Church I stood identified with her, and one in her councils. True it is that the gifts and callings of God are without repentance [Romans 11:29]; not because I was better than the rest of mankind was I called; but, to fulfill the purposes of God, he called me to a high and holy calling.

I wrote with my own pen the entire Book of Mormon (save a few pages) as it fell from the lips of the Prophet Joseph Smith, as he translated it by the gift and power of God by the means of the Urim and Thummim, or, as it is called by that book, 'holy interpreters.' I beheld with my eyes, and handled with my hands, the gold plates from which it was transcribed. I also saw with my eyes and handled with my hands the 'holy interpreters.' That book is true. Sidney Rigdon did not write it. Mr. Spaulding did not write it. I wrote it myself as it fell from the lips of the Prophet. It contains the everlasting Gospel, and came forth to the children of men in fulfillment of the revelations of John, where he says he saw an angel come with the everlasting Gospel to preach to every nation, kindred, tongue and people. It contains principles of salvation; and if you, my hearers, will walk by its light and obey its precepts, you will be saved with an everlasting salvation in the kingdom of God on high. Brother Hyde has just said that it is important that we keep in the true channel, in order to avoid the sand-bars. This is true. The channel is here. The Holy Priesthood is here.

I was present with Joseph when an holy angel from God came down from heaven and conferred on us, or restored the lesser or Aaronic Priesthood, and said to us at the same time, that it should remain upon the earth while the earth stands.

I was also present with Joseph when the higher or Melchizedek Priesthood was conferred by the holy angels from on high. This Priesthood we then conferred on each other, by the will and commandment of God. This Priesthood, as was then declared, is also to remain upon the earth until the last remnant of time. This Holy Priesthood, or authority, we conferred upon many, and is just as good and valid as though God had done it in person.

I laid my hands upon that man—Yes I laid my right hand upon his head (pointing to Brother Hyde), and I conferred upon him the Priesthood, and he holds that Priesthood now. He was also called through me, by the prayer of faith, an apostle of the Lord Jesus Christ (Joseph Fielding Smith, *Essentials in Church History*, [Salt Lake City: Deseret Book, 1979], 386–87).

David Whitmer

It having been represented by one John Murphy of Polo [Caldwell County], Missouri, that I had in a conversation with him last summer, denied my testimony as one of the three witnesses to the Book of Mormon—

To the end thereof, that he may understand me now if he did not then, and that the world may know the truth, I wish now, standing as it were, in the very sunset of life, and in the fear of God, once [and] for all to make this public statement:

That I have never at any time, denied that testimony or any part thereof, which has so long since been published with that book, as one of the three witnesses.

Those who know me best, well know that I have always adhered to that testimony—And that no man may be misled or doubt my present views in regard to the same, I do now again affirm the truth of all my statements as then made and published.

He that hath an ear to hear, let him hear: It was no delusion. What is written is written, and he that readeth let him understand (as cited in Joseph Fielding Smith, in Conference Report, October 1956, 20).

David Whitmer

(David bore his testimony three days before his death.)

David Whitmer never denied his testimony to the truth of the Book of Mormon, through all the years of his separation from The Church, but repeatedly reaffirmed it, especially in the closing years of his life. Three days previous to his death, which occurred on the 25th of January, 1888, he called his family and a number of his friends to his bedside, and turning to his physician, said:

"Dr. Buchanan, I want you to say whether or not I am in my right mind, before I give my dying testimony."

The doctor answered: "Yes, you are in your right mind, for I have just had a conversation with you."

He then addressed himself to all around his bedside in these words: "Now, you must all be faithful in Christ. I want to say to you all, the Bible and the record of the Nephites (Book of Mormon) is true, so that you can say that you heard me bear my testimony on my death-bed. All be faithful in Christ, and your reward will be according to your works. God bless you all. My trust is in Christ forever, worlds without end. Amen" (*Richmond Democrat* [2 February 1888], as cited in B. H. Roberts, *The Missouri Persecutions* [Salt Lake City: Bookcraft, 1965], 182–83).

Martin Harris

(To Elder William H. Homer in December 1869.)

Young man ... do I believe it! Do you see the sun shining! Just as surely as the sun is shining on us and gives us light, and the moon and stars give us light by night ... so surely do I know that the Book of Mormon was divinely translated. I saw the plates; I saw the Angel; I heard the voice of God. I know that the Book of Mormon is true and that Joseph Smith was a true prophet of God. I might as well doubt my own existence as to doubt the divine authenticity of the Book of Mormon or the divine calling of Joseph Smith (William H. Homer, "The Passing of Martin Harris," *Improvement Era* 29 [March 1926]: 470).

Martin Harris

(15 September 1853)

Be it known to all whom this may concern that I, David B. Dille, of Ogden city, Weber County, Salt Lake, *en route* to Great Britain, having business with one Martin Harris, formerly of the Church of Latter-day Saints, and residing in Kirtland, Lake County, Ohio, did personally wait upon him at his residence, and found him sick in bed ...

I ... addressed Mr. Harris relative to his once high and exalted station in the Church, and his then fallen and afflicted condition. I afterwards put the following questions to Mr. Harris, to which he severally replied with the greatest cheerfulness:—"What do you think of the Book of Mormon? Is it a divine record?"

Mr. Harris replied and said—"I was the right-hand man of Joseph Smith, and I know that he was a prophet of God. I know the Book of Mormon is true." Then smiting his fist on the table, he said—"*And you know that I know that it is true.* I know that the plates have been translated by the gift and power of God, for his voice declared it unto us; therefore I know of a surety that the work is true. For," continued Mr. Harris, "did I not at one time hold the plates on my knee an hour-and-a-half, whilst in conversation with Joseph, when we went to bury them in the woods, that the enemy might not obtain them? Yes, I did. And as many of the plates as Joseph Smith translated I handled with my hands, plate after plate." Then describing their dimensions, he pointed with one of the fingers of his left hand to the back of his right hand and said, "I should think they were so long, or about eight inches, and about so thick, or about four inches; and each of the plates was thicker than the thickest tin" (David B. Dille, "Additional Testimony of Martin Harris (One of the Three Witnesses) to the Coming Forth of the Book of Mormon," *Millennial Star* 21 [20 August 1859]: 545).

THE EIGHT WITNESSES
(June 1829)

Lucy Mack Smith

The following day [the day after the Three Witnesses had viewed the plates] we returned [to our home in Manchester], a cheerful, happy company. In a few days we were followed by Joseph, Oliver, and the Whitmers, who came to make us a visit, and make some arrangements about getting the book printed. Soon after they came, all the male part of the company, with my husband, Samuel, and Hyrum, retired to a place where the family were in the habit of offering up their secret devotions to God. They went to this place, because it had been revealed to Joseph that the plates would be carried thither by one of the ancient Nephites. Here it was, that those eight witnesses, whose names are recorded in the

Book of Mormon, looked upon them and handled them. . . .

After these [eight] witnesses returned to the house, the angel again made his appearance to Joseph at which time Joseph delivered up the plates into the angel's hands. The ensuing evening we held a meeting, in which all the witnesses bore testimony to the facts as stated above; and all of our family, even to Don Carlos, who was but fourteen years of age, testified of the truth of the latter-day dispensation—that it was then ushered in (*Biographical Sketches*, 166–68).

The Testimony of Eight Witnesses

Be it known unto all nations, kindreds, tongues, and people, unto whom this work shall come: That Joseph Smith, Jun., the translator of this work, has shown unto us the plates of which hath been spoken, which have the appearance of gold; and as many of the leaves as the said Smith has translated we did handle with our hands; and we also saw the engravings thereon, all of which has the appearance of ancient work, and of curious workmanship. And this we bear record with words of soberness, that the said Smith has shown unto us, for we have seen and hefted, and know of a surety that the said Smith has got the plates of which we have spoken. And we give our names unto the world, to witness unto the world that which we have seen. And we lie not, God bearing witness of it.

CHRISTIAN WHITMER
JACOB WHITMER
PETER WHITMER, JUN.
JOHN WHITMER
HIRAM PAGE
JOSEPH SMITH, SEN.
HYRUM SMITH
SAMUEL H. SMITH

(The Book of Mormon, "The Testimony of Eight Witnesses")

John Whitmer

David Whitmer, Oliver Cowdery, and Martin Harris, were the three witnesses whose names are attached to the Book of Mormon according to the prediction of the book, who knew and saw, for a surety, into whose presence the angel of God came and showed them the plates, the ball, the directors, etc. And also other witnesses even eight, viz., Christian Whitmer, Jacob Whitmer, John Whitmer, Peter Whitmer Jr., Hiram Page, Joseph Smith, Hyrum Smith, and Samuel H. Smith, are the men to whom Joseph Smith, Junior, showed the plates. These witnesses' names go forth also of the truth of this work in the last days, to the convincing or condemning of this generation in the last day.

To say that the Book of Mormon is a revelation from God, I have no hesitance; but with all confidence have signed my name to it as such. . . . I desire to testify to all that will come to the knowledge of this address; that I have most assuredly seen the plates from whence the Book of Mormon is translated, and that I have handled these plates, and know of a surety that Joseph Smith Jr. has translated the Book of Mormon by the gift and power of God. . . . I know that the Bible, Book of Mormon and book of Doctrine and Covenants of the church of the Latter Day Saints, contain the revealed will of heaven (John Whitmer, *John Whitmer's History* [LDS Church Archives, Church Historical Department, The Church of Jesus Christ of Latter-day Saints, Salt Lake City], 25; as cited in *Eyewitness Accounts of the Restoration*, 161–62).

Hyrum Smith

Having given my testimony to the world of the truth of the book of Mormon . . . I thought that it might be strengthening to my beloved brethren, to give them a short account of my sufferings, for the truth's sake, and the state of my mind and feelings, while under circumstances of the most trying and afflicting nature . . . Prior to my settlement in Missouri . . . [I] endured almost all manner of abuse, which was poured out upon the church of Latter Day Saints, from its commencement . . . After enduring many privations and much fatigue, . . . I arrived with my family in Far West. [In the fall of 1838, I was imprisoned with my brethren] for more than four months, and suffered much for want of proper food, and from the nauseous cell in which I was confined . . . How inadequate is language to express the feelings of my mind, . . . knowing that I was innocent of crime, and that I had been dragged from my family at a time, when my assistance was most needed; that I had been abused and thrust into a dungeon, and confined for months on account of my faith, and the "testimony of Jesus Christ."

However I thank God that I felt a determination to die, rather than deny *the things which my eyes had seen, which my hands had handled, and which I had borne testimony to. . . . I* can assure my beloved brethren that I was enabled to bear as strong a testimony, when nothing but death presented itself, as ever I did in my life. . . . I yet feel a determination to do the will of God, in spite of persecutions, imprisonments or death (Hyrum Smith, "Hyrum Smith to the Saints Scattered Abroad," *Times & Seasons* 2 [December 1839]: 20–23).

Samuel Smith

Samuel talked with [Rhoda Young Greene] a short time and then binding his knapsack upon his shoulders, he rose to leave the house. But as he crossed the doorsill, a strong impression was made upon his mind that he must not take the book away with him. And he turned round and handing the book to Mrs. Green said, "I will give you this book, for the Spirit of God forbids my taking it away."

She was so overcome with gratitude that she burst into tears and exclaimed, "Mr. Smith, will (you) stop and pray with me?" He did as she desired and left his blessing upon the home. And she afterwards told me that she never saw a man that had such an appearance or ever heard such a prayer in her life. . . . "It seemed as though the very heavens were rent and the Spirit of God was poured down upon us." After this he explained to her the most profitable manner of reading the book which he had put into her hands, which was this: that she should take it with the Bible and ask God to give you a testimony of the truth of the work, and you will feel a burning sensation in your breast, which is the Spirit of God. She promised that she would, and he left her (Lucy Mack Smith, *Copy of an Old Notebook* [L. Tom Perry Special Collections, Harold B. Lee Library, Brigham Young University, Provo, Utah], 31–34; spelling, punctuation, and capitalization standardized).

Parley P. Pratt

(After being introduced to the Book of Mormon, Parley P. Pratt was filled with an intense desire to meet the witnesses whose names were recorded in the book.)

I read it carefully and diligently, a great share of it, without knowing that the Priesthood had been restored—without ever having heard of anything called "Mormonism," or having any idea of such a Church and people.

There were the witnesses and their testimony to the book, to its translation, and to the ministration of angels; and there was the testimony of the translator; but I had not seen them, I had not heard of them, and hence I had no idea of their organization or of their Priesthood. . . . But as I read, I was convinced that it was true; . . .

This same spirit led me to enquire after and search out the translator, Joseph Smith; and I traveled on foot during the whole of a very hot day in August, blistering my feet, in order to go where I heard he lived; and at night I arrived in the neighbourhood of the little village of Manchester, then in Ontario County, New York. On the way, I overtook a man driving some cows, and enquired for Joseph Smith, the finder and translator of the Book of Mormon. He told me that he lived away off . . . in the State of Pennsylvania. I then enquired for the father of the Prophet, and he pointed to the house, but said that the old gentleman had gone a journey to some distant place. After awhile, in conversation,

Parley P. Pratt
(Courtesy of the Church Archives, The Church of Jesus Christ of Latter-day Saints)

the man told me that his name was Hyrum Smith, and that he was a brother to the Prophet Joseph. This was the first Latter-day Saint that I had ever seen.

He invited me to his home, where I saw mother Smith and Hyrum Smith's wife, and sister Rockwell . . . We sat up talking nearly all night; for I had not much spare time, having two appointments out, and a long day's journey for a man to walk. . . .

During that conversation, I learned something of the rights of the Church, its organization, the restoration of the Priesthood, and many important truths. I felt to go back and fill the two appointments given out, and that closed my ministry, as I felt that I had no authority . . .

I attended to my appointments, and was back again the next morning to brother Hyrum's. He made me a present of the Book of Mormon . . . He took me to a place, about twenty-five miles off, in Seneca county, New York. He there introduced me to the three witnesses whose names appear at the beginning of the Book of Mormon, also to the eight witnesses. I conversed with Oliver Cowdery, one of the three witnesses, and on the next day we repaired to Seneca Lake, where I was baptized by Oliver Cowdery, then the second Apostle in this Church, and a man who had received the ministration of an angel, as you can learn by reading his testimony (in *Journal of Discourses*, 26 vols. [London: Latter-day Saints' Book Depot, 1854–86], 5:193–95).

Samuel Smith

(In an interview)

The Book of Mormon, or, as it is called by some, the Golden Bible . . . is a revelation from God. . . . If you will read this book with a prayerful heart, and ask God to give you a witness, you will know of the truth of this work. . . . I know the book to be a revelation from God, translated by the gift and power of the Holy Ghost, and that my brother Joseph Smith, jun., is a Prophet, Seer, and Revelator (George Q. Cannon, "History of Brigham Young," *Millennial Star* 25 [6 June 1863]: 360–61).

Joseph Smith Sr.

Most of [the Smith's] former neighbors and friends shunned them; some actively lied about them. Others took advantage of them, ransacked their property, and pressed petty lawsuits.

To Joseph and Lucy's credit, they did not become bitter and vindictive. "We doubled our diligence in prayer before God that [our son] Joseph might be more fully instructed and preserved," wrote Lucy. They were the first to know of and accept Joseph Jr.'s calling, sorrowed with him when the first 116 pages of the Book of Mormon were lost, helped guard the plates, heard the testimony of the Three Witnesses, and were among the earliest to be baptized. Joseph Sr. and two sons, Hyrum and Samuel, were among the Eight witnesses. . . .

A Palmyra resident purchased Joseph Sr.'s note and demanded instant payment but offered to forgive the debt if he would burn the Book of Mormon. Even though he was ill, Joseph refused and went to debtors' prison for several weeks" (Donald L. Enders, "Faithful From the First," *Ensign*, January 2001, 56).

P. Wilhelm Poulson, M.D.

John Whitmer received me as a dear father would receive a son, and answered readily all my questions. I said: I am aware that your name is affixed to the testimony in the Book of Mormon, that you saw the plates?

He—It is so, and that testimony is true.

I—Did you handle the plates with your hands?

He—I did so!

I—Then they were a material substance?

He—Yes, as material as anything can be.

I: They were heavy to lift?

He—Yes, and as you know gold is a heavy metal, they were very heavy.

I—How big were the leaves?

He—So far as I recollect, 8 by 6 or 7 inches.

I—Were the leaves thick?

He—Yes, just so thick, that characters could be engraven on both sides.

I—How were the leaves joined together?

He—In three rings, each one in the shape of a D with the straight line towards the centre.

I—In what place did you see the plates[?]

He—In Joseph Smith's house; he had them there.

I—Did you see them covered with a cloth?

He—No. He handed them uncovered into our hands, and we turned the leaves sufficient to satisfy us.

I—Were you all eight witnesses present at the same time?

He—No. At that time Joseph showed the plates to us, we were four persons present in the room, and at another time he showed them to four persons more. . . .

He was firm as a rock in his faith, and when Joseph Smith [III], living in Plano [Illinois], sent word to John Whitmer to reaffirm his testimony, his answer was: "I have never recalled it, and I have nothing to reaffirm."

In regard to joining the Church, he said: 'I have a testimony within me, that testimony I got when I was raised up as a witness—that testimony has never left my bosom, it is by me to this day, and I am in the very place where I have to be, according to the Book of Mormon, which is the law that came out from Zion, which center stake is never to be taken away from here, in Jackson County, Mo.' He had a firm and most absolute faith in the restoration and triumph of Zion on this continent, and the building of temples in Independence and Far West, Mo." (P. Wilhelm Poulson, "Letter to Editors of Deseret News from P. Wilhelm Poulson," *Deseret Weekly News* [14 August 1878]: 434–35).

John Christian Whitmer

(Son of Jacob Whitmer)

I was closely connected with Hiram Page in business transactions and other matters, he being married to my aunt. I knew him at all times and under all circumstances to be true to his testimony concerning the divinity of the Book of Mormon. I was also at the death bed of Oliver Cowdery in 1850, and I heard him speak to my uncle David (Whitmer) and say: "Brother David, be faithful to our testimony to the Book of Mormon, for we know that it is of God and that it is verily true." He then closed his eyes in death. My father, Jacob Whitmer, was always faithful and true to his testimony to the Book of Mormon, and confirmed it on his death bed. Of my uncle John (Whitmer) I will say that I was with him a short time before he died at Far West, Missouri, when he confirmed to me what he had done so many times previously that he knew the Book of Mormon was true. I was also with Uncle David (Whitmer), who died here in January last, and heard him bear his last testimony in the presence of many witnesses whom he had called together for the occasion. He solemnly declared that the record of the Nephites, as he always called the Book of Mormon, was of God, and his testimony concerning it true (Andrew Jensen, *Infancy of the Church* [Salt Lake City: s.n., 1889], 10).

PUBLICATION OF THE BOOK OF MORMON
(1829–1830)

Joseph Smith Jr.

Meantime our translation drawing to a close, we went to Palmyra, Wayne county, N[ew] Y[ork]: Secured the copyright; and agreed with Mr. Egbert B. Grandin to print five thousand copies, for the sum of three thousand dollars.

I wish also to mention here, that the title page of the Book of Mormon is a literal translation, taken from the very last leaf, on the left hand side of the collection or book of plates, which contained the record which has been translated; the language of the whole running the same as all Hebrew writing in general; and that, said title page is not by any means a modern composition either of mine or of any other man's who has lived or does live in this generation. Therefore, in order to correct an error which generally exists concerning it, I give below that part of the title page of the English version of the Book of Mormon, which is a genuine and literal translation of the title page of the original Book of Mormon, as recorded on the plates.

The Book of Mormon Title Page

An account written by the hand of Mormon, upon plates, taken from the plates of Nephi.

"Wherefore, it is an abridgement of the record of the people of Nephi, and also of the Lamanites; written to the Lamanites, who are a remnant of the house of Israel; and also to Jew and Gentile: written by way of commandment, and also by the spirit of prophecy and of revelation.

Written, and sealed up, and hid up unto the Lord, that they might not be destroyed; to come forth by the gift and power of God unto the interpretation thereof: sealed by the hand of Moroni, and hid up unto the Lord, to come forth in due time by the way of Gentile; the interpretation thereof by the gift of God.

An abridgement taken from the book of Ether, also; which is a record of the people of Jared; who were scattered at the time the Lord confounded the language of the people when they were building a tower to get to heaven: which is to show unto the remnant of the house of Israel what great things the Lord hath done for their fathers; and that they may know the covenants of the Lord, that they are not cast off forever; and also to the convincing of the Jew and Gentile that Jesus is the Christ, the eternal God, manifesting himself unto all nations. And now if there are faults, they are the mistakes of men; wherefore condemn not the things of God, that ye may be found spotless at the judgment seat of Christ."

The remainder of the title page is of course, modern ("History of Joseph Smith," *Times & Seasons* 3 [15 October 1842]: 943).

Pomeroy Tucker

In June [probably should be July or August], 1829, Smith the prophet, his brother Hyrum, Cowdery the scribe, and Harris the believer, applied to Mr. Egbert B. Grandin, then publisher of the *Wayne Sentinel* at Palmyra (now deceased), for his price to do the work of one edition of three thousand copies. Harris offered to pay or secure payment if a bargain should be made. Only a few sheets of the manuscript, as a specimen, with the title-page, were exhibited at this time, though the whole number of folios was stated, whereby could be made a calculation of the cost. Mr. Grandin at once expressed his disinclination to entertain the proposal to print at any price, believing the whole affair to be a wicked imposture and a scheme to defraud Mr. Harris, who was his friend, and whom he advised accordingly. This admonition was kindly but firmly resisted by Harris. . . . Further interviews followed, Grandin being earnestly importuned to reconsider his opinion and determination. He was assured by Harris, that if he refused to do the work, it would be procured elsewhere. And the subject was temporarily dropped, except that Grandin complied with Harris's request for an approximate estimate of the cost of the proposed edition. . . .

[After learning that arrangement had been made with Elihu F. Marshall to print the book] Mr. Grandin, on taking the advice of several discreet, fair-minded neighbors, finally reconsidered his course of policy, and entered into contract for the printing and binding of five thousand copies of the Book of Mormon at the price of $3,000, taking Harris's bond and mortgage as offered in security for payment (Pomeroy Tucker, *Origin, Rise, and Progress of Mormonism* [Palmyra, New York: D. Appleton and Company, 1867], 50–53).

Lucy Mack Smith

[After] making a contract with ... E.B. Grandin [and] ... before [returning] ... to Pennsylvania, where he had left his wife, he [Joseph Smith] received a commandment, which was, in substance, as follows:

First, that Oliver Cowdery should transcribe the whole manuscript. Second, that he should take but one copy at a time to the office, so that if one copy should get destroyed, there would still be a copy remaining. Third, that in going to and from the office, he should always have a guard to attend him, for the purpose of protecting the manuscript. Fourth, that a guard should be kept constantly on the watch, both night and day, about the house, to protect the manuscript from malicious persons, who would infest the house for the purpose of destroying the manuscript. All these things were strictly attended to, as the Lord commanded Joseph. After giving these instructions, Joseph returned to Pennsylvania (*Biographical Sketches*, 168–70).

Pomeroy Tucker

In the beginning of the printing the Mormons professed to hold their manuscripts as "sacred," and insisted upon maintaining constant vigilance for their safety during the progress of the work, each morning carrying to the printing-office the installment required for the day, and withdrawing the same at evening. No alteration from copy in any manner was to be made. These things were "strictly commanded," as they said. Mr. John H. Gilbert, as printer, had the chief operative trust of the type-setting and press-work of the job. After the first day's trial he found the manuscripts in so very imperfect a condition, especially in regard to grammar, that he became unwilling further to obey the "command," and so announced to Smith and his party; when, finally, upon much friendly expostulation, he was given a limited discretion in correcting, which was exercised in the particulars of syntax, orthography, punctuation, capitalizing, paragraphing, etc. ... Very soon, too—after some ten days—the constant vigilance by the Mormons over the manuscripts was relaxed by reason of the confidence they came to repose in the printers (*Origin, Rise, and Progress of Mormonism*, 53–54; spelling standardized).

Lucy Mack Smith

The work of printing still continued with little or no interruption, until one Sunday afternoon, when Hyrum became very uneasy as to the security of the work left at the printing-office, and requested Oliver to accompany him thither, to see if all was right. Oliver hesitated for a moment, as to the propriety of going on Sunday, but finally consented, and they set off together.

On arriving at the printing establishment, they found it occupied by an individual by the name of Cole, an ex-justice of the peace, who was busily employed in printing a newspaper. Hyrum was much surprised at finding him there, and remarked, "How is it, Mr. Cole, that you are so hard at work on Sunday?"

Mr. Cole replied that he could not have the press in the daytime during the week, and was obliged to do his printing at night, and on Sundays.

Upon reading the prospectus of his paper, they found that he had agreed with his subscribers to publish one form of "Joe Smith's Gold Bible" each week, and thereby furnish them with the principle portion of the book in such a way that they would not be obliged to pay the Smiths for it. His paper was entitled, *Dogberry Paper on Winter Hill.* In this he had thrown together a parcel of the most vulgar, disgusting prose, and the meanest, and most low-lived doggerel, in juxtaposition with a portion of the Book of Mormon, which he had pilfered. At this perversion of common sense and moral feeling, Hyrum was shocked, as well as indignant at the dishonest course which Mr. Cole had taken, in order to possess himself of the work.

"Mr. Cole," said he, "what right have you to print the Book of Mormon in this manner? Do you not known that we have secured the copyright?"

"It is none of your business," answered Cole; "I have hired the press, and will print what I please; so help yourself."

"Mr. Cole," rejoined Hyrum, "that manuscript is sacred, and I forbid your printing any more of it."

"Smith," exclaimed Cole, in a tone of anger, "I don't care a d—n for you: that d—d gold bible is going into my paper, in spite of all you can do."

Hyrum endeavored to dissuade him from his purpose, but finding him inexorable, left him to issue his paper, . . . he had already issued six or eight numbers, and by taking them ten or twenty miles into the country, had managed to keep them out of our sight.

On returning from the office, they asked my husband what course was best for them to pursue, relative to Mr. Cole. He told them that he considered it a matter with which Joseph ought to be made acquainted. Accordingly, he set out himself for Pennsylvania, and returned with Joseph the ensuing Sunday. The weather was so extremely cold that they came near perishing before they arrived at home; nevertheless, as soon as Joseph made himself partially comfortable, he went to the printing-office, where he found Cole employed, as on the Sunday previous. "How do you do, Mr. Cole," said Joseph. "You seem hard at work."

"How do you do, Mr. Smith," answered Cole, dryly.

Joseph examined his *Dogberry Paper*, and then said firmly, "Mr. Cole, that book [the Book of Mormon], and the right of publishing it, belongs to me, and I forbid you meddling with it any further."

At this Mr. Cole threw off his coat, rolled up his sleeves, and came towards Joseph, smacking his fists together with vengeance, and roaring out, "Do you want to fight, sir? Do you want to fight? I will publish just what I please. Now, if you want to fight, just come on."

Joseph could not help smiling at his grotesque appearance, for his behavior was too ridiculous to excite indignation. "Now, Mr. Cole," said he, "you had better keep your coat on—it is cold, and I am not going to fight you; nevertheless, I assure you, sir, that you have got to stop printing my book, for I know my rights, and shall maintain them."

"Sir," bawled out the wrathy gentleman, "if you think you are the best man, just pull off you coat and try it."

"Mr. Cole," said Joseph, in a low, significant tone, "there is law, and you will find that out, if you do not understand it, but I shall not fight you, sir."

At this, the ex-justice began to cool off a little, and finally concluded to submit to an arbitration, which decided that he should stop his proceedings forthwith, so that he made us no further trouble.

Joseph, after disposing of this affair, returned to Pennsylvania, but not long to remain there, for when the inhabitants of the surrounding country perceived that the work still progressed, they became uneasy, and again called a large meeting. At this time, they gathered their forces together, far and near, and organizing themselves into a committee of the whole, they resolved, as before, never to purchase one of our books, when they should be printed. They then appointed a committee to wait upon E. B. Grandin, and inform him of the resolutions which they had passed, and also to explain to him the evil consequences which would result to him therefrom. The men who were appointed to do this errand fulfilled their mission to the letter, and urged upon Mr. Grandin the necessity of his putting a stop to the printing, as the Smiths had lost all their property, and consequently would be unable to pay him for his work, except by the sale of the books. And this they would never be able to do, for the people would not purchase them. This information caused Mr. Grandin to stop printing, and we were again compelled to sent for Joseph. These trips, back and forth, exhausted nearly all our means, yet they seemed unavoidable.

When Joseph came, he went immediately with Martin Harris to Grandin, and succeeded in removing his fears, so that he went on with the work, until the books were printed, which was in the spring of eighteen hundred and thirty (*Biographical Sketches*, 176–80).

Pomeroy Tucker

The contract [with Grandin regarding publishing the Book of Mormon] was faithfully and satisfactorily fulfilled by both parties, and the book in its entire edition as bargained for was completed and delivered early in the summer [should be spring] of 1830 . . .

Meanwhile, Harris and his wife had separated by mutual arrangement, on account of her persistent unbelief in Mormonism and refusal to be a party to the mortgage. The family estate was divided, Harris giving her about eighty acres of the farm, with a comfortable house and other property as her share of the assets; and she occupied this property until the time of her death. The main farm and homestead, about one hundred and fifty acres of land, was retained by himself, the mortgage covering only this portion. . . . The farm mortgaged was sold by Harris in 1831 at private sale, not by foreclosure, and a sufficiency of the avails [proceeds] went to pay Grandin . . . $3,000 (*Origin, Rise, and Progression of Mormonism*, 54–55; as cited in *Eyewitness Accounts of the Restoration*, 184).

John H. Gilbert

(John was a printer who helped set the type for the publication of the Book of Mormon.)

In the forepart of June, 1829, Mr. E. [Egbert] B. Grandin, the printer of the *Wayne Sentinel*, came to me and said he wanted I should assist him in estimating the cost of printing 5,000 copies of a book that Martin Harris wanted to get printed, which was called the "Mormon Bible."

John H. Gilbert
(Courtesy of the Church Archives, The Church of Jesus Christ of Latter-day Saints)

It was the second application of Harris to Grandin to do the job—Harris assuring Grandin that the book would be printed in Rochester if he declined the job again.

Harris proposed to have Grandin do the job, if he would, as it would be quite expensive to keep a man in Rochester during the printing of the book, who would have to visit Palmyra two or three times a week for manuscript, etc. Mr. Grandin consented to do the job if his terms were accepted.

A few pages of the manuscript were submitted as a specimen of the whole, and it was said there would be about 500 pages.

The size of the page was agreed upon, and an estimate of the number of ems in a page, which would be 1,000, and that a page of manuscript would make more than a page of printed matter, which proved to be correct.

The contract was to print, and bind with leather, 5,000 copies for $3,000. Mr. Grandin got a new font of small pica, on which the body of the work was printed.

When the printer was ready to commence work, [Martin] Harris was notified, and Hyrum Smith brought the first installment of manuscript, of 24 pages, closely written on common foolscap paper—he had it under his vest, and vest and coat closely buttoned over it. At night [Hyrum] Smith came and got the manuscript, and with the same precaution carried it away. The next morning with the same watchfulness, he brought it again, and at night took it away. This was kept up for several days. The title page was first set up, and after proof was read and corrected, several copies were printed for Harris and his friends. On the second day—[Martin] Harris and [Hyrum] Smith being in the office—I called their attention to a grammatical error, and asked whether I should correct it? [Martin] Harris consulted with [Hyrum] Smith a short time, and turned to me and said, "The Old Testament is ungrammatical, set it as it is written."

After working a few days, I said to [Hyrum] Smith on his handing me the manuscript in the morning, "Mr. [Hyrum] Smith, if you would leave this manuscript with me, I would take it home with me at night and read and punctuate it, and I could get along faster in the daytime, for now I have frequently to stop and read half a page to find how to punctuate it." His reply was, "We are commanded not to leave it." A few mornings after this, when [Hyrum] Smith handed me the manuscript, he said to me, "If you will give your word that this manuscript shall be returned to us when you get through with it, I will leave it with you." I assured Smith that it should be returned all right when I got through with it. For two or three nights I took it home with me and read it, and punctuated it with a lead pencil. This will account for the punctuation marks in pencil, which is referred to in the Mormon Report, an extract from which will be found below.

Martin Harris, Hyrum Smith and Oliver Cowdery, were very frequent visitors to the office during the printing of the Mormon Bible [Book of Mormon]. The manuscript was supposed to be in the handwriting of [Oliver] Cowdery. Every chapter, if I remember correctly, was one solid paragraph, without a punctuation mark, from beginning to end.

Names of persons and places were generally capitalized, but sentences had no end. The character or short "&" was used almost invariably where the word "and" occurred, except at the end of a chapter. I punctuated it to make it read as I supposed the author intended, and but very little punctuation was altered in proofreading. The Bible [Book of Mormon] was printed sixteen pages at a time, so that one sheet of paper made two copies of sixteen pages each, requiring 2,000 sheets of paper for each form of sixteen pages. There were thirty-seven forms of sixteen pages each—570 pages in all.

The work was commenced in August 1829, and finished in March 1830—seven months. Mr. J. H. Bortles and myself did the presswork until December taking nearly three days to each form.

In December Mr. Grandin hired a journeyman pressman, Thomas

McAuley, or "Whistling Tom," as he was called in the office, and he and Bortles did the balance of the presswork. The Bible [Book of Mormon] was printed on a "Smith" Press, single pull, and old-fashioned "Balls" ... were used—composition rollers not having come into use in small printing offices.

The printing was done in the third story of the west end of "Exchange Row," and the binding by Mr. Howard, in the second story; the lower story being used as a bookstore, by Mr. Grandin, and now—1892—by Mr. M. Story as a dry goods store.

[Oliver] Cowdery held and looked over the manuscript when most of the proofs were read. Martin Harris once or twice, and Hyrum Smith once, Grandin supposing these men could read their own writing as well, if not better, than anyone else; and if there are any discrepancies between the Palmyra edition and the manuscript these men should be held responsible.

Joseph Smith Jr., had nothing to do whatever with the printing or furnishing copy for the printers, being but once in the office during the printing of the Bible [Book of Mormon], and then not over fifteen or twenty minutes.

... Martin was in the office when I finished setting up the testimony of the Three Witnesses—([Martin] Harris—[Oliver] Cowdery and [David] Whitmer). I said to him, "Martin, did you see those plates with your naked eyes?" Martin looked down for an instant, raised his eyes up, and said, "No, I saw them with a spiritual eye" (John Gilbert, "John Gilbert Autobiography," in *Writings of Early Latter-day Saints and Their Contemporaries, A Database Collection*, comp. Milton V. Backman [Provo, Utah: BYU Religious Studies Center, 1996], 1–4).

IMPACT OF THE BOOK OF MORMON

Henry A. Wallace

(U.S. vice president from 1941 to 1945 and secretary of commerce under Presidents Roosevelt and Truman.)

Of all the American books of the nineteenth century, it seems probable that the Book of Mormon was the most powerful. It reached perhaps only one percent of the United States, but it affected this one percent so powerfully and lastingly that all the people of the United States have been affected, especially by its contribution in opening up one of the great frontiers (Henry A. Wallace, "Speech at the New York Times Book Fair, 5 November 1937"; as cited in Hugh B. Brown, Conference Report, October 1958, 62).

Emma Smith

"I sat across the table from my husband. I wrote with my own pen the words as they fell from his inspired lips. I would give him the pronunciation after he would spell the word out."

One particular word she remembered was the word *Sariah*. Joseph could spell it but he couldn't pronounce it. And at another time, while they were working, she said:

"Joseph looked up. . . . He said, 'Emma, does Jerusalem have a wall around it?'"

She said: "Yes, Joseph, Jerusalem has a wall around it. Everybody knows that." He said, "Thank goodness; I thought I was being deceived." And he went right on translating the record. . . .

"I knew it would be impossible for a learned man to produce or fabricate that work, much less the unlearned man I knew my husband to be" (R. Scott Lloyd, "Events in life of prophet, 'elect lady,'" *Church News* [10 September 1994]: 7).

Emma Smith

(To her son, Joseph Smith III.)

My belief is that the Book of Mormon is of divine authenticity—I have not the slightest doubt of it. I am satisfied that no man could have dictated the writing of the manuscript unless he was inspired; for, when [I was] acting as his scribe, your father would dictate to me hour after hour; and when returning after meals, or after interruptions, he would at once begin where he had left off, without either seeing the manuscript or having any portion of it read to him. . . . It would have been improbable that a learned man could do this; and, for one so . . . unlearned as he was, it was simply impossible (W. W. Blair, "Last Testimony of Sister Emma," *The Saints' Advocate* 26 [1 October 1879]: 52; as cited in Francis W. Kirkham, *A New Witness For Christ in America* [Salt Lake City: Utah Printing Co., 1967], 195–96).

Solomon Chamberlain

(Chamberlain had a vision in or about the year 1807 of three heavens, graded hierarchically according to their different degrees of glory. In another vision in 1816, he learned that the true church was not upon the earth but that it soon would be, and that its arrival would be connected with the publication of another book of scripture, much like the Bible. At about the time the Book of Mormon was being printed, but before he had yet heard of it, Solomon was divinely led to the Smiths' neighborhood in upstate New York.)

I was a stranger in that part of the country, a town where I never before had set my foot, and knew no one in the town. It was now about sundown, and my guide [the Spirit of the Lord] directed me to put up for the night, which I did to a farm house. In the morning, the people of the house asked me if I had heard of the Gold Bible. When they said Gold Bible, there was a power like electricity went from the top of my head to the end of my toes.

[He went to the Smith home, where he met Joseph Smith's brother Hyrum and found that the revelations he had received agreed in precise detail with those granted to the Prophet. He was baptized by Joseph Smith in the waters of Seneca Lake shortly after the establishment of the Church] (Solomon Chamberlain, *Solomon Chamberlain, Autobiography* [LDS Church Archives]; as cited in Susan Easton Black, *Stories from the Early Saints Converted by the Book of Mormon* [Salt Lake City: Bookcraft, 1992], 34–37).

Sidney Rigdon

(Within a few days of obtaining a copy of the Book of Mormon, Sidney Rigdon knew, by direct revelation, that it was true.)

Flesh and blood hath not revealed it unto me, but my Father which is in heaven (*History of the Church*, 1:125).

Luman Shurtliff

I heard a sweet melodious voice about me say, "Joseph Smith Jr. is a prophet of the Most High God, raised up ... and the Book of Mormon which you hold under your arm is true" (Luman Andros Shurtliff,

"Biographical Sketch of the Life of Luman Andros Shurtliff" [BYU Special Collections], 25; as cited in *Stories from the Early Saints Converted by the Book of Mormon*, 71–72).

Harrison Burgess

Testified that "a glorious personage clothed in white" came to him and showed him the plates from which the Book of Mormon had been translated (Harrison Burgess, *Autobiography* [LDS Church Archives], 65–66; as cited in *Stories from the Early Saints Converted by the Book of Mormon*, 27).

Benjamin Brown

Found himself strongly rebuked by two of the Three Nephites for his lack of faith in the Book of Mormon, and then heard "the Spirit of the Lord" say to him, "Now, you know for yourself! You have seen and heard! If you now fall away, there is no forgiveness for you" (Benjamin Brown, *Testimonies for the Truth* [Liverpool: S. W. Richards, 1853], 5; as cited in *Stories from the Early Saints Converted by the Book of Mormon*, 31).

Oliver Granger

Granger saw the angel Moroni who bore witness to him of the truthfulness of the Book of Mormon (Augusta Joyce Crocheron, *Representative Women of Deseret* [Salt Lake City: J. C. Graham and Co. 1884], 24; as cited in *Stories from the Early Saints Converted by the Book of Mormon*, 10).

George Cannon

(Father of George Q. Cannon, who later served as a counselor to four presidents of the Church, was converted in Liverpool in 1840 by Elder John Taylor of the Council of the Twelve, his brother-in-law. Elder Taylor left a copy of the Book of Mormon with the family. George read the book through twice before stating the following.)

No wicked man could write such a book as this; and no good man would write it, unless it were true and he were commanded of God to do so (*Cannon Family Historical Treasures*, ed. Beatrice Cannon Evans and

Jonathan Russell Canon [Salt Lake City: George Cannon Family Association, 1967], 35; as cited in *Stories from the Early Saints Converted by the Book of Mormon*, 26).

Willard Richards

George Q. Cannon
(Courtesy of the Church Archives, The Church of Jesus Christ of Latter-day Saints)

(When he first received the book, he opened it to an arbitrarily chosen passage and began to read. Before completing half a page, he declared the following.)

God or the devil has had a hand in that book, for man never wrote it (*Testimonies of our Leaders*, ed. Forace Green [Salt Lake City: Bookcraft, 1958], 61–62; as cited in *Stories from the Early Saints Converted by the Book of Mormon*, 66).

Willard Richards
(Courtesy of the Church Archives, The Church of Jesus Christ of Latter-day Saints)

Jacob Hamblin

(In February 1842, Jacob heard a Latter-day Saint missionary preach.)

I shall never forget the feeling that came over me when I saw his face and heard his voice. He preached that which I had long been seeking for; I felt that it was indeed the gospel (as cited in *Three Mormon Classics*, ed. Preston Nibley [Salt Lake City: Bookcraft, 1988], 203–5; as cited in Susan Easton Black, *Stories from the Early Saints Converted by the Book of Mormon*, 40–41).

Rachel Ridgeway Ivins

And oh, what joy filled my being! I could sing all the day long and rejoice in the glorious promises of the gospel (Mary Grant Judd, "Rachel Ridgeway Ivans Grant," *Relief Society Magazine* 30 [April 1943]: 228–29; as cited in *Stories from the Early Saints Converted by the Book of Mormon*, 40).

David Pettigrew

In the year of our Lord and Savior Jesus Christ, eighteen hundred and forty, I, David Pettigrew, commenced to write somewhat of a history of my life. . . .

I made no profession of religion until the year eighteen hundred and twenty-three, when I became much concerned about my own welfare. I mourned and lamented much, for I had sinned against my God, and feared that . . . if I did not change my sinful ways my soul must be lost. I cried much unto the Lord for mercy, but I feared that I had gone beyond redemption and that I must see and feel the damnation of hell, but through the mercies of the Almighty God, I found rest to my soul. I was now determined to lead a new life and to serve my God the remainder of my days. I frequently called upon my neighbors to repent and become Christians, and pray unto the Lord with their families, and also in secret, and I was blessed in so doing and a few of my neighbors soon professed to be converted. I thought that the Methodist Church was the nearest correct of any of the professing world, therefore we applied to them, and we were soon organized into a class in our neighborhood, and I was chosen class leader. I strove to do good according to the light I had. I was exceedingly anxious to know why we could not attain to the same religion of the Apostles, or to the same faith and work. I believed that there was but one right way, and I was much troubled concerning that matter. . . .

And thus I passed my days until the year eighteen hundred and thirty-one, when I felt more convinced that some great event was at hand, but what it would be I could not divine, but my prayers to my God [were] that I might know his ways and his will concerning the sons of men. On the first day of the year thirty-two, as I was reading in my room before prayers, some person knocked at my door. I bid him to walk in, and behold, it was a man whom I had had some acquaintance with some years before, which I considered a just and upright man, but not very intelligent. I enquired what was the news, and what sects were doing the most in the cause of religion. He answered that the Methodists he thought were doing the best of any. We conversed a while upon different topics, and at length he asked me if I had heard of a people called the Mormons. I replied, that I never had, only from what I had read in the Christian's Advocate, printed at New York. I there read some slurs about a people that were gathering in the upper part of the state of Missouri, and supposed they were a fit people for the penitentiary.

I asked him if he knew anything about them, to which he replied that he did and believed them to be a good people and that he had a book of their religion upon which I asked him to let me see it, and he handed me the Book of Mormon, this was indeed new to me, and I thought a trick, as he looked upon this book as sacred as on the Bible. I opened the book. It was the second book of Nephi, and the fifth chapter. I read on awhile my thoughts were very active, what to think I knew not. It was entirely a new thing to me and I began to mind what I was reading, although I observed to my wife that I did not think that it was the words of him that had a devil. This was on the Sabbath morning, I read until meeting time, I then invited the gentleman to meetings house. The people had gathered together for meeting. I informed the congregation that this gentleman that was with me was a professor of religion, and if it was their desire that he should occupy the pulpit the forenoon, there was no objection, and he opened the meeting with prayers, and then read the twenty-ninth chapter of Isaiah, and then spoke of the Book of Mormon and that God had brought it forth by raising up a prophet and it was the fullness of the everlasting gospel, and after he had spoken what he saw fit, he sat down, and I immediately arose and spoke as follows: Brethren there has been certainly strange things come to our ears, that we had not thought of, which [are] entirely new to us, therefore, I recommend that we be wise and not hasty in making up our minds concerning this matter, for if it is of man, it will be good for nothing and will soon come to naught, but if it should be of God, and we should be found at variance with it, we would be exceedingly sorry in days to come. I know not whether it is of God or of man, but this much I do know, that there is no harm in being wise in these things, and I took my seat.

Neighbor Beach, Esq., arose and said, "Strange delusion. We read that strange things will take place in the last days, and here they are already amongst us, it is intolerable to think or suppose that such could be the fact. It is blasphemy in the highest, and astonishing to think, that a man possessed with the least common sense should think to be imposed upon in this manner. High delusion it is for us all to awake or we shall be grossly deceived." He took his seat, and I took notice as he spoke that he was much excited, for he trembled and looked angry. I saw that we were about to have confusion, and I called the class to order, and spoke to the class as usual, and soon after dismissed them. The Gentleman of the Mormon Church went on his way, and in a few weeks returned again. I now made up my mind to purchase from him the Book of Mormon, which I did and intended to read it through and keep it to myself. I soon found that the report of my purchase had spread abroad like wild fire. The news rolled around the circuit that brother Pettigrew was ruined, and it was fearful he would be lost. Soon the preacher came who had charge of our circuit; his name was Oglesby. He took his text in the third chapter, first verse, in Galatians. "O foolish Galatians who hath bewitched you that you should not obey the truth." He labored diligently to show the danger of believing any other gospel, or anything else but the holy Bible, and remarked that if an angel, or a plenipotentiary should descend from heaven with any other Gospel then we had in the Bible, he would say let him be accursed and God would say let him be accursed, and Paul would say let him be accursed, and thus he warned us from the Book of Mormon. I persuaded him to take the book with him around the circuit and read it, and I requested him to note all the places that he should find contrary to the gospel of the Bible and bring them to me, which he promised to do. Upon his return the second time, I enquired of him if he had read the book, to which he answered, "No brother Pettigrew, it is not worth reading, it is the most unmeaning thing I ever read. I can show you in a minute." And [he] began to look to find the places, but could not find but one, and that was concerning the hundred and sixteen pages, he thought that if they had been translated once, it might easily be done again, but he too soon saw his mistake and Satan had put it into their hearts to change the words that it should not read the same. The time had now arrived for public preaching, and [he] took his text in the second chapter of Isaiah, and the last verse. "And in that day, a man shall cast his idols of silver and his idols of gold, which every one of them had made for himself to worship to the moles and to the bats, to go into to the cliffs of the rocks and into the tops of the cragged rocks for fear of the Lord, and for the glory of his majesty, when he ariseth to shake terribly the earth, cease ye from man whose breath is in his nostrils, for wherewith is he to be accounted of." Thus was the foundation which he took to build his sermon upon, and after he had gotten through with his sermon he then, exclaimed, "Brother Pettigrew, I now exhort you to call in you[r] neighbors and take your Book of Mormon and burn it a sacrifice to old Molock and let all witness the sight." This gave me peculiar feelings to see a man in the high standing of Doctor Oglesby to treat so lightly upon things which I knew he did not understand. I thought then, "Poor man, he will want to be first into the tops of the cragged rocks, to hide from the glory of his majesty when he ariseth to shake terribly the earth." I cried unto the Lord for help and to give the understanding which would guide me to my duty, and that I might get rid of my office in the class, for my mind was now enlightened and I thought it would not do for me to partake of the sacrament administered in the Methodist Church, as formerly. I kept this to myself and pondered well over these things in my heart. Soon after, I was advised by Doctor Oglesby to withdraw from the class. My place in the class was soon filled by another and I was accordingly released to my heart's desire, and was loosed from the church without any difficulty on my part. These things caused me to draw nearer to the Lord, and he to me and he witnessed to me that he had now begun his work for the last days, and that the Book of Mormon was the true book and by it, I saw that the Lord was the same Lord, and its gospel was the same and its ordinances were the same as those I had been thought to observe. But man, poor man, had changed or transgressed the law, changed the ordinances, and had broken the everlasting covenant, and yet the Lord had spared the earth notwithstanding the many ways, parties, and sects, we had been divided into, and yet none right; but all had gone astray. I truly saw that God was of long suffering and of much patience. My heart was poured out in prayer to my God, and the solemnity of eternity rested upon my mind . . . I, therefore, searched the prophesies and I plainly saw that there was much yet to be fulfilled, and the world was still in the dark as regarding this matter, and my heart was pained and weighed down with sorrow because of the gross darkness that covered the minds of the people . . . I saw that the days of my peace and enjoyment were over if I remained at my place of residence. I, therefore, resolved to change my location. I had heard that the people that believed in the Book of Mormon were gathering in the upper part of the state of Missouri, thither I was determined to go (David Pettigrew, *Autobiography and diary, 1840–1863* [BYU Special Collections], 1–10).

Mary E. Rollins Lightner

(October 1830)

There was a meeting that evening, and we learned that Brother Morley had the Book in his possession the only one in that part of the country. I went to his house just before the meeting was to commence, and asked to see the book; Brother Morley put it in my hand, as I looked at it, I felt such a desire to read it, that I could not refrain from asking him to let me take it home and read it, while he attended meeting. He said it would be too late for me to take it back after meeting, and another thing, he had hardly had time to read a chapter in it himself, and but few of the brethren had even seen it, but I pled so earnestly for it, he finally said, "Child, if you will bring this book home before breakfast tomorrow morning, you may take it." He admonished me to be very careful, and see that no harm came to it.

If any person in this world was ever perfectly happy in the possession of any coveted treasure I was when I had permission to read that wonderful book. Uncle and Aunt were Methodists, so when I got into the house, I exclaimed, "Oh, Uncle, I have got the 'Golden Bible.'" Well, there was consternation in the house for a few moments, and I was severely reprimanded for being so presumptuous as to ask such a favor, when Brother Morley had not read it himself. However, we all took turns reading it until very late in the night as soon as it was light enough to see, I was up and learned the first verse in the book. When I reached Brother Morley's they had been up for only a little while. When I handed him the book, he remarked, "I guess you did not read much in it." I showed him how far we had read. He was surprised and said, "I don't believe you can tell me one word of it." I then repeated the first verse, also the outlines of the history of Nephi. He gazed at me in surprise, and said, "child, take this book home and finish it, I can wait."

Before or about the time I finished the last chapter, the Prophet Joseph Smith arrived in Kirtland, and moved into a part of Newel K. Whitney's house . . . while waiting for his goods to be put in order. Brother Whitney brought the Prophet Joseph to our house and introduced him to the older ones of the family (I was not in at the time.) In looking around he saw the Book of Mormon on the shelf, and asked how that book came to be there. He said, "I sent that book to Brother Morley." Uncle told him how his niece had obtained it. He asked, "Where is your niece?" I was sent for; when he saw me he looked at me so earnestly, I felt almost afraid. After a moment or two he came and put his hands on my head and gave me a great blessing, the first I ever received, and made me a present of the book, and said he would give Brother Morley another. He came in time to rebuke the evil spirits, and set the church in order.

We all felt that he was a man of God, for he spoke with power, and as one having authority in very deed (Mary Lightner, "Mary Elizabeth Rollins Lightner," *The Utah Genealogical and Historical Magazine* 17 [July 1926]: 193–205, 250–60; grammar standardized).

Parley P. Pratt

(Speaking of his first encounter with the Book of Mormon.)

I read it all day; eating was a burden, I had no desire for food; sleep was a burden when the night came, for I preferred reading to sleep.

As I read, the spirit of the Lord was upon me, and I knew and comprehended that the book was true, as plainly and manifestly as a man comprehends and knows that he exists. My joy was now full, as it were, and I rejoiced sufficiently to more than pay me for all the sorrows, sacrifices and toils of my life. I soon determined to see the young man who had been the instrument of its discovery and translation (Parley P. Pratt, *Autobiography of Parley Parker Pratt*, ed. Parley P. Pratt Jr. [Salt Lake City: Deseret Book, 1985], 20).

The joy which filled my bosom in reading that sacred record, waking up our minds and giving us the knowledge of the past dealings of God with the inhabitants of this vast western hemisphere, and of a nation of people as ancient as that of Abraham or of the Jaredites, and giving us a knowledge also of a branch of scattered Israel led away from the land of their fathers 600 years before Christ, and the glorious fact, the most important of all others in the book, that the risen Jesus in his glorified immortal flesh and bones set his feet upon this western hemisphere and ministered publicly to thousands and thousands of the Nephites, blessed them, revealed to them his Gospel in its fulness, and was glorified in their presence ... all these things received in faith in my heart, and by the spirit of knowledge and of light and of understanding, and of hope and joy, and charity filled my heart in a way that I never can express to any being; to have the same joy understood, it must be experienced (*Journal of Discourses*, 3:308).

What would this Gospel do for the people of any age if they would obey it as a people? Whether it were a neighborhood, a town, a city, a nation, or a world ... ? I will tell you. There would be no thieving there any longer, no cheating, no deceiving, no intentional breaking of promises, no wrong dealing, no extortion, no hatred, no envy, and no evil speaking. . . . Because obedience to the Gospel implies repentance, which means nothing more nor less than putting away all our evils, and ceasing to do them. Among the people that obeyed the Gospel there would be no longer adulterers, nor fornicators, nor any other evil that you can name (*Journal of Discourses*, 3:179).

Catherine Smith Salisbury

(Joseph Smith's sister said the following in 1886.)

Many times when I have read its sacred pages, I have wept like a child, while the Spirit has borne witness with my spirit of its truth ("Dear Sisters," *Saints' Herald* 33 [1 May 1886]: 260; as cited in *Stories from the Early Saints Converted by the Book of Mormon*, 19).

Daniel Spencer Jr.

(In 1840, Spencer was a highly successful businessman in West Stockbridge, Massachusetts, when the missionaries arrived. He listened to their message and gave it serious consideration. "One day, when his son was with him in his study, he suddenly burst into a flood of tears, and exclaimed" the following.)

My God, the thing is true, and as an honest man I must embrace it; but it will cost me all I have got on earth.

[He accepted baptism and moved to Nauvoo, where he eventually succeeded Joseph Smith as mayor of the city. He accompanied the smitten Saints in their enforced exodus into the wilderness beyond the Mississippi and, from 1849 to his death in 1868, presided over the Salt Lake Stake] (Andrew Jenson, *Latter-day Saint Biographical Encyclopedia*, 4 vols. [Salt Lake City: Western Epics, 1971], 1:287; as cited in *Stories from the Early Saints Converted by the Book of Mormon*, 74–76).

William E. McLellin

When I first joined the church in 1831, soon I became acquainted with all the Smith family and the Whitmer family, and I heard all their testimonies, which agreed in the main points;

William E. McLellin *(Courtesy of the Church Archives, The Church of Jesus Christ of Latter-day Saints)*

and I believed them then and I believe them yet (Larry C. Porter, "William E. McLellan's Testimony of the Book of Mormon," *BYU Studies* 10 [Summer 1970]: 486).

Luke Johnson

At a conference in Orange, Cuyahoga co., Ohio, I was ordained a High Priest by Joseph Smith. At this Conference the eleven witnesses to the Book of Mormon, with uplifted hands, bore their solemn testimony to the truth of that book, as did also the Prophet Joseph (Luke Johnson, "History of Luke Johnson," *Deseret Weekly News* [26 May 1858]: 57).

Luke Johnson
(Courtesy of the Church Archives, The Church of Jesus Christ of Latter-day Saints)

Joseph Smith Sr.

Most of their former neighbors and friends shunned them; some actively lied about them. Others took advantage of them, ransacked their property, and pressed petty lawsuits.

To Joseph and Lucy's credit, they did not become bitter and vindictive. "We doubted our diligence in prayer before God that [our son] Joseph might be more fully instructed and preserved," wrote Lucy.

A Palmyra resident purchased Joseph Sr.'s note and demanded instant payment but offered to forgive the debt if he would burn the Book of Mormon. Even though he was ill, Joseph refused and went to debtors' prison for several weeks (Donald E. Enders, "Faithful From the First," *Ensign*, January 2001, 56).

$\sim 10 \sim$

JOSEPH AND EMMA

Emma Hale was married to Joseph Smith Jr. on 18 January 1827, in South Bainbridge (now Afton), Chenango County, New York. He was twenty-one years old, and she was twenty-two. They became the parents of nine children and adopted two others. Emma remained a stalwart companion throughout the trials and persecutions that befell her husband, often bearing a large portion of the burdens by herself.

Joseph Smith Jr.

As my father's worldly circumstances were very limited, we were under the necessity of laboring with our hands, hiring out by day['\]s work and otherwise as we could get opportunity, sometimes we were at home and sometimes abroad and by continued labor were enabled to get a comfortable maintenance.

In the year eighteen hundred and twenty-four my father's family met with a great affliction by the death of my eldest brother Alvin. In the month of October eighteen hundred and twenty-five I hired with an old gentleman, by the name of Josiah Stoal who lived in Chenango county State of New York. He had heard something of a silver mine having been opened by the Spaniards in Harmony Susquehanna county State of Pennsylvania, and had previous to my hiring with him been digging in order if possible to discover the mine. After I went to live with him he took me among the rest of his hands to dig for the silver mine, at which I continued to work for nearly a month without success in our undertaking, and finally I prevailed with the old gentleman to cease digging after it. Hence arose the very prevalent story of my having been a money digger.

During the time that I was thus employed I was put to board with a Mr. Isaac Hale of that place; it was there that I first saw my wife (his daughter) Emma Hale. On the eighteenth of January eighteen hundred and twenty-seven we were married while yet I was employed in the service of Mr. Stoal.

Owing to my still continuing to assert that I had seen a vision persecution still followed me, and my wife's father's family were very much opposed to our being married. I was therefore under the necessity of taking her elsewhere so we went and were married at the house of Squire Tarbell, in South Bainbridge Chenango county, New York. Immediately after my marriage I left Mr. Stoal's and went to my father's and farmed with him that season ("History of Joseph Smith," *Times and Seasons* 3 [2 May 1842]: 771–72).

MARRIAGE OF JOSEPH AND EMMA
(18 January 1827)

Lucy Mack Smith

Having made the acquaintance of a couple of gentlemen from Pennsylvania, Mr. Stowell and Mr. Knight, who were desirous of purchasing a quantity of wheat, which we had down on the place, we agreed with them that if they would furnish us with a sum of money requisite for the liquidation of this debt, the wheat should be carried to them in flour the ensuing season. . . .

When the time had nearly come for my husband to set out for Pennsylvania to get the money, Joseph called Mr. Smith and myself aside and told us that he had felt so lonely ever since Alvin's death, that he had come to the conclusion of getting married if we had no objections. He thought that no young woman that he ever was acquainted with was better calculated to render the man of her choice happy than Miss Emma Hale, a young lady whom he had been extremely fond of since his first introduction to her. His father was highly pleased with Joseph's choice, and told him that he was not only willing that he should marry her but desired him to bring her home with him, that we might have the pleasure of her society (Lucy Mack Smith, *The Revised and Enhanced History of Joseph Smith by His Mother,* ed. Scot Facer Proctor and Maurine Jensen Proctor [Salt Lake City: Bookcraft, 1996], 126).

Joseph Knight

Joseph then went to Mr. Stowel's [Stowell] where he had lived some-time before. But Mr. Stowel could not pay him money for his work very well and he came to me perhaps in November and worked for me until about the time that he was married, which I think was in February. And I paid him the money and I furnished him with a horse and cutter [sleigh] to go and see his girl down to Mr. Hales. And soon after this he was married and Mr. Stowel moved him and his wife to his [Joseph's] father's in Palmyra, Ontario County (Joseph Knight, *Reminiscences of Joseph Knight* [LDS Church Archives, Church Historical Department, The Church of Jesus Christ of Latter-day Saints, Salt Lake City]; as cited in Dean C. Jessee, "Joseph Knight's Recollection of Early Mormon History," *BYU Studies* 17 [Autumn 1876]: 32; spelling and capitalization standardized).

Emma Smith

(She recounts to her oldest son a visit she paid to the Stowell home, twenty-five miles from Harmony, where she lived with her parents at the time.)

I was married at South Bainbridge, New York; at the house of Squire Tarbell . . . when I was in my 22nd or 23rd year . . . I was visiting at Mr. Stowell's, who lived in Bainbridge, and saw your father there. I had no intention of marrying when I left home; but, during my visit at Mr. Stowell's, [Joseph] . . . urged me to marry him, and preferring to marry him to any other man I knew, I consented. We went to Squire Tarbell's and were married. . . . The account in Mother Smith's History is substantially correct as to date and place ("Last Testimony of Sister Emma," *The Saints' Herald* 26 [1 October 1879]: 289–90; as cited in Milton V. Backman Jr. *Eyewitness Accounts of the Restoration* [Salt Lake City: Deseret Book, 1986], 54; see also *The Revised and Enhanced History of Joseph Smith*, 136n6).

EMMA SMITH'S CHARACTER

Lucy Mack Smith

(Lucy notes Emma's courageous determination during times of trial.)

Emma's health at this time was quite delicate, yet she did not favor herself on this account, but whatever her hands found to do, she did with her might ... I have never seen a woman in my life, who would endure every species of fatigue and hardship, from month to month, and from year to year, with that unflinching courage, zeal, and patience, which she has ever done; ... She has been tossed upon the ocean of uncertainty—she has breasted the storms of persecution, and buffeted the rage of men and devils, which would have borne down almost any other woman (Lucy Mack Smith, *History of Joseph Smith by His Mother,* ed. Preston Nibley [Salt Lake City: Bookcraft, 1958], 190–91).

Joseph Smith Jr.

(1842)

With what unspeakable delight, and what transports of joy swelled my bosom, when I took by the hand, on that night, my beloved Emma—she that was my wife, even the wife of my youth, and the choice of my heart. Many were the reverberations of my mind when I contemplated for a moment the many scenes we had been called to pass through, the fatigues and the toils, the sorrows and sufferings, and the joys and consolations, from time to time, which had strewed our paths and crowned our board. Oh what a commingling of thought filled my mind for the moment, again she is here, even in the seventh trouble—undaunted, firm, and unwavering—unchangeable, affectionate Emma! (Joseph Smith, *History of The Church of Jesus Christ of Latter-day Saints,* 7 vols., ed. B. H. Roberts [Salt Lake City: Deseret Book, 1964], 5:107).

Emma's Last Dream

Gracia N. Jones

(Gracia was a great-great-granddaughter of Emma and Joseph.)

Emma lived almost thirty-five years after the martyrdom of her Prophet-husband. She died 30 April 1879 in her seventy-fifth year. In her last years she was greatly loved, and in the last hours of her life she was attended by her family: Louis Bidamon, Julia, Joseph III, and Alexander. According to Alexander, Emma seemed to sink away, but then she raised up and stretched out her hand, calling, "Joseph! Joseph!" Falling back on Alexander's arm, she clasped her hands on her bosom, and her spirit was gone. Both Alexander and Joseph thought she was calling for her son Joseph, but later, Alexander learned more about the incident. Sister Elizabeth Revel, Emma's nurse, explained that a few days earlier Emma had told her that Joseph came to her in a vision and said, "Emma, come with me, it is time for you to come with me." "As Emma related it, she said, 'I put on my bonnet and my shawl and went with him; I did not think that it was anything unusual. I went with him into a mansion, and he showed me through the different apartments of that beautiful mansion.' And one room was the nursery. In that nursery was a babe in the cradle. She said, "I knew my babe, my Don Carlos that was taken from me.' She sprang forward, caught the child up in her arms, and wept with joy over the child. When Emma recovered herself sufficient she turned to Joseph and said, 'Joseph, where are the rest of my children.' He said to her, 'Emma, be patient and you shall have all of your children.' Then she saw standing by his side a personage of light, even the Lord Jesus Christ."

Finding this testimony reminded me how precious each soul is in the sight of our Savior, whose compassion and power to save is beyond all comprehension. All of us make mistakes and are in need of repentance. Whenever we withdraw from the fellowship of the Saints and cease to partake of the sacrament on a regular basis, we tend to lose our way and become subject to misunderstanding—especially if our course has been set by real or imagined injury to our feelings, or pride. This could happen to any of us, including my dear great-great-grandmother. . . .

Joseph III recalled in his memoirs that Emma said, as she turned her gaze upward, "Yes, yes, I am coming!"—as if she saw or heard someone beckoning or calling to her (Gracia N. Jones, "My Great-Great-Grandmother, Emma Hale Smith," *Ensign*, August 1992, 37–39).

Joseph Smith Jr.

(In a letter dated 13 October 1832, Joseph Smith expressed his deep affection for his wife.)

My Dear Wife:

This day I have been walking through . . . the City of New Y[ork]. . . . After beholding all that I had any desire to behold, . . . the thoughts of home of Emma and Julia rushed upon my mind like a flood and I could wish for [a] moment to be with them. My breast is filled with all the feelings and tenderness of a parent and a husband, and could I be with you I would tell you many things. . . . I hope you will excuse me for writing this letter so soon after writing, for I feel as if I wanted to say something to you to comfort you in your peculiar trial and present affliction. I hope God will give you strength that you may not faint. I pray God to soften the hearts of those around you to be kind to you and take [the] burden off your shoulders, as much as possible, and not afflict you. I feel for you for I know your state and that others do not, but you must comfort yourself knowing that God is your friend in heaven and that you have one true and living friend on Earth, your husband (*The Personal Writings of Joseph Smith*, 278–79; spelling, grammar, capitalization, and punctuation standardized).

⟫ 11 ⟪

RESTORATION OF THE AARONIC AND MELCHIZEDEK PRIESTHOODS

RESTORATION OF THE AARONIC PRIESTHOOD
(15 May 1829)

Orson Pratt

In the year 1829, Mr. Smith and Mr. Cowdery, having learned the correct mode of baptism, from the teachings of the Savior to the ancient Nephites, as recorded in the "Book of Mormon," had a desire to be baptized; but knowing that no one had authority to administer that sacred ordinance in any denomination, they were at a loss to know how the authority was to be restored, and while calling upon the Lord with a desire to be informed on the subject, a holy angel appeared and stood before them, and laid his hands upon their heads, and ordained them, and commanded them to baptize each other, which they accordingly did (Orson Pratt, *An Interesting Account of Several Remarkable Visions* [Edinburgh: Ballantyne and Hughes, 1840], 23; spelling standardized).

Joseph Smith Jr.

We still continued the work of translation, when, in the ensuing month (May, 1829), we on a certain day went into the woods to pray and inquire of the Lord respecting baptism for the remission of sins, that we found mentioned in the translation of the plates. While we were thus employed, praying and calling upon the Lord, a messenger from heaven descended in a cloud of light, and having laid his hands upon us, he ordained us, saying:

Upon you my fellow servants, in the name of Messiah, I confer the Priesthood of Aaron, which holds the keys of the ministering of angels, and of the gospel of repentance, and of baptism by immersion for the remission of sins; and this shall never be taken again from the earth until the sons of Levi do offer again an offering unto the Lord in righteousness.

He said this Aaronic Priesthood had not the power of laying on hands for the gift of the Holy Ghost, but that this should be conferred on us hereafter; and he commanded us to go and be baptized, and gave us directions that I should baptize Oliver Cowdery, and that afterwards he should baptize me.

Accordingly we went and were baptized. I baptized him first, and afterwards he baptized me—after which I laid my hands upon his head and ordained him to the Aaronic Priesthood, and afterwards he laid his hands on me and ordained me to the same Priesthood—for so we were commanded.

The messenger who visited us on this occasion and conferred this Priesthood upon us, said that his name was John, the same that is called John the Baptist in the New Testament, and that he acted under the direction of Peter, James and John, who held the keys to the Priesthood of Melchizedek, which Priesthood, he said, would in due time be conferred on us, and that I should be called the first Elder of the Church, and he (Oliver Cowdery) the second. It was on the fifteenth day of May, 1829, that we were ordained under the hand of this messenger, and baptized.

Immediately on our coming up out of the water after we had been baptized, we experienced great and glorious blessings from our Heavenly Father. No sooner had I baptized Oliver Cowdery, than the Holy Ghost fell upon him, and he stood up and prophesied many things which should shortly come to pass. And again, as soon as I had been baptized by him, I also had the spirit of prophecy, when, standing up, I prophesied concerning the rise of this Church, and many other things connected with the Church, and this generation of the children of men. We were filled with the Holy Ghost, and rejoiced in the God of our salvation (Joseph Smith–History 1:68–73).

Oliver Cowdery

(Commenting on his experience in helping to translate the Book of Mormon and on seeing John the Baptist appear as a resurrected being.)

These were days never to be forgotten—to sit under the sound of a voice dictated by the *inspiration* of heaven, awakened the utmost gratitude of this bosom! . . .

No men in their sober senses, could translate and write the directions given to the Nephites, from the mouth of the Savior, of the precise manner in which men should build up his church, and especially, when corruption had spread an uncertainty over all forms and systems practiced among men, without desiring a privilege of showing the willingness of the heart by being buried in the liquid grave, to answer a "good conscience by the resurrection of Jesus Christ."

After writing the account given of the Savior's ministry to the remnant of the seed of Jacob, upon this continent, it was easily to be seen, as the prophet said would be, that darkness covered the earth and gross darkness the minds of the people. On reflecting further, it was as easily to be seen, that amid the great strife and noise concerning religion, none had authority from God to administer the ordinances of the gospel. For, the question might be asked, have men authority to administer in the name of Christ, who deny revelations? when *his* testimony is no less than the spirit of prophecy? and his religion based, built, and sustained by immediate revelations in all ages of the world, when he has had a people on earth? If these facts were buried, and carefully concealed by men whose craft would have been in danger, if once permitted to shine in the faces of men, they were no longer to us; and we only waited for the commandment to be given, "Arise and be baptized."

This was not long desired before it was realized. The Lord, who is rich in mercy, and ever willing to answer the consistent prayer of the humble, after we had called upon him in a fervent manner, aside from the abodes of men, condescended to manifest to us his will. On a sudden, as from the midst of eternity, the voice of the Redeemer spake peace to us, while the veil was parted and the angel of God came down clothed with glory, and delivered the anxiously looked for message, and the keys of the gospel of repentance!—What joy! what wonder! what amazement! While the world were racked and distracted—while millions were grouping as the blind for the wall, and while all men were resting upon uncertainty, as a general mass, our eyes beheld—our ears heard. As in the "blaze of day;" yes, more—above the glitter of the May Sun beam, which then shed its brilliancy over the face of nature! Then his voice, though mild, pierced to the center, and his words, "I am thy fellow-servant," dispelled every fear. We listened—we gazed—we admired! 'Twas the voice of the angel from glory—'twas a message from the Most High! and as we heard we rejoiced, while his love enkindled upon our souls, and we were rapt in the vision of the Almighty! Where was room for doubt? No where: uncertainty had fled, doubt had sunk, no more to rise, while fiction and deception had fled forever!

But, dear brother think, further think for a moment, what joy filled our hearts and with what surprise we must have bowed, (for who would not have bowed the knee for such a blessing?) when we received under his hand the holy priesthood, as he said, "upon you my fellow servants, in the name of Messiah I confer this priesthood and this authority, which shall remain upon earth, that the sons of Levi may yet offer an offering unto the Lord in righteousness!"

I shall not attempt to paint to you the feelings of this heart, nor the majestic beauty and glory which surrounded us on this occasion; but you will believe me when I say, that earth, nor men, with the eloquence of time, cannot begin to clothe language in as interesting and sublime a manner as this holy personage. No; nor has this earth power to give the joy, to bestow the peace, or comprehend the wisdom which was contained in each sentence [as] they were delivered by the power of the Holy Spirit! Man may deceive his fellow man; deception may follow deception, and the children of the wicked one may have power to seduce the foolish and untaught, till nought but fiction feeds the many, and the fruit of falsehood carries in its current the giddy to the grave; but one touch with the finger of his love, yes, one ray of glory from the upper world, or one word from the mouth of the Savior, from the bosom of eternity, strikes it *all* into insignificance, and blots it forever from the mind! The assurance that we were in the presence of an angel; the certainty that we heard the voice of Jesus, and the truth unsullied as it flowed from a pure personage, dictated by the will of God, is to me, past description, and I shall ever look upon this expression of the Savior's goodness with wonder and thanksgiving while I am permitted to tarry, and in those mansions where perfection dwells and sin never comes, I hope to adore in that DAY which shall never cease! (Oliver Cowdery,

"Address," *Messenger and Advocate* 1 [October 1834]: 11, 15–16).

Joseph Smith Jr.

[John the Baptist] laid his hands upon my head, and ordained me to a Priest after the order of Aaron, and to hold the keys of this Priesthood, which office was to preach repentance and baptism for the remission of sins, and also to baptize. But I was informed that this office did not extend to the laying on of hands for the giving of the Holy Ghost; that that office was a greater work, and was to be given afterward. . . . [John the Baptist also said] that he acted under the direction of Peter, James and John, who held the keys of the Priesthood of Melchizedek, which Priesthood he said would in due time be conferred on us [Joseph and Oliver] (Joseph Smith, *History of The Church of Jesus Christ of Latter-day Saints*, 7 vols., ed. B. H. Roberts [Salt Lake City: Deseret Book, 1965], 6:250, 1:40–41; punctuation standardized).

RESTORATION OF THE MELCHIZEDEK PRIESTHOOD
(Late May or Early June 1829)

Joseph Smith Jr.

I received the holy priesthood by the ministering of angels to administer the latter of the gospel. I received the high priesthood after the holy order of the son of the living God. I received the power [and the authority] to preach the gospel and administer in the ordinances [thereof]. The keys of the kingdom [were also] conferred upon me (A combination of Joseph Smith Jr. *1832 History* and *1842 History*, as cited in Milton V. Backman Jr., *Eyewitness Accounts of the Restoration* [Salt Lake City: Deseret Book, 1986], 112; this quotation has been changed from third to first person).

Joseph Smith Jr.

(Milton V. Backman has combined various recitals written by Joseph Smith to create the following narrative.)

The Priesthood is everlasting. The Savior, Moses, and Elias gave the keys to Peter, James, and John on the mount, when they were transfigured before him . . . How have we . . . [obtained] the Priesthood in the last days? It came down, in regular succession. Peter, James, and John had it given to them and they gave it to others (*History of the Church*, 3:387).

[The Lord] sent unto [me, Joseph Smith] . . . Peter, James, and John in the wilderness between Harmony, Susquehanna County, and Colesville, Broome County, on the Susquehanna River, declaring themselves as possessing the keys of the kingdom, and of the dispensation of the fullness of times . . . [and] by whom I [was] ordained . . . and confirmed . . . to be apostles, and especial witnesses. [D&C Section 27:12–13, 128:20].

There are, in the Church, two priesthoods, namely, the Melchizedek and Aaronic, including the Levitical Priesthood.

Why the first is called the Melchizedek Priesthood is because Melchizedek was such a great high priest.

Before his day it was called the Holy Priesthood, after the Order of the Son of God.

But out of respect or reverence to the name of the Supreme Being, to avoid the too frequent repetition of his name, they, the Church, in ancient days, called that priesthood after Melchizedek, or the Melchizedek Priesthood. [See D&C Section 107:1–4] (*Eyewitness Accounts of the Restoration*, 113; spelling standardized).

Oliver Cowdery

We [Joseph Smith and Oliver Cowdery] received the high and holy priesthood . . . after . . . we . . . were baptized. I . . . stood in the presence of John, with our departed Joseph, to receive the Lesser Priesthood— and in the presence of Peter, to receive the Greater (Oliver Cowdery, *Oliver Cowdery to Phineas Young, 23 March 1846* [LDS Church Archives, Church Historical Department, The Church of Jesus Christ of Latter-day Saints, Salt Lake City]; as cited in *Eyewitness Accounts of the Restoration*, 114).

Oliver Cowdery

Long after the authority to administer in holy things had been taken away, the Lord opened the heavens and sent forth his word for the salvation of Israel. In fulfillment of the sacred Scripture the everlasting Gospel was proclaimed by the mighty angel, (Moroni) who, clothed with the authority of his mission, gave glory to God in the highest. This Gospel is the "stone taken from the mountain without hands." John the Baptist, holding the keys of the Aaronic Priesthood; Peter, James and John holding the keys of the Melchizedek Priesthood, have also ministered for those who shall be heirs of salvation, and with these ministrations ordained men to the same Priesthoods. These Priesthoods, with their authority, are now, and must continue to be, in the body of the Church of Jesus Christ of Latter-day Saints . . . In connection with Joseph the Seer, [I] was blessed with the above ministrations (Oliver Cowdery, *Statement of Oliver Cowdery to Samuel W. Richards, 13 Jan. 1849* [LDS Church Archives], n.p.; spelling standardized).

Orson Pratt

A revelation and restoration to the earth of the *everlasting gospel* through the angel Moroni would be of no benefit to the nations, unless some one should be ordained with authority to preach it and administer its ordinances. Moroni might reveal a book containing a beautiful and glorious system of salvation, but no one could obey even its first glorious principles without a legally authorized administrator, ordained to preach, baptize, lay on hands for the gifts of the Holy Ghost, etc. Did Moroni ordain Mr. Smith to the apostleship, and command him to administer ordinances? No, he did not. But why not confer authority by ordination, as well as reveal the everlasting gospel? Because in all probability he had no right so to do. All angels have not the same authority—they do not all hold the same keys. . . . How then did Mr. Smith obtain the office of an apostle, if Moroni had no authority to ordain him to such office? Mr. Smith testifies that Peter, James, and John came to him in the capacity of ministering angels, and by the laying on hands ordained him an apostle, and commanded him to preach, baptize, lay on hands for the gift of the Holy Ghost, and administer all the ordinances of the gospel as they themselves did in ancient days.

We consider the restoration of the Aaronic priesthood [by John the Baptist] to be among some of the most important events of the last dispensation. . . . As this priesthood has not authority to administer the laying on of hands for the gift of the Holy Ghost . . . Peter, James, and John appeared as ministering angels, and conferred the Apostleship upon Joseph Smith and others; after which they were authorized to confirm the Church by the laying on of hands (Orson Pratt, *Divine Authority of the Book of Mormon* [Liverpool, England: R. James, 1850], 59; as cited in *Eyewitness Accounts of the Restoration,* 114–15).

Joseph Smith Jr.
(Original punctuation and capitalization have been preserved.)

We continued to translate, at intervals, when not necessitated to attend to the numerous enquirers, that now began to visit us; some for the sake of finding the truth, others for the purpose of putting hard questions, and trying to confound us. Among the latter class were several learned priests who generally came for the purpose of disputation: however the Lord continued to pour out upon us his Holy Spirit, and as often as we had need, he gave us in that moment what to say; so that although unlearned, and inexperienced in religious controversies, yet were we able to confound those learned Rabbis of the day, whilst at the same time, we were enabled to convince the honest in heart, that we had obtained (through the mercy of God) to the true and everlasting gospel of Jesus Christ, so that almost daily we administered the ordinance of baptism for the remission of sins, to such as believed. We now became anxious to have that promise realized to us, which the angel that conferred upon us the Aaronic Priesthood had given us, viz: that provided we continued faithful; we should also have the Melchizedek Priesthood, which holds the authority of the laying on of hands for the gift of the Holy Ghost. We had for some time made this matter a subject of humble prayer, and at length we got together in the chamber of Mr. Whitmer's house in order more particularly to seek of the Lord what we now so earnestly desired: and here to our unspeakable satisfaction did we realize the truth of the Savior's promise; "Ask, and you shall receive, seek, and you shall find, knock and it shall be opened unto you;" for we had not long been engaged in solemn and fervent prayer, when the word of the Lord, came unto us in the chamber, commanding us; that I should ordain Oliver Cowdery to be an elder in the church of Jesus Christ, and that he also should ordain me to the same office, and then to ordain others as it should be made known to us, from time to time: we were however commanded to defer this our ordination until, such times, as it should be practicable to have our brethren, who had been and who should be baptized, assembled together, when we must have their sanction to our thus proceeding to ordain each other, and have them decide by vote whether they were willing to accept us as spiritual teachers, or not, when also we were commanded to bless bread and break it with them, and to take wine, bless it, and drink it with them, [and] afterward proceed to ordain each other according to commandment, then call out such men as the spirit should dictate, and ordain them, and then attend to the laying on of hands for the gift of the Holy Ghost, upon all those whom we had previously baptized; doing all things in the name of the Lord.

The following commandment will further illustrate the nature of our calling to this Priesthood as well as that of others who were yet to be sought after.

Revelation to Joseph Smith, Jr. Oliver Cowdery and David Whitmer, making known the calling of twelve apostles in these last days, and also, instructions relative to building up the church of Christ, according to the fullness of the gospel: given in Fayette, New York, June, 1829. [See also D&C 18:1–2, 9, 14–15, 26–27, 37–39.]

Now behold, because of the thing which you, my servant Oliver Cowdery, have desired to know of me, I give unto you these words: behold I have manifested unto you, by my Spirit in many instances, that the things which you have written are true: wherefore you know that they are true . . .

And now Oliver Cowdery, I speak unto you, and also unto David Whitmer, by the way of commandment: . . . you are called to cry repentance unto this people. And if it so be that you should labor all your days, in crying repentance unto this people, and bring save it be one soul unto me, how great shall be your joy with him in the kingdom of my Father? . . .

And now behold, there are others who are called to declare my gospel, both unto Gentile and unto Jew: yea, even twelve. and the twelve shall be my disciples, and they shall take upon them my name: and the twelve are they who shall desire to take upon them my name, with full purpose of heart . . .

And now behold I give unto you, Oliver Cowdery, and also unto David Whitmer, that you shall search out the twelve who shall have the desires of which I have spoken; and by their desires and their works, you shall know them: and when you have found them you shall show these things unto them ("History of Joseph Smith," *Times and Seasons* 3 [15 September 1842]: 915–17; spelling standardized).

David Whitmer

In June, 1829 ... I was baptized, confirmed, and ordained an Elder ... by Bro. Joseph Smith. Previous to this, Joseph Smith and Oliver Cowdery had baptized, confirmed and ordained each other to the office of an Elder (David Whitmer, *An Address to All Believers in Christ* [Richmond, Missouri: David Whitmer, 1887], 32).

David Whitmer
(Courtesy of the Church Archives, The Church of Jesus Christ of Latter-day Saints)

~ 12 ~

ORGANIZATION OF THE CHURCH

While translating the Book of Mormon, Joseph received a revelation to organize the Church of Jesus Christ. In accordance with the outline the Lord revealed to him concerning the day and manner the organization was to occur, the restored church became lawfully organized on Tuesday, 6 April 1830. Thus, The Church of Jesus Christ of Latter-day Saints was established in harmony with four undergirding principles, namely: in agreement with the laws of the land; by the consent of the people; with the authority of the holy priesthood; and according to the will of God, by His divine directive. It will therefore roll on, as Daniel prophesied, until it fills the whole earth (see Daniel 2:34–35). It will be preached to all nations. As the Savior declared, "This gospel of the kingdom shall be preached in all the world for a witness unto all nations; and then shall the end come" (Matthew 24:14). And though it may be few in number compared to other organizations, it will eventually cover the entire earth just as the ancient prophets Enoch and Nephi foresaw (see Moses 7:62 and 1 Nephi 14:12).

Joseph Smith Jr.

The Lord continue[d] to give us instructions from time to time, concerning the duties which now devolved upon us; and among many other things of the kind, we obtained of Him the following, by the spirit of prophecy and revelation; which not only gave us much information, but also pointed out to us the precise day [April 6, 1830]upon which, according to His will and commandment, we should proceed to organize His Church once more here upon the earth (Joseph Smith, *History of The Church of Jesus Christ of Latter-day Saints*, 7 vols., ed. B. H. Roberts [Salt Lake City: Deseret Book, 1978], 1:64).

Joseph Smith Jr.

We had not long been engaged in solemn and fervent prayer, when the word of the Lord came unto us in the chamber [of the Whitmer home], commanding us that I should ordain Oliver Cowdery to be an

Peter Whitmer Home
(Courtesy of the Church Archives, The Church of Jesus Christ of Latter-day Saints)

Elder in the Church of Jesus Christ; and that he also should ordain me to the same office; and then to ordain others, as it should be made known unto us from time to time. We were, however, commanded to defer this our ordination until such times as it should be practicable to have our brethren, who had been and who should be baptized, assembled together, when we must have their sanction ... to ordain each other, and have them decide by vote whether they were willing to accept us as spiritual teachers or not; when also we were commanded to bless bread and break it with them, and to take wine, bless it, and drink it with them; afterward proceed to ordain each other according to the commandment; then call out such men as the Spirit should dictate, and ordain them; and then attend to the laying on of hands for the gift of the Holy Ghost, upon all those whom we had previously baptized, doing all things in the name of the Lord (*History of the Church*, 1:60–61).

Joseph Smith Jr.

Whilst the Book of Mormon was in the hands of the printer, we still continued to bear testimony and give information, as far as we had opportunity; and also made known to our brethren, that we had received commandment to organize the Church, and accordingly we met together for that purpose, at the house of the above mentioned Mr. [Peter] Whitmer [Sr.], (being six in number) on Tuesday, the sixth day of April, A. D. one thousand eight hundred and thirty. [See *History of the Church*, 1:74.]

Having opened the meeting by solemn prayer to our Heavenly Father we proceeded (according to previous commandment) to call on our brethren to know whether they accepted us as their teachers in the things of the kingdom of God, and whether they were satisfied that we should proceed and be organized as a church according to said commandment which we had received. To these they consented by an unanimous vote. I then laid my hands upon Oliver Cowdery and ordained him an elder of the "Church of Jesus Christ of Latter-day Saints;" after which he ordained me also to the office of an elder of said Church. We then took bread, blessed and brake it with them; also wine, blessed it, and drank it with them. We then laid our hands on each individual member of the Church present that they might receive the gift of the Holy Ghost, and be confirmed members of the Church of Christ. The Holy Ghost was poured out upon us to a very great degree—some prophesied, whilst we all praised the Lord and rejoiced exceedingly. Whilst yet together, I received the following commandment:

Behold, there shall be a record kept among you; and in it thou shalt be called a seer, a translator, a prophet, an apostle of Jesus Christ, an elder of the church through the will of God the Father, and the grace of your Lord Jesus Christ, being inspired of the Holy Ghost to lay the foundation thereof, and to build it up unto the most holy faith. Which church was organized and established in the year of your Lord eighteen hundred and thirty, in the fourth month, and on the sixth day of the month which is called April.

Wherefore, meaning the church, thou shalt give heed unto all his words and commandments which he shall give unto you as he receiveth them, walking in all holiness before me; for his word ye shall receive, as if from mine own mouth, in all patience and faith. . . .

For, behold, I will bless all those who labor in my vineyard with a mighty blessing, and they shall believe on his words, which are given him through me by the Comforter, which manifesteth that Jesus was crucified by sinful men for the sins of the world, yea, for the remission of sins unto the contrite heart. Wherefore it behooveth me that he [Joseph Smith] should be ordained by you, Oliver Cowdery mine apostle; this being an ordinance unto you, that you are an elder under his hand, he being the first unto you, that you might be an elder unto this church of Christ, bearing my name—And the first preacher of this church unto the church, and before the world, yea, before the Gentiles; yea, and thus saith the Lord God, lo, lo! to the Jews also. Amen. [See D&C Section 21:1–5, 9–12.]

We now proceeded to call out and ordain some others of the brethren to different offices of the priesthood, according as the Spirit manifested unto us; and after a happy time spent in witnessing and feeling for ourselves the powers and the blessings of the Holy Ghost, through the grace of God bestowed upon us, we dismissed with the pleasing knowledge that we were now individually members of, and acknowledged of God, "The Church of Jesus Christ," organized in accordance with commandments and revelations given by him to ourselves in the last days, as well as according to the order of the Church as recorded in the New Testament.

Several persons who had attended the above meeting and got convinced of the truth, came forward shortly after, and were received into the Church; among the rest, my own father and mother were baptized, to my great joy and consolation; and about the same time Martin Harris and A. [Orrin Porter] Rockwell (A combination of "History of Joseph Smith," *Times & Seasons* 3 [15 October 1842]: 944–45; "History of Joseph Smith," *Times & Seasons* 4 [15 November 1842]: 12; and Joseph Smith Jr., "Church History," *Times & Seasons* 3 [1 March 1842]: 708; as cited in Milton V. Backman Jr. *Eyewitness Accounts of the Restoration* [Salt Lake City: Deseret Book, 1986], 187–89).

Doctrine and Covenants 20:1–12

(These verses reveal the day the Church was to be organized.)

The rise of the Church of Christ in these last days, being one thousand eight hundred and thirty years since the coming of our Lord and Savior Jesus Christ in the flesh, it being regularly organized and established agreeable to the laws of our country, by the will and commandments of God, in the fourth month, and on the sixth day of the month which is called April—

Which commandments were given to Joseph Smith, Jun., who was called of God, and ordained an apostle of Jesus Christ, to be the first elder of this church;

And to Oliver Cowdery, who was also called of God, an apostle of Jesus Christ, to be the second elder of this church, and ordained under his hand; and this according to the grace of our Lord and Savior Jesus Christ, to whom be all glory, both now and forever. Amen.

After it was truly manifested unto this first elder that he had received a remission of his sins, he was entangled again in the vanities of the world;

But after repenting, and humbling himself sincerely, through faith, God ministered unto him by an holy angel, whose countenance was as lightning, and whose garments were pure and white above all other whiteness;

And gave unto him commandments which inspired him;

And gave him power from on high, by the means which were before prepared, to translate the Book of Mormon;

Which contains a record of a fallen people, and the fullness of the gospel of Jesus Christ to the Gentiles and to the Jews also;

Which was given by inspiration, and is confirmed to others by the ministering of angels, and is declared unto the world by them—

Proving to the world that the holy scriptures are true, and that God does inspire men and call them to his holy work in this age and generation, as well as in generations of old;

Thereby showing that he is the same God yesterday, today, and forever. Amen.

David Whitmer

The reason why we met on that day [April 6, 1830] was this; the world had been telling us that we were not a regularly organized church, and we had no right to officiate in the ordinance of marriage, hold church property, etc., and that we should organize according to the laws of the land. On this account we met at my father's house in Fayette, N.Y., on April 6, 1830, to attend to this matter of organizing according to the laws of the land (David Whitmer, *An Address to All Believers in Christ* [Richmond, Missouri: David Whitmer, 1887], 33).

David Whitmer

In June, 1829, the Lord gave us the name by which we must call the church, being the same as He gave the Nephites. We obeyed His commandment, and called it THE CHURCH OF CHRIST (*An Address to All Believers in Christ*, 73).

[On April 6, 1830, the Church was originally named *The Church of Jesus Christ*, and in an 1835 revelation the name was designated as *The Church of Jesus Christ of Latter-day Saints* (see D&C 115:1–4).]

Oliver Cowdery

(Taken from an 1846 letter to Phineas Young.)

You say you are having a meeting on the 6th of April. Brother Phineas, I could be with you, and tell you about the 6th of April 1830, when but six men then only belonged to the Church, and how we looked forward to the future (Oliver Cowdery, *Letter from Oliver Cowdery to Phineas H. Young, 23 March 1846* [LDS Church Archives, Church Historical Department, The Church of Jesus Christ of Latter-day Saints, Salt Lake City]; as cited in Larry E. Morris, *A Treasury of Latter-day Saint Letters* (Salt Lake City: Eagle Gate, 2001), 79).

Events in the Organizing Meeting

W. Jeffrey Marsh

David Whitmer recalled that the meeting took place about noon (Edward Stevenson, *Letter of Edward Stevenson to Orson Pratt, 23 December 1877*; as cited in Larry C. Porter, "Organizational Origins of the Church of Jesus Christ, 6 April 1830," *Regional Studies in Latter-day Saint Church History: New York*, ed. Larry C. Porter, Milton V. Backman Jr., and Susan Easton Black [Provo, Utah: Brigham Young University, 1992], 158).

Joseph stood before the others and explained the purpose of the meeting, indicating it was being held according to the instructions he had received by revelation. Joseph then invited all present to kneel with him in solemn prayer.

Joseph arose and extended to those present the privilege to express their willingness to accept Joseph Smith and Oliver Cowdery as "their teachers in the things of the Kingdom of God." The group unanimously assented. Joseph also asked "whether they were satisfied that [they] should proceed and be organized as a Church according to said commandment . . . They [again] consented by a unanimous vote" (*History of the Church*, 1:77).

This introduced the doctrine of common consent, according to the commandment of the Lord, as a principle of Church practice. All decisions in the Church should be presented to the membership and sustained by them—a practice that continues today.

"After securing the consent of all present, the Prophet ordained Oliver Cowdery an elder in the Church of Jesus Christ. Following his ordination, Oliver laid his hands upon the head of Joseph and ordained him to the office of elder in Christ's church" (Ivan J. Barrett, *Joseph Smith and the Restoration* [Provo, Utah: Brigham Young University, 1974)] 129). They had both previously received the Melchizedek priesthood under the hands of Peter, James and John, but were instructed to defer ordaining each other to the specific office of Elder until the Church was organized (*History of the Church*, 1:61).

The Sacrament of the Lord's Supper was then administered. Joseph and Oliver blessed and passed the emblems of the Sacrament (the bread and wine of the Lord's Supper) with those present. The prayers for blessing the Sacrament had been received earlier by revelation (D&C 20:75–59).

Joseph and Oliver then confirmed, by laying on of hands, those who had been previously baptized, as members of the Church of Christ and bestowed upon them the gift of the Holy Ghost. The effect was immediate: "The Holy Ghost was poured out upon us to a very great degree—some prophesied, whilst we all praised the Lord, and rejoiced exceedingly" (*History of the Church*, 1:78).

Joseph said, "We then proceeded to call out and ordain some others of the brethren to different offices of the Priesthood, according as the Spirit manifested unto us: and after a happy time spent in witnessing and feeling for ourselves the powers and blessings of the Holy Ghost, through the grace of God bestowed upon us, we dismissed with the pleasing knowledge that we were now individually members of, and acknowledged of God, 'The Church of Jesus Christ,' organized in accordance with commandments and revelations given by Him to ourselves in these last days, as well as according to the order of the Church as recorded in the New Testament" (*History of the Church*, 1:79).

Another impressive event occurred that same day when the Prophet Joseph received a revelation, later designated as Doctrine and Covenants Section 21. In it, the Lord indicated that a record was to be kept and that Joseph was called to be a "seer, a translator, a prophet, an apostle of Jesus Christ, [and] an elder" (D&C 21:1). Members of the Church were further commanded by the Lord:

Wherefore, meaning the church, thou shalt give heed unto all his words and commandments which he shall give unto you as he receiveth them, walking in all holiness before me; For his word ye shall receive, as if from mine own mouth, in all patience and faith. For by doing these things the gates of hell shall not prevail against you; yea, and the Lord God will disperse the powers of darkness from before you, and cause the heavens to shake for your good, and his name's glory. (D&C 21:4–6)

In the same revelation, Oliver was called to be the first preacher in the Church (D&C 21:12). He delivered the first public discourse in the Whitmer home the following Sunday on April 11, 1830.

At some point during the April 6th meeting, the small congregation was called upon to ratify a document called the *Articles and Covenants of the Church*, later known as Doctrine and Covenants Section 20. It stipulated that the members of the Church were "to meet in conference once in three months, or from time to time as said conferences shall direct or appoint."[11] The first of these general conferences was convened, as directed, three months later on June 9, 1830 in the Whitmer home with approximately thirty members assembled. Joseph Smith read Ezekiel chapter fourteen and then offered a prayer. Of the experience that followed, the Saints recorded:

> Much exhortation and instruction was given, and the Holy Ghost was poured out upon us in a miraculous manner—many of our number prophesied, whilst others had the heavens opened to their view . . . The goodness and the condescension of a merciful God . . . create[d] within us sensations of rapturous gratitude, and inspire[d] us with fresh zeal and energy, in the cause of truth. ("History of Joseph Smith," *Times and Seasons* [December 1842]: 4:23)

～ 13 ～

EARLY MEETINGS AND
CONFERENCES OF THE CHURCH

"THE VISIONS OF HEAVEN WERE
OPENED TO MY VIEW"
(April 1830)

Joseph Smith Jr.

*(During a meeting held in 1830, Joseph Smith Jr. performed the
restored Church's first miracle by casting an evil spirit out of
Newel Knight; original punctuation and capitalization have
been preserved.)*

During this month of April I went on a visit to the residence of
Mr. Joseph Knight, of Colesville, Broome co. N. Y., . . . We held several
meetings in the neighborhood, we had many friends, and some enemies.
Our meetings were well attended, and many began to pray fervently
to Almighty God, that he would give them wisdom to understand the
truth. Amongst those who attended our meetings regularly, was Newel
Knight son to Joseph Knight. He and I had many and serious conversations on the important subject of man's eternal salvation: we had got
into the habit of praying much at our meetings and Newel had said that
he would try and take up his cross, and pray vocally during meeting; but
when we again met together he rather excused himself; I tried to prevail
upon him making use of the figure, supposing that he should get into a
mud-hole would he not try to help himself out? and that we were willing

now to help him out of the mud-hole, he replied that provided he had got into a mud-hole through carelessness, he would rather wait and get out himself, than have others to help him, and so he would wait until he should get into the woods by himself, and there he would pray. Accordingly, he deferred praying until [the] next morning, when he retired into the woods; where (according to his own account afterwards) he made several attempts to pray but could scarcely do so, feeling that he had not done his duty, but that he should have prayed in the presence of others. He began to feel uneasy, and continued to feel worse both in mind and body, until upon reaching his own house, his appearance was such as to alarm his wife very much. He requested her to go and bring me to him. I went and found him suffering very much in his mind, and his body acted upon in a very strange manner. His visage and limbs distorted and twisted in every shape and appearance possible to imagine; and finally he was caught up off the floor of the apartment and tossed about most fearfully. His situation was soon made known to his neighbors and relatives, and in a short time as many as eight or nine grown persons had got together to witness the scene. After he had thus suffered for a time, I succeeded in getting hold of him by the hand, when almost immediately he spoke to me, and with great earnestness requested of me, that I should cast the devil out of him, saying that he knew he was in him, and that he also knew that I could cast him out. I replied, "if you know that I can it shall be done," and then almost unconsciously I rebuked the devil; and commanded him in the name of Jesus Christ to depart from him; when immediately Newel spoke out and said that he saw the devil leave him and vanish from his sight.

This was the first miracle which was done in this church or by any member of it, and it was done not by man nor by the power of man, but it was done by God, and by the power or godliness: therefore let the honor and the praise, the dominion and the glory be ascribed to the Father, Son, and Holy Spirit for ever and ever Amen ("History of Joseph Smith," *Times & Seasons* 4 [15 November 1842]: 12–13; spelling standardized).

Joseph Smith Jr.

(Immediately after the evil spirit was cast out, the Prophet was wrapped in heavenly vision.)

The scene was now entirely changed, for as soon as the devil had departed from our friend, his countenance became natural, his distortions of body ceased, and almost immediately the spirit of the Lord descended upon him, and the visions of eternity were opened to his view.—He afterwards related his experience as follows: "I now began to feel a most pleasing sensation resting upon me, and immediately the visions of heaven were opened to my view. I felt myself attracted upward, and remained for some time enwrapped in contemplation, insomuch that I knew not what was going on in the room. By and by I felt some weight pressing upon my shoulder and the side of my head; which served to recall me to a sense of my situation, and I found that the spirit of the Lord had actually caught me up off the floor, and that my shoulder and head were pressing against the beams."

All this was witnessed by many, to their great astonishment and satisfaction, when they saw the devil thus cast out; and the power of God and his holy spirit thus made manifest. So soon as consciousness returned, his bodily weakness was such that we were obliged to lay him upon his bed and wait upon him for some time. As may be expected, such a scene as this contributed much to make believers of those who witnessed it, and finally, the greater part of them became members of the Church.

Soon after this occurrence I returned to Fayette, Seneca County. The Book of Mormon, ('The stick of Joseph in the hands of Ephraim') had now been published for some time, and as the ancient prophet had predicted of it: "It was accounted as a strange thing." No small stir was created by its appearance; great opposition and much persecution followed the believers of its authenticity; but it had now come to pass that truth had sprung out of the earth; and righteousness had looked down from heaven—so we feared not our opponents, knowing that we had both truth and righteousness on our side; that we had both the Father and the Son, because we had the doctrines of Christ, and abided in them; and therefore we continued to preach, and to give information to all who were willing to hear ("History of Joseph Smith," *Times & Seasons* 4 [1 December 1842]: 22; original capitalization and punctuation preserved; spelling standardized).

First General Conference of the Church
(9 June 1830)

The first general conference of the Church was held in the home of Peter and Mary Whitmer, three months after the Church was organized. In addition to spiritual instruction, the members also received numerous spiritual manifestations throughout the proceedings. In this first general conference, convened three months after the Church was organized, the Saints recorded:

Joseph Smith Jr.

Much exhortation and instruction was given, and the Holy Ghost was poured out upon us in a miraculous manner—many of our number prophesied, whilst others had the heavens opened to their view . . . The goodness and condescension of a merciful God . . . create[d] within us sensations of rapturous gratitude, and inspire[d] us with fresh zeal and energy in the cause of truth (Joseph Smith, *History of The Church of Jesus Christ of Latter-day Saints*, 7 vols., ed. B. H. Roberts [Salt Lake City: Deseret Book, 1978], 1:84–86).

Joseph Smith Jr.

On the ninth day of June, 1830, we held our first conference as an organized Church. Our numbers were about thirty, besides whom many assembled with us, who were either believers or anxious to learn. Having opened by singing and prayer, we partook together of the emblems of the body and blood of our Lord Jesus Christ. We then proceeded to confirm several who had lately been baptized, after which we called out and ordained several to the various offices of the Priesthood. Much exhortation and instruction was given, and the Holy Ghost was poured out upon us in a miraculous manner—many of our number prophesied, whilst others had the heavens opened to their view, and were so overcome that we had to lay them on beds or other convenient places; among the rest was Brother Newel Knight, who had to be placed on a bed, being unable to help himself. By his own account of the transaction, he could not understand why we should lay him on the bed, as he felt no sense of weakness. He felt his heart filled with love, with glory, and pleasure unspeakable, and could discern all that was going on in the room; when all of a sudden a vision of the future burst upon him. He saw there represented the great work which through my instrumentality was yet to be accomplished. He saw heaven opened, and beheld the Lord Jesus Christ, seated at the right hand of the majesty on high, and had it made plain to his understanding that the time would come when he would be admitted into His presence to enjoy His society for ever and ever. When their bodily strength was restored to these brethren, they shouted hosannas to God and the Lamb, and rehearsed the glorious things which they had seen and felt, whilst they were yet in the spirit.

Such scenes as these were calculated to inspire our hearts with joy unspeakable, and fill us with awe and reverence for that Almighty Being, by whose grace we had been called to be instrumental in bringing about, for the children of men, the enjoyment of such glorious blessings as were now at this time poured out upon us. To find ourselves engaged in the very same order of things as observed by the holy Apostles of old; to realize the importance and solemnity of such proceedings; and to witness and feel with our own natural senses, the like glorious manifestations of the powers of the Priesthood, the gifts and blessings of the Holy Ghost, and the goodness and condescension of a merciful God unto such as obey the everlasting Gospel of our Lord Jesus Christ, combined to create within us sensations of rapturous gratitude, and inspire us with fresh zeal and energy in the cause of truth (*History of the Church*, 1:84–86).

Jeffrey R. Holland

There they were, approximately 30 members of the Church meeting in that tiny Peter Whitmer home in Fayette, planning to overthrow the Prince of Darkness and establish the kingdom of God in all the world. All the world? What presumption! Were they demented? Had they lost all power to reason? Thirty very average, garden variety Latter-day Saints willing to work with the rest of their lives? To what end? Persecution and pain and maybe 30 more members—for a grand total of 60? Perhaps they did see how limited their immediate personal success would be and maybe they even saw the trouble ahead, but they saw something more. It was all in that business of the influence of the Holy

Ghost and heavens being opened to their view. President John Taylor said later of that experience:

"A few men assembled in a log cabin; they saw the visions of heaven, and gazed upon the eternal world; they looked through the rent vista of futurity, and beheld the glories of eternity; . . . they were laying a foundation for the salvation of the world" (*History of the Church*, 6: 295) (Jeffrey R. Holland, "However Long and Hard the Road," *The New Era* [September 1983]: 38).

FALSE VISIONS OF HIRAM PAGE
(1830)

In 1830, Hiram Page, one of the eight witnesses to the Book of Mormon, possessed a stone through which he claimed to receive revelations about the building of Zion and the order of the Church. Oliver Cowdery, the Whitmer family, and others believed these claims. However, the Prophet Joseph Smith said the claims "were entirely at variance with the order of God's house, as laid down in the New Testament, as well as in our late revelations" (*History of the Church*, 1:109–10).

The Prophet prayed about the matter and received a revelation in which the Lord made it clear that only the President of the Church has the right to receive revelations for the Church (see D&C 28). The Lord instructed Oliver Cowdery to tell Hiram Page that the revelations that came through the stone were from the Adversary (see D&C 28:11). After hearing the Lord's instructions, "Brother Page, as well as the whole Church who were present, renounced the said stone, and all things connected therewith" (*History of the Church*, 1:115).

Doctrine and Covenants 28:1–7, 11–13

Behold, I say unto thee, Oliver, that it shall be given unto thee that thou shalt be heard by the church in all things whatsoever thou shalt teach them by the Comforter, concerning the revelations and commandments which I have given.

But, behold, verily, verily, I say unto thee, no one shall be appointed to receive commandments and revelations in this church excepting my servant Joseph Smith, Jun., for he receiveth them even as Moses.

And thou shalt be obedient unto the things which I shall give unto him, even as Aaron, to declare faithfully the commandments and the revelations, with power and authority unto the church.

And if thou are led at any time by the Comforter to speak or teach, or at all times by the way of commandment unto the church, thou mayest do it.

But thou shalt not write by way of commandment, but by wisdom;

And thou shalt not command him who is at they head, and at the head of the church;

For I have given unto him the keys of the mysteries, and the revelations which are sealed, until I shall appoint unto them another in his stead.

And again, thou shalt take thy brother, Hiram Page, between him and thee alone, and tell him that those things which he hath written from that stone are not of me and that Satan deceiveth him;

For, behold, these things have not been appointed unto him, neither shall anything be appointed unto any of this church contrary to the church covenants.

For all things must be done in order, and by common consent in the church, by the prayer of faith.

THIRD GENERAL CONFERENCE OF THE CHURCH
(January 1831)

In January of 1831, it was decided that a third general conference should be held. During this time, section 38 of the Doctrine and Covenants was revealed. The commandments in this revelation required much sacrifice from the saints, including moving from their homes from New York to Ohio, for their protection and safety. They were promised great blessings for their faithfulness (see D&C 38: 31–32).

John Whitmer

(John recorded the reactions of the Saints to this challenging commandment.)

The time had now come for the general conference to be held. Which was the first of January 1831, and according to this appointment the Saints assembled themselves together. After transacting the necessary business, Joseph the Seer addressed the congregation and exhorted them to stand fast, looking forward considering the end of their salvation. The solemnities of eternity rested on the congregation and having previously received a revelation to go to Ohio, they desired to know somewhat more concerning this matter. Therefore, the Seer enquired of the Lord in the presence of the whole congregation, and thus came the word of the Lord saying: (see D&C 38.)

After the Lord had manifested the above words, through Joseph the Seer, there were some divisions among the congregations, some would not receive the above as the word of the Lord: but that Joseph had invented it himself to deceive the people that in the end he might get gain. Now this was because, their hearts were not right in the sight of the Lord, for they wanted to serve God and man; but our Savior has declared that it was impossible to do so.

The conference was now closed, and the Lord had manifested his will to his people. Therefore they made preparations to journey to the Ohio, with their wives, and children and all that they possessed, to obey the commandment of the Lord (John Whitmer, "The Book of John Whitmer Kept by Commandment," in *Writings of Early Latter-day Saints and Their Contemporaries, A Database Collection*, comp. Milton V. Backman [Provo, Utah: BYU Religious Studies Center, 1996], n.p.; original punctuation preserved).

FOURTH GENERAL CONFERENCE OF THE CHURCH
(3 June 1831)

On June 3, 1831, the fourth general conference of the Church was held at Isaac Morley's home in Kirtland, Ohio. During this conference the spirit was poured out in great abundance upon the Saints. At the same time, the Adversary also made his presence known amongst the Lord's people, requiring the faithful Saints to call upon the name of the Lord for deliverance.

Joseph Smith Jr.

On the 3rd of June, the Elders from the various parts of the country where they were laboring, came in; and the conference before appointed, convened in Kirtland; and the Lord displayed His power to the most perfect satisfaction of the Saints. The man of sin was revealed, and the authority of the Melchizedek Priesthood was manifested and conferred for the first time upon several of the Elders. It was clearly evident that the Lord gave us power in proportion to the work to be done, and strength according to the race set before us, and grace and help as our needs required. Great harmony prevailed; several were ordained; faith was strengthened; and humility, so necessary for the blessing of God to follow prayer, characterized the Saints (*History of the Church*, 1:175–77).

John Whitmer

June 3, 1831, a general conference was called, and a blessing promised, if the elders were faithful, and humble before him. Therefore, the elders assembled from the East and the West, from the North and the South. And also many members. Conference was opened by prayer and exhortation by Joseph Smith, Jr., the Revelator. After the business of the Church was attended to according to the covenants. The Lord made manifest to Joseph that it was necessary that such of the elders as were considered worthy, should be ordained to the High Priesthood.

The spirit of the Lord fell upon Joseph in an unusual manner. And prophesied that John the Revelator was then among the ten tribes of

Israel who had been led away by Salmanasar King of Israel [should be Assyria], to prepare them for their return, from their long dispersion, to again possess the land of their fathers. He prophesied many more things that I have not written. After he had prophesied he laid his hands upon Lyman Wight [and ordained him] to the High Priesthood after the Holy Order of God. And the spirit fell upon Lyman, and he prophesied, concerning the coming of Christ, he said that there were some in the congregation that should live until the Savior should descend from heaven, with a shout, with all the holy angels with him. He said the coming of the Savior should be, like the sun rising in the east, and will cover the whole earth, so will the coming of the Son of man be, yea, he will appear in his brightness and consume all before him. And the hills will be laid low, and the valleys be exalted; and the crooked be made straight; and the rough smooth. And some of my brethren shall suffer martyrdom, for the sake of the religion of Jesus Christ, and seal the testimony of Jesus with their blood.

He saw the heavens opened, and the Son of man sitting on the right hand of the Father. Making intercession for his brethren, the Saints. He said that God would work a work in these last days that tongue cannot express, and the mind is not capable to conceive. The glory of the Lord shone around.

At the conference these were ordained to the high priesthood, namely, Lyman Wight, Sidney Rigdon, John Murdock, Reynolds Cahoon, Harvey Whitlock and Hyrum Smith [they] were ordained by Joseph Smith, Jr., except Sidney Rigdon.

. . . Joseph Smith, Jr., prophesied the day previous that the man of sin should be revealed. While the Lord poured out his spirit upon his servants, the devil took a notion, to make known his power, he bound Harvey Whitlock and John Murdock so that they could not speak, and others were affected but the Lord showed to Joseph the Seer, the design of the thing, he commanded the devil in the name of Christ and he departed to our joy and comfort.

Therefore a part of the revelation given at Fayette, New York, was fulfilled. The churches of the state of New York had moved to Ohio, with their wives and their children, and all their substance, some purchased farms others rented, and thus they situated themselves as convenient as they could. The day being now far spent and the conference was adjourned ("The Book of John Whitmer Kept by Commandment," n.p.).

Zebedee Coltrin

(Coltrin describes an incident that occurred during the conference. The Apostle Paul prophesied that before the Second Coming of the Lord, the "man of sin" (Satan) must be revealed (see 2 Thessalonians 2:1–3). Lucifer's plans and works have been abundantly revealed or manifest in various ways since the Restoration. At the 3 June 1831 conference, "the man of sin was revealed" when several of those in attendance were overcome by the devil, whom the Prophet Joseph Smith rebuked and cast out. Zebedee was an eyewitness to what occurred)

Zebedee Coltrin
(Courtesy of the Church Archives, The Church of Jesus Christ of Latter-day Saints)

During the meeting the powers of darkness were made manifest in a remarkable degree, causing some to make horrid noises, and others to throw themselves violently around. One man of the name of Leman Copley standing at the back of the house, was taken by a supernatural power, and thrown into a window, then Joseph said to Lyman Wight, go and cast the devil out of Leman, he did so, and the devil entered into the body of Harvey Green, and threw him upon the floor in convulsions, then Joseph laid hands upon him, and rebuked the spirit from him and from the house upon which the spirit left him and went outside, among the crowd of men standing near the door, and made a swath among them several feet wide, throwing them violently to the ground. Joseph said this was a fulfillment of the scriptures where it says the man of sin should be revealed *(Minutes of a high priests meeting held at Spanish Fork, Utah, 5 February 1878 [LDS Church Archives, Church Historical Department, The Church of Jesus Christ of Latter-day Saints, Salt Lake City]; as cited in Calvin R. Stephens, "The Life and Contributions of Zebedee Coltrin," Masters Thesis, Brigham Young University, 1974, 13–14).*

Jared Carter

(3 June 1831)

Brother Joseph notwithstanding he is not naturally talented for a speaker yet he was filled with the power of the Holy Ghost so that he spoke as I never heard man speak for God by the power of the Holy Ghost spoke in him and marvelous was the display of the power of the spirit among the Elders present (Jared Carter, *Autobiography* (1830–33), [LDS Church Archives]; as cited in Davis Bitton, *Guide to Mormon Diaries and Autobiographies* [Provo, Utah: Brigham Young University Press, 1977], 62; capitalization standardized).

PRIESTHOOD ORDINATIONS

(4 June 1831)

On 4 June 1831, after the fourth general conference of the church, High Priests were ordained for the first time in this dispensation.

Levi Hancock

The Fourth of June came and we all met in a little string of buildings under the hill near Isaac Morley's in Kirtland, Geauga County, Ohio. Then we all went to a school house on the hill about one fourth of a mile ascending nearly all the way. The building was built of logs. It was filled with slab benches. Here the elders were seated and the meeting was opened as usual . . .

Joseph put his hands on Harvey Whitlock and ordained him to the high priesthood. . . .

Then he ordained Jacob Scott and some others to the High Priesthood (Levi Hancock, "Levi Hancock, Autobiography," in *Writings of Early Latter-day Saints and Their Contemporaries, A Database Collection*, 33).

(8 March 1833)

Joseph Smith Jr.

(Counselors to the Prophet Joseph Smith were ordained and set apart, creating the First Presidency of the Church.)

Elder Rigdon expressed a desire that himself and Brother Frederick G. Williams should be ordained to the offices to which they had been called, viz., those of the Presidents of the High Priesthood, and to be equal in holding the keys of the kingdom with Brother Joseph Smith, Jun., according to the revelation given on the 8th of March, 1833 (see D&C 90). Accordingly I laid my hands on Brothers Sidney and Frederick, and ordained them to take part with me in holding the keys of this last kingdom, and to assist in the Presidency of the High Priesthood, as my Counselors (*History of the Church*, 1:334).

⋙ 14 ⋘

EARLY MISSIONARIES AND CONVERTS

Since 1830, hundreds of thousands of people have served as full-time missionaries for The Church of Jesus Christ of Latter-day Saints. Although missionaries are required to make immeasurable sacrifices of their time, talent, and monetary means, the impact these men and women have had on blessing mankind is abundantly evident worldwide. Following are stories of some of the first missionaries and converts to the restored church of Jesus Christ.

Joseph Smith Jr.

Some few were called and ordained by the Spirit of revelation and prophecy, and began to preach as the Spirit gave them utterance, and though weak, yet were they strengthened by the power of God, and many were brought to repentance, were immersed in the water, and were filled with the Holy Ghost by the laying on of hands. They saw visions and prophesied, devils were cast out, and the sick healed by the laying on of hands. From that time the work rolled forth with astonishing rapidity (Joseph Smith, *History of The Church of Jesus Christ of Latter-day Saints*, 7 vols., ed. B. H. Roberts [Salt Lake City: Deseret Book, 1978], 4:538–39).

The Mission of Samuel Smith
(April 1830)

In April 1830, Samuel Smith began traveling to neighboring towns in New York to preach the gospel and introduce people to the Book of Mormon. He had little success, although he did sell a copy to a man named Phineas Young. In June 1830, Samuel was set apart by the Prophet Joseph to take a missionary journey to the east. He walked twenty-five miles the first day and stopped at many houses, but the people ignored him. The next day he left a copy of the Book of Mormon with John P. Greene, a Methodist minister. John Greene's wife, Rhoda, was Phineas Young's sister.

Facing rejection from almost everyone he contacted, Samuel felt that his mission had been unsuccessful. However, the books he left with Phineas Young and John P. Greene led to their conversions and the conversion of many others. For example, Phineas Young and Rhoda Greene had a brother named Brigham, who was converted and later became the second President of the Church. Brigham Young's friend Heber C. Kimball also joined the Church. He later served in the First Presidency. Both Brigham Young and Heber C. Kimball were instrumental in the conversion of thousands of others in the United States and England.

Phineas Young
(Recounts receiving the Book of Mormon from Samuel Smith.)

In April, 1830, having received the Book of Mormon, as I was on my way home from the town of Lima, where I had been to preach, I stopped at the house of a man by the name of Tomlinson, to get some dinner. While engaged in conversation with the family, a young man came in, and walking across the room to where I was sitting, held a book toward me, saying,—"There is a book, sir, I wish you to read." The thing appeared so novel to me that for a moment I hesitated, saying—"Pray, sir, what book have you?"

"The Book of Mormon, or, as it is called by some, the Golden Bible."

"Ah, sir, then it purports to be a revelation."

"Yes," said he, "it is a revelation from God."

I took the book, and by his request looked at the testimony of the witnesses. Said he—"If you will read this book with a prayerful heart, and ask God to give you a witness, you will know the truth of this work."

I told him I would do so, and then asked him his name. He said his name was Samuel H. Smith.

"Ah," said I, ["]you are one of those witnesses."

"Yes," said he, "I know the book to be a revelation from God, translated by the gift and power of the Holy Ghost, and that my brother Joseph Smith, jun., is a Prophet, Seer and Revelator."

. . . I bought the book and went home, and told my wife I had got a week's work laid out, and I hoped that nothing would occur to prevent my accomplishing my task. She said, "Have you anything new to attend to?"

I replied, "I have got a book here, called the Book of Mormon, and it is said to be a revelation, and I wish to read it and make myself acquainted with its errors, so that I can expose them to the world."

I commenced and read every word in the book the same week. The week following I did the same, but to my surprise I could not find the errors I anticipated, but felt a conviction that the book was true.

On the next Sabbath I was requested to give my views on the subject, which I commenced to do. I had not spoken ten minutes in defense of the book when the Spirit of God came upon me in a marvelous manner, and I spoke at great length on the importance of such a work, quoting from the Bible to support my position, and finally closed by telling the people that I believed the book. The greater part of the people agreed with my views, and some of them said they had never heard me speak so well and with such power. My father then took the book home with him, and read it through. I asked him his opinion of it. He said it was the greatest work and the clearest of error of anything he had ever seen, the Bible not excepted.

I then lent the book to my sister Fanny Murray. She read it and declared it a revelation. Many others did the same (George Q. Cannon, "History of Brigham Young," *Millennial Star* 25 [June 1863]: 360–61).

JOSEPH SMITH SR. SHARES THE
GOSPEL WITH HIS FAMILY
(August 1830)

Lucy Mack Smith

(Before the Church was restored, Lucy Mack Smith had a dream in which she learned that her husband would accept the gospel but that his brother would not.)

I thought that I stood in a large and beautiful meadow, which lay a short distance from the house in which we lived, and that everything around me wore an aspect of peculiar pleasantness. The first thing that attracted my special attention in this magnificent meadow was a very pure and clear stream of water which ran through the midst of it; and as I traced this stream, I discovered two trees standing upon its margin, both of which were on the same side of the stream. These trees were very beautiful. They were well proportioned, and towered with majestic beauty to a great height. Their branches, which added to their symmetry and glory, commenced near the top and spread themselves in luxurious grandeur around. I gazed upon them with wonder and admiration, and after beholding them a short time, I saw one of them was surrounded with a bright belt that shone like burnished gold, but far more brilliantly. Presently, a gentle breeze passed by, and the tree encircled with this golden zone bent gracefully before the wind and waved its beautiful branches in the light air. As the wind increased, this tree assumed the most lively and animated appearance and seemed to express in its motions the utmost joy and happiness. If it had been an intelligent creature, it could not have conveyed by the power of language the idea of joy and gratitude so perfectly as it did; and even the stream that rolled beneath it shared, apparently, every sensation felt by the tree, for, as the branches danced over the stream, it would swell gently, then recede again with a motion as soft as the breathing of an infant, but as lively as the dancing of a sunbeam. The belt also partook of the same influence, and, as it moved in unison with the motion of the stream and of the tree, it increased continually in refulgence and magnitude until it became exceedingly glorious.

I turned my eyes upon its fellow, which stood opposite; but it was not surrounded with the belt of light as the former, and it stood erect and fixed as a pillar of marble. No matter how strong the wind blew over it, not a leaf was stirred, not a bough was bent, but obstinately stiff it stood, scorning alike the zephyr's breath, or the power of the mighty storm.

I wondered at what I saw, and said in my heart, What can be the meaning of all this? And the interpretation given me was that these personated my husband and his oldest brother, Jesse Smith; that the stubborn and unyielding tree was like Jesse; that the other, more pliant and flexible, was like Joseph, my husband; that the breath of heaven, which passed over them, was the pure and undefiled gospel of the Son of God, which gospel Jesse would always resist, but which Joseph, when he was more advanced in life, would hear and receive with his whole heart and rejoice therein; and unto him would be added intelligence, happiness, glory, and everlasting life (Lucy Mack Smith, *The Revised and Enhanced History of Joseph Smith by His Mother*, ed. Scot Facer Proctor and Maurine Jensen Proctor [Salt Lake City: Bookcraft, 1996], 59–60).

Lucy Mack Smith

Joseph Smith, Sr., was filled with the testimony of the truth, and was always anxious to share it with others. He was almost sixty when he made the tedious journey . . . to carry the gospel to his father and mother, his sisters and brothers. Soon after his return [home,] he was imprisoned for a small debt of fourteen dollars, rather than deny the divinity of the Book of Mormon and be forgiven the debt! He was cast into a cell with a condemned murderer and left for four days without food. Later he was transferred to the prison workyard where he preached the gospel and converted two persons whom he later baptized. He was in prison a full month before his family was able to obtain his release (E. Cecil McGavin, *The Family of Joseph Smith* [Provo, Utah: Brigham Young University, 1963], 68; see also Lucy Mack Smith, *History of Joseph Smith by His Mother*, ed. Preston Nibley [Salt Lake City: Bookcraft, 1958], 172–73, 179–86; as cited in Church Educational System, *Doctrine and Covenants and Church History Teacher's Manual* [Salt Lake City: The Church of Jesus Christ of Latter-day Saints, 2003], 59).

MISSION TO THE LAMANITES
(1830–1831)

After receiving commandment by way of revelation, Oliver Cowdery, Peter Whitmer Jr., Ziba Peterson, and Parley P. Pratt were called to serve a mission in "the borders by the Lamanites" (D&C 28:9). Although this mission had little success with the Lamanite people, it was successful in bringing in hundreds of faithful saints of other nationalities, including Sidney Rigdon, Isaac Morley, Levi Hancock, Lyman Wight and John Murdock, and their families.

Parley P. Pratt

(He recounts their success preaching to the Delaware tribe and recorded a speech given by Oliver Cowdery.)

Passing through the tribe of Shawnees we tarried one night with them, and the next day crossed the Kansas river and entered among the Delawares. We immediately inquired for the residence of the principal Chief, and were soon introduced to an aged and venerable looking man, who had long stood at the head of the Delawares, and been looked up to as the Great Grandfather, or Sachem of ten nations or tribes.

He was seated on a sofa of furs, skins and blankets, before a fire in the center of his lodge; which was a comfortable cabin, consisting of two large rooms.

His wives were neatly dressed, partly in calicoes and partly in skins; and wore a vast amount of silver ornaments. As we entered his cabin he took us by the hand with a hearty welcome, and then motioned us to be seated on a pleasant seat of blankets, or robes. His wives, at his bidding, set before us a tin pan full of beans and corn boiled up together, which proved to be good eating; although three of us made use alternately of the same wooden spoon.

There was an interpreter present and through him we commenced to make known our errand, and to tell him of the Book of Mormon. We asked him to call the council of his nation together and give us a hearing in full. He promised to consider on it till next day, in the meantime recommending us to a certain Mr. Pool for entertainment; this was their blacksmith, employed by government.

The man entertained us kindly and comfortably. Next morning

we again called on Mr. Anderson, the old chief, and explained to him something of the Book. He was at first unwilling to call his council; made several excuses, and finally refused; as he had ever been opposed to the introduction of missionaries among his tribe.

We continued the conversation a little longer, till he at last began to understand the nature of the Book. He then changed his mind; became suddenly interested, and requested us to proceed no further with our conversation till he could call a council. He dispatched a messenger, and in about an hour had some forty men collected around us in his lodge, who, after shaking us by the hand, were seated in silence; and in a grave and dignified manner awaited the announcement of what we had to offer. The chief then requested us to proceed; or rather, begin where we began before, and to complete our communication. Elder Cowdery then commenced as follows:

"Aged Chief and Venerable Council of the Delaware nation; we are glad of this opportunity to address you as our red brethren and friends. We have traveled a long distance from towards the rising sun to bring you glad news; we have traveled the wilderness, crossed the deep and wide rivers, and waded in the deep snows, and in the face of the storms of winter, to communicate to you great knowledge which has lately come to our ears and hearts; and which will do the red man good as well as the pale face.

"Once the red men were many; they occupied the country from sea to sea—from the rising to the setting sun; the whole land was theirs; the Great Spirit gave it to them, and no pale faces dwelt among them. But now they are few in numbers; their possessions are small, and the pale faces are many.

"Thousands of moons ago, when the red men's forefathers dwelt in peace and possessed this whole land, the Great Spirit talked with them, and revealed His law and His will, and much knowledge to their wise men and prophets. This they wrote in a Book; together with their history, and the things which should befall their children in the latter days.

"This Book was written on plates of gold, and handed down from father to son for many ages and generations.

"It was then that the people prospered, and were strong and mighty; they cultivated the earth; built buildings and cities, and abounded in all good things, as the pale faces now do.

"But they became wicked; they killed one another and shed much blood; they killed their prophets and wise men, and sought to destroy the Book. The Great Spirit became angry, and would speak to them no more; they had no more good and wise dreams; no more visions; no more angels sent among them by the Great Spirit; and the Lord commanded Mormon and Moroni, their last wise men and prophets, to hide the Book in the earth, that it might be preserved in safety, and be found and made known in the latter day to the pale faces who should possess the land; that they might again make it known to the red man; in order to restore them to the knowledge of the will of the Great Spirit and to His favor. And if the red man would then receive this Book and learn the things written in it, and do according thereunto, they should cease to fight and kill one another; should become one people; cultivate the earth in peace, in common with the pale faces, who were willing to believe and obey the same Book, and be good men and live in peace.

"Then should the red men become great, and have plenty to eat and good clothes to wear, and should be in favor with the Great Spirit and be his children, while he would be their Great Father, and talk with them, and raise up prophets and wise and good men amongst them again, who should teach them many things.

"This Book, which contained these things, was hid in the earth by Moroni, in a hill called by him, Cumorah, which hill is now in the State of New York, near the village of Palmyra, in Ontario County.

"In that neighborhood there lived a young man named Joseph Smith, who prayed to the Great Spirit much, in order that he might know the truth; and the Great Spirit sent an angel to him, and told him where this Book was hid by Moroni; and commanded him to go and get it. He accordingly went to the place, and dug in the earth, and found the Book written on golden plates.

"But it was written in the language of the forefathers of the red man; therefore this young man, being a pale face, could not understand it; but the angel told him and showed him, and gave him knowledge of the language, and how to interpret the Book. So he interpreted it into the language of the pale faces, and wrote it on paper, and caused it to be printed, and published thousands of copies . . . among them; and then sent us to the red men to bring some copies of it to them, and to tell them this news. So we have now come from him, and here is a copy of the Book, which we now present to our red friend, the chief of the

Delawares, and which we hope he will cause to be read and known among his tribe; it will do them good."

We then presented him with a Book of Mormon.

There was a pause in the council, and some conversation in their own tongue, after which the chief made the following reply:

"We feel truly thankful to our white friends who have come so far, and been at such pains to tell us good news, and especially this new news concerning the Book of our forefathers; it makes us glad in here"—placing his hand on his heart.

"It is now winter, we are new settlers in this place; the snow is deep, our cattle and horses are dying, our wigwams are poor; we have much to do in the spring—to build houses, and fence and make farms; but we will build a council house, and meet together, and you shall read to us and teach us more concerning the Book of our fathers and the will of the Great Spirit" (Parley P. Pratt, *Autobiography of Parley P. Pratt*, ed. Scot Facer Proctor and Maurine Jensen Proctor [Salt Lake City: Deseret Book, 2000], 61–65; spelling standardized).

MISSIONARIES SPEAK TO SIDNEY RIGDON'S CONGREGATION

Joseph Smith Jr.

(The missionaries requested permission to speak to Sidney Rigdon's congregation in Mentor, Ohio. He granted them permission and later accepted the gospel.)

The appointment was accordingly published, and a large and respectable congregation assembled. Oliver Cowdery and Parley P. Pratt severally addressed the meeting. At the conclusion, Mr. Rigdon arose, and stated to the congregation that the information they had that evening received was of an extraordinary character, and certainly demanded their most serious consideration: and as the Apostle advised his brethren to "prove all things, and hold fast that which is good," so he would exhort his brethren to do likewise, and give the matter a careful investigation, and not turn against it without being fully convinced of its being an imposition, lest they should, possibly, resist the truth (*History of the Church*, 1:124).

Lyman Wight

(As recorded in his journal.)

Lyman Wight
(Courtesy of the Church Archives, The Church of Jesus Christ of Latter-day Saints)

When I had my goods about half loaded, there came along four men (namely P. Pratt, O. Cowdery, P. Whitmer, and Ziba Peterson) and brought with them the Book of Mormon, which they wished to introduce to us. I desired they would hold on till I got away, as my business was of vital importance, and I did not wish to be troubled with romances nor idle speculations. But nothing daunted, they were not to be put off, but were as good-natured as you please. Curiosity got uppermost, and I concluded to stop for a short time. We called meeting, and one testified that he had seen angels, and another that he had seen plates, and that the gifts were back in the church again, etc. The meeting became so interesting withal that I did not get away till the sun was about an hour high at night, and it was dark before I arrived at my new home (*Saints' Herald* 29 [1882]: 192; as cited in Karl Ricks Anderson, *Joseph Smith's Kirtland* [Salt Lake City: Deseret Book, 1989], 5–6).

MISSIONARIES IN KIRTLAND
(1830–1833)

As the good news of the restored gospel of Jesus Christ began to spread, citizens in Ohio took notice of the marvelous message of angels and a "gold bible." The following article is taken from a newspaper in Painesville shortly after missionaries began teaching in that area.

Painesville Telegraph

(The Telegraph *was a local newspaper in Painesville, Ohio.)*

About two weeks since some persons came along here with the book [of Mormon], one of whom pretends to have seen Angels, and assisted in translating the plates. He proclaims . . . that the ordinances of the gospel, have not been regularly administered since the days of the Apostles, till the said Smith and himself commenced the work. . . . In the neighboring township of Kirtland, we understand that twenty or thirty have been immersed into the new order of things; many of whom had been previously baptized (n.a., "The Golden Bible," *Painesville Telegraph* [16 November 1830]: 3).

CALLED TO SERVE

Many Saints experienced great hardships and sacrificed much in order to faithfully respond to the call to preach the gospel. Despite the hardships, these early missionaries were instrumental in spreading the good news of the Restoration and often witnessed monumental conversions.

Daniel Tyler

About December, 1832, Elder Hyrum Smith, brother to the prophet, came to our neighborhood. My father told him that his daughter, who was present, was bent on being baptized into his church, stating at the same time, that the Elder who baptized her would do so at his peril. The Elder quite mildly remarked in substance as follows: "Mr. Tyler, we shall not baptize your daughter against your wishes. If our doctrine be true, which we testify it is, if you prevent your daughter from embracing it, the sin will be on your head, not on ours or your daughter's."

This remark pricked him to the heart. He began to think that possibly the "Mormons" were right and he was wrong. He therefore decided to counsel his daughter in the matter and then permit her to exercise her free agency. He would thus relieve himself of any responsibility.

His remarks to my sister were to the effect that if this new religion was true, it was the best religion in the world, but, if false, it was the worst. "These men," said he, "know whether it is true or false, but I do not." He wished her to reflect upon all these things before making a move in the matter. She replied that she had weighed them long ago and believed it to be her duty to be baptized. He took her on an ox-sled to Lake Erie, a distance of two miles, where, after a hole was cut through three feet of solid ice, she was baptized and confirmed into the Church by Elder Hyrum Smith" (Daniel Tyler, "Incidents of Experience," *Scraps of Biography* [Salt Lake City: Juvenile Instructor Office, 1883], 26).

Levi Hancock

(Levi served valiantly as a member of Zion's Camp. In February 1835, he was chosen as one of the presidents of the Seventy.)

I have to be honest before God and do all the good I can for this kingdom or woe is me. I care not for the world nor what they say. They have to meet my Testimony at the Judgment seat. I mean that my conduct shall be such that my words will be believed, the Lord being my helper (Don L. Searle, "It Is the Truth, I Can Feel It," *Ensign,* July 1999, 48–50).

Levi Hancock
(Courtesy of the Church Archives, The Church of Jesus Christ of Latter-day Saints)

John E. Page

John E. Page
(Courtesy of the Church Archives, The Church of Jesus Christ of Latter-day Saints)

On the 31st day of May, 1836, I started on a mission to Canada West, Leeds county. I was gone from my family seven months and twenty days.

On the 16th day of February 1837, I again left Kirtland with my family of wife and two small children, taking with me all the earthly good I possessed, which consisted of one bed and our wearing apparel of the plainest kind, to continue my mission in the same region of country as before.

In July following, the commandment came forth for me to occupy a place in the Quorum of the Twelve.

[At the time brother Page was called to go on a mission to Canada, he objected because he was destitute of clothing. Brother Joseph Smith took off his coat, gave it to him, told him to go, and said the Lord would bless him abundantly on his mission]

(John E. Page, "History of John E. Page," *Millennial Star* 27 [18 February 1865]: 103).

President Thomas S. Monson

(Recites the story of Brother Page's call to Canada.)

We demonstrate our love by how well we serve our God. Remember when the Prophet Joseph Smith went to John E. Page and said to him, "Brother Page, you have been called on a mission to Canada."

Brother Page, struggling for an excuse, said, "Brother Joseph, I can't go to Canada. I don't have a coat to wear."

The Prophet took off his own coat, handed it to John Page, and said, "Wear this, and the Lord will bless you."

John Page went on his mission to Canada. In two years he walked something like 5,000 miles and baptized 600 converts. (See Andrew Jenson, "John E. Page," *The Historical Record*, 5:572.) He was successful because he responded to an opportunity to serve his God (Thomas S. Monson, "How Do We Show Our Love," *Ensign*, January 1998, 2).

Lydia Knight

(On hearing the Prophet preach in Mount Pleasant, Ontario, Canada, in 1833.)

The Prophet commenced by relating the scenes of his early life. He told how the angel visited him, of his finding the plates and the translation of them, and gave a short account of the matter contained in the Book of Mormon.

As the speaker continued his wonderful narrative, I was listening and watching him intently. I saw his face become white and a shining glow seemed to beam from every feature. . . .

I was filled with a bright, peaceful influence and was full of gratitude that God had spared me to hear and accept His glorious gospel. As a lonely girl, I had thought of death and its rest with a longing heart. But here was life—life eternal. After I was baptized, I was constrained to cry aloud, "Glory to God in the highest. Thanks be to His holy name that I have lived to see this day and be a partaker of this great blessing" (Lydia Knight, "Lydia Knight's History, 14–23," *Journal History* [LDS Church Archives, Church Historical Department, The Church of Jesus Christ of Latter-day Saints, Salt Lake City], 19 October 1833;

as cited in *They Knew the Prophet,* ed. Hyrum L. Andrus and Helen Mae Andrus [Salt Lake City: Deseret Book, 1999], 48–50).

Parley P. Pratt

(Describes his call on a mission in April 1836.)

Spring at length returned, and the Elders prepared to take leave of each other, and to go on their several missions. As to myself, I was deeply in debt for the expenses of life during the winter, and on account of purchasing a lot, and building thereon. I, therefore, knew not what to do, whether to go on a mission or stay at home, and endeavor by industry to sustain my family and pay my debts.

It was now April; I had retired to rest one evening at an early hour, and was pondering my future course, when there came a knock at the door. I arose and opened it, when Elder Heber C. Kimball and others entered my house, and being filled with the spirit of prophecy, they blessed me and my wife, and prophesied as follows:

"Brother Parley, thy wife shall be healed from this hour, and shall bear a son, and his name shall be Parley; and he shall be a chosen instrument in the hands of the Lord to inherit the priesthood and to walk in the steps of his father. He shall do a great work in the earth in ministering the Word and teaching the children of men. Arise, therefore, and go forth in the ministry, nothing doubting. Take no thoughts for your debts, nor the necessaries of life, for the Lord will supply you with abundant means for all things" (Parley P. Pratt, *Autobiography of Parley Parker Pratt,* ed. Parley P. Pratt Jr. [Salt Lake City: Deseret Book, 1964], 162–65).

EARLY CONVERSION EXPERIENCES

For many, the decision to be baptized into the true church required significant sacrifice. Many new Saints gave up social status, wealth, and the respect of their friends and family. At times, these individuals were forced to choose between the eternal rewards of God and the temporal enticing of the world.

CONVERSION OF SIDNEY RIGDON
(November 1830)

Joseph Smith Jr.

(On the trials Sidney Rigdon faced in deciding to be baptized.)

The honors and applause of the world were showered down upon him, his wants were abundantly supplied, and were anticipated. He was respected by the entire community, and his name was a tower of strength. His counsel was sought for, respected and esteemed.—But if he should unite with the Church of Christ, his prospects of wealth and affluence would vanish; his family dependent upon him for support, must necessarily share his humiliation and poverty. He was aware that his character and his reputation must suffer in the estimation of the community ("History of Joseph Smith," *Times & Seasons* 4 [1 September 1843]: 304).

Sidney Rigdon and his wife, Phebe

(The couple counted the costs and chose to join with the Saints.)

[*Sidney Rigdon:*] [M]y dear, you have once followed me into poverty, are you again willing to do the same? . . .

[*Phebe Rigdon:*] I have weighed the matter, I have contemplated on the circumstances in which we may be placed; I have counted the cost, and I am perfectly satisfied to follow you; it is my desire to do the will of God, come life or come death ("History of Joseph Smith," *Times & Seasons* 4 [1 September 1843]: 304).

CONVERSION OF PHILO DIBBLE
(November 1830)

Philo Dibble

(Speaking of his baptism)

When I came out of the water, I knew that I had been born of water and of the spirit, for my mind was illuminated with the Holy Ghost.

I spent that evening at Dr. F. G. Williams. While in bed that night I felt what appeared to be a hand upon my left shoulder and a sensation like fibers of fire immediately enveloped my body. . . . I was enveloped in a heavenly influence, and could not sleep for joy.

The next morning I started home a happy man (Philo Dibble, "Philo Dibble's narrative," *Early Scenes in Church History* [Salt Lake City: Juvenile Instructor Office, 1882], 76).

CONVERSION OF ORSON SPENCER

Reverend Orson Spencer was a graduate of two colleges and extensively known particularly in the New England states as a Baptist preacher. He had a congregation in Massachusetts which included the governor of the state. His brother Daniel called the nature and origin of the Book of Mormon to his attention. Reverend Spencer bought a copy. He later describes his reaction in 1842 [see *Spencer's Letters*, ed. 6 (1879), 10–11]:

"I read diligently the Book of Mormon from beginning to end, in close connection with the comments of Origen Bachelor, Laroy Sunderland, and Dr. Hurlbut, together with newspapers and some private letters obtained from the surviving friends of Mr. Spaulding, the supposed author of the book. I arose from its perusal with a strong conviction on my mind, that its pages were graced with the pen of inspiration."

He was converted and with great sacrifice joined the Church. He said:

"I only ask the friends of pure religion to read the Book of Mormon with the same unprejudiced, prayerful and teachable spirit that they would recommend unbelievers in the ancient scriptures to read those records" (Franklin S. Harris Jr., *The Book of Mormon Message and Evidences* [Salt Lake City: Deseret Book, 1953], 172–73).

CONVERSION OF JOHN TAYLOR
(May 1836)

In 1836 Elder Parley P. Pratt, a member of the Quorum of the Twelve, was called to serve a mission to Canada. On his way to Toronto, "a stranger gave him a letter of introduction to John Taylor, a Methodist lay preacher in Toronto. Taylor was affiliated with a group who believed existing churches did not correspond with New Testament Christianity. For two years this group had met several times a week for the 'purpose of seeking truth, independent of any sectarian organization." In Toronto, Elder Pratt was courteously received by the Taylors, but they were not at first enthusiastic about his message.

John Taylor
(Courtesy of the Church Archives, The Church of Jesus Christ of Latter-day Saints)

Discouraged at being unable to secure a place to preach, Parley decided to leave Toronto. Before going, he stopped at the Taylors to get some of his luggage and to say good-bye. While he was there, Leonora Taylor told her friend Mrs. Isabella Walton about Parley's problem and said she was sorry he was leaving.

"He may be a man of God," she said. Mrs. Walton replied that she had been inspired by the Spirit to visit the Taylors that morning because she was willing to let Elder Pratt stay at her home and preach. He did so and was eventually invited to attend a meeting of John Taylor's group, in which John read the New Testament account of Philip's preaching in Samaria. "Now," said he, "where is our Philip? Where is our receiving the Word with joy, and being baptized *when we believed?* Where is our Peter and John? Our apostles? Where is our Holy Ghost by the laying on of hands? . . ." When Parley was invited to speak, he declared that he had answers to John Taylor's questions.

For three weeks John Taylor attended Elder Pratt's meetings making detailed notes of his sermons and carefully comparing them with the scriptures. Gradually he became convinced that the true gospel of Jesus Christ was restored. He and his wife, Leonora, were baptized on 9 May 1836 (*Church History in the Fulness of Times,* Prepared by the Church Educational System [Salt Lake City: The Church of Jesus Christ of Latter-day Saints, 1989], 157).

CONVERSION OF EDWARD HUNTER

Bishop Edward Hunter, the third presiding bishop of the Church, was converted to Mormonism largely through the efforts of the missionaries. But it wasn't because of what they did for him as much as what he did for them.

Always a deeply religious man, Hunter had often asked the Lord in prayer, "How can I worship thee acceptably?" But he had not received a satisfactory answer. So he continued to worship as he thought best, and do what he could to ensure others that same privilege.

Believing that all people should be free to voice their convictions, Hunter donated some land and helped construct a community building with that objective in mind. The building, called the West Nantmeal Seminary, served its purpose well until 1839 when some Mormon missionaries asked to use it for a public meeting.

The request caused quite an uproar. Many of the community's leading citizens vehemently declared that "Mormons are unfit to use the building." It appeared unlikely that the missionaries would be granted a hearing until Edward Hunter came to their defense. A powerful and influential man in the community, he saw to it that the elders were allowed to conduct their meeting. From that time on, he seemed compelled to take the side of the Mormons, even against great opposition.

On another occasion a young LDS missionary was being insulted and threatened by a mob in a nearby town. When word reached Hunter that the young man was in danger, he promptly rode to the elder's rescue.

Later that evening, questioning his unexplained loyalty to these missionaries, he asked the Lord in prayer, "Why have I taken such a decided stand for these strangers? Are these Mormons thy servants?" Hunter later recorded that "instantly a light came into the room at the top of the door, so great that I could not endure it."

Soon thereafter, Joseph Smith passed through town, and Hunter arranged for him to preach at the seminary. So impressed was he with the young prophet that when Orson Hyde stopped to visit on his way to dedicate the land of Palestine, Hunter asked to be baptized. Because so many of his neighbors followed his example, the area they lived in— Brandywine Valley, Pa.—became known as "Mormon Hollow" (Joseph Walker, "Service brings conversion," *Church News* [5 June 1983]: 16).

⚜ 15 ⚜

THE JOSEPH SMITH TRANSLATION
OF THE BIBLE

On 6 April 1830 (the day The Church of Jesus Christ of Latter-day Saints was organized, and just a few days after the Book of Mormon was published), the Savior declared to the assembled Saints that Joseph Smith was a "seer, a *translator*, a prophet, an apostle of Jesus Christ" (D&C 21:1). When we speak of Joseph Smith as a *translator*, we tend to think only of the Prophet's work with the Book of Mormon, but, in fact, Joseph Smith spent most of his life laboring as a translator of ancient scriptures, restoring a variety of records from every former dispensation. Elder LeGrand Richards of the Quorum of the Twelve noted, "The Prophet Joseph Smith brought us the Book of Mormon, the Doctrine and Covenants, the Pearl of Great Price, and many other writings. As far as our records show, he has given us more revealed truth than any prophet who has ever lived upon the face of the earth" (LeGrand Richards, "Call of the Prophets," *Ensign*, May 1981, 33).

Immediately following the organization of the Church, the Prophet Joseph Smith was divinely commissioned to begin an intense study of the Bible and make an inspired translation. His efforts occupied an immense amount of his time during the next three years, from June 1830 to July 1833.

The Explanatory Introduction to the Doctrine and Covenants

(Describes how important the Joseph Smith Translation was to the formation of the Doctrine and Covenants.)

Several of the earlier sections involve matters regarding the translation and publication of the Book of Mormon (see sections 3, 5, 10, 17, 19). Some later sections reflect the work of the Prophet Joseph Smith in making an inspired translation of the Bible, during which many of the great doctrinal sections were received (see, for example, Sections 37, 45, 73, 76, 77, 86, 91, and 132, each of which has some direct relationship to the Bible translation).

COMMENTS ABOUT THE JOSEPH SMITH TRANSLATION OF THE BIBLE

Doctrine and Covenants 35:20–21

(Sidney Rigdon, a prominent preacher in Ohio who had joined the Church in 1830, was given this direction by the Lord just six months after Joseph Smith had begun his translation of the Bible.)

And a commandment I give unto thee—that thou shalt write for him; and the scriptures shall be given, even as they are in mine own bosom, to the salvation of mine own elect;

For they will hear my voice, and shall see me, and shall not be asleep, and shall abide the day of my coming; for they shall be purified, even as I am pure.

Joseph Smith Jr.

(Promises that the Spirit will bear witness of the truth of the Joseph Smith Translation.)

Search the scriptures—*search the revelations which we publish*, and ask your Heavenly Father, in the name of His Son Jesus Christ, to manifest the truth unto you, and if you do it with an eye single to His glory nothing doubting, He will answer you by the power of His Holy

Spirit. You will then know for yourselves and not for another. You will not then be dependent on man for the knowledge of God; nor will there be any room for speculation. No; for when men receive their instruction from Him that made them, they know how He will save them. Then again we say: Search the Scriptures, search the Prophets and learn what portion of them belongs to you and the people of the nineteenth century (*Teachings of the Prophet Joseph Smith*, ed. Robert J. Matthews [Salt Lake City: Deseret Book, 1976], 11; italics added).

Moses 1:39–41

(Promise given to Moses concerning the Joseph Smith Translation.)

For behold, this is my work and my glory—to bring to pass the immortality and eternal life of man.

And now, Moses, my son, I will speak unto thee concerning this earth upon which thou standest; and thou shalt write the things which I shall speak.

And in a day when the children of men shall esteem my words as naught and take many of them from the book which thou shalt write, behold, I will raise up another like unto thee; and they shall be had again among the children of men—among as many as shall believe.

Doctrine and Covenants 76:15–23

(Joseph Smith's work in translating the Bible led to many great doctrinal revelations, including one of the greatest revelations ever given about the salvation of mankind—the vision of the degrees of glory earth's inhabitants will inherit in the resurrection (see D&C 76). Joseph Smith commented that he and Sidney Rigdon were working on the JST when this marvelous revelation was received.)

For while we were doing the work of translation, *which the Lord had appointed unto us*, we came to the twenty-ninth verse of the fifth chapter of John, which was given unto us as follows—

Speaking of the resurrection of the dead, concerning those who shall hear the voice of the Son of Man:

And shall come forth; they who have done good, in the

resurrection of the just; and they who have done evil, in the resurrection of the unjust.

Now this caused us to marvel, for it was given unto us of the Spirit.

And while we meditated upon these things, the Lord touched the eyes of our understandings and they were opened, and the glory of the Lord shone round about.

And we beheld the glory of the Son, on the right hand of the Father, and received of his fulness;

And saw the holy angels, and them who are sanctified before his throne, worshiping God, and the Lamb, who worship him forever and ever.

And now, after the many testimonies which have been given of him, this is the testimony, last of all, which we give of him: That he lives!

For we saw him, even on the right hand of God; and we heard the voice bearing record that he is the Only Begotten of the Father—

The Red Brick Store
(Courtesy of the Church Archives, The Church of Jesus Christ of Latter-day Saints)

Howard Coray

(Coray served as secretary to the Prophet Joseph Smith. He shared a spiritual experience he had while working with Joseph in an upstairs room of the Red Brick Store.)

One morning, I went as usual, into the Office to go to work: I found Joseph sitting on one side of a table and Robert B. Thompson on the opposite side, and the understanding I got was that they were examining or hunting in the manuscript of the new translation of the Bible for something on Priesthood, which Joseph wished to present, or have read to the people the next Conference: Well, they could not find what they wanted and Joseph said to Thompson "put the manuscript [to] one side, and take some paper and I will tell you what to write." Bro[ther] Thompson took some foolscap paper that was at his elbow and made himself ready for the business. I was seated probably 6 or 8 feet on Joseph's left side, so that I could look almost squarely into [the side of Joseph's eye]. Well, the Spirit of God descended upon him, and a measure of it upon me, insomuch that I could fully realize that God, or the Holy Ghost, was talking through him. I never, neither before or since, have felt as I did on that occasion. I felt so small and humble I could have freely kissed his feet (Dean Jessee, "Howard Coray's Recollections of Joseph Smith," *BYU Studies* 17 [Spring 1977]: 344; original punctuation and capitalization preserved).

Doctrine and Covenants 93:53

(Instructions given in May 1833 to Joseph Smith to finish the Joseph Smith Translation)

It is my will that you should hasten to translate my scriptures.

Doctrine and Covenants 94:10

And again, verily I say unto you, the second lot on the south shall be dedicated unto me for the building of a house unto me, for the work of the printing of the translation of my scriptures, and all things whatsoever I shall command you.

Doctrine and Covenants 104:58–59

And for this purpose I have commanded you to organize yourselves, even to print my words, the fulness of my scriptures, the revelations which I have given unto you, and which I shall, hereafter, from time to time give unto you—

For the purpose of building up my church and kingdom on the earth, and to prepare my people for the time when I shall dwell with them, which is nigh at hand.

Joseph Smith III

(A son of Joseph Smith Jr. and Emma Smith, Joseph Smith III describes how his mother felt about the responsibility to safeguard the JST manuscript.)

When Mother made demand for [Father's papers] they were denied to her on the plea that as her husband had been President of the church all his correspondence and public documents were the property of the organization. His private records, biography, portions of history— family and general—manuscripts, memoranda, and parts of his library were all included in this refusal to comply with Mother's request. She did have possession, however, of the manuscript of the *Inspired Translation of the Scriptures*, which she retained, notwithstanding the fact that numerous requests for it were made from time to time. It had been placed in her charge, she had been appointed a guardian over it, and . . . she felt the grave responsibility of safely keeping it until such time as the Lord would permit or direct its publication (Mary Audentia Smith Anderson, "The Memoirs of President Joseph Smith III (1832–1914)," *The Saints' Herald* [29 January 1935]: 144).

Emma Smith

(A letter to her son Joseph Smith III in 1867, when he was about to publish the Joseph Smith Translation.)

My own dear Joseph. . . . Now as it regards the Ms [manuscript] of the New Translation, if you wish to keep them you may do so, but if not I would like to have them. I have often thought the reason our house did not burn down when it was so often on fire was because of them, and I still feel there is a sacredness attached to them (Emma Smith Bidamon,

"Letter to Joseph Smith III, December 2, 1867," *The Emma Bidamon Papers* [Independence, Missouri: RLDS Church Archives], 4 f. 39).

MODERN COMMENTARY ON THE IMPORTANCE OF THE JOSEPH SMITH TRANSLATION OF THE BIBLE

Bruce R. McConkie

When the Joseph Smith Translation of the Bible—included in this revelation [see D&C 42:56–58] under the designation "fulness of my scriptures"—came forth, then teachers were to use it and the various additional direct revelations. This, then, is a command to teach the changes and additions now found in the so-called Inspired Version. . . .

Unless and until men believe the doctrines of the restoration they can never—never, never, never—worlds without end, prepare themselves to abide the day of our Lord's return; to dwell with Enoch and his fellows in the returning Zion; to stand with the elect of Israel in building up their ancient homeland; to perform miracles; to glory in the gifts of the Spirit; and to find full fellowship with the Saints of that God who has bought us with his blood. . . .

It was [the Lord's] design and purpose to bring forth the Book of Mormon as a new and added witness of the Lord Jesus Christ. . . .

After this—as a crowning achievement—he would begin the perfection of the Bible, a work destined to be greater and have more significance than any of us have yet realized. . . .

Let me speak plainly. Satan hates and spurns the scriptures. The less scripture there is, and the more it is twisted and perverted, the greater is the rejoicing in the courts of hell.

There has never been a book—not even the Book of Mormon—that has been so maligned and cursed and abused as the Bible. . . .

[The Bible] is now in the hands of intellectuals and unbelievers and ministers whose delight it is to twist and pervert its doctrines and to spiritualize away the plain meanings of all its important parts. And it once was in the sole and exclusive care and custody of an abominable organization, founded by the devil himself, likened prophetically unto a great whore, whose great aim and purpose was to destroy the souls of men in the name of religion. . . .

May I be pardoned if I say that negative attitudes and feelings about the Joseph Smith Translation are simply part of the devil's program to keep the word of truth from the children of men. . . .

Yes, the Inspired Version is inspired. Yes, the Joseph Smith Translation of the Bible is holy scripture. In one sense of the word it is the crowning part of the doctrinal restoration. . . .

God grant us the wisdom to walk in the light of that great beacon of understanding that he [Joseph Smith] lighted for our benefit and blessing (Bruce R. McConkie, "The Doctrinal Restoration," *The Joseph Smith Translation*, 1–22).

Bruce R. McConkie

The Joseph Smith Translation, though completed to the point that the early Brethren were going to publish it at one time, has not been completed in the full and true sense. But for that matter neither has the Book of Mormon. I am as anxious to read and study what is in the sealed portion of the Book of Mormon as I am to give the same attention to those parts of the Bible yet to be revealed ("The Doctrinal Restoration," 15).

Bruce R. McConkie

Use and rely on the Joseph Smith Translation [of the Bible] . . . This counsel . . . can scarcely be stated with too great an emphasis. The Joseph Smith Translation, or Inspired Version, is a thousand times over the best Bible now existing on earth. It contains all that the King James Version does, plus pages of additions and corrections and an occasional deletion. It was made by the spirit of revelation, and the changes and additions are the equivalent of the revealed word in the Book of Mormon and the Doctrine and Covenants.

For historical and other reasons there have been, among some members of the Church in times past, some prejudice and misunderstanding of the place of the Joseph Smith Translation. I hope this has now all vanished away. The Latter-day Saint edition of the Bible footnotes many of the major changes made in the Inspired Version and has a seventeen-page section that sets forth excerpts that are too lengthy for inclusion in the footnotes. Reference to this section and to the footnotes themselves will give anyone who has spiritual insight a deep appreciation of this revelatory work of the Prophet Joseph Smith. It is one of the great evidences of his prophetic call.

I am pleased to say that . . . we have the world's foremost authority on the Joseph Smith Translation. His contributions in this field of gospel scholarship rank with the best works published in our dispensation. He is of course Brother Robert J. Matthews . . . His published work, "'A Plainer Translation': Joseph Smith's Translation of the Bible, A History and Commentary," is deserving of your careful study (Bruce R. McConkie, "The Bible, A Sealed Book," *Eighth Annual Church Educational System Religious Educators' Symposium* [Salt Lake City: The Church of Jesus Christ of Latter-day Saints, 1984], 5).

Dallin H. Oaks

Those who understand that the importance of the scriptures is what the Lord would have us understand today are anxious for revelatory insight into the current significance of scriptural texts and concepts. They understand that some things we have already received are hard to understand without the Lord's help (see 1 Nephi 15: 1, 3, 8, 11), and that we can never receive enough of the word of God. Persons with this attitude are anxious to have every source of revelation to help us to know what the Lord would have us understand from the scriptures today. Such persons will welcome the revelatory insights—even additions—by the prophets of this dispensation.

Dallin H. Oaks
(Courtesy of the Church Archives, The Church of Jesus Christ of Latter-day Saints)

. . . There should be no doubt about the current status of the Joseph Smith Translation of the Bible. It is a member of the royal family of scripture. . . . As a member of the royal family of scripture it should be noticed and honored on any occasion when it is present (Dallin H. Oaks, "Scripture Reading, Revelation, and the Joseph Smith Translation of the Bible," *Plain and Precious Truths Restored: The Doctrinal and Historical Significance of the Joseph Smith Translation,* ed. Robert L. Millett and Robert J. Matthews [Salt Lake City: Bookcraft, 1995], 13).

Bruce R. McConkie

The added truths [Joseph Smith] placed in the Bible and the corrections he made raise the resultant work to the same high status as the Book of Mormon and the Doctrine and Covenants. It is true that he did not complete the work, but it was far enough along that he intended to publish it in its present form in his lifetime (Bruce R. McConkie, "Come: Hear the Voice of the Lord," *Ensign*, December 1985, 58).

Robert L. Millet

There is so much beauty and depth of doctrine and insight to be had within the Joseph Smith Translation of the Bible that it is foolish to study and teach without it; to do so is tantamount to being choosy about what we will receive from the Lord and what we will not. Such an attitude is certainly foreign to the genuine truth-seeker. Those who love and revere the name and labors of Joseph Smith should be pleased and enthusiastic to receive whatever God has chosen to reveal through his modern seer and lawgiver ("A Historical Overview," 46).

Robert J. Matthews

Question: Can and should we purchase Joseph Smith's translation of the Bible to use in teaching classes in the Church? Would it be appropriate to do so?

Dr. Robert J. Matthews: . . . Yes, you can; Yes, you should; Yes, it would be appropriate (Robert J. Matthews, "The JST: Retrospect and Prospect—A Panel," *The Joseph Smith Translation: the Restoration of Plain and Precious Things*, ed. Monte S. Nyman and Robert L. Millet [Provo, Utah: Brigham Young University, 1987], 301).

Spencer W. Kimball

Since . . . 1820, additional scripture has continued to come, including the numerous and vital revelations flowing in a never-ending stream from God to his prophets on the earth. Many of these revelations are recorded in . . . the Doctrine and Covenants. Completing our Latter-day Saint scriptures is the Pearl of Great Price, another record of revelation and translated writings of both ancient and modern prophets.

There are those who would assume that with the printing and

binding of these sacred records, that would be the "end of the prophets." But again we testify to the world that revelation continues and that the vaults and files of the Church contain these revelations which come month to month and day to day. We testify also that there is, since 1830 when The Church of Jesus Christ of Latter-day Saints was organized, and will continue to be, so long as time shall last, a prophet, recognized of God and his people, who will continue to interpret the mind and will of the Lord (Spencer W. Kimball, "Revelation: The Word of the Lord to His Prophets," *Ensign*, April 1977, 78).

Robert J. Matthews

The Doctrine and Covenants contains instruction about Joseph Smith's translation of the Bible—when to begin the translation, when to stop, who is to be scribe, how to get it printed, and so on. It also contains revelations which were not intended as part of the Bible text but grew out of the translation experience, such as sections 76, 77, 86, 91, and probably 132.

Many verses in the Doctrine and Covenants are unintelligible to a reader unless he knows that the subject of those verses is the translation of the Bible. Just as some early sections of the Doctrine and Covenants revolve around the translation of the Book of Mormon (sections 3, 5, 8, 9, 10, and 17), some later sections revolve around the translation and intended printing of the Bible—parts of 35, 37, 41, 42, 45, 73, 74, 93, 94, 104, and 124, and all of sections 76, 77, 86, and 91 (Robert J. Matthews, *A Bible! A Bible!* [Salt Lake City: Bookcraft, 1990], 16).

Robert J. Matthews

Every member of the Church since 1831 has been influenced in some way by the Joseph Smith Translation of the Bible (JST), even if he or she has never heard of it and does not know even one corrected verse. This is true because many doctrines and practices of the Church were first made known, or enlarged upon, through the Prophet's translation of the Bible. These included the age of accountability at eight years, the degrees of glory, the ministry of Enoch and his city, the concept of Zion, and the doctrines of premortal existence. The JST is not just a better Bible, it is a major vehicle of the Restoration and a contribution to the Doctrine and Covenants. It was a branch of the Prophet's ministry

(Robert J. Matthews, "The Role of the Bible in the Restoration of the Gospel: What Every Teacher Should Know About the JST," Handout prepared for the CES symposium on the Doctrine and Covenants/Church History 10–12 August 1993, Brigham Young University, 1).

Translation of the Bible, by Liz Lemon Swindle
(Courtesy of Liz Lemon Swindle, Foundation Arts)

Joseph F. McConkie

When it came to the Bible, Joseph Smith spoke as one having authority, and rightly so, for save Jesus only, no man ever walked the face of the earth that had greater knowledge of the Bible than he had. A library containing every whit the world knows about the book would not rival his understanding. It is one thing to read the book and quite another to be instructed by its authors. Who among the world's scholars can boast of having stood face to face with Adam, Enoch, Noah, a messenger from Abraham's dispensation, Moses, John the son of Zacharias, Peter, James, and John? While religious leaders were claiming that the heavens were sealed to them, Joseph Smith was being personally tutored by the ancient prophets who laid their hands upon his head and conferred upon him the power, keys, and authority they held (Joseph F. McConkie, "Joseph Smith and the Poetic Writings," *The Joseph Smith Translation: the Restoration of Plain and Precious Things,* ed. Monte S. Nyman and Robert L. Millet [Provo, Utah: Brigham Young University, 1987], 118).

Robert J. Matthews

The translation process was a learning experience for Joseph Smith. He learned new things by reading the Bible and by receiving the inspiration of the Lord in response to his study. It was a process of inquiry. It required effort, prayer, energy, desire, and serious contemplation. Had he not been willing to follow these requirements, he would not have gained the insight or received the revelation, and none of us would have had the benefit of a new translation (*A Bible! A Bible!*, 92).

16

GATHERING TO THE OHIO

In December 1830, the Lord commanded the Saints to move to Ohio (see D&C 37:3). The following January, the Saints from various branches in New York met in the Peter Whitmer Sr. home in Fayette. They asked about the commandment to move to Ohio, and the Prophet Joseph Smith prayed and received the following revelation:

> I tell you these things because of your prayers; where-fore, treasure up wisdom in your bosoms . . . [and] if ye are prepared ye shall not fear.
>
> And that ye might escape the power of the enemy, and be gathered unto me a righteous people, without spot and blameless—
>
> Wherefore, for this cause I gave unto you the com-mandment that ye should go to the Ohio; and there I will give unto you my law; and there you shall be endowed with power from on high. (D&C 38:30–32)

Within a few weeks, the Prophet and his wife, Emma, set out on the three-hundred-mile trek to Kirtland with Sidney Rigdon and Edward Partridge. They journeyed in a borrowed sleigh belonging to Joseph Knight. Between the end of January 1831 and May 1831, most of the Saints in New York sold their property and traveled in three separate groups to Ohio.

Elizabeth Ann Whitney

(Whitney recites the spiritual impression she and her husband received in Kirtland, Ohio, to prepare them for the arrival of the Prophet Joseph Smith.)

One night . . . it was midnight—as my husband and I, in our house at Kirtland, were praying to the father to be shown the way, the Spirit rested upon us and a cloud overshadowed the house. It was as though we were out of doors. The house passed away from our vision. We were not conscious of anything but the presence of the Spirit and the cloud that was over us. We were wrapped in the cloud. A solemn awe pervaded us. We saw the cloud and felt the spirit of the Lord. Then we heard a voice out of the cloud, saying, "Prepare to receive the word of the Lord, for it is coming." At this we marveled greatly; but from that moment we knew that the word of the Lord was coming to Kirtland (O. F. Whitney, "The Aaronic Priesthood," *The Contributor* 6 [January 1885]:125).

B. H. Roberts

About the first of February, 1831, a sleigh containing four persons drove through the streets of Kirtland and drew up in front of the store of Gilbert and Whitney. One of the men, a young and stalwart personage alighted, and springing up the steps walked into the store and to where the junior partner was standing. "Newel K. Whitney! Thou art the man!" he exclaimed, extending his hand cordially, as if to an old and familiar acquaintance. "You have the advantage of me," replied the merchant, as he mechanically took the proffered hand, "I could not call you by name as you have me." "I am Joseph the Prophet," said the stranger smiling. "You've prayed me here, now what do you want of me?" The Prophet, it is said, while in the East had seen the Whitneys, in vision, praying for his coming to Kirtland. "Mother Whitney" also tells how on a certain night prior to the advent of Elder Cowdery and his companions, while she and her husband were praying to the Lord to know how they might obtain the gift of the Holy Ghost, which of all things they desired, they saw a vision as of a cloud of glory resting upon their house, and heard a voice from heaven saying, "Prepare to receive the word of the Lord, for it is coming" (Joseph Smith, *History of The Church of Jesus Christ of Latter-day Saints*, 7 vols., ed. B. H. Roberts [Salt Lake City: Deseret Book, 1980], 1:146).

Lucy Mack Smith

(In order for the Saints to relocate to Kirtland, they needed to separate into different parties. One of these parties was headed by the Prophet's mother, Lucy Mack Smith. Her untiring spunk, fortitude, and resilience encouraged and inspired her weary party as they encountered many trials along the way. During one part of the journey, Lucy Mack Smith's group found themselves stranded as the barge they were waiting to board had been iced in.)

Here we found the brethren from Colesville, who informed us that they had been detained one week at this place, waiting for the navigation to open. Also, that Mr. Smith and Hyrum had gone through to Kirtland by land, in order to be there by the first of April.

I asked them if they had confessed to the people that they were "Mormons." "No, indeed," they replied, "neither must you mention a word about your religion, for if you do you will never be able to get a house, or a boat either."

I told them I should tell the people precisely who I was; "and," continued I, "if you are ashamed of Christ, you must not expect to be prospered; and I shall wonder if we do not get to Kirtland before you."

While we were talking with the Colesville brethren, another boat landed, having on board about thirty brethren, among whom was Thomas B. Marsh, who immediately joined us, and, like the Colesville brethren, he was decidedly opposed to our attending to prayer, or making known that we were professors of religion. He said that if our company persisted in singing and praying, as we had hitherto done, we should be mobbed before the next morning.

"Mob it is, then," said I, "we shall attend to prayer before sunset, mob or no mob." Mr. Marsh, at this, left considerably irritated. I then requested brothers Humphry and Page to go around among the boatmen, and inquire for one Captain Blake, who was formerly captain of a boat belonging to my brother, General Mack, and who, upon my brother's decease, purchased the boat and still commanded the same. They went in search of the man, and soon found him, and learned from him that his boat was already laden with the usual amount of passengers and freight. He said, however, that he thought he could make room for us if we would take a deck passage. As this was our only opportunity, we moved our goods on board the next day, and by the time that we fairly settled ourselves, it began to rain. This rendered our situation very uncomfortable, and some of the sisters complained bitterly because we had not hired a house till the boat was ready to start. In fact their case was rather a trying one, for some of them had sick children; in consequence of which, Brother Page went out for the purpose of getting a room for the women and sick children, but returned unsuccessful. At this the sisters renewed their complaints, and declared that they would have a house, let the consequences be what they might. In order to satisfy them, I set out myself, with my son William, although it was still raining very fast, to see if it were possible to procure a shelter for them and their children.

I stopped at the first tavern, and inquired of the landlord if he could let me have a room for some women and children who were sick. The landlord replied that he could easily make room for them. At this, a woman who was present turned upon him very sharply, saying, "I have put up here myself, and I am not a-going to have anybody's things in my way. I'll warrant the children have got the whooping cough or measles, or some other contagious disease, and, if they come, I will go somewhere else."

"Why, madam," said the landlord, "that is not necessary, you can still have one large room."

"I don't care," said she, "I want 'em both, and if I can't have 'em, I won't stay—that's it."

"Never mind," said I, "it is no matter; I suppose I can get a room somewhere else, just as well."

"No, you can't though," rejoined the lady, "for we hunted all over the town and we could not find one single one till we got here."

I left immediately and went on my way. Presently I came to a long row of rooms, one of which appeared to be almost vacant. I inquired if it could be rented for a few days. The owner of the buildings I found to be a cheerful old lady, near seventy years of age. I mentioned the circumstances to her, as I before had done to the landlord.

"Well, I don't know," said she; "where be you going?"

"To Kirtland," I replied.

"What be you?" said she. "Be you Baptists?"

I told her that we were "Mormons."

"Mormons!" ejaculated she, in a quick, good-natured tone. "What be they? I never heard of them before."

"I told you that we were 'Mormons,'" I replied, "because that is what the world calls us, but the only name we acknowledge is Latter-day Saints."

"Latter-day Saints!" rejoined she, "I never heard of them either."

I then informed her that this Church was brought forth through the instrumentality of a prophet, and that I was the mother of this prophet.

"What!" said she, "a prophet in these days! I never heard of the like in my life; and if you will come and sit with me, you shall have a room for your sisters and their children, but you yourself must come and stay with me, and tell me all about it."

This I promised to do, and then returned to the boat and had the sisters and their sick children removed to the old lady's house; and after making them comfortable, I went into her room. We soon fell into conversation, in which I explained to her, as clearly as I could, the principles of the gospel. On speaking of the laying on of hands for the reception of the Holy Ghost, she was as much surprised as those disciples were whom Paul found at Ephesus, and she asked me, "What do you mean by the Holy Ghost?" I continued my explanations until after two o'clock the next morning, when we removed to the boat again. On arriving there, Captain Blake requested the passengers to remain on board, as he wished, from that time, to be ready to start at a moment's warning; at the same time he sent out a man to measure the depth of the ice, who, when he returned, reported that it was piled up to the height of twenty feet, and that it was his opinion that we would remain in the harbor at least two weeks longer....

Just then William whispered in my ear, "Mother, do see the confusion yonder; won't you go and put a stop to it!"

I went to that part of the boat where the principal portion of our company was. There I found several of the brethren and sisters engaged in a warm debate, others murmuring and grumbling, and a number of young ladies were flirting, giggling, and laughing with gentlemen passengers, who were entire strangers to them, whilst hundreds of people on shore and on other boats were witnessing this scene of clamor and vanity among our brethren with great interest. I stepped into their midst. "Brethren and sisters," said I, "we call ourselves Saints, and profess to have come out from the world for the purpose of serving God at the expense of all earthly things; and will you, at the very onset, subject the cause of Christ to ridicule by your own unwise and improper conduct? You profess to put your trust in God, then how can you feel to murmur and complain as you do! You are even more unreasonable than the children of Israel were; for here are my sisters pining for their rocking chairs, and brethren from whom I expected firmness and energy, declare that they positively believe they shall starve to death before they get to the end of their journey. And why is it so? Have any of you lacked? Have not I set food before you every day, and made you, who had not provided for yourselves, as welcome as my own children? Where is your faith? Where is your confidence in God? Can you not realize that all things were made by him, and that he rules over the works of his own hands? And suppose that all the Saints here should lift their hearts in prayer to God, that the way might be opened before us, how easy it would be for him to cause the ice to break away, so that in a moment we could be on our journey!"

Just then a man on shore cried, "Is the Book of Mormon true?"

"That book," replied I, "was brought forth by the power of God, and translated by the gift of the Holy Ghost; and, if I could make my voice sound as loud as the trumpet of Michael, the Archangel, I would declare the truth from land to land, and from sea to sea, and the echo should reach to every isle, until every member of the family of Adam should be left without excuse. For I do testify that God has revealed himself to man again in these last days, and set his hand to gather his people upon a goodly land, and, if they obey his commandments, it shall be unto them for an inheritance; whereas, if they rebel against his law, his hand will be against them to scatter them abroad, and cut them off from the face of the earth; and that he has commenced a work which will prove a savor of life unto life, or of death unto death, to every one that stands here this day—of life unto life—if you will receive it, or of death unto death, if you reject the counsel of God, for every man shall have the desires of his heart; if he desires the truth, he may hear and live, but if he tramples upon the simplicity of the word of God, he will shut the gate of heaven against himself." Then, turning to our own company, I said, "Now, brethren and sisters, if you will all of you raise your desires to heaven, that the ice may be broken up, and we be set at liberty, as sure as the Lord lives, it will be done." At that instant a noise was heard, like bursting thunder. The captain cried, "Every man to his post." The ice parted, leaving barely a passage for the boat, and so narrow that as the boat passed through the buckets of the waterwheel were torn off with a crash, which, joined to the word of command from the captain, the hoarse answering of the sailors, the noise of the ice, and the cries and confusion of the spectators, presented a scene truly terrible. We had barely passed through the avenue when the ice closed together again, and the Colesville brethren were left in Buffalo, unable to follow us.

As we were leaving the harbor, one of the bystanders exclaimed, "There goes the 'Mormon' company! That boat is sunk in the water nine inches deeper than ever it was before, and, mark it, she will sink—there is nothing surer." In fact, they were so sure of it that they went straight to the office and had it published that we were sunk, so that when we arrived at Fairport we read in the papers the news of our own death (Lucy Mack Smith, *History of Joseph Smith by His Mother*, ed. Preston Nibley [Salt Lake City: Bookcraft, 1958], 199–205).

Oliver B. Huntington

We left Sackets Harbor . . . but [were] driven back, the wind blowing a perfect gale; we landed in Rochester the next morning before sunrise. . . . From Rochester we took the canal to Buffalo and from Buffalo to Fairport, 12 miles from Kirtland we sailed on a steamboat, and in four days from the time we left Sackets we were in Kirtland. We all walked the 12 miles with joy, rejoicing at the privilege of getting there no matter how (Oliver B. Huntington, *Diary, 1842–1847* [L. Tom Perry Special Collections, Harold B. Lee Library, Brigham Young University, Provo, Utah], 1, 6–27).

Amasa Lyman

Elders Orson Pratt and Lyman E. Johnson passed through the section of New Hampshire where young Lyman lived, on a preaching tour. He believed the message proclaimed by these new evangels and was baptized on the 27th of April, 1832. . . . In consequence of the ill feelings which arose in his uncle's family [where he was living], owing to his joining the Church, Amasa departed from the home of his kindred, and set out on foot for the gathering place of the Saints in Ohio. After a journey of some seven hundred miles, in which he endured many hardships—for much of the journey was made on foot and with but scant means of subsistence—he arrived at Hiram in Portage county. . . .

Amasa Lyman
*(Courtesy of the Church
Archives, The Church of
Jesus Christ of Latter-day
Saints)*

About the first of July [1832] ... Amasa had the joy of meeting the Prophet of the new dispensation. Of that meeting and the impressions it produced, he says:

Of the impressions produced I will here say, although there was nothing strange or different from other men in his personal appearance, yet when he grasped my hand in that cordial way (known to those who have met him in the honest simplicity of truth), I felt as one of old in the presence of the Lord (*History of the Church,* 1:332).

Brigham Young

When we arrived in Kirtland [in September 1833], if any man that ever did gather with the Saints was any poorer than I was—it was because he had nothing. . . . I had two children to take care of—that was all. I was a widower. "Brother Brigham, had you any shoes?" No; not a shoe to my foot, except a pair of borrowed boots. I had no winter clothing, except a homemade coat that I had had three or four years. "Any pantaloons?" No. "What did you do? Did you go without?" No; I borrowed a pair to wear till I could get another pair. I had traveled and preached and given away every dollar of my property. I was worth a little property when I started to preach . . . I had traveled and preached until I had nothing left to gather with; but Joseph said: "come up;" and I went up the best I could (in *Journal of Discourses,* 26 vols. [London: Latter-day Saints' Book Depot, 1854–86], 6:25; spelling standardized).

Phoebe Carter

My friends marveled at my course, as did I, but something within me impelled me on. My mother's grief at my leaving home was almost more than I could bear; and had it not been for the spirit within I should have faltered at the last. My mother told me she would rather see me buried than going thus alone out into the heartless world. "Phoebe," she said, impressively, "will you come back to me if you find Mormonism false?" I answered, "[Y]es, mother; I will, thrice." These were my words, and she knew I would keep my promise. My answer relieved her trouble; but it cost us all much sorrow to part. When the time came for my departure I dared not trust myself to say farewell; so I wrote my good-byes to each, and leaving them on my table, ran downstairs and jumped into the carriage. Thus I left the beloved home of my childhood to link my life with the saints of God (Edward W. Tullidge, *The Women of Mormondom* [Salt Lake City: s.n., 1975], 412; as cited in Karl Ricks Anderson, *Joseph Smith's Kirtland* [Salt Lake City: Deseret Book, 1989], 13).

Warren Cowdery

(Commenting on what occurred as the Saints gathered to Kirtland in 1831.)

The noise and bustle of teams with lumber, brick, stone, lime or merchandise, were heard from the early dawn of morning till the grey twilight of evening. . . . The starting up, as if by magic, of buildings in every direction around us, [was] evincive to us of buoyant hope, lively anticipation, and a firm confidence that our days of pinching adversity had passed by, that the set time of the Lord to favor Zion had come ("Kirtland Ohio, June 1837," *Messenger and Advocate* 3 [June 1837]: 520).

Caroline Crosby

About the middle of July a co[mpany] came from Boston Mass [to Kirtland, Ohio]. . . . And no house could be found for their accommodation. John [Boynton] was building, but could not get it ready in season. He therefore came to us and offered to give us four times the amount of rent we paid, if we would go in with sister Sabre Granger, a maiden lady near by us, who was living alone, and let him have our house for his friends. My husband left it with me to say, to which I hesitated some time, but at length consented, rather reluctantly. The remuneration I considered no object; [but] to leave my pleasant little house, to go in with another, after living by ourselves so short a time; but the idea of accommodating friends, stimulated me to make the sacrifice.

Sister Granger's house was small, only one room, besides cellar, pantry, a small closet, and chamber. She had however a stove room, outside where she cooked her food. She had many peculiarities, which in some respects were not as agreeable to us, as we could wish. Notwithstanding being kindhearted, and friendly, atoned in my estimation, for many imperfections (as cited in *Joseph Smith's Kirtland*, 13–14).

～ 17 ～

GATHERING TO MISSOURI

DEDICATION OF INDEPENDENCE, MISSOURI, TEMPLE SITE
(2 August 1831)

After receiving the revelation that Independence, Jackson County, Missouri, would be the new gathering place for the Saints, the Prophet and several others journeyed to Independence in order to dedicate the land for this purpose.

Oliver Cowdery

After many struggles and afflictions, being persecuted by our enemies, we received intelligence by letter from our brethren, who were at the East, that br[others] Joseph and Sidney, and many other elders, were commanded to take their journey to this land, the Land of Missouri. Which [land] was promised unto us [to] be the land of the inheritance of the Saints, and the place of the gathering in these last days. Which intelligence cheered our hearts, and caused us to rejoice exceedingly. And by the special protection of the Lord, br[other] Joseph Smith Jr. and Sidney Rigdon, in company with eight other elders, with the church from Colesville, New York, consisting of about sixty souls, arrived in the month of July and by revelation the place was made known where the temple shall stand, and the city should commence. And by commandment, twelve of us assembled ourselves together, viz., Elder Joseph Smith Jr., the Seer, Oliver Cowdery, Sidney Rigdon, Newel Knight, William W. Phelps, and Ezra Booth, who denied the faith.

On the second day of August 1831, Brother Sidney Rigdon stood up and asked saying: Do you receive this land for the land of your inheritance with thankful hearts from the Lord? Answer from all, we do. Do you pledge yourselves to keep the laws of God on this land, which you have never kept in your own land? We do. Do you pledge yourselves to see that others of your brethren, who shall come hither, do keep the laws of God? We do. After prayer he arose and said, I now pronounce this land consecrated and dedicated to the Lord for a possession and inheritance for the Saints, (in the name of Jesus Christ having authority from him,) and for all the faithful servants of the Lord to the remotest ages of time. Amen.

The day following, eight elders, viz., Joseph Smith Jr., Oliver Cowdery, Sidney Rigdon, Peter Whitmer Jr., Frederick G. Williams, Wm. W. Phelps, Martin Harris, and Joseph Coe, assembled together where the temple is to be erected. Sidney Rigdon dedicated the ground where the city is to stand, and Joseph Smith Jr. laid a stone at the northeast corner of the contemplated temple in the name of the Lord Jesus of Nazareth. After all present had rendered thanks to the great ruler of the universe, Sidney Rigdon pronounced this spot of ground wholly dedicated unto the Lord forever. Amen (*From Historian to Dissident: The Book of John Whitmer*, ed. Bruce N. Westergren [Salt Lake City: Signature Books, 1995], 85–87; grammar, punctuation and spelling standardized).

Joseph Smith Jr.

(An account of his arrival in Missouri and the dedication of the temple site at Independence.)

The First Act in the Founding of Zion. On the second day of August, I assisted the Colesville branch of the Church to lay the first log, for a house, as a foundation of Zion in Kaw township, twelve miles west of Independence. The log was carried and placed by twelve men, in honor of the twelve tribes of Israel. At the same time, through prayer, the land of Zion was consecrated and dedicated by Elder Sidney Rigdon for the gathering of the Saints. It was a season of joy to those present, and afforded a glimpse of the future, which time will yet unfold to the satisfaction of the faithful.

Description of the Land of Zion. As we had received a command-ment for Elder Rigdon to write a description of the land of Zion, we sought for all the information necessary to accomplish so desirable an object. The country is unlike the timbered states of the East. As far as the eye can reach the beautiful rolling prairies lie spread out like a sea of meadows; and are decorated with a growth of flowers so gorgeous and grand as to exceed description; and nothing is more fruitful, or a richer stockholder in the blooming prairie than the honey bee. Only on the water courses is timber to be found. There in strips from one to three miles in width, and following faithfully the meanderings of the streams, it grows in luxuriant forests. The forests are a mixture of oak, hickory, black walnut, elm, ash, cherry, honey locust, mulberry, coffee bean, hackberry, boxelder, and bass wood; with the addition of cotton-wood, butterwood, pecan, and soft and hard maple upon the bottoms. The shrubbery is beautiful, and consists in part of plums, grapes, crab apple, and persimmons.

Agricultural Products; Animals, Domestic and Wild. The soil is rich and fertile; from three to ten feet deep, and generally composed of a rich black mold, intermingled with clay and sand. It yields in abundance, wheat, corn, sweet potatoes, cotton and many other common agricul-tural products. Horses, cattle and hogs, though of an inferior breed, are tolerably plentiful and seem nearly to raise themselves by grazing in the vast prairie range in summer, and feeding upon the bottoms in winter. The wild game is less plentiful of course where man has com-menced the cultivation of the soil, than in the wild prairies. Buffalo, elk, deer, bear, wolves, beaver and many smaller animals here roam at plea-sure. Turkeys, geese, swans, ducks, yea a variety of the feathered tribe, are among the rich abundance that grace the delightful regions of this goodly land—the heritage of the children of God.

The Climate. The season is mild and delightful nearly three quarters of the year, and as the land of Zion, situated at about equal distances from the Atlantic and Pacific oceans, as well as from the Alleghany and Rocky mountains, in the thirty-ninth degree of north latitude, and between the sixteenth and seventeenth degrees of west longitude, it bids fair—when the curse is taken from the land—to become one of the most blessed places on the globe. The winters are milder than the Atlantic states of the same parallel of latitude, and the weather is more agreeable; so that were the virtues of the inhabitants only equal to the blessings of the Lord which He permits to crown the industry of those inhabitants, there would be a measure of the good things of life for the benefit of the Saints, full, pressed down, and running over, even an hundred-fold. The disadvantages here, as in all new countries, are self-evident—lack of mills and schools; together with the natural privations and inconveniences which the hand of industry, the refinement of society, and the polish of science, overcome.

The Future Glory of Zion. But all these impediments vanish when it is recollected what the Prophets have said concerning Zion in the last days; how the glory of Lebanon is to come upon her; the fir tree, the pine tree, and the box tree together, to beautify the place of His sanctuary, that He may make the place of His feet glorious. Where for brass, He will bring gold; and for iron, He will bring silver; and for wood, brass; and for stones, iron; and where the feast of fat things will be given to the just; yea, when the splendor of the Lord is brought to our consideration for the good of His people, the calculations of men and the vain glory of the world vanish, and we exclaim, "Out of Zion the perfection of beauty, God hath shined."

Dedication of the Temple Site. On the third day of August, I proceeded to dedicate the spot for the Temple, a little west of Independence, and there were also present Sidney Rigdon, Edward Partridge, W. W. Phelps, Oliver Cowdery, Martin Harris and Joseph Coe.

The 87th Psalm was read:—

His foundation is in the holy mountains.

The Lord loveth the gates of Zion more than all the dwellings of Jacob.

Glorious things are spoken of thee, O city of God. Selah.

I will make mention of Rahab and Babylon to them that know me: behold Philistia, and Tyre, with Ethiopia; this man was born there.

And of Zion it shall be said, This and that man was born in her: and the Highest Himself shall establish her.

The Lord shall count, when he writeth up the people, that this man was born there. Selah.

As well the singers as the players on instruments shall be there: all my springs are in thee.

The scene was solemn and impressive.

First Conference in Zion. On the 4th I attended the first conference in the land of Zion. It was held at the house of Brother Joshua Lewis, in Kaw township, in the presence of the Colesville branch of the Church. The Spirit of the Lord was there (Joseph Smith, *History of The Church of Jesus Christ of Latter-day Saints,* 7 vols., ed. B. H. Roberts [Salt Lake City: Deseret Book, 1964], 1:196–99).

DESCRIPTIONS OF THE LAND OF ZION
(Jackson County, Missouri)

W. W. Phelps

(Writing from Independence in 1831.)

The prairies are beautiful beyond description (*Ontario Phoenix* [7 Sep. 1831]; as cited in Richard L. Anderson, "New Data for Revising the Missouri 'Documentary History,'" *BYU Studies* 14 [Summer 1974]: 500).

Sidney Rigdon

The season is mild and delightful nearly three quarters of the year, and as the land of Zion, situated at about equal distances from the Atlantic and Pacific oceans, as well as from the Alleghany and Rocky mountains, in the thirty-ninth degree of north latitude, and between the sixteenth and seventeenth degrees of west longitude, it bids fair—when the curse is taken from the land—to become one of the most blessed places on the globe (*History of the Church,* 1:198).

Sidney Rigdon
(Courtesy of the Church Archives, The Church of Jesus Christ of Latter-day Saints)

W. W. Phelps

(1832)

Zion, according to the prophets, is to become like Eden or the garden of the Lord (*History of the Church*, 1:279).

Wilford Woodruff

President Young said Joseph the Prophet told me that the garden of Eden was in Jackson Co. Missouri (Wilford Woodruff, *Wilford Woodruff's Journal*, 9 vols., ed. Scott G. Kenney [Midvale, Utah: Signature Books, 1985], 129).

W. W. Phelps
(Courtesy of the Church Archives, The Church of Jesus Christ of Latter-day Saints)

COLESVILLE, NEW YORK, SAINTS GATHER TO MISSOURI
(1831)

Emily Partridge Smith Young

On 4 February 1831, my father was called by revelation [D&C 41:9] to be a bishop in Zion, and was ordained to that office soon after. Some time in June following, Brother Joseph, with several of the brethren stated for Missouri, my father being one of the number. They reached Independence, Jackson County, Missouri, about the middle of July. After locat[ing] Zion (in Independence, or that town being the center spot) and transacting other necessary business, the brethren returned home, leaving my father to remain in Zion as he had been appointed by revelation to labor in that place and to take up his residence there and send for his family (Emily Young, "Emily Partridge Smith Young," in *Writings of Early Latter-day Saints and Their Contemporaries, A Database Collection*, comp. Milton V. Backman [Provo, Utah: BYU Religious Studies Center, 1996], 7).

Newel Knight

We were not accustomed to a frontier life, so things around us seemed new and strange and the work we had to do was of a different nature to that which had been done in the East. Yet we took hold with cheerful hearts, and a determination to do our best, and with all diligence went to work to secure food and prepare for the coming winter (Newel Knight, *Scraps of Biography* [L. Tom Perry Special Collections, Harold B. Lee Library, Brigham Young University, Provo, Utah], 72; as cited in *Church History in the Fulness of Times*, Prepared by the Church Educational System [Salt Lake City: The Church of Jesus Christ of Latter-day Saints, 1989], 108).

Parley P. Pratt

They had arrived late in the summer, and cut some hay for their cattle, sowed a little grain, and prepared some ground for cultivation, and were engaged during the fall and winter in building log cabins, etc. The winter was cold, and for some time about ten families lived in one log cabin, which was open and unfinished, while the frozen ground served for a floor. Our food consisted of beef and a little bread made of corn, which had been grated into coarse meal by rubbing the ears on a tin grater. This was rather an inconvenient way of living for a sick person; but it was for the gospel's sake, and all were very cheerful and happy . . .

There was a spirit of peace and union, and love and good will manifested in this little Church in the wilderness, the memory of which will be ever dear to my heart (Parley P. Pratt, *Autobiography of Parley Parker Pratt*, ed. Parley P. Pratt Jr. [Salt Lake City: Deseret Book, 1964], 71–72; spelling standardized).

Bruce A. Van Orden

It was not what Zion was, but what it could become, that buoyed them up and lifted sagging spirits (Bruce A. Van Orden, "Causes and Consequences: Conflict in Jackson County," *Regional Studies in Latter-day Saint Church History: Missouri*, ed. Arnold K. Garr and Clark V. Johnson [Provo, Utah: Brigham Young University, 1994], 339).

Emily M. Corburn

It was a strange sight indeed, to see four of five yoke of oxen turning up the rich soil. Fencing and other improvements went on in rapid succession. Cabins were built and prepared for families as fast as time, money and labor could accomplish the work; and our homes in this new country presented a prosperous appearance—almost equal to Paradise itself—and our peace and happiness, as we flattered ourselves, were not in a great degree deficient to that of our first parents in the garden of Eden, as no labor or painstaking was spared in the cultivation of flowers and shrubbery of a choice selection (Emily M. Austin, *Mormonism; or, Life among the Mormons* [New York: AMS Press, 1971], 67).

JOSEPH AGAIN JOURNEYS TO MISSOURI
(1832)

While attending to church business in early April of 1832, Joseph Smith was obligated to travel to Missouri without his family. Due to mounting persecution in Ohio, Emma moved in with Newel K. and Elizabeth Whitney during her husband's absence, but was obliged to move in with another family until Joseph's return. This was a time of deep trial for Emma and Joseph for six months, they corresponded solely via letters.

Joseph Smith Jr.

(1 April 1832)

She [Emma] went to Kirtland, to brother Whitney's, and Sister Whitney's aunt, Sarah Smith, (who was then living with her,) inquired of her niece if my wife was going to stay there; and on being answered in the affirmative, said she should go away, for there was not room enough for the both of them; accordingly sister Whitney invited my wife to leave, which she did immediately; having enjoyed about two hours visit. She then went to brother Reynolds Cahoon's, and father Smith's, and doctor Williams', where I found her, very disconsolate on my return ("History of Joseph Smith," *Times & Seasons* 5 [2 September 1844]: 624).

Joseph Smith Jr.

(Relating an incident that occurred during this trip.)

On the 6th of May [1832] I gave the parting hand to the brethren in Independence, and, in company with Brothers Rigdon and Whitney, commenced a return to Kirtland, by stage to St. Louis, from thence to Vincennes, Indiana; and from thence to New Albany, near the falls of the Ohio River. Before we arrived at the latter place, the horses became frightened, and while going at full speed Bishop Whitney attempted to jump out of the coach, but having his coat fast, caught his foot in the wheel, and had his leg and foot broken in several places; at the same time I jumped out unhurt. We put up at Mr. Porter's public house, in Greenville, for four weeks, while Elder Rigdon went directly forward to Kirtland. During all this time, Brother Whitney lost not a meal of victuals or a night's sleep, and Dr. Porter, our landlord's brother, who attended him, said it was a pity we had not got some "Mormon" there, as they could set broken bones or do anything else. I tarried with Brother Whitney and administered to him till he was able to be moved. While at this place I frequently walked out in the woods, where I saw several fresh graves; and one day when I rose from the dinner table, I walked directly to the door and commenced vomiting most profusely. I raised large quantities of blood and poisonous matter, and so great were the muscular contortions of my system, that my jaw in a few moments was dislocated. This I succeeded in replacing with my own hands, and made my way to Brother Whitney (who was in bed), as speedily as possible; he laid his hands on me and administered to me in the name of the Lord, and I was healed in an instant, although the effect of the poison was so powerful, as to cause much of the hair to become loosened from my head. Thanks be to my Heavenly Father for His interference in my behalf at this critical moment, in the name of Jesus Christ. Amen (*History of the Church*, 1:271).

Joseph Smith Jr.

(This letter was written around the time the above experience occurred.)

Dear Wife:

I would inform you that Brother Martin has arrived here and brought the pleasing news that our families were well when he left there, which greatly cheered our hearts and revived our Spirits. We thank our Heavenly Father for his Goodness unto us and [all of you] . . . My situation is a very unpleasant one, although I will endeavor to be contented, the Lord assisting me. I have visited a grove which is just back of the town almost every day, where I can be secluded from the eyes of any mortal, and there give vent to all the feelings of my heart in meditation and prayer. I have called to mind all the past moments of my life and am left to mourn [and] shed tears of sorrow for my folly in suffering the adversary of my soul to have so much power over me as he has [had in times past]; but God is merciful and has forgiven my sins and I rejoice that he sendeth forth the Comforter unto as many as believe and humbleth themselves before him. I was grieved to hear that Hiram had [lost] his little Child. I think we can in, some degree, sympathize with him, but we all must be reconciled to our lots and say the will [of the Lord] be done. Sister Whitney wrote a letter to [her husband] which was very cheering and being unwell at the time and filled with much anxiety, it would have been very consoling to me to have received a few lines from you . . . I hope you will excuse . . . my inability in conveying my ideas in writing . . . I should like [to] see little Julia and once more take her on my knee and converse with you on all the subjects which concern us . . . I subscribe myself your husband. The Lord bless you. Peace be with [you]. So farewell until I return (*The Personal Writings of Joseph Smith*, ed. Dean C. Jessee [Salt Lake City: Deseret Book, 2002], 264–65; spelling, grammar, capitalization and punctuation standardized).

JOSEPH SMITH'S PLAT FOR THE CITY OF ZION

The plat Joseph Smith designed for the city of Zion at Independence, Missouri, is a good example of his forward-thinking. This city-plan was later used by Brigham Young to lay out over 300 cities in the west. With the temple in the center, streets were laid out according to the compass points. Joseph Smith's city-design was given an award in 1996 by the 30,000 member American Planning Association for its practicality and ingenuity. Today, a copy of the plat of Zion hangs in the LDS Visitors' Center in Independence, Missouri, and in Brigham Young Historic Park in Salt Lake City.

LDS Church News

In the spring of 1833, Joseph Smith envisioned a plan for the "city of Zion," a city plat of square, wide streets that eventually influenced hundreds of cities in the West.

Now, more than century and half later, the genius of the prophet has been officially recognized by the 30,000-member American Planning Association. The association awarded the Church and Joseph Smith the 1996 Planning Landmark Award, presented by the Planning Landmarks and Pioneers Jury.

Elder F. Burton Howard of the Seventy and counselor in the North American Southeast Area presidency represented the First Presidency at an awards dinner recently at the association's annual conference in Orlando, Fla. He received a plaque honoring the Church and its founder. At the banquet, Joseph Smith and Brigham Young were praised for their vision and practical application that resulted in major and smaller cities and towns being established throughout the Mountain West. The city of Zion plan "assured, in general, a highly organized community life. . . . It also made possible a more advantageous utilization of the lands."

The association also will donate an 18-by-24-inch bronze plaque to be displayed in the Brigham Young Historic Park in Salt Lake City.

That plat was nominated by Eugene E. Carr, adjunct professor of urban planning at the University of Utah and a member of the Planning Landmarks and Pioneers Jury.

"The planning and founding of more than 500 communities in the American West is regarded by many planning historians as one of the most significant accomplishments in the history of American city development," said Bruce Parker, president of the Utah chapter of the American Planning Association.

"The plat placed high value on the quality of the urban environment and the importance of a coherent community. The cities of Zion were to be a 'gathering place,' and during Brigham Young's lifetime they accommodated some 80,000 converts to the Church.

"The Mormon communities were agriculturally sustainable. They were laid out in a grid of 10-acre blocks, with a community center containing cultural, school, religious and commercial activities. Farming was conducted in surrounding greenbelts outside the city. That plat provided for neighborhood structure (wards), modern zoning (separation of incompatible uses), and land use regulations (residences set back from the street with a fine, well-maintained gardens, or groves in the front yard)."

He said that he hopes the award will "rekindle an awareness among all Utahns of their heritage—an appreciation for attractive and socially cohesive communities, and careful stewardship of the land and the environment" ("1833 'Plat of Zion' wins national honor," *LDS Church News* [25 May 1996]: 11).

Joseph Smith Jr.

(The Prophet intended to use the plat of Zion as a pattern to build numerous other cities as they filled up with Saints. The following comes from a handwritten note in the margin.)

Lay off another [city] in the same way, and so fill up the world in these last days; and let every man live in the city, for this is the city of Zion" (*History of the Church*, 1:358).

ADAM-ONDI-AHMAN
(1838)

The place called Adam-ondi-Ahman is a large valley located twenty-five miles northeast of Far West, on a bend in the Grand River in Daviess County, Missouri. The first LDS settler was Lyman Wight, who arrived in February 1838. Joseph Smith first visited the site 19 May 1838. He received D&C 116 and learned that this was the area where Adam and Eve dwelt after leaving the Garden of Eden. Joseph declared the area to be "Adam-ondi-Ahman." Orson Pratt said this phrase, in the pure Adamic language, means "The valley of God where Adam dwelt" (See *Journal of Discourses*, 26 vols. [London: Latter-day Saints' Book Depot, 1854–86], 18:343).

The Saints called it Di-ahman. W. W. Phelps wrote a hymn about Adam-ondi-Ahman called "Our Earth Was Once a Garden Place," which was sung at the dedication of the Kirtland Temple and included in the first LDS hymnbook, in 1835. There were perhaps 1,500 people living in Adam-ondi-Ahman in 1838, with about two hundred log cabins. Most residences were located on the long, gentle, western and southern slopes of what is known as Spring Hill. Spring Hill was planned to be in the center of the city.

D&C 107:53–57

(Revealed in Kirtland, Ohio, on 28 March 1835, this revelation describes a meeting Adam held in this valley, which is a type of the meeting that will yet occur in this same place.)

Three years previous to the death of Adam, he called Seth, Enos, Cainan, Mahalaleel, Jared, Enoch, and Methuselah, who were all high priests, with the residue of his posterity who were righteous, into the valley of Adam-ondi-Ahman, and there bestowed upon them his last blessing.

And the Lord appeared unto them, and they rose up and blessed Adam, and called him Michael, the prince, the archangel.

And the Lord administered comfort unto Adam, and said unto him: I have set thee to be at the head; a multitude of nations shall come of thee, and thou art a prince over them forever.

And Adam stood up in the midst of the congregation; and, notwithstanding he was bowed down with age, being full of the Holy Ghost, predicted whatsoever should befall his posterity unto the latest generation.

These things were all written in the book of Enoch, and are to be testified of in due time.

Joseph Smith Jr.

In the afternoon I went up the river about half a mile to Wight's Ferry, accompanied by President Rigdon, and my clerk, George W. Robinson, for the purpose of selecting and laying claim to a city plat near said ferry in Daviess County, township 60, ranges 27 and 28, and sections 25, 36, 31, and 30, which the brethren called "Spring Hill," but by the mouth of the Lord it was named Adam-ondi-Ahman, because, said He, it is the place where Adam shall come to visit his people, or the Ancient of Days shall sit, as spoken of by Daniel the Prophet (*History of the Church*, 3:35).

Heber C. Kimball

The Prophet Joseph called upon Brother Brigham, myself and others, saying, "Brethren, come, go along with me, and I will show you something." He led us a short distance to a place where were the ruins of three altars built of stone, one above the other, and one standing a little back of the other, like unto the pulpits in the Kirtland Temple, representing the order of three grades of Priesthood; "There," said Joseph, "is the place where Adam offered up sacrifice after he was cast out of the garden." The altar stood at the highest point of the bluff (Orson F. Whitney, *Life of Heber C. Kimball* [Salt Lake City: Deseret Book, 1945], 209).

Heber C. Kimball

I could tell you a thousand things that happened in that early day. I have been, as I have already told you, to where Adam offered sacrifices and blessed his sons, and I felt as though there were hundreds of angels there, and there were angels there like unto the three Nephites (*Journal of Discourses*, 12:191).

Wilford Woodruff

Again President Young said Joseph the Prophet told me that the garden of Eden was in Jackson Co Missouri, & when Adam was driven out of the garden of Eden He went about 40 miles to the Place which we Named Adam Ondi Ahman, & there built an Altar of Stone & offered Sacrifice. That Altar remains to this day. I saw it as Adam left it as did many others, & through all the revolutions of the world that Altar had not been disturbed (Wilford Woodruff, *Wilford Woodruff's Journal*, 9 vols., ed. Scott G. Kenney [Midvale, Utah: Signature Books, 1983], 7:129; original capitalization preserved; spelling standardized).

A.O. [Abrahm O.] Smoot told W. Woodruff that He & Alanson Ripley while surveying out Adam Ondi Ahman about 22 Miles North of Jackson County Missouri they Came across a Stone wall in the midst of a dens forest & underbrush. The wall was 30 feet long 3 feet thick, and about 4 feet high above the ground and laid in mortar or Cement. When Joseph Smith the Prophet visited the place and Examined the wall He said it was the remains of an Altar Built By Father Adam where he offered Sacrifice after he was driven from the Garden of Eden which was located in Jackson County Missouri. The whole town which was laid out and named Adam Ondi Ahman was in the midst of a thick & heavy forest of timber and the place named after Adams Altar. The Prophet Joseph said it was upon this Altar where Adam blessed his sons and Posterity Before his death. Let Historians of the Church note this. (*Wilford Woodruff's Journal*, 8:172; original capitalization preserved; spelling standardized).

Joseph Smith Jr.

Daniel in his seventh chapter speaks of the Ancient of Days; he means the oldest man, our Father Adam, Michael, he will call his children together and hold a council with them to prepare them for the coming of the Son of Man. He (Adam) is the father of the human family, and presides over the spirits of all men, and *all that have had the keys must stand before him in this grand council. This may take place before some of us leave this stage of action.* The Son of Man stands before him, and there is given him glory and dominion. Adam delivers up his stewardship to Christ, that which was delivered to him as holding the keys of the universe, but retains his standing as head of the human family (*History of the Church*, 3:386–87).

Edward Stevenson

I stood with Joseph Smith and others when he pointed out the sacred spot of Adam's altar. Turning to the lovely valley below us, in a large bend of [the] Grand River, he said, "Here is the real valley where Father Adam called his posterity together and blessed them" (Edward Stevenson, *Autobiography of Edward Stevenson* [LDS Church Archives, Church Historical Department, The Church of Jesus Christ of Latter-day Saints, Salt Lake City]; as cited in *Encyclopedia of Joseph Smith's Teachings*, ed. Larry E. Dahl and Donald Q. Cannon [Salt Lake City: Bookcraft, 1997], 23).

Orson Pratt

I will read a new revelation upon the subject given May 18, 1838, almost thirty-nine years ago. It was given when the Prophet Joseph Smith, and the Latter-day Saints, had gathered themselves together in Missouri, about forty or fifty miles north of Jackson County. They had assembled at a place that they called Spring Hill, and the Lord revealed to Joseph, on that occasion, things concerning this great event. This place, Spring Hill, is alluded to by the Lord, in this revelation, as being anciently called Adam-ondi-Ahman, because it is the place where Adam shall come to visit his children, or the place where the Ancient of Days shall sit, as spoken of by Daniel the Prophet. Here, then, we have a key to the important personage, called the Ancient of Days, that he is our father Adam, and that he is to sit in judgment, among certain numbers of his children, in that certain region of country. . . .

Orson Pratt
(Courtesy of the Church Archives, The Church of Jesus Christ of Latter-day Saints)

We have then an understanding that it was the place where Adam dwelt. Perhaps you may be anxious to know what "Ondi-Ahman" means. It means the place where Adam dwelt. "Ahman" signifies God. The whole term means Valley of God, where Adam dwelt. It is in the original language spoken by Adam, as revealed to the Prophet Joseph (*Journal of Discourses*, 18:342).

Orange L. Wight

(Son of Lyman Wight, Orange was the first man to settle at Adam-ondi-Ahman.)

I was now eleven years old. Father was again called on a mission, but returned shortly and we made arrangements to move to Caldwell County, Missouri. We moved to Caldwell County and settled about three miles from Far West—most of the Saints moved from Clay to Caldwell. Also we had a great many newcomers from the east so we began to number the Saints by thousands instead of hundreds. The county population increased to such an extent that it was thought proper to establish a settlement in another county; hence, we moved to Daviess County and our principle settlement at a place on Grand River called—afterwards Adam-ondi-Ahman, named by the Prophet Joseph Smith from the fact as the Prophet Joseph told us that it was the place where Adam offered his holy sacrifice. The altar was still there and not far from our house when we went there. Our family was among the first to move to that county and father bought land of one Adam Black; you will see his name mentioned in most of the church histories.

I wish now to give a description of the [Adam's] altar, more particular the situation and also other things in the neighborhood including some things that are [cached] there. . . . Adam-ondi-Ahman was visited a number of times by the Prophet Joseph Smith and I became still better acquainted with him being now 14 years old, I could comprehend and appreciate all or nearly all he would say. He was very kind and sociable with both young and old. We often bathed in the limped waters of Grand River. . . . At one time we had a jolly time—yes and at other times. There was Joseph the Prophet, my father [Lyman Wight], Sidney Rigdon, and several others, our amusement consisted in part seeing Brother Rigdon swim. He was so corpulent that he was forced to lay on his back to swim, he would swim in that way until his shoulders would strike the sand bar then he could turn but would flop back in deep water (Orange L. Wight, "Autobiography," in *Writings of Early Latter-day Saints and Their Contemporaries, A Database Collection*, 3–4).

John Taylor

In speaking with the Prophet Joseph once on this subject, he traced it from the first down to the last, until he got to the Ancient of Days. He wished me to write something for him on this subject, but I found it a very difficult thing to do. He had to correct me several times. We are told that the "judgment shall sit and the books be opened." He spoke of the various dispensations and of those holding the keys thereof, and said there would then be a general giving up or accounting for. I wrote that each one holding the keys of the several dispensations would deliver them up to his predecessor, from one to another, until the whole kingdom should be delivered up to the Father, and then God would be "all in all." Said he, "That is not right." I wrote it again, and again he said it was not right. It is very difficult to find language suitable to convey the meaning of spiritual things. The idea was that they should deliver up or give an account of their administrations, in their several dispensations, but that they would all retain their several positions and Priesthood. The Bible and Doctrine and Covenants speaks about certain books which should be opened; and another book would be opened, called the

Book of Life, and out of the things written in these books would men be judged at the last day (*Journal of Discourses*, 18:330).

Orson F. Whitney

Adam was the first to receive and obey the Gospel, revealed to him out of Eternity at the very beginning of Time. Since his day it has been upon the earth repeatedly, in a series of dispensations, of which this is the greatest and the last. Adam presides over all the gospel dispensations, including the Dispensation of the Fullness of Times—he presides over them all, just as the President of the Church presides over all the Stakes of Zion and all the outside Missions, though each has its own immediate presiding authority. Joseph Smith is the immediate head of this dispensation, and Adam is the general head of all. Standing next to Church in the Priesthood, whenever that divine power is revealed from heaven to earth, "it is by Adam's authority." So says Joseph Smith.

The world has not seen the last of Father Adam. He is coming again, as the Ancient of Days, to fulfill the prophecy of Daniel. He will come to the valley of Adam-ondi-Ahman, where of old he blessed his posterity, foretelling what should befall them to the latest generation. He will call a council and assemble his righteous descendants, to prepare them for the glorious advent of the King of Kings.

This is a part of the divine program, as made known by modern revelation (Orson F. Whitney, in Conference Report, October 1925, 101).

Benjamin F. Johnson

On our arrival at Diahman, our camp was pitched upon the town plat which had just been surveyed by direction of the Prophet and of course each one was anxious to obtain the most eligible, or the first choice of lots. As I was young and unmarried my choice would come near the last under the rule of "oldest served first." So when it was my choice I found I must take the top lot on the promontory overlooking the Grand River valley, or go farther away and lower down than I wished to. So I chose the upper, which at first appeared rocky, but which made the other lots appear almost enviable. When, after a few days, the Prophet accompanied us to this spot, and pointed out those rocks as the ones of which Adam built an altar and offered sacrifice upon this spot, where he stood and blessed the multitude of his children, when they called him Michael, and where he will again sit as the Ancient Days, then I was not envious of anyone's choice for a city lot in Adam-ondi-Ahman. Yet I would not have inferred that my inheritance there, or those given me elsewhere are to be especially guaranteed to have in future (Benjamin F. Johnson, *My Life's Review* [Mesa, Arizona: 21st Century Printing, 1992], 35–36).

Bruce R. McConkie

With reference to the use of sacramental wine on our day, the Lord said to Joseph Smith: "You shall partake of none except it is made new among you; yea, in this my Father's kingdom which shall be built up on the earth." In so stating, he is picking up the language he used in the upper room. Then he says: "The hour cometh that I will drink of the fruit of the vine with you on the earth." Jesus is going to partake of the sacrament again with his mortal disciples on earth. But it will not be with mortals only. He names others who will be present and who will participate in the sacred ordinance. These include Moroni, Elias, John the Baptist, Elijah, Abraham, Isaac, Jacob, Joseph (who was sold into Egypt), Peter, James, and John, "and also with Michael, or Adam, the father of all, the prince of all, the ancient of days." Each of these is named simply by way of illustration. The grand summation of the whole matter comes in these words: "And also with all those whom my Father hath given me out of the world" (D&C 27:4–14). The sacrament is to be administered in a future day, on this earth, when the Lord Jesus is present, and when all the righteous of all ages are present. This, of course, will be a part of the grand council at Adam-ondi-Ahman (Bruce R. McConkie, *The Millennial Messiah* [Salt Lake City: Deseret Book, 1982], 587).

W. W. Phelps

(Poem about Adam-ondi-Ahman)

This earth was once a garden place,
With all her glories common,
And men did live a holy race,
And worship Jesus face to face,
In Adam-ondi-Ahman.

We read that Enoch walked with God,
Above the pow'r of mammon,
While Zion spread herself abroad,
And Saints and angels sang aloud,
In Adam-ondi-Ahman.
Her land was good and greatly blest,
Beyond all Israel's Canaan;
Her fame was known from east to west,
Her peace was great, and pure the rest
Of Adam-ondi-Ahman.
Hosanna to such days to come,
The Savior's second coming,
When all the earth in glorious bloom
Affords to Saints a holy home,
Like Adam-ondi-Ahman
(William W. Phelps, "Adam-ondi-Ahman," *Hymns of the Church
of Jesus Christ of Latter-day Saints* [Salt Lake City: The Church of Jesus
Christ of Latter-day Saints, 1985], 49)

⤚ 18 ⤙

VISION OF THE THREE DEGREES
OF GLORY

In February 1832, while working on the inspired revision of the Bible in the home of John Johnson in Hiram, Ohio, Joseph Smith and Sidney Rigdon studied John 5:29, which discusses the resurrection of the just and the unjust. While pondering this topic, they received a sequence of visions concerning the three degrees of glory in the resurrection. The sole participants in these visions were Joseph and Sidney. Others were present in the room, and although they were not able to view "the Vision," it was apparent to them that the Prophet and Elder Rigdon were receiving a revelation. Philo Dibble, for example, reported that he witnessed marked changes in the Prophet and could see and feel the glory of the Spirit but was not privileged to see what Sidney and Joseph saw. These visions are now recorded as section 76 in the Doctrine and Covenants.

Elder Melvin J. Ballard of the Quorum of the Twelve has commented on the significance of this vision, saying: "The greatest revelation the Lord, Jesus Christ, has ever given to man, so far as record is made, was given to the Prophet Joseph Smith on the 16th of April, 1832, known as the 76th section of the book of Doctrine & Covenants, commonly called for years and still known as 'The Vision.' I say, this to my mind is the climax of all wonderful revelations that have come from the Lord from the days of Father Adam until the present moment" (Melvin J. Ballard, *Three Degrees of Glory* [Salt Lake City: Magazine Printing and Publishing, 1975], 3).

Joseph Smith Jr.

Upon my return from [the] Amherst conference, I resumed the translation of the Scriptures. From sundry revelations which had been received, it was apparent that many important points touching the salvation of man, had been taken from the Bible, or lost before it was compiled. It appeared self-evident from what truths were left, that if God rewarded every one according to the deeds done in the body the term "Heaven," as intended for the Saints' eternal home[,] must include more kingdoms than one. Accordingly, on the 16th of February, 1832, while translating St. John's Gospel, myself and Elder Rigdon saw the following vision. [See D&C 76] (Joseph Smith, *History of The Church of Jesus Christ of Latter-day Saints*, 7 vols., ed. B. H. Roberts [Salt Lake City: Deseret Book, 1980], 1:245).

Doctrine and Covenants 76:20–21

We beheld the glory of the Son, on the right hand of the Father, and received of his fulness;

And saw the holy angels, and them who are sanctified before his throne, worshiping God, and the Lamb, who worship him forever and ever.

Joseph Smith Jr.

I know God. I have gazed upon the glory of God, the throne, visions and glories of God, and the visions of eternity in days gone by (*History of the Church*, 6:290).

Joseph Smith Jr.

All your losses will be made up to you in the resurrection, provided you continue faithful. By the vision of the Almighty I have seen it (*History of the Church*, 5:362).

Joseph Smith Jr.

Could you gaze into heaven five minutes, you would know more than you would by reading all that ever was written on the subject (*History of the Church*, 6:50).

Joseph Smith Jr.

I could explain a hundred fold more than I ever have of the glories of the kingdoms manifested to me in the vision, were I permitted, and were the people prepared to receive them (*History of the Church*, 5:402).

Joseph Smith Jr.

Nothing could be more pleasing to the Saints upon the order of the kingdom of the Lord, than the light which burst upon the world through the foregoing vision [D&C 76]. Every law, every commandment, every promise, every truth, and every point touching the destiny of man, from Genesis to Revelation, where the purity of the scriptures remains unsullied by the folly of men, go to show the perfection of the theory [of different degrees of glory in the future life] and witnesses the fact that that document is a transcript from the records of the eternal world. The sublimity of the ideas; the purity of the language; the scope for action; the continued duration for completion, in order that the heirs of salvation may confess the Lord and bow the knee; the rewards for faithfulness, and the punishments for sins, are so much beyond the narrow-mindedness of men, that every honest man is constrained to exclaim: "*It came from God*" (*History of the Church*, 1:252–53).

Philo Dibble

The vision which is recorded in the Book of Doctrine and Covenants was given at the house of "Father Johnson," in Hyrum, Ohio, and during the time that Joseph and Sidney were in the spirit and saw the heavens open, there were other men in the room, perhaps twelve, among whom I was one during a part of the time—probably two-thirds of the time,—I saw the glory and felt the power, but did not see the vision.

The events and conversation, while they were seeing what is written (and many things were seen and related that are not written,) I will relate as minutely as is necessary.

Joseph would, at intervals, say: "What do I see?" as one might say while looking out the window and beholding what all in the room could not see. Then he would relate what he had seen or what he was looking at. Then Sidney replied, "I see the same." Presently Sidney would say "what do I see?" and would repeat what he had seen or was seeing, and

Joseph would reply, "I see the same."

This manner of conversation was repeated at short intervals to the end of the vision, and during the whole time not a word was spoken by any other person. Not a sound nor motion made by anyone but Joseph and Sidney, and it seemed to me that they never moved a joint or limb during the time I was there, which I think was over an hour, and to the end of the vision.

Joseph sat firmly and calmly all the time in the midst of a magnificent glory, but Sidney sat limp and pale, apparently as limber as a rag, observing which, Joseph remarked, smilingly, "Sidney is not used to it as I am" (Philo Dibble, "Recollections of the Prophet Joseph Smith," *Juvenile Instructor* 27 [15 May 1892]: 303–4).

Wilford Woodruff

Before I saw Joseph I said I did not care how old he was, or how young he was; I did not care how he looked—whether his hair was long or short; the man that advanced that revelation [D&C 76] was a prophet of God (Wilford Woodruff, *The Discourses of Wilford Woodruff*, ed. G. Homer Durham [Salt Lake City: Bookcraft, 1969], 29).

Wilford Woodruff

I will refer to the "Vision" alone, as a revelation which gives more light, more truth, and more principle than any revelation contained in any other book we ever read (*The Discourses of Wilford Woodruff*, 47).

Brigham Young

When God revealed to Joseph Smith and Sidney Rigdon that there was a place prepared for all, according to the light they had received and their rejection of evil and practice of good, it was a great trial to many, and some apostatized because God was not going to send to everlasting punishment heathens and infants, but had a place of salvation, in due time, for all, and would bless the honest and virtuous and truthful, whether

Brigham Young
(Courtesy of the Church Archives, The Church of Jesus Christ of Latter-day Saints)

they ever belonged to any church or not (in *Journal of Discourses*, 26 vols. [London: Latter-day Saints' Book Depot, 1854–86], 16:42).

JOSEPH SMITH'S INSPIRED POEM

William W. Phelps was a close friend of the Prophet but became disaffected from the Church and was subsequently excommunicated in 1838. He found no peace in his apostasy. Humbled and penitent, he petitioned for reinstatement. In response to his plea, Joseph penned a letter filled with the spirit of reconciliation and forgiveness. Knowing Phelps to be a poet, the Prophet closed his letter with a short poem of his own:

> Dear Brother Phelps:—I must say that it is with no ordinary feelings I endeavor to write a few lines to you in answer to yours of the 29th ultimo; at the same time I am rejoiced at the privilege granted me.
>
> You may in some measure realize what my feelings, as well as Elder Rigdon's and Brother Hyrum's were, when we read your letter—truly our hearts were melted into tenderness and compassion when we ascertained your resolves, &c...
>
> It is true, that we have suffered much in consequence of your behavior—the cup of gall, already full enough for mortals to drink, was indeed filled to overflowing when you turned against us. One with whom we had oft taken sweet counsel together, and enjoyed many refreshing seasons from the Lord—"had it been an enemy, we could have borne it."
> . . .
>
> However, the cup has been drunk, the will of our Father has been done, and we are yet alive, for which we thank the Lord. And having been delivered from the hands of wicked men by the mercy of our God, we say it is your privilege to be delivered from the powers of the adversary, be brought into the liberty of God's dear children, and again take your stand among the Saints of the Most High, and by diligence, humility, and love unfeigned, commend yourself to our God, and your God, and to the Church of Jesus Christ.
>
> Believing your confession to be real, and your repentance genuine, I shall be happy once again to give you the right

hand of fellowship, and rejoice over the returning prodigal.

Your letter was read to the Saints last Sunday, and an expression of their feeling was taken, when it was unanimously *Resolved*, That W. W. Phelps should be received into fellowship.

"Come on, dear brother, since the war is past,
For friends at first, are friends again at last."
Yours as ever,
Joseph Smith, Jun.
(*History of the Church*, 4:162–64; original capitalization and punctuation preserved)

So moved by the Prophet's forgiveness and charity, Brother Phelps returned to the church and later expressed his immense gratitude in a poem to the Prophet he entitled "Vade Mecum," or "Go With Me":

Go with me, will you go to the saints that have died,—
To the next, better world, where the righteous reside;
Where the angels and spirits in harmony be
In the joys of a vast paradise? Go with me.
Go with me where the truth and the virtues prevail;
Where the union is one, and the years never fail;
Not a heart can conceive, nor a nat'ral eye see
What the Lord has prepar'd for the just. Go with me.
Go with me where there is no destruction or war;
Neither tyrants, or sland'rers, or nations ajar;
Where the system is perfect, and happiness free,
And the life is eternal with God. Go with me.
Go with me, will you go to the mansions above,
Where the bliss, and the knowledge, the light, and the love,
And the glory of God do eternally be?—
Death, the wages of sin, is not there. Go with me.
Nauvoo, January, 1843
(W. W. Phelps, "From W. W. Phelps to Joseph Smith: The Prophet. Vade Mecum, (translated) Go With Me"; *Times & Seasons* 4 [1 February 1843]: 81–82; as cited in *Encyclopedia of Joseph Smith's Teachings*, ed. Larry E. Dahl and Donald Q. Cannon [Salt Lake City: Bookcraft, 1997], 164–65)

The Prophet Joseph spent the next month drafting a response. The February issue of the *Times and Seasons* printed Phelps's poem, followed by "The Answer: A Vision"—a 312-line poetic response by Joseph Smith. It is an incredible poem, and one of the greatest commentaries on The Vision ever recorded. It is included here in its entirety:

A Vision

I will go, I will go, to the home of the Saints,
Where the virtue's the value, and life the reward;
But before I return to my former estate
I must fulfill the mission I had from the Lord.

Wherefore, hear, O ye heavens, and give ear O ye earth;
And rejoice ye inhabitants truly again;
For the Lord he is God, and his life never ends,
And besides him there ne'er was a Saviour of men.

His ways are a wonder; his wisdom is great;
The extent of his doings, there's none can unveil;
His purposes fail not; from age unto age
He still is the same, and his years never fail.

His throne is the heavens, his life time is all
Of eternity *now*, and eternity *then*;
His union is power, and none stays his hand,—
The Alpha, Omega, for ever: Amen.

For thus saith the Lord, in the spirit of truth,
I am merciful, gracious, and good unto those
That fear me, and live for the life that's to come;
My delight is to honor the saints with repose;

That serve me in righteousness true to the end;
Eternal's their glory, and great their reward;
I'll surely reveal all my myst'ries to them,—
The great hidden myst'ries in my kingdom stor'd—

From the council in Kolob, to time on the earth.
And for ages to come unto them I will show
My pleasure & will, what my kingdom will do:
Eternity's wonders they truly shall know.

Great things of the future I'll show unto them,

Yea, things of the vast generations to rise;
For their wisdom and glory shall be very great,
And their pure understanding extend to the skies:

And before them the wisdom of wise men shall cease,
And the nice understanding of prudent ones fail!
For the light of my spirit shall light mine elect,
And the truth is so mighty 't will ever prevail.

And the secrets and plans of my will I'll reveal;
The sanctified pleasures when earth is renew'd,
What the eye hath not seen, nor the ear hath yet heard;
Nor the heart of the natural man ever hath view'd.

I, Joseph, the prophet, in spirit beheld,
And the eyes of the inner man truly did see
Eternity sketch'd in a vision from God,
Of what was, and now is, and yet is to be.

Those things which the Father ordained of old,
Before the world was, or a system had run,—
Through Jesus the Maker and Savior of all;
The only begotten, (Messiah) his son.

Of whom I bear record, as all prophets have,
And the record I bear is the fullness,—yea even
The truth of the gospel of Jesus—*the Christ*,
With whom I convers'd, in the vision of heav'n.

For while in the act of translating his word,
Which the Lord in his grace had appointed to me,
I came to the gospel recorded by John,
Chapter fifth and the twenty ninth verse, which you'll see.

Which was given as follows:

"Speaking of the resurrection of the dead,—
"Concerning those who shall hear the voice of the son
of man—
"And shall come forth:—
"They who have done good in the resurrection of the just.
"And they who have done evil in the resurrection of the
unjust."

I marvel'd at these resurrections, indeed!
For it came unto me by the spirit direct:—
And while I did meditate what it all meant,
The Lord touch'd the eyes of my own intellect:—

Hosanna forever! they open'd anon,
And the glory of God shone around where I was;
And there was the Son, at the Father's right hand,
In a fullness of glory, and holy applause.

I beheld round the throne, holy angels and hosts,
And sanctified beings from worlds that have been,
In holiness worshipping God and the Lamb,
Forever and ever, amen and amen!

And now after all of the proofs made of him,
By witnesses truly, by whom he was known,
This is mine, last of all, that he lives; yea, he lives!
And sits at the right hand of God, on his throne.

And I heard a great voice, bearing record from heav'n,
He's the Saviour, and only begotten of God—
By him, of him, and through him, the worlds were all
made,
Even all that career in the heavens so broad,

Whose inhabitants, too, from the first to the last,
Are sav'd by the very same Saviour of ours;
And, of course, are begotten God's daughters and sons,
By the very same truths, and the very same pow'rs.

And I saw and bear record of warfare in heav'n;
For an angel of light, in authority great,
Rebell'd against Jesus, and sought for his pow'r,
But was thrust down to woe from his Godified state.

And the heavens all wept, and the tears drop'd like dew,
That Lucifer, son of the morning had fell!
Yea, is fallen! is fall'n, and become, Oh alas!
The son of Perdition; the devil of hell!

And while I was yet in the spirit of truth,
The commandment was: write ye the vision all out;

For Satan, old serpent, the devil's for war,—
And yet will encompass the saints round about.

And I saw, too, the suff'ring and mis'ry of those,
(Overcome by the devil, in warfare and fight,)
In hell-fire, and vengeance, the doom of the damn'd;
For the Lord said, the vision is further: so write.

For thus saith the Lord, now concerning all those
Who know of my power and partake of the same;
And suffer themselves, that they be overcome
By the power of Satan; despising my name:—

Defying my power, and denying the truth;—
They are they—of the world, or of men, most forlorn,
The Sons of Perdition, of whom, ah! I say,
'T were better for them had they never been born!

They're vessels of wrath, and dishonor to God,
Doom'd to suffer his wrath, in the regions of woe,
Through the terrific night of eternity's round,
With the devil and all of his angels below:

Of whom it is said, no forgiveness is giv'n,
In this world, alas! nor the world that's to come;
For they have denied the spirit of God.
After having receiv'd it: and mis'ry's their doom.

And denying the only begotten of God,—
And crucify him to themselves, as they do,
And openly put him to shame in their flesh,
By gospel they cannot repentance renew.

They are they, who must go to the great lake of fire,
Which burneth with brimstone, yet never consumes,
And dwell with the devil, and angels of his,
While eternity goes and eternity comes.

They are they, who must groan through the great second
death,
And are not redeemed in the time of the Lord;
While all the rest are, through the triumph of Christ,

Made partakers of grace, by the power of his word

The myst'ry of Godliness truly is great;—
The past, and the present, and what is to be;
And this is the gospel—glad tidings and all,
Which the voice from the heavens bore record to me:

That he came to the world in the middle of time,
To lay down his life for his friends and his foes,
And bear away sin as a mission of love;
And sanctify earth for a blessed repose.

'Tis decreed, that he'll save all the work of his hands,
And sanctify them by his own precious blood;
And purify earth for the Sabbath of rest,
By the agent of fire, as it was by the flood.

The Savior will save all his Father did give,
Even all that he gave in the regions abroad,
Save the Sons of Perdition: They're lost; ever lost,
And can never return to the presence of God.

They are they, who must reign with the devil in hell,
In eternity now, and eternity then,
Where the worm dieth not, and the fire is not quench'd;—
And the punishment still, is eternal. Amen.

And which is the torment apostates receive,
But the end, or the place where the torment began,
Save to them who are made to partake of the same,
Was never, nor will be, revealed unto man.

Yet God shows by vision a glimpse of their fate,
And straightway he closes the scene that was shown:
So the width, or the depth, or the misery thereof,
Save to those that partake, is forever unknown.

And while I was pondering, the vision was closed;
And the voice said to me, write the vision: for lo!
'Tis the end of the scene of the sufferings of those,
Who remain filthy still in their anguish and woe.

And again I bear record of heavenly things,

Where virtue's the value, above all that's pric'd—
Of the truth of the gospel concerning the just,
That rise in the first resurrection of Christ.

Who receiv'd and believ'd, and repented likewise,
And then were baptis'd, as a man always was,
Who ask'd and receiv'd a remission of sin,
And honored the kingdom by keeping its laws.

Being buried in water, as Jesus had been,
And keeping the whole of his holy commands,
They received the gift of the spirit of truth,
By the ordinance truly of laying on hands.

For these overcome, by their faith and their works,
Being tried in their life-time, as purified gold,
And seal'd by the spirit of promise, to life,
By men called of God, as was Aaron of old.

They are they, of the church of the first born of God,—
And unto whose hands he committeth all things;
For they hold the keys of the kingdom of heav'n,
And reign with the Savior, as priests, and as kings.

They're priests of the order of Melchisedek,
Like Jesus, (from whom is this highest reward,)
Receiving a fullness of glory and light;
As written: They're Gods; even sons of the Lord.

So all things are theirs; yea, of life, or of death;
Yea, whether things now, or to come, all are theirs,
And they are the Savior's, and he is the Lord's
Having overcome all, as eternity's heirs.

'Tis wisdom that man never glory in man,
But give God the glory for all that he hath;
For the righteous will walk in the presence of God,
While the wicked are trod under foot in his wrath.

Yea, the righteous shall dwell in the presence of God,
And of Jesus, forever, from earth's second birth—
For when he comes down in the splendor of heav'n,
All these he'll bring with him, to reign on the earth.

These are they that arise in their bodies of flesh,
When the trump of the first resurrection shall sound;
These are they that come up to Mount Zion, in life,
Where the blessings and gifts of the spirit abound.

These are they that have come to the heavenly place;
To the numberless courses of angels above:
To the city of God; e'en the holiest of all,
And the home of the blessed, the fountain of love:

To the church of old Enoch, and of the first born:
And gen'ral assembly of ancient renown'd,
Whose names are all kept in the archives of heav'n,
As chosen and faithful, and fit to be crown'd.

These are they that are perfect through Jesus' own blood,
Whose bodies celestial are mention'd by Paul,
Where the sun is the typical glory thereof,
And God, and his Christ, are the true judge of all.

Again I beheld the terrestrial world,
In the order and glory of Jesus, go on;
'Twas not as the church of the first born of God,
But shone in its place, as the moon to the sun.

Behold, these are they that have died without law;
The heathen of ages that never had hope,
And those of the region and shadow of death,
The spirits in prison, that light has brought up.

To spirits in prison the Savior once preach'd,
And taught them the gospel, with powers afresh;
And then were the living baptiz'd for their dead,
That they might be judg'd as if men in the flesh.

These are they that are hon'rable men of the earth;
Who were blinded and dup'd by the cunning of men:
They receiv'd not the truth of the Savior at first;
But did, when they heard it in prison, again.

Not valiant for truth, they obtain'd not the crown,
But are of that glory that's typ'd by the moon:
They are they, that come into the presence of Christ,

But not to the fullness of God, on his throne.

Again I beheld the telestial, as third,
The lesser, or starry world, next in its place,
For the leaven must leaven three measure of meal,
And every knee bow that is subject to grace.

These are they that receiv'd not the gospel of Christ,
Or evidence, either, that he ever was;
As the stars are all diff'rent in glory and light,
So differs the glory of these by the laws.

These are they that deny not the spirit of God,
But are thrust down to hell, with the devil, for sins,
As hypocrites, liars, whoremongers, and thieves,
And stay 'till the last resurrection begins.

'Till the Lamb shall have finish'd the work he begun;
Shall have trodden the wine press, in fury alone,
And overcome all by the pow'r of his might:
He conquers to conquer, and save all his own.

These are they that receive not a fullness of light,
From Christ, in eternity's world, where they are,
The terrestrial sends them the Comforter, though;
And minist'ring angels, to happify there.

And so the telestial is minister'd to,
By ministers from the terrestrial one,
As terrestrial is, from the celestial throne;
And the great, greater, greatest, seem's stars, moon, and
sun.

And thus I beheld, in the vision of heav'n,
The telestial glory, dominion and bliss,
Surpassing the great understanding of men,—
Unknown, save reveal'd, in a world vain as this.

And lo, I beheld the terrestrial, too,
Which excels the telestial in glory and light,
In splendor, and knowledge, and wisdom, and joy,
In blessings, and graces, dominion and might.

I beheld the celestial, in glory sublime;
Which is the most excellent kingdom that is,—
Where God, e'en the Father, in harmony reigns;
Almighty, supreme, and eternal, in bliss.

Where the church of the first born in union reside,
And they see as they're seen, and they know as they're
known;
Being equal in power, dominion and might,
With a fullness of glory and grace, round his throne.

The glory celestial is one like the sun;
The glory terrestr'al is one like the moon;
The glory telestial is one like the stars,
And all harmonize like the parts of a tune.

As the stars are all different in luster and size,
So the telestial region, is mingled in bliss;
From the least unto greatest, and greatest to least,
The reward is exactly as promis'd in this.

These are they that came out for Apollos and Paul;
For Cephas and Jesus, in all kinds of hope;
For Enoch and Moses, and Peter, and John;
For Luther and Calvin, and even the Pope.

For they never received the gospel of Christ,
Nor the prophetic spirit that came from the Lord;
Nor the covenant neither, which Jacob once had;
They went their own way, and they have their reward.

By the order of God, last of all, these are they,
That will not be gather'd with saints here below,
To be caught up to Jesus, and meet in the cloud:—
In darkness they worshipp'd; to darkness they go.

These are they that are sinful, the wicked at large,
That glutted their passion by meanness or worth;
All liars, adulterers, sorc'rers, and proud;
And suffer, as promis'd, God's wrath on the earth.

These are they that must suffer the vengeance of hell,
'Till Christ shall have trodden all enemies down,

And perfected his work, in the fullness of times;
And is crown'd on his throne with his glorious crown.

The vast multitude of the telestial world—
As the stars of the skies, or the sands of the sea;—
The voice of Jehovah echo'd far and wide,
Ev'ry tongue shall confess, and they all bow the knee.

Ev'ry man shall be judg'd by the works of his life,
And receive a reward in the mansions prepar'd;
For his judgments are just, and his works never end,
As his prophets and servants have always declar'd.

But the great things of God, which he show'd unto me,
Unlawful to utter, I dare not declare;
They surpass all the wisdom and greatness of men,
And only are seen, as has Paul, where they are.

I will go, I will go, while the secret of life,
Is blooming in heaven, and blasting in hell;
Is leafing on earth, and a budding in space:—
I will go, I will go, with you, brother, farewell.

JOSEPH SMITH

(Joseph Smith Jr., "The Answer To W. W. Phelps, Esq.
A Vision," *Times & Seasons* 4 [1 February 1843]: 82–85)

҉ 19 ҉

APOSTASY AND PERSECUTIONS
IN KIRTLAND

While Kirtland served as the headquarters for the Church, many valuable instructions were given by revelation, the power of God was made manifest among the Saints, Joseph Smith and Sidney Rigdon continued their work on the Inspired Version of the Bible, numerous revelations now contained in the Doctrine and Covenants were received, and a temple was built—but all this was accompanied by intense poverty and false displays of spirituality. The spirit of apostasy overcame many, and severe persecution followed. In addition to the magnificent outpouring of the Holy Spirit while the Saints resided in Kirtland, many false spirits and false forms of spirituality made themselves manifest.

"Many false spirits were introduced, many strange visions were seen, and wild, enthusiastic notions were entertained; men ran out of doors under the influence of this spirit, and some of them got upon the stumps of trees and shouted, and all kinds of extravagances were entered into by them; . . . many ridiculous things were entered into, calculated to bring disgrace upon the Church of God, to cause the Spirit of God to be withdrawn" (Joseph Smith, *History of The Church of Jesus Christ of Latter-day Saints,* 7 vols., ed. B. H. Roberts [Salt Lake City: Deseret Book, 1976], 4:580).

This chapter captures some of the hardships suffered by those striving to build and uphold the kingdom of God in Kirtland at this time.

Tarring and Feathering of the Prophet Joseph Smith

As persecution against the Saints continued, Joseph Smith and Sidney Rigdon were forcefully taken from their homes on March 24, 1832, beaten, and tarred and feathered. "During the attack, a little child, Joseph Smith Murdock, was exposed to the night air, being sick with the measles, and died in consequence. That little baby boy is sometimes called the first martyr of the Church" (Andrew Jenson, *Encyclopedic History of The Church of Jesus Christ of Latter-day Saints* [Salt Lake City: Deseret News Publishing Co., 1941], 338). Following is the official account about the events of that fateful evening:

On the 24th of March [1832], the twins before mentioned, which had been sick of the measles for some time, caused us [Joseph and Emma Smith] to be broken of our rest in taking care of them, especially my wife. In the evening I told her she had better retire to rest with one of the children, and I would watch with the sicker child. In the night she told me I had better lie down on the trundle bed, and I did so, and was soon after awakened by her screaming murder, when I found myself going out of the door, in the hands of about a dozen men; some of whose hands were in my hair, and some had hold of my shirt, drawers and limbs. The foot of the trundle bed was towards the door, leaving only room enough for the door to swing open. My wife heard a gentle tapping on the windows which she then took no particular notice of (but which was unquestionably designed for ascertaining whether or not we were all asleep), and soon after the mob burst open the door and surrounded the bed in an instant, and, as I said, the first I knew I was going out of the door in the hands of an infuriated mob. I made a desperate struggle, as I was forced out, to extricate myself, but only cleared one leg, with which I made a pass at one man, and he fell on the door steps. I was immediately overpowered again; and they swore by G—, they would kill me if I did not be still, which quieted me. As they passed around the house with me, the fellow that I kicked came to me and thrust his hand, all covered with blood, into my face and with an exulting horse laugh, muttered, "Ge, gee, G—d—ye, I'l[1] fix ye."

They then seized me by the throat and held on till I lost my breath. After I came to, as they passed along with me, about thirty rods from the house, I saw Elder Rigdon stretched out on the ground, whither they had dragged him by his heels. I supposed he was dead.

I began to plead with them, saying, "You will have mercy and spare my life, I hope." To which they replied, "G—d—ye, call on yer God for help, we'll show ye no mercy;" and the people began to show themselves in every direction; one coming from the orchard had a plank; and I expected they would kill me, and carry me off on the plank; They then turned to the right, and went on about thirty rods farther; about sixty rods from the house, and thirty from where I saw Elder Rigdon, into the meadow, where they stopped, and one said, "Simonds, Simonds," (meaning, I supposed, Simonds Rider,) "pull up his drawers, pull up his drawers, he will take cold." Another replied: "Ain't ye going to kill 'im? ain't ye going to kill 'im?" when a group of mobbers collected a little way off, and said: "Simonds, Simonds, come here;" and "Simonds" charged those who had hold of me to keep me from touching the ground (as they had done all the time), lest I should get a spring upon them. They held a council, and as I could occasionally overhear a word, I supposed it was to know whether or not it was best to kill me. They returned after a while, when I learned that they had concluded not to kill me, but to beat and scratch me well, tear off my shirt and drawers, and leave me naked. One cried, "Simonds, Simonds, where is the tar bucket?" "I don't know," answered one, "where 'tis, Eli's left it."

They ran back and fetched the bucket of tar, when one exclaimed, with an oath, "Let us tar up his mouth"; and they tried to force the tar-paddle into my mouth; I twisted my head around, so that they could not; and they cried out, "G—d—ye, hold up yer head and let us giv ye some tar." They then tried to force a vial into my mouth, and broke it in my teeth. All my clothes were torn off me except my shirt collar; and one man fell on me and scratched my body with his nails like a mad cat, and then muttered out: "G—d—ye, that's the way the Holy Ghost falls on folks!"

They then left me, and I attempted to rise, but fell again; I pulled the tar away from my lips, so that I could breathe more freely, and after a while I began to recover, and raised myself up, whereupon I saw two lights. I made my way towards one of them, and found it was Father Johnson's. When I had come to the door I was naked, and the tar made me look as if I were covered with blood, and when my wife saw me she thought I was all crushed to pieces, and fainted. During the affray abroad, the sisters of the neighborhood had collected at my room. I called for a blanket, they threw me one and shut the door; I wrapped it around me and went in.

In the meantime, Brother John Poorman heard an outcry across the corn field, and running that way met Father Johnson, who had been fastened in his house at the commencement of the assault, by having his door barred by the mob, but on calling to his wife to bring his gun, saying he would blow a hole through the door, the mob fled, and Father Johnson, seizing a club, ran after the party that had Elder Rigdon, and knocked down one man, and raised his club to level another, exclaiming, "What are you doing here?" when they left Elder Rigdon and turned upon Father Johnson, who, turning to run toward his own house, met Brother Poorman coming out of the corn field; each supposing the other to be a mobber, an encounter ensued, and Poorman gave Johnson a severe blow on the left shoulder with a stick or stone, which brought him to the ground. Poorman ran immediately towards Father Johnson's, and arriving while I was waiting for the blanket, exclaimed, "I'm afraid I've killed him." "Killed who?["] asked one; when Poorman hastily related the circumstances of the encounter near the corn field, and went into the shed and hid himself. Father Johnson soon recovered so as to come to the house, when the whole mystery was quickly solved concerning the difficulty between him and Poorman, who, on learning the facts, joyfully came from his hiding place.

My friends spent the night in scraping and removing the tar, and washing and cleansing my body; so that by morning I was ready to be clothed again. This being the Sabbath morning, the people assembled for meeting at the usual hour of worship, and among them came also the mobbers; viz.: Simonds Rider, a Campbellite preacher and leader of the mob; one McClentic, who had his hands in my hair; one Streeter, son of a Campbellite minister; and Felatiah Allen, Esq., who gave the mob a barrel of whisky to raise their spirits. Besides these named, there were many others in the mob. *With my flesh all scarified and defaced, I preached to the congregation as usual, and in the afternoon of the same day baptized three individuals* [by cutting a hole in the iced-over river].

The next morning I went to see Elder Rigdon, and found him crazy, and his head highly inflamed, for they had dragged him by his heels, and those, too, so high from the ground that he could not raise his head from the rough, frozen surface, which lacerated it exceedingly; and when he saw me he called to his wife to bring him his razor. She asked him what he wanted of it; and he replied, to kill me. Sister Rigdon left the room, and he asked me to bring his razor; I asked him what he wanted of it, and he replied he wanted to kill his wife; and he continued delirious some days. The feathers which were used with the tar on this occasion, the mob took out of Elder Rigdon's house. After they had seized him, and dragged him out, one of the banditti returned to get some pillows; when the women shut him in and kept him a prisoner some time.

During the mobbing one of the twins contracted a severe cold, [and] continued to grow worse until Friday, and then died. The mobbers were composed of various religious parties, but mostly Campbellites, Methodists and Baptists, who continued to molest and menace Father Johnson's house for a long time (*History of the Church*, 1:261–65; emphasis added).

PERSECUTION AND MOBOCRACY IN KIRTLAND

During the 1830s, the Saints were suffering intense persecution in both Ohio and Missouri. The mob violence was relentless, and many Saints lived each day in fear.

Joseph Smith III

It must be remembered that from 1830 to the time of [Joseph Smith's] death, he and his people were never safe from invasion and persecution from which the Saints were well worn out. Raids from savages were not more dangerous than the illegal attacks from white men. The Saints had fled from Kirtland to the West to build up a peaceful settlement upon the borders of civilization; and there they had been met not only by ridicule, bigotry, intolerance, and bitter religious opposition, but also by injury, oppression, and loss of life and property (as cited in Joseph Smith III, *Memories of Old Nauvoo*, ed. Paul V. Ludy [Bates City, Missouri: Paul V. Ludy and Associates, 2001], 7–8).

Joseph Smith Jr.

[The Kirtland period was a] long seven years of servitude, persecution, and affliction in the midst of our enemies (Joseph Smith, *History of the Church*, 3:11).

Benjamin F. Johnson

Much of my time in boyhood was spent in assisting to prepare arms for the protection of the Saints. The lower story of my mother's house in Kirtland was at that time used by Brother M. C. Davis as a gunsmith shop, for the manufacture of defensive weapons for the use of the people (Benjamin F. Johnson, *My Life's Review* [Mesa, Arizona: 21st Century Printing, 1992], 24).

Ira Ames

Ever since my arrival in Kirtland, I had stood guard at night in consequence of the mob and persecutions we endured. Especially this winter of 1835, I [was] frequently taking my blanket and sleeping in Joseph's house and guarding my portion of the time and continued as one of Joseph's body guards until I left Kirtland (Max H. Parkin, *Conflict at Kirtland* [Provo, Utah: Department of Seminaries and Institutes of Religion, 1967], 206–7).

George A. Smith

In consequence of the persecution which raged against the Prophet Joseph and the constant threats to do him violence, it was found necessary to keep continual guard to prevent his being murdered by his enemies . . . During the fall and winter I took a part of this service going [two and a half] miles to guard at President Rigdon's (George A. Smith, "George A. Smith," in *Writings of Early Latter-day Saints and Their Contemporaries, A Database Collection*, comp. Milton V. Backman [Provo, Utah: BYU Religious Studies Center, 1996], 76).

Joseph Smith Jr.

All of the church in Kirtland had to lie every night for a long time upon our arms to keep off mobs, of forties, of eighties, & of hundreds to save our lives and the press, and that we might not be scattered & driven to the four winds! (*Personal Writings of Joseph Smith*, ed. Dean C. Jessee [Salt Lake City: Deseret Book, 2002], 336).

Oliver Cowdery

Our enemies have threatened us, but thank the Lord we are yet on earth. They came out on the 8th about 12 o'clock at night, a little west & fired cannon, we supposed to alarm us, but no one was frightened, but all prepared to defend ourselves if they made a sally upon our houses (Oliver Cowdery, *Oliver Cowdery Letterbooks*, [San Marino, California: Huntington Library, n.d.], January 21, 1834; as cited in Karl Ricks Anderson, *Joseph Smith's Kirtland* [Salt Lake City: Deseret Book, 1989], 25).

Hepzibah Richards

All our friends design leaving this place soon as possible.... The feeling seems to be that Kirtland must be trodden down by the wicked for a season.... Probably several hundred families will leave within a few weeks (Hepzibah Richards, *Letter from Hepzibah Richards to Willard Richards, 22 January 1838* [LDS Church Archives, Church Historical Department, The Church of Jesus Christ of Latter-day Saints, Salt Lake City]; as cited in *Church History in the Fulness of Times*, Prepared by the Church Educational System [Salt Lake City: The Church of Jesus Christ of Latter-day Saints, 1993], 178).

VEXATIOUS LAWSUITS AT KIRTLAND

Heber C. Kimball

Joseph was sued before a magistrate's court in Painesville on a vexatious suit. I carried him from Kirtland to Painesville, with four or five others, in my wagon every morning for five days, and brought them back in the evening. We were often waylaid, but managed to elude our enemies by rapid driving and taking different roads. Esq. Bissell defended the Prophet.

Mobs were organized around Kirtland, who were enraged against us, ready to destroy us (Daniel H. Wells, "History of Brigham Young," *Millennial Star* 26 [20 August 1864]: 535).

Joseph Smith Jr.

(27 July 1837)

We were detained all day by malicious and vexatious lawsuits. About sunset I got into my carriage to return home to Kirtland; at this moment the sheriff sprang into the carriage, seized my lines, and served another writ on me (*History of the Church*, 1:502).

ECONOMIC HARDSHIPS SUFFERED IN KIRTLAND

Newel K. Whitney

(18 September 1837)

It is a fact well known that the Saints in the city of Kirtland have been called to endure great affliction for the truth's sake, and to bear a

Newel K. Whitney
(Courtesy of the Church Archives, The Church of Jesus Christ of Latter-day Saints)

heavy burden in order that the foundation of the kingdom of God might be laid on a sure and certain basis ... The exertions of the enemy ... have given to the Saints great trouble, and caused them much expense. In addition to this, they have had to publish the word of the Lord, which has been attended with great expense. These things, together with building the House of the Lord, have embarrassed them very much; for when subscriptions failed they went on and accomplished the work of building the house themselves, plighting all that they had, property, credit, and reputation, and by these means accomplished this great work which is the wonder and admiration of the world. This they have done in faith . . . And besides all this there have been a large number of poor who have had to receive assistance from the donations of the Church, which have tended to increase its embarrassments (*History of the Church*, 2:515).

George A. Smith

In the spring of 1835 a majority of the inhabitants of Kirtland combined together and warned all the Saints to leave the town. This was done to prevent any of our people becoming a town charge in case of poverty. They then bought up all the grain that was for sale in the country around, and refused to sell a particle of it to our people. Mr. Lyman, a Presbyterian owning the Kirtland Mills, was at the head of the movement. He accumulated several thousand bushels of grain in his mill and refused to sell the least portion of it to any of the Saints. This arrangement was brought about by a combination of all religious sects in the vicinity. Mr. Chase, a Presbyterian neighbor of ours, who had a quantity of grain on hand and had refused to sell a particle at any price, came to my father one morning and asked him if he could board the school mistress his portion, assigning as a reason that he had not got provisions to feed her on. My father, although he had eaten the last morsel of bread stuff we had, for breakfast, told him he could board her as well as not. This was done to ascertain our straitened circumstances.

But Joseph on learning the plan of our enemies, got the brethren to put their mites together and sent to Portage County and bought a supply of wheat at a reasonable price and carried to a mill owned by one of the brethren several miles from town; so that our Christian friends not only had the mortification of not starving out the Saints, but had when harvest came around a large quantity of grain on hand and no market for it, as our people had raised a supply for themselves (George A. Smith, "George A. Smith," in *Writings of Early Latter-day Saints*, 368–69).

Oliver Huntington

My poor old father who but six months ago was in affluent circumstances, and surrounded with everything to make him comfortable, and render life desirable; [with] a farm of upwards of 230 acres; a good stone house and two frame barns . . . from all these earthly comforts and conveniences, in six months he was brought to live by day's work, and that but very poorly, still my mother was the same mother and the same wife.

It was a torment to each, to see the other in want and still more see their children cry for bread and have none to give them nor know where the next was coming from, and after all their trials and sufferings not only there but elsewhere, never did I hear either of them utter a murmuring or complaining word against any of the authorities of the Church, or express a doubt of the truth of the work. . . . John and I, though small, felt for them as much as our age would and could be expected; we often would kneel beside each other in the woods, and in the barn, daily, and pray to God to have mercy and bless father and mother, that they should not want nor see us want for bread (Oliver Huntington, "Oliver Huntington," *Writings of Early Latter-day Saints*, 28–29).

Brigham Young

You have frequently heard me refer to my poverty when I moved to Kirtland in the fall of 1833. Not a man ever gathered with the Saints, so far as I have known, but had more property than I had. When I came into the church I distributed my substance and went to preaching, and when I gathered with the Saints I had nothing. . . . I went to work for brother Cahoon, one of the Kirtland Temple Committee. He had little or no means, and only a shell of a house. I helped him, and the Lord threw things in his path, and he paid me for my labor (in *Journal of Discourses*, 26 vols. [London: Latter-day Saints' Book Depot, 1854–86], 8:277–78).

Jonathan Crosby

Shortly after we got to Kirtland, Brother B. Young, H. C. Kimball, [and] P. P. Pratt came to me to borrow money. I had nearly 100 dol[lar]s . . . they were very poor. Pres. Young said he had nothing in the house to eat, and he knew not where to get it. . . . He stood in the door of the printing office thinking of his condition and he felt so bad the sweat [rolled off] him. Soon P. P. Pratt came along, and he said to him, "What shall we do?" I have nothing to eat and I don't know where to get it. Broth[er] Pratt said there was a brother and his wife just come to my house he got some money and I think he will lend us some (I had let Brother Pratt have 7 doll[ar]s before). So they all came and gave me their joint note and I let them have 75 doll[ar]s—25 each, this was Jan. of [18]35 (Jonathan Crosby, *Jonathan Crosby Autobiography* [LDS Church Archives], 15; as cited in *Conflict at Kirtland*, 161).

APOSTASY IN KIRTLAND

The Apostasy of Simonds Ryder

(Some members are deceived because they become critical of Church leaders' imperfections. The following story illustrates how Simonds Ryder was deceived in this way.)

Simonds Ryder was converted to the Church in 1831. Later he received a letter signed by the Prophet Joseph Smith and Sidney Rigdon, informing him that it was the Lord's will, made manifest by the Spirit, that he preach the gospel. Both in the letter he received and in the official commission to preach, his name was spelled Rider instead of Ryder. (See *History of the Church*, 1:261.) Simonds Ryder "thought if the 'Spirit' through which he had been called to preach could err in the matter of spelling his name, it might have erred in calling him to the ministry as well; or, in other words, he was led to doubt if he were called at all by the Spirit of God, because of the error in spelling his name!" (*History of the Church*, 1:261).

Simonds Ryder later apostatized from the Church. He led the mob that tarred and feathered Joseph Smith and Sidney Rigdon. Ironically, when he died, Simonds name was misspelled on his headstone. It displays his name as "Rider" not "Ryder." (See Robert J. Woodford, "The Articles and Covenants of the Church of Christ and the Book of Mormon," *Doctrines for Exaltation: The 1989 Sperry Symposium on the Doctrine and Covenants*, ed. Susan Easton Black et al. [Salt Lake City: Deseret Book, 1989], 271.)

Eliza R. Snow

A spirit of speculation had crept into the hearts of some of the Twelve, and nearly, if not every quorum was more or less infected. Most of the Saints were poor, and now prosperity was dawning upon them—the Temple was completed, and in it they had been recipients of marvelous blessings, and many who had been humble and faithful to the performance of every duty—ready to go and come at every call of the Priesthood, were getting haughty in their spirits, and lifted up in the pride of their hearts. As the Saints drank in the love and spirit of the world, the Spirit of the Lord withdrew from their hearts, and they were filled with pride and hatred toward those who maintained their integrity. They linked themselves together in an opposing party—pretended that they constituted the Church, and claimed that the Temple belonged to them, and even attempted to hold it (*History of the Church*, 2:487–88).

Joseph Smith Jr.

As the fruits of this spirit, evil surmisings, fault-finding, disunion, dissension, and apostasy followed in quick succession . . . it seemed as though all the powers of earth and hell were combining their influence in an especial manner to overthrow the Church at once, and make a final end. . . . No quorum in the Church was entirely exempt from the influence of those false spirits who are striving against me for the mastery; even some of the Twelve were so far lost to their high and responsible calling, as to begin to take sides, secretly, with the enemy (*History of the Church*, 2:487–88).

Mary Fielding Smith

(In a letter to her sister Mercy, 1 September 1837.)

I do thank my heavenly Father for the comfort and peace of mind I now enjoy in the midst of all the confusion and perplexity, and raging of the devil against the work of God in this place. For although here is

Mary Fielding Smith
(Courtesy of the Church Archives, The Church of Jesus Christ of Latter-day Saints)

a great number of faithful precious souls, yea the Salt of the Earth is here, yet it may be truly called a place where Satan has his seat. He is frequently stirring up some of the people to strife & contention and dissatisfaction with things they do not understand. . . . I pray God to have mercy upon us all and preserve us from the power of the great enemy who knows he has but a short time to work in. . . . I believe the voice of prayer has sounded in the House of the Lord some days from morning till night and it has been by these means that we have hitherto prevailed and it is by this means only that I for one expect to prevail (Kenneth W. Godfrey, Audrey M. Godfrey and Jill Mulvay Derr, *Women's Voices* [Salt Lake City: Deseret Book, 1982], 63–64; spelling and capitalization standardized).

Benjamin F. Johnson

Brethren who had borne the highest priesthood and who had for years labored, traveled, ministered and suffered together, and even placed their lives upon the same altar, now were governed by a feeling of hate and a spirit to accuse each other, and all for the love of *Accursed Mammon*. All their former companionship in the holy anointing in the Temple of the Lord, where filled with the Holy Ghost, the heavens were opened, and in view of the glories before them they had together shouted "Hosanna to God and the Lamb," all was now forgotten by many, who were like Judas, ready to sell or destroy the Prophet Joseph and his followers. And it almost seemed to me that the brightest stars in our firmament had fallen. Many to whom I had in the past most loved to listen, their voices seemed now the most discordant and hateful to me. From the Quorum of the Twelve fell four of the brightest: Wm. E. McLellin, Luke and Lyman Johnson and John Boyington; of the First Presidency, F. G. Williams; the three Witnesses to the Book of Mormon, Oliver Cowdery, David Whitmer and Martin Harris. Of other very prominent elders were Sylvester Smith, Warren Cowdery, Warren Parrish, Joseph Coe and many others who apostatized or became enemies to the Prophet. I

Benjamin F. Johnson
(Courtesy of the Church Archives, The Church of Jesus Christ of Latter-day Saints)

was then nineteen years of age, and as I now look back through more than fifty years of subsequent experience, to that first great Apostasy, I regard it as the greatest sorrow, disappointment and test through which I have ever passed; the first real experience among false brethren, the greatest sorrow and test for the faithful. But with all my faults I did not forget the Lord nor His chosen servants. And in this day of great affliction and separation by apostasy, I felt to call mightily upon His name, that He would never leave me to follow these examples, but that He would keep me humble, even though in poverty and affliction, so only that I fail not (*My Life's Review*, 28–29).

Lyman Johnson

(To Brigham Young)

If I could believe 'Mormonism' . . . as I did when I traveled with you and preached, if I possessed the world I would give it. I would give anything, I would suffer my right hand to be cut off, if I could believe it again. Then I was full of joy and gladness. My dreams were pleasant. When I awoke in the morning my spirit was cheerful. I was happy by day and by night, full of peace and joy and thanksgiving. But now it is darkness, pain, sorrow, misery in the extreme. I have never since seen a happy moment (*Journal of Discourses*, 19:41).

Lyman Johnson
(Courtesy of the Church Archives, The Church of Jesus Christ of Latter-day Saints)

Brigham Young

(On one occasion, several members of the Twelve, the witnesses of the Book of Mormon, and other authorities of the Church met in the upper room of the temple to determine a way to depose the Prophet Joseph Smith and appoint David Whitmer as president of the Church. Several men present were opposed to such an action. Brigham Young was one of them.)

I rose up, and in a plain and forcible manner told them that Joseph was a Prophet, and I knew it, and that they might rail and slander him as much as they pleased, they could not destroy the appointment of the Prophet of God, they could only destroy their own authority, cut the thread that bound them to the Prophet and to God and sink themselves to hell. Many were highly enraged at my decided opposition to their measures, and Jacob Bump (an old pugilist) was so exasperated that he could not be still. Some of the brethren near him put their hands on him, and requested him to be quiet; but he writhed and twisted his arms and body saying, "How can I keep my hands off that man?" I told him if he thought it would give him any relief he might lay them on. This meeting was broken up without the apostates being able to unite on any decided measures of opposition. This was a crisis when earth and hell seemed leagued to overthrow the Prophet and Church of God. The knees of many of the strongest men in the Church faltered.

During this siege of darkness I stood close by Joseph, and, with all the wisdom and power God bestowed upon me, put through my utmost energies to sustain the servant of God and unite the Quorums of the Church (Elden Jay Watson, *Manuscript History of Brigham Young 1801–1844* [Salt Lake City: Smith Secretarial Service, 1968], 16–17).

Heber C. Kimball

[A] man's life was in danger the moment he spoke in defense of the Prophet of God. During this time I had many days of sorrow and mourning, for my heart sickened to see the awful extent that things were getting to. The only source of consolation I had, was in bending my knees continually before my Father in Heaven, and asking Him to sustain me and preserve me from falling into snares, and from betraying my brethren as others had done; for those who apostatized sought every means and opportunity to draw others after them. They also entered into combinations to obtain wealth by fraud and every means that was evil (Orson F. Whitney, *Life of Heber C. Kimball* [Salt Lake City: Deseret Book, 1945], 101).

Parley P. Pratt

After I had returned from Canada, there were jarrings and discords in the Church at Kirtland, and many fell away and became enemies and apostates. There were also envyings, lyings, strifes and divisions, which caused much trouble and sorrow. By such spirits I was also accused, misrepresented and abused. And at one time, I also was overcome by the same spirit in a great measure, and it seemed as if the very powers of darkness which war against the Saints were let loose upon me. But the Lord knew my faith, my zeal, my integrity of purpose, and he gave me the victory.

I went to brother Joseph Smith in tears, and, with a broken heart and contrite spirit, confessed wherein I had erred in spirit, murmured, or done or said amiss. He frankly forgave me, prayed for me and blessed me. Thus, by experience, I learned more fully to discern and to contrast the two spirits, and to resist the one and cleave to the other. And, being tempted in all points, even as others, I learned how to bear with, and excuse, and succor those who are tempted (Parley P. Pratt, *Autobiography of Parley Parker Pratt*, ed. Parley P. Pratt Jr. [Salt Lake City: Deseret Book, 1964], 168).

Mary Fielding Smith

(Commenting on a mob's attempt to capture Joseph Smith and his companions.)

They were to come home in Dr [Sampson] Avards carriage and expected to arrive about 10 O clock at night but to their great disappointment they were prevented in a most grievous manner. They had got within 4 miles of home after a very fatiguing journey . . . when they were surrounded with a Mob and taken back to Painesville and secured as was supposed in a Tavern where they intended to hold a mock trial. But to the disappointment of the wretches the Housekeeper was a Member of the Church who assisted our beloved Brethren in making their escape, but as Br[other] J[oseph] S[mith] says not by a Basket let down through a Window, but by the Kitchen Door. . . .

The first step they took was to find the Woods as quick as possible where they thought they should be safe. But in order [to reach] thereto they had to lay down in a swamp or by an old log just w[h]ere they happened to be so determinately were they pursued by their mad enemy in every direction. Sometimes so closely that Br[other] J[oseph] was obliged to entreat Bro Rigdon, after his exertion in running, while lying by a log to breath[e] more softly if he meant to escape.

When they would run or walk they took each other by the hand and covenanted to live and die together. Owing to the darkness of the night their pursuers had to carry lighted torches which was one means of the escape of our beloved sufferers as they could see them in every direction while they were climbing over fences or traveling through brush or corn fields until about 12 O clock. When after traveling as they suppose in this manner 5 or 6 miles they found the road which led homeward and saw no more of their pursuers. After traveling on foot along muddy slippery roads till near 3 in the morning they arrived safe at home . . . I suppose all these things will only add another gem to their Crown (*Women's Voices*, 64–65; spelling standardized).

Oliver B. Huntington

It was the life and glory of the apostates to hatch up vexatious lawsuits and strip the brethren of their property and means of removing. It seemed as though all power was given them to torment the saints. The real Mormons were designated by the appellation of Lick skillets, and every Lick skillet had to suffer; the principal ones left were hunted like rabbits and foxes who sculk and hide in holes, and so did they. Numbers lay concealed in our house day after day, until their families could be got out of the place, one after another would come and go until we had served a variety with the best we had, and was glad of the privilege of showing favor to the righteous . . . and even the mummies were secreted there to keep them from being destroyed. . . .

Many who turned away and denied the faith . . . became the most bitter enemies of the church, and used to try every means to make a disturbance among the brethren, every day of the week, Sundays not excepted. I remember one Sunday of seeing men jumping out of the windows, I ran to see what the fuss was, and found the apostates had tried to make a real muss, as they had frequently tried before, but on this occasion I saw a dagger, the door keeper held, that was wrenched from one of their hands whilst making his way to the stand. I heard the women scream and saw the men jump out of the windows, them that had chickens hearts, and I shall always remember the sensation that came over me (Oliver B. Huntington, *Diary* [LDS Church Archives], 29; as cited in *Joseph Smith's Kirtland*, 219–20; spelling standardized).

Lucy Mack Smith

Joseph then went to Cleveland in order to transact some business pertaining to the bank, and as he was absent the ensuing Sunday, my husband preached to the people. In speaking of the bank affair, he reflected somewhat sharply upon Warren Parrish. Although the reflection was just, Parrish was highly incensed and made an attempt to drag him [Joseph Smith Sr.] out of the stand. My husband appealed to Oliver Cowdery, who was justice of the peace, to have him brought to order, but Oliver never moved from his seat. William, seeing the abuse which his father was receiving, sprang forward and caught Parrish, and carried him in his arms nearly out of the house. At this John Boynton stepped forward, and drawing a sword from his cane, presented it to William's breast, and said, "if you advance one step further, I will run you through." Before William had time to turn himself, several gathered around him, threatening to handle him severely, if he should lay the weight of his finger upon Parrish again. At this juncture of affairs, I left the house, not only terrified at the scene, but likewise sick at heart, to see that the apostasy of which Joseph had prophesied was so near at hand (Lucy Mack Smith, *History of Joseph Smith by His Mother*, ed. Preston Nibley [Salt Lake City: Bookcraft, 1958], 241).

Caroline Crosby

(Caroline witnessed a mob burn down the printing house in Kirtland.)

About the 15th of Jan., I was awakened one night near the middle of the night, by sister Sherwood calling to me and Jane, crying fire. I awoke and as I lay near the window I looked out, and beheld the ground as light as day, while the sky was as black as a thundercloud. A deep solemnity pervaded my mind, and a very strange sensation ran through my whole system. We arose immediately, and opened the door, and beheld the printing office all in flames, and men assembling from every direction in great haste. But they were all too late, they merely threw out a few books, and some of them were scorched. The sparks and shingles were carried to an immense distance. It was the nearest building to the temple but the wind was favorable in protecting it from the flames (Caroline Barnes Crosby, *Autobiography* [LDS Church Archives]; as cited in *Conflict at Kirtland*, 265; see also *Joseph Smith's Kirtland*, 222).

Hepzibah Richards

(23 March 1838)

For the last three months we as a people have been tempest tossed, and at times the waves have well nigh overwhelmed us . . .

A dreadful spirit reigns in the breasts of those who are opposed to this Church. They are above law and beneath whatever is laudable. Their leading object seems to be to get all the property of the Church for little or nothing, and drive them out of the place. The house of our nearest neighbor has been entered by a mob and ransacked from the top to the bottom under pretense of finding goods which it is thought they had stolen themselves. An attempt has since been made to set the same house on fire while the family were sleeping in bed (*Women's Voices,* 76).

LEAVING KIRTLAND

The mobocracy in Kirtland reached such a dangerous point that the Saints were forced to flee the city in 1838. They left behind their homes, land, and temple to join with the Saints in Missouri. Although the abandonment of Kirtland took place later, related eyewitness accounts appear here to give a more complete picture of the persecution during the Kirtland era.

Reynolds Cahoon

We turned the key and locked the door of our homes, leaving our property and all we possessed in the hands of enemies and strangers, never receiving a cent for anything we owned (*Reynolds Cahoon and His Stalwart Sons,* ed. Stella Cahoon Shurtleff and Brent Farrington Cahoon [n.p.: Stella Cahoon Shurtleff, 1960], 28; as cited in *Church History in the Fulness of Times,* 169).

Lucy Mack Smith

(Remarking on a prophetic statement made by her son.)

One evening, before finishing his preparations for the contemplated journey, he sat in council with the brethren at our house. After giving them directions as to what he desired them to do, while he was absent from them, and, as he was about leaving the room, he said, "Well, brethren, I do not recollect anything more, but one thing, brethren, is certain, I shall see you again, let what will happen, for I have a promise of life five years, and they cannot kill me until that time is expired" (*History of Joseph Smith*, 247–48).

Joseph Smith Jr.

A new year [1838] dawned upon the Church in Kirtland in all the bitterness of the spirit of apostate mobocracy; which continued to rage and grow hotter and hotter, until Elder Rigdon and myself were obliged to flee from its deadly influence, as did the Apostles and Prophets of old, and as Jesus said, "when they persecute you in one city, flee to another." On the evening of the 12th of January, about ten o'clock, we left Kirtland, on horseback, to escape mob violence, which was about to burst upon us under the color of legal process to cover the hellish designs of our enemies, and to save themselves from the just judgment of the law.

We continued our travels during the night, and at eight o'clock on the morning of the 13th, arrived among the brethren in Norton Township, Medina county, Ohio, a distance of sixty miles from Kirtland. Here we tarried about thirty-six hours, when our families arrived; and on the 16th we pursued our journey with our families, in covered wagons towards the city of Far West, in Missouri. . . .

The weather was extremely cold, we were obliged to secrete ourselves in our wagons, sometimes, to elude the grasp of our pursuers, who continued their pursuit of us more than two hundred miles from Kirtland, armed with pistols and guns, seeking our lives. They frequently crossed our track, twice they were in the houses where we stopped, once we tarried all night in the same house with them, with only a partition between us and them; and heard their oaths and imprecations, and threats concerning us, if they could catch us; and late in the evening they came in to our room and examined us, but decided we were not the men. At other times we passed them in the streets, and gazed upon them, and they on us, but they knew us not (*History of the Church*, 3:1–3).

Hepzibah Richards

(Early 1838)

We suffer from fear, but we hope these days of suffering will not always last (*Women's Voices*, 76).

Lucy Mack Smith

Sometimes we lay in our tents, through driving storms; at other times we were traveling on foot through marshes and quagmires. Once in particular, we lay all night exposed to the rain, which fell in torrents, so that when I arose in the morning, I found that my clothing was perfectly saturated with the rain. However, I could not mend the matter by a change of dress, for the rain was still falling rapidly, and I wore my clothes in this situation, three days; in consequence of which I took a severe cold, so that when we arrived at the Mississippi river, I was unable to walk or sit up. After crossing this river, we stopped at a . . . hut, a most unlovely place, yet the best shelter we could find. This hut was the birth-place of Catharine's son Alvin.

The next day my husband succeeded in getting a comfortable place, about four miles distant, for Catherine and her infant, and they were carried thither on a lumber wagon, the same day (*History of Joseph Smith*, 251–52).

Elias Smith

(10 March 1838)

The Spirit of the Lord came down in mighty power, and some of the Elders began to prophesy that if the quorum would go up in a body together, and go according to the commandments and revelations of God, pitching their tents by the way, that they should not want for anything on the journey that would be necessary for them to have; and further that there should be nothing wanting towards removing the whole quorum of Seventies that would go in a body, but that there should be a sufficiency of all things for carrying such an expedition into effect (*History of the Church*, 3:88).

Zerah Pulsipher

One evening, while we were in the attic story of the Lord's House, and while Joseph Young, I think, was at prayer, I saw a Heavenly messenger, who appeared to be a very tall man dressed in a white robe from head to foot. He cast his eyes on me and on the rest of the Council and said, "Be one, and you shall have enough," and soon after the way was opened before us, so that we received money and means for clothing for the poor and to prepare for our removal. James Foster and Jonathan Dunham also saw the angel at the same time I did (Max H. Parkin, *Conflict at Kirtland* [Salt Lake City: M. H. Parkin, 1966], 269; as cited in *Joseph Smith's Kirtland*, 239).

Hepzibah Richards

(To Rhoda Richards, 23 March 1838.)

Probably an hundred and 25 families or more remain [in Kirtland]. They will go in large wagons covered square on the top with canvas or something that will turn water. Will take their clothing, beds, and cooking utensils and tent by the way. Fifty [yards] of common sheeting will make a tent that will accommodate eighteen persons. Women and children will sleep in the wagons. Some will take along light crick bedsteads, and other measures will be taken to prevent sleeping on the ground as much as possible. They will have runners to go before and lay up provisions, that the inhabitants may not take advantage of their necessities to increase their prices. They will travel five days in a week; stop on Saturdays to bake and wash. Sabbath hold meetings. Will be eight or ten weeks on the road. They design to take along the poor and the lame, deeming it wrong to leave those who have a desire to go but have no means. It will be required of them to refund it as fast as they are able. This will probably be accomplished, but it must be by mighty effort. Duck will be prefer[r]ed for tent cloth—will turn rain better. The camp will move but slowly. The men will walk much of the way (*Women's Voices*, 78).

Christopher Crary

(Citizen of Kirtland)

When their bank failed, all their imaginary wealth vanished; their money was gone; their teams were gone; their provisions were gone; their credit was gone; their stores of goods disappeared. No community could be left in more destitute circumstances, and the only alternative was for them to leave—leave their Temple, their homes, all that they had held dear, and go to, they knew not where. And how to go was a serious question. . . . In 1838 the camp was ready to start, and left in a body, making a string of teams more than a mile long (Christopher G. Crary, *Pioneer and Personal Reminiscences* [Marshalltown, Iowa: Marshall Printing Co., 1893], 35; as cited in *Joseph Smith's Kirtland*, 240–41).

Elias Smith

On the road near Bellefontaine one of the sons of Martin H. Peck, had a wagon wheel run over his leg, but as the Lord would have it, and to the astonishment of all—considering the weight of the load on the wagon—he received no particular injury, although the wheel ran over the boy's leg on a hard road without any obstruction whatever. The wheel made a deep cut in the limb, but after hands were laid on him in the name of the Lord, the boy was able to walk considerable in the course of the afternoon. This was one, but not the first, of the wonderful manifestations of God's power unto us on the journey (*History of the Church*, 3:113).

～ 20 ～

Settlement in and Expulsion from Jackson County, Missouri (1831–1833)

Descriptions of the Land in and Around Jackson County

Washington Irving

(Written from Independence in 1824)

Many parts of these prairies of the Missouri are extremely beautiful, resembling cultivated countries, embellished with parks and groves, rather than the savage rudeness of the wilderness. Yesterday I was out on a deer hunt in the vicinity of this place, which led me through some scenery that only wanted a castle, or a gentleman's seat here and there interspersed, to have equaled some of the most celebrated park scenery of England. The fertility of all this western country is truly astonishing. The soil is like that of a garden, and the luxuriance and beauty of the forests exceed any that I have seen. We have gradually been advancing, however, toward rougher and rougher life, and are now at a straggling frontier village [Independence] that has only been five years in existence (Pierre Irving, *Works of Washington Irving*, 14 vols. [Philadelphia: University Library Association, n.d.], 2:249).

Sidney Rigdon

The country is unlike the timbered states of the East. As far as the eye can reach the beautiful rolling prairies lie spread out like a sea of meadows; and are decorated with a growth of flowers so gorgeous and grand as to exceed description; and nothing is more fruitful, or a richer stockholder in the blooming prairie than the honey bee. Only on the water courses is timber to be found. There in strips from one to three miles in width, and following faithfully the meanderings of the streams, it grows in luxuriant forests. The forests are a mixture of oak, hickory, black walnut, elm, ash, cherry, honey locust, mulberry, coffee bean, hackberry, boxelder, and bass wood; with the addition of cottonwood, butterwood, pecan, and soft and hard maple upon the bottoms. The shrubbery is beautiful, and consists in part of plums, grapes, crab apple, and persimmons.

The soil is rich and fertile; from three to ten feet deep, and generally composed of a rich black mould, intermingled with clay and sand. It yields in abundance, wheat, corn, sweet potatoes, cotton and many other common agricultural products. Horses, cattle and hogs, though of an inferior breed, are tolerably plentiful and seem nearly to raise themselves by grazing in the vast prairie range in summer, and feeding upon the bottoms in winter. The wild game is less plentiful of course where man has commenced the cultivation of the soil, than in the wild prairies. Buffalo, elk, deer, bear, wolves, beaver and many smaller animals here roam at pleasure. Turkeys, geese, swans, ducks, yea a variety of the feathered tribe, are among the rich abundance that grace the delightful regions of this goodly land—the heritage of the children of God.

The season is mild and delightful nearly three quarters of the year, and as the land of Zion, situated at about equal distances from the Atlantic and Pacific oceans, as well as from the Alleghany and Rocky mountains, in the thirty-ninth degree of north latitude, and between the sixteenth and seventeenth degrees of west longitude, it bids fair—when the curse is taken from the land—to become one of the most blessed places on the globe (Joseph Smith, *History of The Church of Jesus Christ of Latter-day Saints*, 7 vols., ed. B. H. Roberts [Salt Lake City: Deseret Book, 1978], 1:197–98).

Wilford Woodruff

President Young said Joseph the Prophet told me that the garden of Eden was in Jackson Co. Missouri (Wilford Woodruff, *Wilford Woodruff's Journal*, 9 vols., ed. Scott G. Kenney [Midvale, Utah: Signature Books, 1985], 129).

W. W. Phelps

(1832)

Zion [Independence, Missouri], according to the Prophets, is to become like Eden, or the garden of the Lord (*History of the Church*, 1:279).

CLASH OF CULTURES IN JACKSON COUNTY

The friction and conflicts between members of The Church of Jesus Christ of Latter-day Saints and the settlers in Jackson County were complicated because of several major factors:

Land: The Latter-day Saints were competing with other settlers for the same land. Jackson County, Missouri, was the western-most boundary of the country at a time when explorers and expansionists were pushing settlements further west. As a border state, Missouri was home to a fairly lawless element of citizens, yet, Jackson County was a consecrated land to the Saints for the building up of Zion.

Slavery: Most Latter-day Saints were nonslave holders, but Missouri was a slave state.

Native-Americans: The Latter-day Saints tried to befriend and convert native Americans, believing that they were a chosen generation, as indicated in the Book of Mormon. However, most settlers feared or distrusted the Native Americans.

Politics: The political power of the Latter-day Saints increased as their numbers grew. Missourians knew that if the Mormons voted together, they could elect the candidates of their choice by sheer majority. The settlers' concerns about the growing political clout was intertwined with their concern over the rapid increase in the Mormon population.

Socioeconomics: The church-owned store and efforts to live the law of consecration were viewed as exclusionary and unfair competition by local merchants.

Religious beliefs and practices: The Latter-day Saints' belief in modern prophets and current revelation was contrary to their neighbors' view of biblical Christianity. Due to the growth of the Latter-day Saint Church membership, there was jealousy and contempt on the part of ministers of other faiths.

Attitudes: The cooperation and zeal for building "Zion" was seen by some settlers as clannishness or self-righteousness.

Culture: The Latter-day Saints were mostly from the northern and eastern states, while most other Missouri settlers were from the South. These regions differed in culture, habits, views of life, and lifestyles. Both groups viewed each other with much suspicion and intolerance. The Saints were fairly well-educated and cultured, while the Prophet observed that the settlers in Jackson County were "nearly a century behind the times" (*History of the Church*, 1:189).

Opposition from the adversary: The adversary simply did not want the Saints to build a temple in Independence, which was prophesied to become Church headquarters during the millennial reign.

Joseph Smith Jr.

It seemed good and pleasant for brethren to meet together in unity. But our reflections were many, coming as we had from a highly cultivated state of society in the east, and standing now upon the confines or western limits of the United States, and looking into the vast wilderness of those that sat in darkness; how natural it was to observe the degradation, leanness of intellect, ferocity, and jealousy of a people that were nearly a century behind the times (*History of the Church*, 1:189).

Emily Partridge Young

The people [of Independence in 1831] were different in their customs and manner of speaking. It was, "I reckon," and "a right smart chance," and instead of carrying things in their hands they would "toat" them on their heads. Large bundles and baskets, churns, tubs and piggins of water or milk, all "toated" on their heads. Little children were "toated" straddle of one hip. In warm weather women went barefoot, and little boys from two to ten years old were running the streets with nothing on but a tow shirt. Everything seemed to be after the back-woods style (Emily Partridge Young, "Autobiography of Emily D. P. Young," *Woman's Exponent* 13 [December 1884]: 103).

John Townsend

(Describing Independence in 1834.)

The site of the town is beautiful, and very well selected, standing on a high point of land, and overlooking the surrounding country, but the town itself is very indifferent; the houses, (about fifty,) are very much scattered, composed of logs and clay, and are low and inconvenient. There are six or eight stores here, two taverns, and a few tip[p]ling houses. As we did not fancy the town, nor the society that we saw there, we concluded to take up our residence at the house of the landing until the time of starting on our journey (John Kirk Townsend, *Across the Rockies to the Columbia* [Lincoln: University of Nebraska Press, 1978), 25–26).

Levi Hancock

We traveled slowly and continued to preach to the people when-ever we got a chance. The people we met were good livers if they were a mind to be but the way they managed was more like beasts than like humans. They had dogs, horses, cows and pigs, and chickens in abun-dance around the house and in the house and mixed together: in the cold weather doors were open night and day. Snow flying and wind blowing through. The cracks were not chinked. They used rags for beds, ground for floors. The children were ragged and dirty. They had corn pudding and dogger to eat with a little bacon and sassafras tea. . . .

When they have an abundance of horses, cattle and cows they might spare and make themselves and family comfortable. Land is all they want (*The Journal of Levi W. Hancock*, ed. Clara E. H. Lloyd [n.p., n.d.], 48; see also *Autobiography of Parley P. Pratt*, 73; spelling and punctua-tion standardized).

Emily Austin

(She recalled that the Mormons were never really welcome in Jackson County.)

On several occasions we received intelligence that the inhabitants of Jackson county were displeased at the idea of so many coming into the county. They said the range for their county would be taken by the Mormon cattle, and the "shuck" devoured by Mormon pigs; and they boldly declared they would not suffer this to be so (Emily M. Austin, *Mormonism, or, Life Among the Mormons* [Madison, Wisconson: n.p., 1882], 68; as cited in *Regional Studies in Latter-day Saint History: Missouri*, ed. Arnold K. Garr and Clark V. Johnson [Provo: Department of Church History and Doctrine, 1994], 296).

Reverend John Mason Peck

(Peck was a Baptist missionary; he comments on the people of St. Louis in 1818.)

One-half, at least, of the Anglo-American population were infidels of a low and indecent grade, and utterly worthless for any useful purpose of society. Of the class I allude to, I cannot recollect an individual who was reclaimed, or who became a respectable citizen. . . .

This class despised and vilified religion in every form, were vulgarly profane, even to the worst forms of blasphemy, and poured out scoffing and contempt on the few Christians in the village. Their nightly orgies were scenes of drunkenness and profane revelry. Among the frantic rites observed were the mock celebration of the Lord's Supper, and burning the Bible. The last ceremony consisted in raking a place in the hot coals of a wood fire, and burying therein the book of God with shoutings, prayers, and songs.

The boast was often made that the Sabbath never had crossed, and never should cross the Mississippi (John Mason Peck, *Forty Years of Pioneer life: Memoirs of John Mason Peck*, ed. Rufus Babcock [Carbondale, Illinois: Southern Illinois University Press, 1965], 87; spelling has been standardized).

Joseph Smith Jr.

(Description of the impact betrayals of traitors and dissenters had on the Saints in Jackson County.)

All the enemies upon the face of the earth may roar and exert all their power to bring about my death, but they can accomplish nothing, unless some who are among us and enjoy our society, have been with us in our councils, participated in our confidence, taken us by the hand, called us brother, saluted us with a kiss, join with our enemies, turn our virtues into faults, and, by falsehood and deceit, stir up their wrath and indignation against us, and bring their united vengeance upon our heads. . . . *We have a Judas in our midst* (*History of the Church*, 6:152).

John C. McCoy

(An 1833 resident of Jackson County.)

Their [the "Mormons'"] exclusiveness, and assumption of holiness, of miraculous gifts in speaking in unknown tongues as at the day of Pentecost and pretended interpretation of the gibberish by those professedly inspired for that purpose and their openly expressed avowal that all the land of this chosen zion, comprising the entire country, had been allotted to the saints by divine authority as made known through his [the Lord's] chosen prophet Joseph, surnamed Smith, these together with other causes which will be alluded to hereafter, gradually created a feeling of bitter hostility against them ("The Mormons," *Kansas City Journal* [18 January 1885]: 8).

Joseph Smith Jr.

But as we could not associate with our neighbors (who were, many of them, of the basest of men, and had fled from the face of civilized society, to the frontier country to escape the hand of justice,) in their midnight revels, their Sabbath breaking, horse racing and gambling; they commenced at first to ridicule, then to persecute [us] (*History of the Church*, 4:538).

Reverend Finis Ewing

Protestant ministers also resented the Mormon intrusion into the county. Latter-day Saints were labeled fanatics and knaves and were denounced as gullible and ignorant because they believed in and frequently experienced miracles, prophecy, healings, and speaking in tongues. Jealousy and fear of losing some from their flocks added to the antagonism of the ministers. The Reverend Finis Ewing of the Cumberland Presbyterian Church asserted, "The 'Mormons' are the common enemies of mankind and ought to be destroyed." A reverend of the Missionary Society (sent to Christianize the American Indians) went "from house to house, seeking to destroy the Church by spreading slanderous falsehoods, to incite the people to acts of violence against the saints" (*Church History in the Fulness of Times*, Prepared by the Church Educational System [Salt Lake City: The Church of Jesus Christ of Latter-day Saints, 1993], 131).

Newel Knight

The sectarian priests and missionaries around us were among the first to come out both secretly and openly against us. Among the more active of these was a Mr. Pixley, who did not content himself in slandering us to the people of Jackson county, but also wrote to eastern papers telling horrible lies about us, with the evident intention of rousing a spirit of hatred against us. His talk was of the bitterest kind, his speeches perfectly inflammatory; and he appeared to have an influence among the people to carry them with him in his hellish designs. Nor did he confine his actions to the white settlers, but tried to stir up the Indians against us, and use every means in his power to accomplish his purposes. His efforts were seconded by such men as Reverends McCoy, Fitzhugh, Bogard, Kavanaugh, Lovelady, Likens, Hunter, and others (Newel Knight, "Newel Knight's Journal," *Scraps of Biography* [Salt Lake City: Juvenile Instructor Office, 1883], 76; see also *History of the Church*, 1:372–73).

Col. Thomas Pitcher

(An avowed enemy of the Latter-day Saints.)

The Mormons, as a rule, were an ignorant and a fanatical people, though there were some very intelligent men among them. The troubles around 1833, which led to their expulsion from the county, were originated by these fanatics making boasts that they intended to posses the entire county, saying that God had promised it to them and they were going to have it. This of course raised ill feeling toward them, which continued to grow more and more bitter, until the final uprising took place (R. Etzenhouser, *From Palmyra, New York, 1830, to Independence, Missouri, 1894* [Independence, Missouri: Ensign Publishing House, 1894], 323).

A Local Resident of Westport, Missouri

(Westport was one of the areas in which the Saints settled. The following account, taken from an 1881 historical record, illustrates a mistaken attitude among some of the Saints.)

About half a mile south, on Brush creek, there lived an old, gray-headed Mormon named Pryor, who was a frequent visitor at our house, having, as he professed, no doubt honestly, great regard and friendship for my father, and who would patiently listen to the harmless nonsense of the garrulous old fanatic while his discourse would often run thus:

"Brother M., I have the greatest regard and friendship for you; pray without ceasing for the Lord to open your eyes to see and understand the near approach of the end, as revealed to us through the chosen prophet, Joseph. This land of promise is already parceled to the Saints by divine authority. Your tract, Brother M., is included in my inheritance and in the Lord's own good time I will possess it, for it is so recorded. But fear not, Brother M. The Lord will either open your eyes to become one of us, or He will make me an instrument for your welfare" ("The Other Side," *Kansas City Daily Journal* [24 September 1881]).

John C. McCoy

One mile west of the Blue, on the old road from Independence to the state line, on what is now the Chouteau farm, there was a country store kept by one Moses G. Wilson, a brigadier general of the militia, a restless partisan, very prominent and influential with a certain class.

This [store] was, during 1833, the rendezvous for the anti-Mormons, where they were wont to meet to discuss the situation and form plans and organize raids upon the Mormon settlements up toward the state line. There was no pretense of legality in any of their proceedings, only a unanimous determination to drive out the Mormons from the country or be themselves driven out ("The Mormons," *Kansas City Journal* [18 January 1885]: 8).

John C. McCoy

I said the Mormons received bad treatment at the hands of the people of Jackson County. I will modify this by saying at the hands of a very small portion of the citizens; for all the outrages were committed by not more than fifty of the roughs of the county ("The Other Side," *Kansas City Journal* [24 April 1881]: 9).

THE LORD'S WARNING ABOUT THE EXPULSION FROM AND REDEMPTION OF JACKSON COUNTY
(A Parable)

Doctrine & Covenants 101:43–62

And now, I will show unto you a parable, that you may know my will concerning the redemption of Zion.

A certain nobleman had a spot of land, very choice; and he said unto his servants: Go ye unto my vineyard, even upon this very choice piece of land, and plant twelve olive-trees;

And set watchmen round about them, and build a tower, that one may overlook the land round about, to be a watchman upon the tower, that mine olive-trees may not be broken down when the enemy shall come to spoil and take upon themselves the fruit of my vineyard.

Now, the servants of the nobleman went and did as their lord commanded them, and planted the olive-trees, and built a hedge round about, and set watchmen, and began to build a tower.

And while they were yet laying the foundation thereof, they began to say among themselves: And what need hath my lord of this tower?

And consulted for a long time, saying among themselves: What need hath my lord of this tower, seeing this is a time of peace?

Might not this money be given to the exchangers? For there is no need of these things.

And while they were at variance one with another they became very slothful, and they hearkened not unto the commandments of their lord.

And the enemy came by night, and broke down the hedge; and the servants of the nobleman arose and were affrighted, and fled; and the enemy destroyed their works, and broke down the olive-trees.

Now, behold, the nobleman, the lord of the vineyard, called upon his servants, and said unto them, Why! what is the cause of this great evil?

Ought ye not to have done even as I commanded you, and—after ye had planted the vineyard, and built the hedge round about, and set watchmen upon the walls thereof—built the tower also, and set a watchman upon the tower, and watched for my vineyard, and not have fallen asleep, lest the enemy should come upon you?

And behold, the watchman upon the tower would have seen the enemy while he was yet afar off; and then ye could have made ready and kept the enemy from breaking down the hedge thereof, and saved my vineyard from the hands of the destroyer.

And the lord of the vineyard said unto one of his servants: Go and gather together the residue of my servants, and take all the strength of mine house, which are my warriors, my young men, and they that are of middle age also among all my servants, who are the strength of mine house, save those only whom I have appointed to tarry;

And go ye straightway unto the land of my vineyard, and redeem my vineyard; for it is mine; I have bought it with money.

Therefore, get ye straightway unto my land; break down the walls of mine enemies; throw down their tower, and scatter their watchmen.

And inasmuch as they gather together against you, avenge me of mine enemies, that by and by I may come with the residue of mine house and possess the land.

And the servant said unto his lord: When shall these things be?

And he said unto his servant: When I will; go ye straightway, and do all things whatsoever I have commanded you;

And this shall be my seal and blessing upon you—a faithful and wise steward in the midst of mine house, a ruler in my kingdom.

And his servant went straightway, and did all things whatsoever his lord commanded him; and after many days all things were fulfilled.

"SECRET CONSTITUTION"

In July 1833, a "secret constitution" was circulated by Jackson County citizens, listing their grievances against the Latter-day Saints and calling for their removal.

The secret constitution contained the following five major points against the Mormons: "(1) that the Mormons claimed to hold personal communion or converse face to face with the Most High God, to receive communications and revelations direct from heaven, to heal the sick by laying on hands, and, in short, to perform all the wonder-working miracles wrought by the inspired apostles and prophets of old; (2) that they were deluded fanatics, weak and designing knaves—the very dregs of society out of which they had come—lazy, idle, and vicious; (3) that they were poor, having brought little property with them, and leaving less behind; (4) that they had tampered with the slaves of the old settlers; and (5) that they claimed Jackson County had been given them by God—it was theirs without purchase" (Ivan J. Barrett, *Joseph Smith and the Restoration* [Provo, Utah: Brigham Young University Press, 1973], 246).

HISTORY OF THE CHURCH

A committee of Missourians declared five restrictions on the Mormons as follows:

1—That no Mormon shall in future move and settle in this county.

2—That those now here, who shall give a definite pledge of their intention, within a reasonable time to remove out of the county, shall be allowed to remain unmolested until they have sufficient time to sell their property, and close their business, without any material sacrifice.

3—That the editor of the *Star* be required forthwith to close his office, and discontinue the business of printing in this county; and as to all other stores and shops belonging to the sect, their owners must in every case strictly comply with the terms of the second article of this declaration; and upon failure prompt and efficient measures will be taken to close the same.

4—That the Mormon leaders here, are required to use their influence in preventing any further emigration of their distant brethren to this county, and to counsel and advise their brethren here to comply with the above requisitions.

5—That those who fail to comply with these requisitions, be referred to those of their brethren who have the gifts of divination, and of unknown tongues, to inform them of the lot that awaits them (*History of the Church*, 1:398).

TEXT OF THE SECRET CONSTITUTION
(Distributed by Jackson County citizens, 15 July 1833)

We, the undersigned, citizens of Jackson county, believing that an important crisis is at hand, as regards our civil society, in consequence of a pretended religious sect of people that have settled, and are still settling in our county, styling themselves "Mormons;" and intending, as we do, to rid our society, "peaceably if we can, forcibly if we must," and believing as we do, that the arm of the civil law does not afford us a guarantee, or at least not a sufficient one, against the evils which are now inflicted upon us, and seem to be increasing, by the said religious sect, deem it expedient, and of the highest importance, to form ourselves into a company for the better and easier accomplishment of our purpose—a purpose which we deem almost superfluous to say, is justified as well by the law of nature, as by the law of self-preservation. It is more than two years since the first of these fanatics, or knaves, (for the one or the other they undoubtedly are) made their first appearance amongst us, and pretending as they did, and now do, to hold personal communication and converse face to face with the Most High God; to receive communications and revelations direct from heaven; to heal the sick by laying on hands; and, in short, to perform all the wonder-working miracles wrought by the inspired Apostles and Prophets of old.

We believed them deluded fanatics, or weak and designing knaves, and that they and their pretensions would soon pass away; but in this we were deceived. The arts of a few designing leaders amongst them have thus far succeeded in holding them together as a society; and since the arrival of the first of them, they have been daily increasing in numbers; and if they had been respectable citizens in society and thus deluded, they would have been entitled to our pity rather than to our contempt and hatred; but from their appearance, from their manners, and from their conduct since their coming among us, we have every reason to fear that, with but very few exceptions, they were of the very dregs of that society from which they came, lazy, idle, and vicious. This we conceive is not idle assertion, but a fact susceptible of proof, for with these few exceptions above named, they brought into our county little or no property with them and left less behind them, and we infer that those only yoke themselves to the "Mormon" car who had nothing earthly or heavenly to lose by the change; and we fear that if some of the leaders amongst them, had paid the forfeit due to crime, instead of being chosen ambassadors of the Most High, they would have been inmates of solitary cells. But their conduct here stamps their characters in their true colors. More than a year since, it was ascertained that they had been tampering with our slaves, and endeavoring to sow dissension and raise sedition amongst them. Of this their "Mormon" leaders were informed, and they said they would deal with any of their members who should again in like case offend. But how spacious are appearances. In a late number of the *Star*, published in Independence by the leaders of the sect, there is an article inviting free negroes and mulattoes from other states to become "Mormons," and remove and settle among us. This exhibits them in still more odious colors. It manifests a desire on the part of their society, to inflict on our society an injury that they know would be to us entirely insupportable, and one of the surest means of driving us from the country; for it would require none of the supernatural gifts that they pretend to, to see that the introduction of such a cast amongst us would corrupt our blacks, and instigate them to bloodshed.

They openly blaspheme the Most High God, and cast contempt on His holy religion, by pretending to receive revelations direct from heaven, by pretending to speak unknown tongues, by direct inspiration, and by divers[e] pretenses derogatory of God and religion, and to the utter subversion of human reason.

They declare openly that their God hath given them this county of land, and that sooner or later they must and will have possession of our lands for an inheritance; and, in fine, they have conducted themselves on many other occasions, in such a manner that we believe it a duty we owe to ourselves, our wives, and children, to the cause of public morals, to remove them from among us, as we are not prepared to give up our pleasant places and goodly possessions to them or to receive into the bosom of our families, as fit companions for our wives and daughters, the degraded and corrupted free negroes and mulattoes that are now invited to settle among us.

Under such a state of things, even our beautiful country would cease to be a desirable residence, and our situation intolerable. We, therefore, agree that after timely warning, and receiving an adequate compensation for what little property they cannot take with them, they refuse to leave us in peace, as they found us—we agree to use such means as will be sufficient to remove them, and to that end we each pledge to each other our bodily powers, our lives, fortunes and sacred honors.

We will meet at the court house, at the town of Independence, on Saturday next, the 20th inst., [July], to consult on subsequent movements (*History of the Church*, 1:374–76).

On 20 July 1833, a meeting of 400–500 Jackson County citizens was held at the Independence Courthouse. A committee declared five restrictions against the Mormons.

Robert Johnson

(The chairman of this committee, he incited the entire group to violence by a speech in which he said the following.)

We are daily told, and not by the ignorant alone, but by all classes of them, that we, (the Gentiles,) of this county are to be cut off, and our lands appropriated by them for inheritances. Whether this is to be accomplished by the hand of the destroying angel, the judgments of God, or the arm of power, they are not fully agreed among themselves (*History of the Church*, 1:396).

As outlined in the Secret Constitution, the Saints were prohibited from printing their newspaper, *The Times and Seasons*. When they were made aware of this stipulation, they asked for three months to consider it and to inform the Church leaders, who, at this time, were residing in Ohio. Their request was denied, and the Saints were only allowed fifteen minutes to make the decision. A short time later, the previously peaceful committee turned mob and destroyed the printing office and the press.

Six Elders Offer Their Lives in Exchange for the Safety of the Saints
(23 July 1833)

B. H. Roberts

On July 23rd the mob, to the number of some five hundred, again came dashing into Independence bearing a red flag, and armed with rifles, pistols, dirks, whips and clubs. They rode in every direction in search of the leading elders, making the day hideous with their inhuman yells and wicked oaths. They declared it to be their intention to whip those whom they captured with from fifty to five hundred lashes each, allow their [slaves] to destroy their crops, and demolish their dwellings. Said they: "We will rid Jackson county of the Mormons peaceably if we can, forcibly if we must. If they will not go without, we will whip and kill the men; we will destroy their children, *and ravish their women!*" (*A Comprehensive History of the Church of Jesus Christ of Latter-day Saints*, 6 vols., ed. B. H. Roberts [Provo, Utah: Brigham Young University Press, 1965], 1:337).

John Whitmer

A committee was appointed at the foregoing meeting and waited on us. Partridge, Corrill, Phelps, etc. [met with] the committee consist[ing] of Lewis Franklin, Mr. Campbell, Jud[ge] Lucas, Judge Fristoe, Russel Hicks, Mr. Simpson, two of the Mr. Wilsons, Captain Tipitts and Mr. Cummings.

To answer them this question, "Will you leave this county or not?" allowing us only fifteen minutes to answer the question. We did not reply at that time. The committee further required of us to shut up our printing office, store, mechanical shops, etc. immediately and leave the county.

Those who waited on the committee were A. S. Gilbert, Edward Partridge, Isaac Morley, John Corrill, W. W. Phelps, and John Whitmer.

When they found that we were unwilling to comply with their requests, they returned to the courthouse and voted to raze the printing [office] to the ground, which they immediately did; and at the same time took Edward Partridge and Charles Allen and tarred and feathered them, threatening to kill us if we did not leave the county immediately.

John Whitmer
(Courtesy of the Church Archives, The Church of Jesus Christ of Latter-day Saints)

They were also determined to demolish the store. A. S. Gilbert prevailed on them to let it stand until Tuesday next, and have time to pack his goods himself.

Tuesday arrived and death and destruction stared us in the face. The whole county turned out and surrounded us. [They] came to W. W. Phelps' and my house and took us upon the public square, as also Partridge, Corrill, Morley, and Gilbert, and were determined to massacre us unless we agreed to leave the county immediately. Finally we agreed to leave upon the following condition:

July 23, 1833.

It is understood that the undersigned members of the said society do give their solemn pledge each for himself as follows: That Oliver Cowdery, W. W. Phelps, W[illiam] E. McLellin, Edward Partridge, Lyman Wight, Simeon Carter, Peter and John Whitmer, and Harvey Whitlock shall remove with their families out of this county on or before the first day [of January] next, and that they, as well as the two herein after named, use all their influence to induce all the brethren now here to move as soon as possible, one half say, by the first of Jan[uary] next, and all by the first day of April next, and to advise and try all means in their power to stop any more of their sect from moving to this county. As to those now on the road and who have no notice of this agreement, they will use their influence to prevent their settling permanently in the county, but that they shall only make arrangement for temporal shelter till a new location is fixed on by the society. John Corrill and A. S. Gilbert are allowed to remain as general agents to wind up the business of the society, so long as necessity shall require, and said Gilbert may sell out his good[s] now on hand, but is to make no new importation. The Star is not again to be published no[r] a press set up by the society in this county.

If the said E. Partridge and W. W. Phelps move their families by the first of Jan[uary] as aforesaid, ... they themselves will be allowed to go and come in order to transact and wind up their business. The committee pledge themselves to use all their influence to prevent any violence being used, so long as a compliance with the foregoing terms is observed by the parties concerned.

Signed, Samuel C. Owens, Leonadas Oldham, G. W. Simpson, W. L. Irvin, John Harris, Henry Childs, Harvey H. Younger, Hugh L. Brazi[a]le, N. K. Olmstead, W[illiam] Bowers, Z. Waller, Harman Gregg, Aaron Overton, Samuel Weston (*From Historian to Dissident: The Book of John Whitmer*, ed. Bruce N. Westergren [Salt Lake City: Signature Books, 1995], 106–8; punctuation and capitalization standardized).

DESTRUCTION OF THE PRINTING OFFICE
(20 July 1833)

Members of the mob, seething with rage against the Saints, and failing to honor their word to avoid violence, destroyed the home of Brother W. W. Phelps and the printing press, which was located upstairs. According to one account, "with yells and curses the mob surrounded the printing office and house of William W. Phelps. Among the mob was a man whose wife had recently been attended in childbirth by Mrs. Phelps. While the decision was being made in the courthouse to destroy Phelps's printing establishment, the man had slipped out and dashed over to warn Mrs. Phelps. After hitching a team to a wagon and assisting Mrs. Phelps with her sick infant into a seat, he grabbed some freshly baked bread, wrapped it in a cloth, and handed the package to her, whispering, 'Go now, Sister Phelps, as far and as fast as you can.' He also warned William W. Phelps of the mob's approach. Phelps fled from the premises and hid. In their hurry to flee before the mob approached, they left two little boys in the building. The mob entered the living quarters of Phelps and threw his furniture out into the yard. They rushed upstairs and threw the press out the window, destroyed the type, and burned most of the written revelations, bookwork, and papers. This done, they completely demolished the brick structure, covering Henry Phelps and his younger brother with broken bricks and debris. Although buried completely, they were not injured and later were rescued by members of the Church" (Ivan J. Barrett, *Joseph Smith and the Restoration* [Provo, Utah: Brigham Young University Press, 1981], 249–50).

John Whitmer

Men entered Phelps' living quarters and threw much of their property into the yard and street. But the mob was mainly concerned with the press. Leaders quickly took a piece of timber up the outside steps and knocked open the door of the pressroom. Chapman Duncan, a church member, reported, "I saw a man [John King] go up the stairs, burst open the door. Others followed." The men took the type and threw it into the street where it could be found for years afterward, a plaything for children. Next, the press itself "was thrown from the upper story," along with the apparatus, bookwork, and paper which were scattered through the streets. In ensuing legal action Phelps described items damaged or destroyed. These included, "other goods and Chattel viz: printing paper, printing ink, blank deeds, blank forms of various other things, unprinted manuscripts, and other unpublished works." The press, broken in the fall, lay in the street until the following February. Chapman related that after the type and press were thrown out the window, "They took a long tree and put it into a window, crossed the corner of the house into another window, and sprung the tree to throw out the corner of the house . . . I did not stay to see it fall." The Reverend Benton Pixley wrote that after the mob pulled down the building, its roof was drawn into the highway. When Mrs. Phelps looked back from a safe distance, she thought the entire building was burning. Though the mob did not burn the building, there may have been flames from burning papers mixed with swirling dust from the falling building (as cited in Ronald E. Romig and John H. Siebert, "First Impressions: The Independence, Missouri, Printing Operation, 1832–1833," *The John Whitmer Historical Association Journal* 10 [n.m. 1990]: 62–63).

Emily Dow Partridge Smith Young

While the destruction of the printing office and store were going on, two young girls [Mary Ann and Caroline Rollins], nieces of A. S. Gilbert had run out of the house and hid in the corner of the fence and were watching the mob, and when they saw them bring a table piled full of papers and set it in the middle of the street and heard them say, "Here is the book of revelations of the damned Mormons;" they watched their opportunity when the mob returned to the house, they ran and gathered up as many of the papers as they could hold in their arms and ran into the cornfield and hid. The mob soon discovered them running with the papers and followed them but could not find them. The cornfields there were so very large and cornstalks grew so high that they were almost like young forests and it is an easy matter for a person to get lost in one of them. These two girls had run so far that they were lost, but after a while succeeded in finding their way out. They went to an old shanty where they found the family of Brother Phelps trying to make themselves a little comfortable. Sister Phelps took the revelations and hid them in her bed. This is how a few of the revelations were preserved. The names of these girls were Mary E. and Caroline Rollins (Emily Young, "Emily Dow Partridge Smith Young Autobiography," in *Writings of Early Latter-day Saints and Their Contemporaries, A Database Collection*, comp. Milton V. Backman [Provo, Utah: BYU Religious Studies Center, 1996], 14).

Mary Elizabeth Rollins Lightner

The mob renewed their efforts again by tearing down the printing office, a two story building, and driving Brother Phelps' family out of the lower part of the house and putting their things in the street. They brought out some large sheets of paper, and said "Here are the Mormon Commandments." My sister Caroline and myself were in a corner of a fence watching them; when they spoke of the commandments I was determined to have some of them. Sister said if I went to get any of them she would go too, but said "they will kill us." While their backs were turned, prying out the gable end of the house, we went, and got our arms full, and were turning away, when some of the mob saw us and called on us to stop, but we ran as fast as we could. Two of them started after us. Seeing a gap in a fence, we entered into a large cornfield, laid the papers on the ground, and hid them with our persons. The corn was from five to six feet high, and very thick; they hunted around considerable, and came very near us but did not find us. After we satisfied ourselves that they had given up the search for us, we tried to find our way out of the field[;] the corn was so high we could not see where to go . . . Soon we came to an old log stable which looked as though it had not been used for years. Sister Phelps and children were carrying in brush and piling it up at one side of the barn to lay her beds on. She asked me what I had—I told her. She then took them from us, which made us feel very bad. They got them bound in small books and sent me one, which I prized very highly (Mary Lightner, "Mary Elizabeth Rollins Lightner," *The Utah Genealogical and Historical Magazine* 17 [July 1926]: 196).

Mary Lightner
(Courtesy of the Church Archives, The Church of Jesus Christ of Latter-day Saints)

Bishop Edward Partridge and Charles Allen Tarred and Feathered

Not being content with the destruction of the Phelps's residence and the printing office, the mob broke into the houses of the Saints, searching for the leading elders. "Men, women, and children ran in all directions, not knowing what would befall them. The mob caught Bishop Edward Partridge and Charles Allen, and dragged them [a half mile] through the maddened crowd, which insulted and abused them along the road to the public square. Here two alternatives were presented them; either they must renounce their faith in the *Book of Mormon* or leave the county. The *Book of Mormon* they would not deny, nor consent to leave the county" (*Comprehensive History of the Church*, 1:333). Bishop Partridge was granted permission to speak. In his autobiography he relates what happened.

Edward Partridge

I was taken from my house by a mob, George Simpson being leader, who escorted me about a half a mile, to the court house, on the public square in Independence; and then and there, a few rods from said court house, surrounded by hundreds of the mob, I was stripped of my hat, coat and vest and daubed with tar from head to foot, and then a quantity of feathers put upon me; and all this because I would not agree to leave the country, and my home where I had lived two years.

Edward Partridge
(Courtesy of the Church Archives, The Church of Jesus Christ of Latter-day Saints)

Before tarring and feathering me I was permitted to speak. I told them that the Saints had suffered persecution in all ages of the world; that I had done nothing which ought to offend anyone; that if they abused me, they would abuse an innocent person; that I was willing to suffer for the sake of Christ, but to leave the country, I was not then willing to consent to it. By this time the multitude made so much noise that I could not be heard: some were cursing and swearing, saying, "call upon your Jesus," etc.; others were equally noisy in trying to still the rest, that they might be enabled to hear what I was saying.

Until after I had spoken, I knew not what they intended to do with me, whether to kill me, to whip me, or what else I knew not. I bore my abuse with so much resignation and meekness, that it appeared to astound the multitude, who permitted me to retire in silence, many looking very solemn, their sympathies having been touched as I thought; and as to myself, I was so filled with the Spirit and love of God, that I had no hatred towards my persecutors or anyone else (*History of the Church*, 1:390–91).

Whitmer Settlement attacked by Mobs
(31 October 1833)

The mobocracy that broke out in July in Independence continued to spread throughout Jackson County. Many citizens joined in the attempt to drive the Saints from their homes.

Parley P. Pratt

A mob of fifty armed men rode upon the Whitmer Branch on the last night of October, threatening the Saints with instant death if they did not renounce Joseph Smith and deny the Book of Mormon. Ramming the windows and doors with poles, they demolished ten houses and unroofed thirteen. Philo Dibble and other leading Mormons fled with their families into the woods and escaped capture. Several Mormon men, among whom were Hiram Page and George Beebe, were brutally whipped with heavy ox goads as their wives and children fled in terror into the woods (Parley P. Pratt, *Persecution of the Saints* [New York: Oswego County Democrat Office, 1840], 31; as cited in *Joseph Smith and the Restoration*, 258).

Bloody Day of Conflict
(4 November 1833)

On November 4, 1833, the Saints faced the height of the conflict as Missourians captured a Mormon ferry on the Big Blue River. The mob and the Saints faced off on opposite banks of the river, the mob fired, and a bloody battle ensued.

One hundred men, led by James Campbell, took possession of the Church-owned ferry on the Big Blue River and drove the Saints away. The mobbers then rode to a store a mile from the ferry and made themselves bold with corn liquor. Nineteen young Saints were on their way to assist their brethren but retreated when they encountered the mob at the store. Upon seeing the nineteen young Mormons retreating, Campbell's men mounted their horses and pursued them unsuccessfully. Having been eluded, the mobbers arrived at the Whitmer settlement and there "fired at the Mormons, who returned the fire. One of

David Whitmer's men, Henry A. Cleveland, received a ball in his left shoulder. Most of the mob made a disorganized retreat after the first fire, leaving some of their horses in Whitmer's cornfield. Two of their number, Hugh L. Brazeale and Thomas Linvill, were killed. . . .

"Andrew Barber, who had led the Mormon attack with a pistol in hand, was mortally wounded. His death occurred the next morning between five and six o'clock. He was the first man in this gospel dispensation to be martyred for the truth's sake. After the battle some of the brethren went to administer to him, but he objected stating that angels were in the room waiting to receive his spirit" (Philo Dibble, "Philo Dibble's Narrative," *Early Scenes in Church History, Faith-Promoting Series,* 8 vols. [Salt Lake City: Juvenile Instructor Office, 1882], 82).

Philo Dibble

We all responded and met the mob in battle, in which I was wounded with an ounce ball and two buck shot, all entering my body just at the right side of my navel. The mob were finally routed, and the brethren chased them a mile away. Several others of the brethren were also shot, and one, named [Andrew] Barber, was mortally wounded. After the battle was over, some of the brethren went to administer to him, but he objected to their praying that he might live, and asked them if they could not see the angels present. He said the room was full of them, and his greatest anxiety was for his friends to see what he saw, until he breathed his last, which occurred at three o'clock in the morning.

A young lawyer named Bazill [Hugh L. Brazeale], who came into Independence and wanted to make himself conspicuous, joined the mob, and swore he would wade in blood up to his chin.

He was shot with two balls through his head, and never spoke. There was another man, whose name I fail to remember, that lived on the Big Blue, who made a similar boast. He was also taken at his word. His chin was shot off, or so badly fractured by a ball that he was forced to have it amputated, but lived and recovered, though he was a horrible sight afterwards.

After the battle I took my gun and powder horn and started for home. When I got about half way I became faint and thirsty. I wanted to stop at Brother Whitmer's to lay down. The house, however, was full of women and children, and they were so frightened that they objected to my entering, as the mob had threatened that wherever they found a wounded man they would kill men, women and children.

I continued on and arrived home, or rather at a house in the field that the mob had not torn down, which was near my own home. There I found my wife and two children and a number of other women who had assembled. I told them I was shot and wanted to lay down.

They got me on the bed, but on thinking of what the mob had said, became frightened, and assisted me up stairs. I told them, however, that I could not stay there, my pain was so great. They then got me down stairs again, and my wife went out to see if she could find any of the brethren. In searching for them she got lost in the woods and was gone two hours, but learned that all the brethren had gone to the Colesville Branch, three miles distant, taking all the wounded with them save myself.

The next morning I was taken farther off from the road, that I might be concealed from the mob. I bled inwardly until my body was filled with blood, and remained in this condition until the next day at five P.M. I was then examined by a surgeon who was in the Black Hawk war, and who said that he had seen a great many men wounded, but never saw one wounded as I was that ever lived. He pronounced me a dead man.

David Whitmer, however, sent me word that I should live and not die, but I could see no possible chance to recover. After the surgeon had left me, Brother Newel Knight came to see me, and sat down on the side of my bed. He laid his right hand on my head, but never spoke. I felt the Spirit resting upon me at the crown of my head before his hand touched me, and I knew immediately that I was going to be healed. It seemed to form like a ring under the skin, and followed down my body. When the ring came to the wound, another ring formed around the first bullet hole, also the second and third. Then a ring formed on each shoulder and on each hip, and followed down to the ends of my fingers and toes and left me. I immediately arose and discharged three quarts of blood or more, with some pieces of my clothes that had been driven into my body by the bullets. I then dressed myself and went out doors and saw the falling of the stars, which so encouraged the Saints and frightened their enemies. It was one of the grandest sights I ever beheld. From that time not a drop of blood came from me and I never afterwards felt the slightest pain or inconvenience from my wounds, except that I was somewhat weak from the loss of blood.

The next day I walked around the field, and the day following I mounted a horse and rode eight miles, and went three miles on foot.

The night of the battle many of the women and children ran into the woods. One sister, not being able to take all of her children with her, left her little boy four years old in a corn shock, where he remained until morning. Some went out on the burnt prairie. The mob gathered and swore they would go and massacre them. When they got ready to go, the heavens were lit up with the falling of stars. This brought to us a perfect redemption at that time.

The night of the battle, the mob took all my household furniture, and after my recovery I crossed the river to Clay County, leaving behind me a drove of hogs, three cows and all of my crop, which I never recovered (*Early Scenes in Church History*, 83–85).

Newel Knight

While fifty or sixty were thus engaged, about thirty of the brethren came upon them and a battle ensued. As soon as the mob saw the brethren coming, some of them called out, "Fire, G—d d—m ye, fire!" and several shots were immediately fired into our party, which were promptly returned, when the mob fled, leaving some of their horses in one of the corn fields, and H. L. Brazile and Thomas Linvill dead on the ground. We also learned that several of their number were wounded. We had two or three wounded. One, a young man named Barber, received a mortal wound; he was the first man in this dispensation, who was martyred for the truth's sake. Another, Philo Dibble, was wounded in the abdomen at the first discharge; he was examined by a surgeon of great experience, who had served in the Mohawk war, and he said he never knew a man to live who was wounded in such a manner. The next day I went to see Brother Dibble, and found the house where he lay surrounded by the mob. I managed to get in, and went to the bed; two men came and seated themselves at the door; as I looked upon Brother Dibble lying there in extreme agony, I drew the bed curtains with one hand and laid the other upon his head, praying secretly to our heavenly Father in his behalf. I then left, as I did not wish to put myself into the power of the mob; and the next day business took me some ten miles from the place, where I met Brother Dibble making his escape from the county. He told me that as soon as I placed my hand upon his head, the pain and soreness seemed gradually to move as before a power driving it, until in a few minutes it left his body. He then discharged about a gallon of putrid matter, and the balls and pieces of clothing which had passed into his body (Newel Knight, "Newel Knight's Journal," *Classic Experiences and Adventures* [Salt Lake City: Bookcraft, 1969], 80–81).

George Albert Smith

There was an old revolutionary soldier, named Brace, in the "Mormon" company, who had fought in many battles under Washington, in the war of Independence. He fired his musket at Campbell without effect, and he fired at the old soldier also without effect; but Campbell being able to load quicker than he could, there was no alternative for Brace but to run at him with the butt end of his gun before he could reload; so he commenced yelling like ten thousand Indians, and charged Campbell with the butt end of his musket. Campbell, to save himself, suddenly wheeled his horse and plied the whip. This gave the old veteran a chance to re-load. He then fired his piece, and killed Campbell's horse as he was jumping over a fence, which left him hanging there; but Campbell in his terror did not know whether he was running on his feet or riding on his horse. So he ran across the country with all the power he possessed, whipping behind him, as he supposed, his horse, crying, "Get up, or the Mormons will kill us!—get up, or the Mormons will kill us" (in *Journal of Discourses*, 26 vols. [London: Latter-day Saints' Book Depot, 1854–86], 7:73–74).

SAINTS EXPELLED AND DRIVEN FROM JACKSON COUNTY
(November–December 1833)

Joseph Smith Jr.

There is great excitement at present among the Missourians, who are seeking if possible an occasion against us. They are continually chafing us, and provoking us to anger if possible, one sign of threatening after another, but we do not fear them, for the Lord God, the Eternal Father is our God, and Jesus . . . is our strength and confidence. . . .

Their father the devil, is hourly calling upon them to be up and doing, and they, like willing and obedient children, need not the second admonition; but in the name of Jesus Christ ... we will endure it no longer, if the great God will arm us with courage, with strength and with power, to resist them in their persecutions. We will not act on the offensive, but always on the defensive (*History of the Church*, 3:67–68).

Elizabeth Haven Barlow
(In a letter to her cousin, Elizabeth Howe Bullard.)

O! how Zion mourns, her sons have fallen in the streets by the cruel hand of the enemy, and her daughters weep in silence. It is impossible for my pen to tell you of our situation, only those who feel it, know. Between five and seven thousand men, women, and children driven from the places of gathering out of the state [Missouri] from houses and lands, in poverty, to seek for habitations where they can find them. The Saints are coming as fast as possible; they have only to the 8th of March to leave the state. The Prophet has sent word to have them make speed, haste out of the state. About twelve families cross the river into Quincy every day, and about thirty are constantly on the other side waiting to cross. It is slow and grimy; there is only one ferry boat to cross in. . . . By the river of Babylon we can sit down, yes, dear E[lizabeth] we weep when we remember Zion. . . .

We look upon our present with sorrow and much anxiety. We must now scatter in every direction just so we can find employment. Some of our dear brethren who have mingled with us in praise and prayer are now buried with the dead; some who a few months ago seemed to run well in the strait and narrow path have to our astonishment and grief forsook us and fled; our Prophet is still in jail, and many others whom we love. To look at our situation at this present time it would seem that Zion is all destroyed, but it is not so; the work of the Lord is on the march. . . .

God moves in a mysterious way, his wonders to perform. Many have been sifted out of the Church, while others have been rooted and ground in love and are the salt of the earth. . . .

It is only those who stand amidst all these trials unto the end that will at last be found worthy of a crown of glory. These scenes try us exceedingly, and we are to be tried (everyone who inhabits the celestial kingdom) like gold seven times purified (as cited in Kenneth W. Godfrey, Audrey M. Godfrey, and Jill Mulvay Derr, *Women's Voices* [Salt Lake City: Deseret Book, 1982], 106–9).

Parley P. Pratt

The shore began to be lined on both sides of the ferry with men, women and children; goods, wagons, boxes, provisions, etc., while the ferry was constantly employed; and when night again closed upon us the cottonwood bottom had much the appearance of a camp meeting. Hundreds of people were seen in every direction, some in tents and some in the open air around their fires, while the rain descended in torrents. Husbands were inquiring for their wives, wives for their husbands; parents for children, and children for parents. Some had the good fortune to escape with their families, household goods, and some provisions; while others knew not the fate of their friends, and had lost all their goods. The scene was indescribable, and, I am sure, would have melted the hearts of any people on the earth, except our blind oppressors, and a blind and ignorant community (Parley P. Pratt, *Autobiography of Parley P. Pratt*, ed. Scot Facer Proctor and Maurine Jensen Proctor [Salt Lake City: Deseret Book, 2000], 121).

Lyman Wight

I saw one hundred and ninety women and children driven thirty miles across the prairie, with three decrepit men only in their company, in the month of November, the ground thinly crusted with sleet; and I could easily follow on their trail by the *blood that flowed from their lacerated feet* on the stubble of the burnt prairie! (*History of the Church*, 3:439).

Benjamin F. Johnson

We were being hemmed in on all sides by our enemies and were without food. All the grain, cattle, hogs, and supplies of every kind were left in the country, or so far from home they could not be obtained except with a strong guard. So our only possible chance was to go out in foraging companies and bring in whatever we could find, without regard to ownership (Benjamin F. Johnson, *My Life's Review* [Mesa, Arizona: 21st Century Printing, 1992], 37).

(At the time the Saints were driven from Jackson County, the Prophet Joseph Smith was residing at Church Headquarters, in Ohio. He made the following observations in letters he wrote to the suffering Saints.)

Joseph Smith Jr.

Brethren if I were with you I should take an active part in your sufferings, and although nature shrinks, yet my spirit would not let me forsake you unto death[,] God helping me (*Personal Writings of Joseph Smith*, ed. Dean C. Jessee [Salt Lake City: Deseret Book, 2002], 306).

Joseph Smith Jr.

Kirtland Mills, Ohio—December 10, 1833.

Edward Partridge, W. W. Phelps, John Whitmer, A. S. Gilbert, John Corrill, Isaac Morley, and all the Saints whom it may concern.

BELOVED BRETHREN:—This morning's mail brought letters from Bishop Partridge, and Elders Corrill and Phelps, all mailed at Liberty, November 19th, which gave us the melancholy intelligence of your flight from the land of your inheritance, having been driven before the face of your enemies in that place.

From previous letters we learned that a number of our brethren had been slain, but we could not learn from the letters referred to above, that there had been more than one killed, and that one Brother Barber, and that Brother Dibble was wounded in the bowels. We were thankful to learn that no more had been slain, and our daily prayers are that the Lord will not suffer His Saints, who have gone up to His land to keep His commandments, to stain His holy mountain with their blood.

I cannot learn from any communication by the Spirit to me, that Zion has forfeited her claim to a celestial crown, notwithstanding the Lord has caused her to be thus afflicted, except it may be some individuals, who have walked in disobedience, and forsaken the new covenant; all such will be made manifest by their works in due time. I have always expected that Zion would suffer some affliction, from what I could learn from the commandments which have been given. But I would remind you of a certain clause in one which says, that after *much* tribulation cometh the blessing. . . .

Now, there are two things of which I am ignorant; and the Lord will not show them unto me, perhaps for a wise purpose in Himself—I mean in some respects—and they are these: Why God has suffered so great a calamity to come upon Zion, and what the great moving cause of this great affliction is; and again, by what means He will return her back to her inheritance, with songs of everlasting joy upon her head. These two things, brethren, are in part kept back that they are not plainly shown unto me (*History of the Church*, 1:453–54).

George A. Smith

(Describing what happened to some of the Jackson County mobbers.)

In the history of our persecutions there have arisen a great many anecdotes; but one will perhaps serve to illustrate the condition in which I wish to see every man that raises in these mountains the hand of oppression upon the innocent. I wish to see such men rigged out with the same honors and comforts as was the honorable Samuel C. Owen, Commander-in-Chief of the Jackson County mob. He, with eleven men, was engaged at a mass meeting, to raise a mob to drive the Saints from Clay County. This was in the year 1834, in the month of June. They had made speeches, and done everything to raise the indignation of the people against the Saints. In the evening, himself, James Campbell, and nine others, commenced to cross the Missouri river on their way home again; and the Lord, or some accident, knocked a hole in the bottom of the boat. When they discovered it, says Commander Owen to the company on the ferry boat, "We must strip to the bone, or we shall all perish." Mr. Campbell replied, "I will go to hell before I will land naked." He had his choice, and went to the bottom. Owen stripped himself of every article of clothing, and commenced floating down the river. After making several attempts he finally landed on the Jackson side of the river, after a swim of about fourteen miles. He rested some time, being perfectly exhausted, and then started into the nettles, which grow very thick and to a great height, in the Missouri bottoms, and which was his only possible chance in making from the river to the settlements. He had to walk four miles through the nettles, which took him the remainder of the night, and when he got through the nettles, he came to a road, and saw a young lady approaching on horseback, who was the belle of Jackson County. In this miserable condition he laid himself behind a log, so that she could not see him. When she arrived opposite the log, he says, "Madam, I am Samuel C. Owen, the Commander-in-Chief of the mob against the Mormons; I wish you to send some men from the next house with clothing, for I am naked." The lady in her philanthropy dismounted, and left him a light shawl and a certain unmentionable under garment, and passed on. So His Excellency Samuel C. Owen, who was afterwards killed in Mexico by foolishly exposing himself, contrary to orders, took up his line of march for the town, in the shawl and petticoat uniform, after his expedition against the "Mormons."

My young friends, have the goodness to use every man so, who comes into your country to mob and oppress the innocent; and LADIES, DON'T LEND HIM ANY CLOTHING (in *Journal of Discourses*, 2:24).

Joseph Smith Jr.

(In August, the Western Monitor, *a newspaper in Fayette, Missouri, ran a series of articles censuring the mob action in Jackson County and suggesting that the Saints seek redress from state authorities for the wrongs they had suffered. Thereupon Church leaders wrote up a petition detailing their grievances and denying the false accusations of the settlers of Jackson County.)*

Influenced by the precepts of our beloved Savior when we have been smitten on the one cheek, we have turned the other also; . . . we have borne the above outrages without murmuring; but we cannot patiently bear them any longer; according to the laws of God and man, we have borne enough (*History of the Church*, 1:414–15).

Alexander Doniphan

If a cohort of angels were to come down, and declare we were innocent, it would all be the same; for he (Judge Austin King) had determined from the beginning to cast us into prison (*History of the Church*, 3:213).

Alexander Doniphan
(Courtesy of the Church Archives, The Church of Jesus Christ of Latter-day Saints)

General Atchison

Things are not so bad in that county [Daviess] as represented by rumor, and, in fact, from affidavits I have no doubt your Excellency [Gov. Lilburn W. Boggs] has been deceived by the exaggerated statements of designing or half crazy men. I have found there is no cause of alarm on account of the Mormons; they are not to be feared; they are very much alarmed (*History of the Church*, 3:85).

Doctrine & Covenants 105:2–5

(Revealed the cause of the expulsion.)

Behold, I say unto you, were it not for the transgressions of my people, speaking concerning the church and not individuals, they might have been redeemed even now. But behold, they have not learned to be obedient to the things which I required at their hands, but are full of all manner of evil, and do not impart of their substance, as becometh saints, to the poor and afflicted among them; And are not united according to the union required by the law of the celestial kingdom; And Zion cannot be built up unless it is by the principles of the celestial kingdom; otherwise I cannot receive her unto myself. (See also *Doctrine & Covenants* 101:6–7.)

Doctrine & Covenants 101:76–77, 86–89

(Commandment to the Saints to importune the government for redress.)

And again I say unto you, those who have been scattered by their enemies, it is my will that they should continue to importune for redress, and redemption, by the hands of those who are placed as rulers and are in authority over you. According to the laws and constitution of the people, which I have suffered to be established, and should be maintained for the rights and protection of all flesh, according to just and holy principles . . . Let them importune at the feet of the judge; And if he heed them not, let them importune at the feet of the governor; And if the governor heed them not, let them importune at the feet of the president; and if the president heed them not, then will the Lord arise and come forth out of his hiding place, and in his fury vex the nation.

Doctrine & Covenants 101:99–100

(Commandment to the Saints to not relinquish their lands in Zion.)

Therefore, it is my will that my people should claim, and hold claim upon that which I have appointed unto them, though they should not be permitted to dwell thereon. Nevertheless, I do not say they shall not dwell thereon; for inasmuch as they bring forth fruit and works meet for my kingdom they shall dwell thereon.

᭞ INDEX ᭞

Aaronic Priesthood, restoration of, 195, 233–37

Abel, 129

Abraham, 128

Adam (Michael), 127–28, 320–27

Adam-ondi-Ahman, 320–28

Adams, Mary Frost, 19

Allen, Charles, 385, 389

Allen, Felatiah, 348

Alma, 129

American Planning Association, 318–20

Ames, Ira, 350

Ancient of Days. *See* Adam

Anderson, Chief, 270–73

Anderson, John, 112–14

Angels: appearances of, to Joseph, 128–30

Anthon, Charles, 151–56

Apostles, early, 128–29

Apostles, Nephite, 129

Appleby, William I., 12

Articles and Covenants of the Church, 250

Atchison, General, 401

Austin, Emily, 374

Avard, Sampson, 360

Bachelor, Origen, 280

Backman, Milton V., Jr.: on camp

meetings, 61–63; compiles Joseph's experiences with Moroni, 117–18, 119, 120–21, 122–23; compiles Joseph's retrieving the plates, 133; compiles Martin Harris accounts of seeking authenticity, 154–55; compiles Orson Pratt account of Martin Harris, 155–56; compiles David Whitmer account of being a witness to gold plates, 190–91; compiles Martin Harris account of being a witness, 192–93; on Joseph receiving Melchizedek Priesthood, 238

Ballard, Melvin J., 329

Baptism, 233–37

Barber, Andrew, 392, 394, 398

Barlow, Elizabeth Haven, 396–97

Beebe, George, 391

Belnap, Gilbert, 4

Benson, Ezra Taft, 78–79

Bent, Samuel, 45

Benton, Mr., 110–11

Bible, translation of, 285–87

Bidamon, Louis, 231

Big Blue River, battle at, 391–95

Black, Adam, 325

Blake, Captain, 301, 303

to translate, 170–75; humility of, to translate, 176; receives help from Joseph Knight Sr., 176–79; receives Aaronic Priesthood, 195, 233–37; receives Melchizedek Priesthood, 195–96, 237–42; shows plates to eight witnesses, 199–200, 204; has Book of Mormon published, 205–14; Emma's description of Joseph translating Book of Mormon, 215; Mary Lightner's experience with, 222–24; organizes the Church, 243–50; instructs saints to move to Ohio, 257–58, 299; preaches in West Nantmeal Seminary, 282; translates the Bible, 285–97; designs city plat of Zion, 318–20; identifies Adam-ondi-Ahman, 320–24; reinstates W. W. Phelps, 333–34; writes "A Vision," 335–44; is tarred and feathered, 346–49; vexatious lawsuits brought against, 351–52, 361; apostates seek to depose, 355–61

Smith, Joseph, Jr., *teachings of:* on keeping records for posterity, xi; on the building up of Zion, xii, 74–75; on the work of the Lord in the last days, xiii; on testimony, xiii; on dispensations, 75; on kingdom of God in last days, 77–78; on move to Ohio, 257, 299

Smith, Joseph, Sr.: other's opinions about, 45–47; has visions and dreams, 46–49; Joseph tells, of Moroni's visit, 123; at time of Joseph retrieving the plates, 142–43; helps Joseph hide the plates, 148; at completion of Book of Mormon, 180; is witness to gold plates, 199–200, 203; family of, is persecuted, 203, 226; is pleased Joseph will marry, 228; baptism of, 246; has strong testimony, 268–69; takes Emma into his home, 316; sees apostasy in Kirtland, 362

Smith, Joseph, III: seeks reaffirmation of John Whitmer's testimony, 204; at Emma's death, 231; wants to publish JST version of Bible, 290; on persecution of Saints, 349

Smith, Julia, 231–32, 318

Smith, Lovina, 148

Smith, Lucy (Joseph's Sister), 50

Smith, Lucy Mack: on mob coming to kill Joseph, 27–29; is a religious woman, 43; seeks to know way of salvation, 43–45, 63; defends Joseph before ministers, 44–45; on her husband's visions and dreams, 47–49; on Joseph's childhood, 54; on childhood illness of Joseph, 55–60; on revivals, 63; on persecution of Joseph, 101–2, 203; on Joseph telling family what Moroni says, 124–25; on Joseph's experience with